Exploring the dynamics and impact of decentralisation on inter-ethnic relations in post-Yugoslav Macedonia, Lyon engages thoroughly with existing theories of conflict management, territorial state construction, and decentralisation and offers a wealth of original empirical analysis. This exceptionally timely contribution to our existing knowledge and understanding provides highly relevant policy recommendations and should be required reading for all serious students and analysts of ethnic conflict in the Western Balkans and beyond.

Stefan Wolff, Professor of International Security,
University of Birmingham, UK

This important study not only contributes to our understanding of contemporary Macedonia, but also makes an important argument about the importance of decentralisation as a tool of conflict management. Macedonia is the prime case study of international mediators seeking to address interethnic relations through decentralisation and local-level power-sharing. Aisling Lyon provides a very well-researched, nuanced assessment of whether decentralisation has delivered. The weaknesses of the Macedonian experience provide useful guidance for policy makers in addressing interethnic conflict elsewhere.

Florian Bieber, Professor of South East European studies,
University of Graz, Austria

Aisling Lyon's *tour de force* critically engages with the assumption that a redistribution of state responsibilities enhances democracy and social harmony. Her vital contribution to debates about decentralisation sets the experiments in the former Yugoslav Republic of Macedonia within the wider context of global trends of fragmentation. Does decentralisation help to pacify societies, leave them to fend for themselves or merely grant them cosmetic authority? This is a book to be savoured as much for its compass as its attention to detail.

Michael Pugh, Emeritus Professor, University of Bradford, UK &
Visiting Professor, Radboud University Nijmegen, Netherlands

Decentralisation and the Management of Ethnic Conflict

Ethnic inequalities in divided societies can exacerbate social divisions and lead to conflict. Reducing these inequalities could have a de-escalating effect, yet there is little consensus on how this can be achieved most effectively and sustainably. Decentralisation is held to improve inter-ethnic relations in multi-ethnic states by allowing territorially concentrated groups greater autonomy over their own affairs, and the case of the Republic of Macedonia offers an example of the successes and failings of decentralisation.

Decentralisation and the Management of Ethnic Conflict offers new insight into the dynamics of conflict management through decentralisation, using an in-depth case study of decentralisation in the Republic of Macedonia between 2005 and 2012. Guided by the concept of horizontal inequalities, the volume identifies the factors which influenced the decision to devolve responsibilities to the municipalities after 2001.Taking an integrative approach to studying the political, administrative and fiscal dimensions of decentralisation and its implementation, the book investigates whether these institutional reforms have indeed contributed to the reduction of inequalities between Macedonia's ethnic groups, and what the obstacles were in those areas in which decentralisation has not reached its full potential. The key lesson of the Macedonian case is that attempts to solve internal self-determination conflicts through decentralisation will fail if local self-governance exists only in form but not in substance.

This book contributes to a more nuanced understanding of the challenges facing different forms of decentralisation in the long term, and as such represents a significant contribution to Conflict Studies, Development Studies and Political Science more generally.

Aisling Lyon obtained her PhD from the Department of Peace Studies, University of Bradford, and has worked internationally on a number of local government capacity-building projects. Her research interests include insti tutional design in multi-ethnic states and the political systems of South-East Europe and Turkey.

Exeter Studies in Ethno Politics
Series Editor: Gareth Stansfield
University of Exeter, UK

Decentralisation and the Management of Ethnic Conflict

Lessons from the Republic of Macedonia

Aisling Lyon

Routledge
Taylor & Francis Group

LONDON AND NEW YORK

First published 2016
by Routledge

2 Park Square, Milton Park, Abingdon, Oxfordshire OX14 4RN
52 Vanderbilt Avenue, New York, NY 10017

Routledge is an imprint of the Taylor & Francis Group, an informa business

First issued in paperback 2019

British Library Cataloguing in Publication Data
A catalogue record for this book is available from the British Library

Library of Congress Cataloguing in Publication Data
Lyon, Aisling.
  Decentralisation and the management of ethnic conflict : lessons from
  the Republic of Macedonia / Aisling Lyon.
    pages   cm. – (Exeter studies in ethno politics)
  1. Decentralization in government–Macedonia (Republic)   2. Central-local
  government relations–Macedonia (Republic)   3. Ethnic conflict–Macedonia
  (Republic)   4. Macedonia (Republic)–Ethnic relations.   5. Macedonia
  (Republic)–Politics and government–1992–
  JN9679.5.A56 D425 2016
  303.6089/094976–dc23   2015020292

ISBN: 978-1-138-94411-4 (hbk)
ISBN: 978-0-367-87437-7 (pbk)

Typeset in Times New Roman
by Out of House Publishing

To my parents Helen and Nick Lyon,
and in memory of my grandmothers Peggy Lyon and Mary Drew.

Contents

Figures

Tables

Foreword

The evidence is in plain sight. The autocrats of the world, past and present, have been united in just one way. They are inveterate centralisers. Stalinists and Nazis favoured hyper-centralisation under one-party control, and today's *Salafists* seek to re-create a fantastic version of the early Islamic caliphate, in which decentralisation has no place. Centralisers have grim friends: dictators, despots or sultans. With enemies like these, the case for decentralisation always has a head-start in political argument. But, sadly, it does not follow that decentralisation is invariably an unmitigated political good.

This model and outstanding study of contemporary Macedonia by Dr Aisling Lyon is very unusual because it critically explores in significant depth and across multiple appropriate dimensions a recurrent piety, namely, the merits of decentralisation, administrative, political and fiscal. She does so through rigorous conceptual control, and very detailed empirical investigation; and she seeks to integrate the insights of both political scientists and economists. The work displays her logical skills, fieldwork, and intensive programme of interviews. The results provide the dispassionate reader with a controlled, moderately worded, but nevertheless astringent evaluation of the Macedonian experience since the Ohrid Framework Agreement of 2001. She does not provide a polemic against decentralisation per se – she firmly believes that political decentralisation can be part of an institutional programme to reduce the ethnic inequalities that may generate conflict. But, she provides a cold bath for the more gushing enthusiasts of decentralisation.

Macedonia has been widely classified as a contemporary case of 'consociation'. This distinctive model of power-sharing displays four features when it is organised in its strong form: parity of the constituent partners through cross-community executive power-sharing; the application of the norm of proportionality throughout public life, especially in representation and in expenditures; community autonomy (especially in matters of language and religion, and therefore education); and, lastly, the allocation of veto-rights to the principal partners. Dr Lyon correctly shows, however, that in Macedonia decentralisation was adopted largely to prevent the Albanian minority, concentrated in the west and north-east of the country, from obtaining an authentic autonomy settlement, whether based on territorial or community government.

Decentralisation, in short, was adopted to divide Albanians across municipalities or local governments, to prevent their collective self-government rather than to enable their collective empowerment as a community. Instead of an Albanian-dominated 'western region', numerous decentralised local government entities have been developed that are supposedly consistent with the European Charter of Local Self-Government. Some have Albanian majorities, more have Macedonian Slav majorities, a smaller number are mixed.

The new state established in 1991 is known to everyone, except Greek nationalists, as Macedonia. Its titular nationality is often called by others 'the Macedonian Slavs'. They mostly wish, however, to be known as *the* Macedonians. Their first constitution also of 1991 proclaimed a mono-lingual, mono-ethnic and mono-national state, with minority protections as an afterthought. The real state of affairs at this juncture was captured in *Before the Rain* (1994), the superb film by director Milcho Manchevski. Its portrait of deep communal divisions was much more accurate as history and forecast than the new constitutional parchment. The political dreaming of the Macedonian Slavs was soon rudely interrupted by an Albanian insurrection at the start of the new millennium. The Macedonian Slavs believed this uprising heralded their long-held nightmare of a Greater Albania, which would either absorb Macedonia, or partition it. Some of them contemplated ethnic expulsions in response. The monster in the Macedonian Slavs' nightmare was not the sovereign state of Albania, however, but the recently successful veterans of the struggle of Albanians in neighbouring Kosovo. The full story was, of course, more complex. Yet recalling 'the Macedonian syndrome' – that a war in and over Macedonia signals the likelihood of a wider regional war – the powers-that-be in Europe intervened more extensively than before.

In the Ohrid Framework Agreement, mediated by European Union foreign policy officials, the leaders of the Macedonian Slavs were obliged to modify their constitution. They had to commit credibly to recognising Macedonia as a multi-ethnic state of all its citizens. These concessions, though painful, were far less than those that might have been entailed in conceding a bi-national state, in which Albanians would have been full and equal partners. The Macedonian Slavs were and remain adamantly opposed to federalising their small post-communist state. They had lived in Yugoslavia. They feared a federative entity could build the institutional infrastructure to support secession. After all, over a decade before, they had executed just such an exit from a federation.

Under the provisions of the Ohrid Framework Agreement, which stopped the Albanian insurrection, and guaranteed the state's territorial integrity, the Macedonian Slav leaders were tacitly obligated by the leaders of the European Union, NATO and the OSCE to accept power-sharing (through regular coalition governments) and proportionality. Neither autonomy nor significant veto-rights (except over future constitutional amendments) were conceded, however. In the language of political science, a partial consociation was envisaged, with just two of its key components, and very partial it has proved to be.

Instead of autonomy, decentralisation was offered – to be applied through-out the new country, in a programme of symmetrical decentralisation, in which each of the local entities would have identical powers. The micro-minorities, those who were neither Macedonian Slav nor Albanian, would achieve full incorporation as equal citizens, and enjoy language, educational and religious freedoms, and any group with over twenty per cent of the popu-lation (not named) in the country or in a local government would have its language upgraded to official status.

What Dr Lyon shows in admirable and convincing detail is that despite some nominal and early promise the Ohrid Framework Agreement has not been implemented in spirit and only partially in letter. The dominant Macedonian Slav party periodically co-opts one of the Albanian parties. The VMRO-DPMNE uses corruption, mass surveillance of its adversaries, numerous electoral manipulations, and the standard techniques of patronage, bribery and intimidation to disorganise opposition. Differently put, normal Balkan democracy applies. The Albanians have fared better than the micro-minorities in securing their language and educational rights, but provision for educa-tion and other services is badly skewed by the systematic failure to develop and apply a genuine fiscal equalisation formula for the funding of 'decentral-isation'. And even if such a formula were developed and applied the centre would likely, as at present, use its grant-supplying and regulatory powers to determine and micro-manage how expenditures are spent. Measures of pro-gress on fiscal decentralisation that rely on data about local revenue-raising are wholly inadequate if the central government retains extensive control over how funds are spent. The difference between decentralisation under a unitary state and decentralisation within a federation is here clearly supplied in Dr Lyon's evidence. The dominant governing party's manipulation of official data is in Shakespeare's words 'a piece of work'. The Macedonian case advertises the necessity of careful thinking about the regulation of political parties as a crit-ical component of post-conflict settlements. Since such parties have to be the vehicles of government, decentralised or not, the problem is profound.

Modern Macedonia has also been widely hailed as an illustration of the merits of preventive diplomacy and light-touch intervention: it showcases two examples of timely, and even skilful, deployment of both European diplomatic soft power and hard NATO military power. In 1999, Dr Alice Ackermann could reasonably publish her intelligent doctoral thesis under the title *Making Peace Prevail: Preventing Violent Conflict in Macedonia* (Syracuse University Press), with a prudent epilogue about future threats to instability. It is certainly true that the OSCE intervention in Macedonia, shortly after its independence, and the joint EU and NATO intervention in 2001, were separately and jointly more timely, less costly, and more effective than the interventions in nearby Bosnia and Herzegovina or Kosovo. And, it is also true that Macedonia has so far been spared neo-colonial or direct pro-tectorate government by EU diplomats and humanitarians. Yet both the events of 2001, triggered in part by the refugee crisis after the NATO intervention in Kosovo, and Dr Lyon's study of the post-Ohrid world, behove us to be cautious about exaggerating Macedonia's place in tales of successful preventive and light-touch intervention.

In the first place had the recognition criteria applied to Macedonia's declaration of independence been more stringent regarding minority rights and power-sharing then the second intervention might not have been necessary. Moreover, interventions, light-touch or otherwise, are rarely successful without vigorous follow-up on monitoring and implementation. Dr Lyon ably shows how the project of decentralisation has fallen far short of expectations partly because of the absence of careful compliance criteria linked to smart sanctions by its EU sponsors. Indeed Macedonia was recognised as a candidate for EU membership in 2005, long before any accurate evaluation could have taken place on the implementation of the Ohrid Framework Agreement. Its constitutional provisions were necessary but not sufficient benchmarks of progress.

Assessing interventions in ethnic conflicts requires evaluation against at least two standards: do they stop and prevent more violence than they create? and do they make post-intervention ethnic relations better? Interventions in Macedonia, so far, have met the first standard. On the second question, the jury remains out, but Dr Lyon's book provides at least as much evidence for the prosecution as the defence. Beset by the economic crises of the Eurozone, the European Union's own constitutional failings, including its crises of expansion and governability – all manifest in the current refugee crisis – it may be too much to hope that the European powers will carefully reappraise their policies toward Macedonia before another intervention becomes warranted. A nineteenth-century Irish agrarian and nationalist radical once argued that, 'Violence is the only way of ensuring a hearing for moderation'. Let us hope that in this case William O'Brien's hypothesis is proved wrong, and that a third major intervention will not be required. Reading Dr Lyon's book will not inspire confidence, but it will leave its reader clearly, and realistically informed.

Brendan O'Leary
Lauder Professor of Political Science
University of Pennsylvania
September 2015

Preface and acknowledgements

This research project began in late 2007 when I was working in Kosovo's Ministry of Local Government Administration. Martti Ahtisaari, the former President of Finland and UN Special Envoy, had offered his 'Comprehensive Proposal for the Kosovo Status Settlement' earlier that year, and colleagues were busy drafting legislation on municipal governance before Kosovo's much-anticipated declaration of independence a few months later. 'Decentralisation' was the 'buzzword' in Kosovo, and many believed it would provide the institutional setting for resolving Kosovo's inter-ethnic tensions, 'as it had done in neighbouring Macedonia', I was frequently told. Having lived and worked in Macedonia intermittently since 2004, I was less convinced of decentralisation's track record of addressing non-majority group grievances. Macedonia's experience with decentralisation needed to be more critically appraised before it could be upheld as a model of ethnic conflict management, to be replicated elsewhere. This study, over eight years later, is the result.

A large number of staff and elected officials from the Macedonian municipalities of Gostivar, Kruševo, Kumanovo, Šuto Orizari and Struga gave their time to me. Representatives from the OSCE, UNDP, Office of the EU Special Representative in Skopje and Soros Foundation were equally generous. I am particularly grateful to Dušica Perišić, Ticiana Garcia-Tapia, Katarina Živković, Kristina Hadzi-Vasileva, Toni Popovski, Mihaela Stojkoska, Liljana Ristovska, Naim Memeti, Ardita Dema-Mehmeti, Albert Musliu, Vesel Memedı, Jeton Aliji and Maja Trajkovska. Without their assistance and advice, my fieldwork would not have been possible. Special thanks also goes to Alan Packer, for inspiring me to work in local government in Kosovo and Macedonia; Nial Memeti, for providing excellent Albanian/Macedonian/Turkish/English interpretation during my fieldwork interviews; and to the Memeti family for providing me with a home away from home for so many years, along with endless glasses of Turkish tea.

I am indebted to Michael Pugh. His comments have guided the development of this research and it is not possible to thank him enough for his time, patience and support. I would like to thank my PhD examiners, Stefan Wolff and Jim Whitman, for providing me with invaluable feedback and advice.

I am especially grateful to Brendan O'Leary for his incredibly rich feedback and continuous encouragement, and to the two anonymous reviewers who commented meticulously on early drafts of my manuscript. I very much enjoyed working with Joe Whiting, Acquisitions Editor at Routledge, and his colleagues, and I thank them all for their hard work and support during this book's journey towards publication. I am also very grateful to my partner Latif Tas, who has been a constant support for me throughout. Final thanks go to my family, and especially my young nephews Drew and Quinn, who have provided me with a welcome distraction from my studies.

Acronyms and abbreviations

ADI	Association for Democratic Initiatives
CDI	Community Development Institute
CICRs	Committees for Inter-Community Relations
CLDD	Center for Local Democracy Development
CoE	Council of Europe
CRPM	Center for Research and Policy Making
CSLD	Center for the Study of Local Democracy
DPA	Democratic Party of Albanians (*Partia Demokratike Shqiptare – PDSH –* in Albanian)
DUI	Democratic Union for Integration (*Bashkimi Demokratik për Integrim – BDI –* in Albanian)
EC	European Commission
ECRI	European Commission against Racism and Intolerance
ESI	European Stability Initative
FCNM	Framework Convention for the Protection of National Minorities
FOSM	Foundation Open Society Macedonia
GDP	Gross Domestic Product
GIZ	*Gesellschaft für Internationale Zusammenarbeit* (German Society for International Co-operation)
GTZ	*Gesellschaft für Technische Zusammenarbeit* (German Society for Technical Co-operation)
HCNM	High Commissioner on National Minorities
HDI	Human Development Index
ICG	International Crisis Group
IMC	Inter-Municipal Co-operation
IMF	International Monetary Fund
IRIS	Institute for Regional and International Studies
IT	Information Technology
MANU	Macedonian Academy of Sciences and Arts
MCIC	Macedonian Center for International Co-operation
MKD	Macedonian Denar
MLGA	Macedonia Local Government Activity
MoES	Ministry of Education and Science
MoLSG	Ministry of Local Self-Government

MoLSP	Ministry of Labour and Social Policy
NALAS	Network of Associations of Local Authorities of South-East Europe
NDP	People's Democratic Party (*Partia Demokratike Popullore – PDP* – in Albanian), but commonly referred to by its Macedonian title (Народна демократска партија)
NGO	Non-Governmental Organisation
NLA	National Liberation Army (*Ushtria Çlirimtare Kombëtare – UÇK* – in Albanian)
ODIHR	Office for Democratic Institutions and Human Rights
OHR	Office of the Higher Representative
OSCE	Organization for Security and Co-operation in Europe
OSI	Open Society Institute
PDP	Party for Democratic Prosperity (*Partia për Prosperitet Demokratik – PPD* – in Albanian)
PER	Project on Ethnic Relations
PIT	Personal Income Tax
RDK	*Rilindja Demokratike Kombëtare* (National Democratic Renaissance)
REF	Roma Education Fund
RM	Republic of Macedonia
SDC	Swiss Agency for Development and Co-operation
SDSM	Social Democratic Union of Macedonia (Социјалдемократски сојуз на Македонија - СДСМ - in Macedonian)
SEC	State Election Commission
SIOFA	Secretariat for Implementation of the Ohrid Framework Agreement
SSO	State Statistical Office of the Republic of Macedonia
UN	United Nations
UNDP	United Nations Development Programme
UNESCAP	United Nations Economic and Social Commission for Asia and the Pacific
UNICEF	United Nations Children's Fund
UNSC	United Nations Security Council
US	United States
USAID	United States Agency for International Development
VAT	Value Added Tax
VMRO-DPMNE	Internal Macedonian Revolutionary Organisation – Democratic Party for Macedonian National Unity (Внатрешна македонска револуционерна организација – Демократска партија за македонско национално единство – ВМРО – ДПМНЕ)
ZELS	Association of the Units of Local Self-Governance of the Republic of Macedonia (Заедница на Единиците на Локалната Самоуправа на Република Македонија – ЗЕЛС)

Introduction

In the nineteenth century the Macedonian question was synonymous with intractable and insoluble ethnic conflict that divided its peoples and spilled across sovereign borders.[1] It gave its name to a fruit salad in French, one in which the component elements refused to dissolve. Mindful of Macedonia's past, in the 1990s European and American policy-makers, with the establishment of both a United Nations and a CSCE preventative mission in Macedonia, moved much more quickly to forestall conflict there than they did, for example, in Bosnia and Herzegovina.[2] In the twenty-first century the question has become whether there is now a distinctively Macedonian answer to ethnic conflict.

Macedonia, as it is known to the world, apart from Greek officials who insist on labelling it FYROM (the Former Yugoslav Republic of Macedonia), experienced ethnic conflict during the spring and summer of 2001. Intense fighting broke out between ethnic Albanian insurgents under the Albanian National Liberation Army – NLA[3] – and state security forces.[4] Hostilities were concentrated in the north and west of the country, near the border with Kosovo, where significant Albanian communities reside. The insurgents claimed to be fighting to improve the rights of fellow Albanians living in Macedonia.

During almost seven months of hostilities, between 150 and 250 people were killed, with a further 650 wounded. More than 100,000 civilians were forced to leave their homes because of the fighting and the state lost control of approximately 20 per cent of the country to the insurgents (Phillips 2004: 16; Daskalovski 2006: 100). The conflict officially ended with the signing of the internationally sponsored Ohrid Framework Agreement in August 2001, within which decentralisation was a major component.[5]

Decentralisation is held, by its proponents, to be capable of improving inter-ethnic relations in multi-ethnic states by allowing territorially concentrated local communities the possibility of realising their aspirations for internal self-determination, while also maintaining the territorial integrity of the existing state. *Internal* as opposed to *external* self-determination claims refer to a group's express preference for territorial self-government or to non-territorial cultural autonomy within an existing state (Wolff 2009: 33).[6]

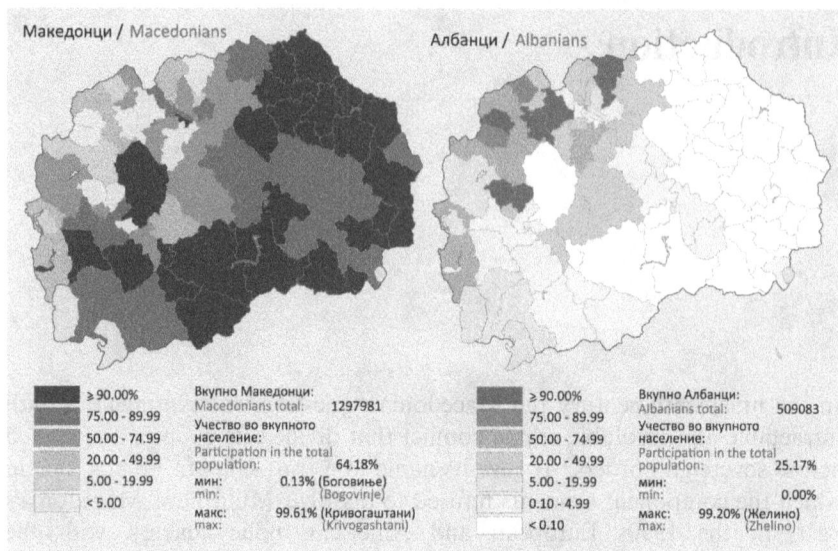

Македонци / Macedonians		Албанци / Albanians	
≥ 90.00%	Вкупно Македонци: Macedonians total: 1297981	≥ 90.00%	Вкупно Албанци: Albanians total: 509083
75.00 - 89.99	Учество во вкупното население:	75.00 - 89.99	Учество во вкупното население:
50.00 - 74.99	Participation in the total population: 64.18%	50.00 - 74.99	Participation in the total population: 25.17%
20.00 - 49.99	мин: 0.13% (Боговиње)	20.00 - 49.99	мин: 0.00%
5.00 - 19.99	min: (Bogovinje)	5.00 - 19.99	min:
< 5.00	макс: 99.61% (Кривогаштани) max: (Krivogashtani)	0.10 - 4.99	макс: 99.20% (Желино) max: (Zhelino)
		< 0.10	

Figure 0.1 The territorial pattern of ethnic demography in the Republic of Macedonia (Macedonian and Albanian communities)

Source: SSO (2014c: 75)

This book identifies the factors distinctive to Macedonia which influenced the decision to devolve responsibilities to municipalities after 2001. It examines the design of Macedonian decentralisation, and demonstrates how local power-sharing mechanisms were intended to address the concerns of both the Albanian and Macedonian communities. The implementation of the political, administrative and fiscal dimensions of decentralisation are considered. An empirical evaluation of whether decentralisation has contributed to the reduction of inequalities between Macedonia's ethnic groups is advanced. The research demonstrates that the reform's ability to contribute to the management of ethnic conflict in Macedonia has so far been mixed. Undemocratic, hierarchical political parties and the prevalence of clientelism at both the central and local levels, together with inadequate fiscal autonomy, have meant that the reform has been only partial. Where decentralisation's potential has not been reached, obstacles to its successful implementation are identified and discussed.

Research into how decentralisation to the local level may facilitate the peaceful management of ethnic conflict used to be neglected by scholars. However, the emerging practice of complex power-sharing has given studies of local government decentralisation a new sense of urgency and significance. Studies on local government decentralisation are needed given the international community's reluctance to accept changes to international boundaries, to grant minorities group rights in general, and territorial autonomy in particular, and the bad press given to multi-national federations.[7] Importantly, not all ethnic conflicts are secessionist in nature. Moreover, the geographical dispersal of a state's ethnic populations may lend itself to territorial autonomy (federal or otherwise) or to independence.[8]

The Macedonian case addresses researchers, practitioners and policy-makers in multi-ethnic countries that have recently embarked upon decentralisation reforms as a means of integrating and appeasing demands for internal self-determination by territorially concentrated ethnic groups. Examples include but are not limited to Indonesia (Diprose 2008), Uganda (Green 2008) and Serbian as well as Turkish communities living in southern Kosovo (Cocozzelli 2008; Gjoni *et al.* 2010; Burema 2013). Macedonian experience in the design – but crucially also the implementation – of decentralisation reforms should be contemplated by any government considering decentralising power locally to territorially concentrated ethnic groups in the future, such as Kosovo's integration of Serbian-majority municipalities in the north of the country and Ukraine's integration of Russian-speaking communities, particularly those living in the eastern regions (Rossi 2014; Gjoni *et al.* 2010; Burema 2013; Emerson 2015). Importantly, decentralisation to the local level represents a mechanism for granting greater autonomy to territorially concentrated minority ethnic groups without necessarily recognising their distinctive ethnic character. In this respect, the findings discussed in this study may be of particular significance to Turkey and its sizable, territorially concentrated yet constitutionally unrecognised Kurdish community (Bookchin 1991; Akkaya and Jongerden 2013).

Scope of the study

This study focuses on only one of a variety of territorial self-government arrangements available for managing ethnopolitical conflict: decentralisation to the local government level, within a unitary state. Other common forms of territorial self-government not examined in this research are federalism, autonomy (sometimes referred to as federacy arrangements) and devolution.[9] Decentralisation, as it is understood here, is a process in which central–local relations are restructured through the devolution of competences from the central to local levels of government (Braathen and Bjerkreim Hellevik 2008: 3; Grasa and Camps 2009: 21). It is understood as a mechanism for sharing power vertically between central and local government politically, administratively and fiscally. Normatively it is guided by the principle of subsidiarity, which means that a central authority should perform only those functions which cannot be performed effectively at a more immediate or local level, and that no authority usurps the authority of another (European Union 2007: Art. 5.3; Council of Europe 1985: Art. 4.3).

Political decentralisation refers to the transfer of political authority to the local level through the establishment of elected local governments and procedures aimed at increasing the participation of citizens and civil society in local decision-making (Grasa and Camps 2009: 21). *Administrative* decentralisation involves the devolution of functional responsibilities to local administrations, e.g. municipalities, regions or counties. Importantly, it does so without removing their accountability to central government. It may also entail the devolution of political decision-making authority over these competences, but this is not a necessary condition (Falleti 2005: 329). Lastly, *fiscal* decentralisation entails the transfer of financial authority from the central to local level, and is essential if institutions are to exercise public policy functions autonomously. It increases the revenues or fiscal autonomy of local governments, e.g. through an increase of transfers from the central government, the creation of new local taxes, or the delegation of tax collection authority that was previously national (Falleti 2005: 329). It may also include local control over the revenues and royalties from the exploitation of natural resources.

Decentralisation requires the legal *devolution* of competences from the central to local levels of government. It enables locally elected representatives to exercise their authority and carry out their functions, based on the confidence that the central government places in them (Siegle and O'Mahony 2007: 2). In this respect it differs significantly from forms of deconcentrated or delegated government. When responsibilities are merely *deconcentrated*, power is not transferred to locally elected representatives, but rather to centrally appointed officials operating at the local level, e.g. prefects. Consequently, central government maintains control over resources and local priorities (Grasa and Camps 2009: 23). In contrast, the *delegation* of central government competences to elected local governments means that some local autonomy may be retained in the implementation of central policies. However, these competences remain the ultimate responsibility of central government and can therefore be retracted at any time.

While decentralisation reforms may entail the extensive devolution of power to local governments, these self-governing entities remain ultimately subordinate to the authority of central government.[10] Unlike federal systems, sovereignty is not divided in decentralised unitary states. Unitary states may possess central and sub-central tiers of government, but in the event of conflict, the central government remains constitutionally sovereign. Exceptionally decentralised unitary states may entrench regional or local governments in their constitutions or organise laws, which usually means that higher thresholds of political support are required to modify the powers of local governments. Typically, however, central executive decisions and legislation cannot be overruled by lower government levels, except, of course, when they are found to be unlawful (Norris 2008: 168). Similarly, devolved responsibilities can, in principle, be legislatively withdrawn at any time and without the need for local consent. The decentralisation of power to local communities is therefore a 'matter of grace, not [a] right' (Elazar 1994: 13).

The absence of a constitutionally entrenched guarantee which requires the consent of all government tiers to authorise amendments is the key legal feature of decentralisation that distinguishes it from other forms of territorial self-government, principally federalism (Rothchild and Hartzell 2000: 261; Coakley 2001: 299; Wolff 2010: 10). Irrespective of the degree of autonomy initially awarded to decentralised local units, their authority remains vulnerable to the encroachment of central governments. Other attributes of federalism that are typically missing in decentralised states are bicameral legislatures, where the second chamber represents the local and regional levels and may compensate smaller units through over-representation; independent mechanisms of judicial review, with supreme arbitral authority to settle disputes over the constitution and inter-governmental relations; and exclusive legislative and judicial powers (Amoretti and Bermeo 2004: 9). Decentralisation also differs from autonomy (territorial and personal) in that the reforms are not generally of an explicitly ethnic nature (Young 1998: 60).[11] They often do not explicitly mention 'autonomy'. Ruth Lapidoth, a leading expert on autonomy, defines territorial autonomy as 'an arrangement aimed at granting a certain degree of self-identification to a group that differs from the majority of the population in the state, and yet constitutes the majority in a specific region' (Lapidoth 1997: 174–5). Finally, decentralisation differs from territorial autonomy, federacy and asymmetric devolution, because it requires territorial sub-divisions across the entire state (Wolff 2010: 10).

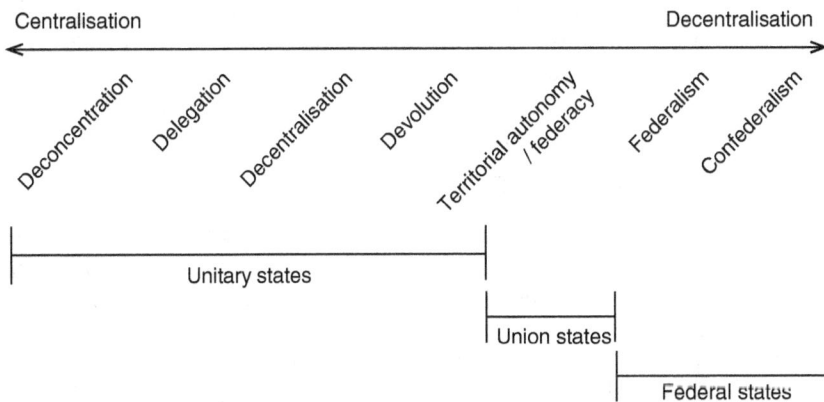

Figure 0.2 Centralisation/decentralisation continuum of territorial self-government arrangements

Note: This illustration represents only an approximation of the degree to which different forms of territorial self-government are either centralised or decentralised. Levels of autonomy will differ depending on the extent to which responsibility is devolved. Stefan Wolff (2009: 9) defines a confederation as a relatively rare form of voluntary association of sovereign member states. Some competences are pooled by treaty, but executive power is not usually granted to the confederal level of government. An example of a confederation is the State Union of Serbia and Montenegro between 2003 and 2006. Examples of union states include India, the United Kingdom and Spain.

Why do governments decentralise?

If the enhanced autonomy that spatially concentrated groups acquire through decentralisation comes at the expense of central government control, why do central governments choose to decentralise? It is an accepted fact that most decentralising states, particularly those which are unitary rather than federal, have conceived and implemented decentralisation reforms on their own initiative ('top-down decentralisation'), and have been relatively free of pressure from below (Manor 1999: 43; Dickovick 2011: 35).[12] Where then does the enthusiasm for decentralisation come from? The motives behind decentralisation, notes Paul Smoke (2010: 194), are 'often much more complex and may be rather less benign', but are crucial to understand since they have a direct bearing on the ways in which reforms are designed and implemented, and on their long-term prospect of success. Decentralisation motivated only by short-term goals, such as immediate electoral incentives, is more likely to be obstructed and/or reversed at a later date (Shah and Thompson 2004: 22).

Exogenous pressures may be placed by regional and international organisations on countries transitioning from a planned to a market economy to decentralise. But decentralisation can bring many recognised benefits to central governments. When threatened with secessionist attempts, federalism or even partition of the state, decentralisation can appear an attractive way of preserving state integrity, regaining control of remote areas, and re-integrating autonomy or secessionist movements (Litvack *et al.* 1998: 108; Schou and Haug 2005: 18). Decentralisation to the municipal level, rather than to the regional level or federal institutions, may be deliberately employed to fragment the local power bases of secessionist groups into smaller, weaker, politically insignificant units (Horowitz 2000: 646; Crook 2002: 300; Ejobowah 2008: 239). Decentralisation may also be used as a mechanism for rejuvenating imperilled governments and for gaining countrywide acceptance of state institutions (Boone 2003: 375; Lake and Rothchild 2005: 122). Finally, central governments may decentralise in times of economic crises to reduce government expenditure levels and budget deficits by offloading responsibility for providing expensive public services on to local bodies (Eaton 2004: 11; Manor 1999: 109; Scott 2009: 7).

Some scholars have questioned the tendency of researchers to under-emphasise and misperceive the political (rather than fiscal or administrative) motives of national politicians when researching decentralisation initiatives (Manor 1999: 53). Since most politicians are generally preoccupied with protecting and enhancing their own influence, political considerations often take precedence over other concerns. For example, political parties in central governments may recognise decentralisation as a strategy for mobilising and strengthening local power bases, and extending their patronage networks (Manor 1999: 44; Khemani 2010: 4). Although scholars have found no connection between political party decisions to decentralise and their ideological convictions, Kathleen O'Neill's research into decentralisation processes in Bolivia, Colombia, Ecuador, Peru and Venezuela does however suggest a link between the adoption of reforms and the electoral concerns of parties (O'Neill 2003, 2005).[13] The premise of her argument is as follows:

> Viewed through the lens of electoral motivations, decentralising reform can be reconciled with the power-seeking motives of politicians: A party distributes political and fiscal power to the arenas in which their political allies seem most likely to gain control .... When political parties predict that they will be unable to control central power in a centralised governing structure and also predict that they could win a substantial proportion of subnational offices were they contested democratically, decentralisation becomes more attractive. Its attractiveness lies in the party's ability to hold real power at subnational levels even as it loses control of the centre.
>
> (O'Neill 2003: 1087)

Decentralisation may therefore require a 'calculation of trade-offs', whereby the parties in government balance relinquishing some of the power held in the present against the opportunity to compete for decentralised power in the future (Rodríguez 1997: 4).

Threats to successful decentralisation

The prominent role political considerations potentially play in decentralisation decisions may affect the long-term success of reforms. Hastily developed reforms, created in response to a political crisis or conflict, are more likely to lack broad-based political support and may result in the adoption of superficial frameworks or outright opposition during implementation (Smoke 2007: 135). Similarly, if decentralisation has been imposed on a country by external agencies, these reforms are also likely to lack legitimacy in the eyes of both majority and minority communities and may become vulnerable to centripetalist tendencies. Peace, observe David Lake and Donald Rothchild, may consolidate majority power, and over time majority communities may use their political strength to recentralise state authority and resources (Lake and Rothchild 2005: 110).

Relatedly, if the decision to decentralise was based on the short-term political calculations of governing parties (e.g. perceived greater electoral strength at the local rather than central level), then the fate of reforms may be sealed if the fortunes of these same parties are reversed at a later date (Eaton 2001: 103). Likewise, the sustainability of decentralisation may be undermined if an alternative party with strong support at the central level is re-elected and believes it would benefit from recentralising power (Manor 1999: 60; O'Neill 2005: 23; Dickovick 2011: 10). This is what David Lake and Donald Rothchild refer to as the 'transient majority problem'. They observe: 'no present majority can bind a future majority. Territorial decentralisation offered today can be retracted tomorrow' (Lake and Rothchild 2005: 128). Finally, if the reforms

Table 0.1 Champions of and challengers to decentralisation

	Comment
Potentially strong supporters	
Citizens and locally elected representatives	Demand for more participation in local government
Parliament	Territorial parliamentarians would like to identify with specific local projects which they can 'bring home'; favour a less transparent, discretionary system
Urban and wealthier municipalities	Often concerned with how their autonomy is restricted and how access to their tax base is limited
Potentially weak supporters	
Ministry of Finance	Advocate strict limits to fiscal decentralisation in order to maintain control of the main fiscal tools for stabilisation policy purposes
Ministry of Economy	Wish to control the types of investments made, in addition to their regional distribution
Line Ministries	Would like to control public service delivery standards and maintain ultimate approval or sign-off power over initiatives
Ambivalent supporters	
Ministry of Local Self-Government	Favours a greater guaranteed fiscal share for municipalities, but would like to control the distribution of these resources
Rural and less wealthy municipalities	Are more interested in fiscal equalisation systems than local tax systems and would like a guaranteed transfer of resources from urban and wealthier municipalities to the rest

Source: Adapted by the author from Bahl (1999: 26)

are a result of negotiations between national representatives rather than grassroots pressure from below (as in most unitary states), the interests that benefit most from decentralisation are rarely sufficiently organised to defend against the reform's reversal (Eaton 2001: 123).

Genuine support for decentralisation at the national level can also vary within political parties and across government. Despite reforms being formally endorsed by their party, national politicians may resist devolving political and fiscal power to local counterparts because these individuals are likely to be their political rivals (Eaton 2001: 117).[14] Similarly, ministries and their bureaucrats may have insufficient incentives to work co-operatively across government and with the sub-central level. Indeed, decentralisation undermines functional departmental control over substantial resources and there may well be competition between ministries for control of the decentralisation agenda and resources (Boone 2003: 135). If the Ministry of Finance, for example, is on record as favouring decentralisation, explains Roy Bahl, it is likely to be a very controlled form of decentralisation with the local level experiencing limited freedom to set tax rates or borrow capital, as well as stringent expenditure mandates (Bahl 1999: 27). Table 0.1 illustrates the possible competing interests in decentralisation across government.

The pace of implementing decentralisation is an important consideration which may undermine the reform's long-term success. Recentralisation, observe Shah and Thompson for the World Bank, is more likely to occur if the process of decentralisation is implemented gradually (Shah and Thompson 2004: 20). A steady, as opposed to a 'Big Bang' approach, such as the reform process implemented in Indonesia after 1998, may be justified by the fear of weak local capacity or low levels of civic participation.[15] However, the slow pace of reforms may give opponents of decentralisation an opportunity to regroup and build support to circumvent it.

Regardless of the motives of political parties and central government bureaucracies concerning decentralisation, important preconditions for successful reforms include a general commitment to popular participation and support for bottom-up decision-making (Kälin 1999: 59; Blunt and Turner 2005: 77). Central government must be genuinely prepared to share power with sub-central units, and both the central and local levels must regard each other as authorised partners in an ongoing process. Sufficient local capacity to implement the devolved competences effectively is also crucial: concern about under-performing local governments is most frequently invoked against decentralisation (Illner 1998: 30; Litvack *et al.* 1998: 122). Impatience, observes Manor, very often destroys the considerable promise of decentralisation (Manor 1999: 72). Finally, democracy and the presence of a vibrant, inclusive civil society within which participatory local government may flourish are other important preconditions for successful decentralisation (Manor 1999: 55; Tranchant 2007: 3; Barter 2008: 3).

Territorial self-government and conflict management

Addressing internal self-determination disputes through various territorial solutions has produced a sizable literature. But it continues to be dominated by studies of federalism in its various forms,[16] and autonomy (territorial and non-territorial), rather than of the devolution of power to the local level.[17] Recent developments in the liberal consociational literature have however created more interest in decentralisation to the local level. For example, in an attempt to address consociationalism's neglect of self-determination conflicts, John McGarry and Brendan O'Leary have emphasised the complementarity of consociational power-sharing and territorial forms of self-governance, as well as the possibility of combining it with power-dividing strategies such as human rights legislation (McGarry and O'Leary 2005, 2008, 2011).

The emerging practice of complex power-sharing, researched extensively by Stefan Wolff (2007, 2008, 2009, 2012) and Marc Weller (Weller, Metzger and Johnson 2008), reflects a growing realisation among scholars and practitioners that neither central power-sharing nor territorial self-government alone is likely to be sufficient to secure sustainable peace in areas where minorities are territorially concentrated (Horowitz 1993: 36; Rothchild and Hartzell 2000: 269; Hoodie and Hartzell 2005: 103). An increasing number of peace agreements have combined territorial self-government with various models of power-sharing at both the central and local levels. Examples include, but are not limited to, Bosnia and Herzegovina (1995), Northern Ireland (1998), Macedonia (2001) and Kosovo (2007).[18]

While the literature on local government decentralisation is extensive and covers a wide range of issues, few researchers have recognised the reform's potential for contributing to the management of ethnic conflict. Common research themes include the deepening of local democracy and civic participation (Sisk 2001), poverty reduction and the implementation of 'pro-poor' policies (Crawford and Hartmann 2008), enhanced local accountability and transparency (Connerley *et al.* 2010) and the more efficient provision of basic public services (Ahmad *et al.* 2005). The impact of clientelism and political patronage on the effectiveness of decentralisation reforms is another popular theme and, as we shall see, is particularly relevant to Macedonia.[19]

An almost entirely separate body of work exists on fiscal decentralisation (Oates 1972; Bahl 1999; Dickovick 2011). However, research into how reforms may unevenly affect different parts of a country is unusual.[20] Studies which jointly address the political, administrative and fiscal aspects of decentralisation are also lacking. Economists typically research fiscal relations between the different levels of government and local economic development,[21] while political scientists focus their attention on issues of institutional design, election results, inter-governmental relations and accountability mechanisms.[22]

Generic studies on decentralisation and ethnic conflict management do exist,[23] and scholars have acknowledged the relevance of other decentralisation-related themes, such as local democracy and poverty alleviation, for reducing inter-ethnic tensions.[24] Short single country case studies have been published on numerous countries, but no monographs have the ambitions pursued here: to demonstrate the distinctive features of (symmetric) decentralisation within unitary states as a conflict-management strategy.[25] Where empirical evidence exists, scholars have generally been preoccupied with assessing whether decentralisation in its broadest sense, i.e. also including federal and federacy arrangements, either exacerbates or inhibits ethnic conflict and secessionist tendencies, rather than examining under what conditions decentralisation is most likely to work.[26] This book's focus on the implementation, rather than just the design, of decentralisation in Macedonia contributes to a more nuanced understanding of the challenges facing different forms of territorial self-governance in the longer term. It demonstrates how the prevalence of clientelism at both the central and local levels, together with limited fiscal autonomy, can undermine the reform's potential to grant meaningful self-government to territorially concentrated minority ethnic groups.

The key arguments advanced

Decentralisation has the potential to address significant inequalities between groups while remaining sensitive to the majority's determination to preserve the state's integrity

While decentralisation alone may not have addressed all of the grievances raised by the Republic of Macedonia's Albanian community before 2001, this research demonstrates its potential to address many of the inequalities that contributed to raising inter-ethnic tensions during the 1990s. Devolving additional competences to the municipal level has enhanced the political control diverse communities have over the management of local affairs. The creation of alternative sites of power for local elites has also expanded the space available for citizens to participate in local government. Further, devolving the management of controversial issues, such as the use of community languages and flags, to the municipal level has gone some way towards tempering the heat generated by Albanian cultural status demands. Finally, decentralising responsibility for the delivery of primary and secondary education has improved access to mother-tongue education and has facilitated a more equitable distribution of public funds.

Despite granting local communities enhanced access to and participation in the management of their own affairs and resources, decentralisation ultimately represents a mechanism for integrating non-majority communities into unitary state structures and for maintaining the territorial integrity of the state. It does so by ensuring that the municipalities remain ultimately subordinate to central government, and are sufficiently numerous to fragment the power base of non-majority communities across multiple local units – in this sense decentralisation may be read as a power-dividing strategy, one that disrupts the possibility of Albanian regionalisation. Decentralisation to the local level also represents a mechanism for granting greater power to persons within minority groups without necessarily recognising their distinctive ethnic character.

Limited fiscal autonomy undermines the benefits of political and administrative decentralisation

This study argues that fiscal inter-governmental relations are inherently political and political forces substantially determine the way in which they are designed and implemented. An examination of the fiscal powers of Macedonian municipalities suggests that decentralisation has done little to restrain central government's monopoly over state power and resources. This outcome is the result of a conscious political decision by coalition government elites (Macedonian and Albanian) to maintain power, rather than a general design feature of decentralisation per se. Consequently, Macedonia appears more decentralised than it really is, because the political and administrative aspects of decentralisation are more visible than the discrete and complex fiscal regulations that undermine the reform's potential. As a result, the reform thus far has only been partial, and advances in the administrative and political aspects of the reform have been undermined by limited progress in its fiscal dimension.

Macedonia's experience with decentralisation between 2005 and 2012 shows that while constitutionally guaranteed decentralisation processes may be harder to reverse than others, it is not impossible. Administrative and political aspects of decentralisation may be constitutionally guaranteed, but a municipality's right to meaningful fiscal autonomy is often defined in legislation that can be easily amended. While the sequencing of different aspects of the reform within a post-conflict environment may be justified in the short term, attempts to solve internal self-determination conflicts through decentralisation in the longer term will fail if self-governance continues to exist only in form but not in fiscal substance.

Decentralisation may not affect all groups and all parts of the country equally

Symmetrical decentralisation may have adverse effects on inter-community relations because the reform only benefits territorially concentrated groups. The dispersal of the Turkish, Roma, Serbian and Vlach communities throughout Macedonia means that in most municipalities these smaller communities fall well below the thresholds required to benefit from rights permitting the enhanced use of community languages and symbols, or influencing the design and delivery of services. Macedonians and Albanians residing in small numbers in municipalities where another ethnic community may be in the majority are subject to a similar fate. Further, consociational-inspired local power-sharing mechanisms have thus far proved ineffective in protecting the interests of smaller local communities. They may also have advanced the interests of (some) ethnic communities at the expense of broader intra-ethnic relations, i.e. between members of different political parties.

Rather than provide for a more equitable distribution of public resources, and creating optimal conditions for expanding citizens' access to basic services in previously marginalised regions, fiscal decentralisation may in fact exacerbate longstanding socio-economic disparities. This is particularly the case for disparities between urban and rural areas, and if fiscal decentralisation relies too heavily on property-related taxes to provide municipal revenues.

Understanding the political and social context to decentralisation is crucial

Macedonia demonstrates that the (limited) success of decentralisation depends as much on contextual factors as on the design of any particular reform model. Democratic institutions are never introduced in a political and economic vacuum, and the motives of political elites, changes to the state's economy and the political configuration of party politics all significantly influence decentralisation's chances of success.

Successful decentralisation requires the central government to be genuinely prepared to share power with sub-central units, and both the central and local levels must regard each other as equally authorised partners. However, this can only happen if the internal structures of political parties are democratic and if party hierarchies take into account the views of their members, because high levels of central control discipline over members implies the subordination of local politicians in party structures at the expense of local democracy. The existence of vertical clientelistic relationships within parties undermines the autonomy of local politicians. Polities based on clientelistic exchange between parties and voters are not conducive to encouraging the development of responsive and accountable local government. Left unchecked, patron–client relations within political parties undermine the benefits associated with decentralisation by limiting the effectiveness of municipal administrations and by making them less accountable to local citizens. What may appear to be representative local governments, responsive to the needs of local citizens, may in reality only be a deconcentration of central government.

Structure of the book

The above conclusions are derived from the evidence supplied in the chapters to follow. Chapter 1 accounts for the adoption and details of Macedonia's decentralisation programme. Its joint use of consociational and integrative measures was intended to address the concerns of both the Albanian and Macedonian communities. Why decentralisation rather than autonomy was the governing theme of the Framework Agreement is explained. Chapter 2 examines the political aspects of decentralisation and considers whether it has contributed to widening effective political participation and strengthening democracy at the local level. It examines whether decentralisation has addressed political and cultural inequalities by improving the political representation of diverse groups in local decision-making processes; deepening local democracy by providing opportunities for local residents to participate in local governance; and enhancing the transparency, accountability and responsiveness of municipal governments.

Chapter 3 examines administrative decentralisation and considers whether devolving responsibility for the provision of public services can satisfy the demands of non-majority groups for greater autonomy over their own affairs. It focuses on the provision of primary and secondary education in Macedonia, and considers whether decentralisation has facilitated the provision of heterogeneous local public services; enhanced participation and transparency in local decision-making regarding the delivery of services; and ensured a more equitable and transparent distribution of public resources.

Chapter 4 assesses fiscal decentralisation and considers whether the reforms have enhanced the fiscal autonomy of Macedonian municipalities. It begins by considering how the short-term political calculations of governing parties at the centre may have influenced both the design and implementation of fiscal decentralisation. The chapter then evaluates the extent to which municipalities are dependent on central government for their revenues; the ability of municipalities to make independent decisions over spending; and the capacity of municipalities to set independent financial contracts with private actors, such as creditors and employees. An appraisal of inter-governmental fiscal relations is necessary to determine whether the political and administrative goals of decentralisation examined in the previous two chapters are viable in the absence of sufficient fiscal autonomy and resources.

Chapter 5 considers the apparent conflict between subsidiarity and solidarity, and examines whether the fiscal autonomy ensuing from decentralisation has been achieved at the expense of economic and territorial cohesion. It does this by examining whether decentralisation in Macedonia has addressed socio-economic inequalities by facilitating a more equitable distribution of public resources throughout Macedonia; creating the optimal conditions for expanding citizens' access to basic services (thereby reducing social exclusion); and reducing longstanding socio-economic disparities between urban and rural areas.

The Conclusion assesses the extent to which decentralisation between 2005 and 2012 has contributed to the management of ethnic conflict in Macedonia. It evaluates whether the reform has lived up to expectations and has indeed contributed to conflict reduction. It also considers whether decentralisation has had any adverse effects on Macedonia's fractious inter-ethnic relations. The obstacles to decentralisation's successful implementation are identified against clear standards. This analysis distinguishes between factors related to the particular design that decentralisation in Macedonia took, and the context within which the reform has so far been implemented. Despite its appropriate design, successful decentralisation in Macedonia requires a central government that is genuinely prepared to share power with sub-central units. Attempts to solve internal self-determination conflicts through decentralisation in the longer term will fail if self-government continues to exist only in form but not in substance.

Notes

1 See notably Weiner (1971). Weiner's model assumes a minimum of three actors: an irredentist state, an anti-irredentist neighbour and a shared ethnic group across the international boundary.
2 The Conference on Security and Co-operation in Europe's (CSCE) Spillover Mission to Skopje was established in September 1992 to prevent a possible spillover of war from neighbouring former Yugoslav republics into Macedonia. Its mandate was to monitor Macedonia's borders with Serbia and Albania, as well as its political, economic and social conditions. United Nations Security Council Resolution 795

authorised the immediate preventive deployment of United Nations peacekeepers to Macedonia's borders with Albania and Serbia in December 1992. The mandate of the United Nations Protection Force (UNPROFOR) 'Macedonia Command' mission (renamed 'United Nations Preventive Deployment Force' or UNPREDEP in March 1995) also included monitoring parts of Macedonia's border areas with Albania and Serbia. In addition, the mission provided preventive forces to strengthening the country's stability and served as a deterrent against possible Serbian aggression. Following Macedonia's decision to establish diplomatic relations with Taiwan, China vetoed a decision to extend UNPREDEP's mandate and the mission was terminated on 1 March 1999 (Ackermann 2000: 112–22, 128 and 134–40). See also UNPREDEP's Chief of Mission Henryk Sokalski's *An Ounce of Prevention* (2003) and UNSC Resolution 795 (1992).

3 *Ushtria Çlirimtare Kombëtare* – UÇK – in Albanian.

4 Hereafter, Macedonia's ethnic communities (ethnic Albanian, ethnic Turkish, etc.) are referred to as 'Albanian', 'Turkish', etc. Where the term 'Macedonian community' is used, it refers to the majority ethnic group.

5 Hereafter referred to as the 'Framework Agreement'.

6 Such claims differ from external self-determination claims, which include demands for independent statehood and unification with another state.

7 In the work of international organisations, autonomy is usually considered from the perspective of maintaining the status quo: where existing, it has been (moderately) endorsed; where not granted, it has been (moderately) discouraged. For the bad press attached to multi-national federations see McGarry and O'Leary (2009).

8 For a review see McGarry and O'Leary (2011).

9 In this context, the term 'devolution' denotes the decentralisation of specific competences by the recognised sovereign centre to a selected territory or territories in an otherwise unitary state. Examples include the United Kingdom (Scotland, Wales and Northern Ireland), and Spain (Catalonia, Basque Country, etc.) (Wolff 2010: 10).

10 The degree of devolved authority may in fact be greater than in federal or autonomous units.

11 Autonomy can also be granted on a non-territorial or 'personal' basis.

12 According to Manor, enthusiasm from local citizens often develops after decentralisation has taken place, rather than beforehand.

13 J. Tyler Dickovick's research on Brazil, South Africa, Peru and Senegal finds no empirical evidence to suggest a link between decentralisation and economic liberalisers or with left-wing politicians, given the policy's association with participation and local action (Dickovick 2011: 24–5).

14 In Macedonia, as elsewhere, a politician often begins their political career at the local level before choosing to compete in national elections once their reputation has been established.

15 For more details of Indonesia's approach to decentralisation, see Diprose (2008, 2009).

16 See for example Elazar (1994), Amoretti and Bermeo (2004), McGarry and O'Leary (2005, 2009), Brancati (2006, 2010), Horowitz (2007) and Burgess and Pinder (2011).

17 See for example Lapidoth (1997), Ghai (2000), Wolff and Weller (2005) and Nimni (2007).

18 For an analysis of the General Framework Agreement for Peace in Bosnia and Herzegovina, also known as the Dayton Agreement, see Bieber (2006). For an analysis of Northern Ireland's Belfast or Good Friday Agreement, see McGarry and O'Leary (2004). For an overview of Macedonia's Ohrid Framework Agreement, see Bieber (2008). For details of the Comprehensive Proposal for the Kosovo Status Settlement, see Ker-Lindsay (2011).

19 See for example Keefer (2005), Chanie (2007), Barter (2008) and Lambright (2011).
20 See, however, Bird and Ebel (2007), Lessmann (2009) and Monastiriotis (2013) for interesting discussions of how fiscal decentralisation may exacerbate socio-economic disparities.
21 See for example Oates (1972), Bahl (1999) and Bird and Ebel (2007).
22 See for example Crook and Manor (1998), Treisman (2007) and Wolff (2010).
23 See for example Kälin (2004), Kauzya (2005), Schou and Haug (2005), Brancati (2006, 2010), GTZ (2006), Siegle and O'Mahoney (2007), Braathen and Bjerkreim Hellevik (2008), Crawford and Hartmann (2008), Grasa and Camps (2009) and Connerley *et al.* 2010). 'GTZ' is an acronym for *Gesellschaft für Technische Zusammenarbeit* (German Society for Technical Co-operation). It was renamed *Gesellschaft für Internationale Zusammenarbeit* (German Society for International Co-operation/GIZ) in 2011.
24 See for example Sisk (2001) and Crawford and Hartmann (2008).
25 For Uganda, see Green (2008) and Schelnberger (2010); for Indonesia, see Diprose (2008, 2009); for Malawi, see Tambulasi (2009); for South Africa, see Hartmann (2010); for Rwanda, see van Tilburg (2010); for Kosovo, see Holohan (2005), Gjoni *et al.* (2010) and Burema (2013). All but Holohan are limited to book chapters and journal articles.
26 Scholars who argue that federal structures reduce the likelihood of ethnic mobilisation by allowing territorially concentrated groups a meaningful degree of self-government include Lijphart (1977, 2002), Gurr (2000) and McGarry and O'Leary (2005). In contrast, others, such as Nordlinger (1972), Bunce (2004), Hale (2004), Roeder and Rothchild (2005) and Brancati (2006, 2010) argue that federalism is subject to strong centripetal and centrifugal pulls and is therefore likely to fail in the long run.

1 How decentralisation came to the new Macedonia

The death of Yugoslavia gave birth to a new Macedonian question.[1] The 'old' Macedonian question, or at least the best known of the old ones, was politically and militarily focused on a nation-building contest between the new Bulgarian, Greek and Serbian nation-states over the national status of the Orthodox villagers of Macedonia – and the joint determination of each of these new states to assimilate or expel the relevant Muslim and Albanian populations, with concomitant implications for instability throughout the Balkans. The new Macedonian question, by contrast, has two related aspects. The most important and largely internal question, and the critical subject of this book, is whether the two major communities of the former Yugoslav Republic, namely Macedonian Slavs and Albanians, can establish a workable democratic coexistence. The former fear being demographically outstripped, and have been known to contemplate expulsion and down-sizing to secure control of 'their' state. The latter, by contrast, have feared a renewed tyranny of the majority. They objected to the new Macedonia formed after the dissolution of Yugoslavia, because it was constitutionally defined as a mono-national state with Macedonian recognised as the only state language. Some of them looked to pan-Albanian sources for support. The second, largely external question, is the new Macedonia's relations with its immediate neighbours. One key diplomatic relationship remains unresolved: Greece refuses to recognise Macedonia by its own preferred name, insisting that it be known as FYROM (the Former Yugoslav Republic of Macedonia), and has managed to dictate European Union diplomacy on the subject. The other is formally resolved on paper. By the terms of the Framework Agreement, and the conditions imposed on Kosovo's recognition, Kosovo has no territorial claims on Macedonia. Nevertheless the possibility of a 'greater Albania' haunts the imagination of Macedonian Slavs.

The immediate origins of armed conflict in Macedonia in 2001 are the subject of continuing polemical and historiographical debate. No effort will be made here to appraise the merits of these various claims. Instead the focus here is squarely on the specific structural causes of group tensions which the Framework Agreement sought to address, and comprehension of which is critical to the appropriateness of decentralisation as a remedy.[2] The persistent external threats to the survival of the Macedonian state, and the debate over the Macedonian nation, are addressed because the insecurity of the dominant Macedonian Slavs contributed to their reluctance to provide timely concessions to non-majority communities and shaped their policy outlook on decentralisation. The particular institutional design of Macedonia's decentralisation, a combination of integrationist and consociational measures,[3] was intended jointly to address the concerns of the Albanian and Macedonian Slav communities.[4] Examining the status and dynamics of the inequalities that existed between Macedonia's two largest ethnic communities before 2001 is therefore essential.

Multiple inequalities in the political, cultural, social and economic spheres, experienced simultaneously by Albanian political elites and the people they represented, made Macedonia prone to ethnic conflict. Regardless of whether these grievances were all genuine or all exaggerated or were extensively manipulated by political entrepreneurs, the only way to build sustainable peace in post-2001 Macedonia was for these inequalities to be addressed. The historic legacy of the continuous occupation of Macedonia by regional and external powers, and its partition in numerous wars in the Balkans, along with persistent identity disputes, largely with its Greek neighbour, during the 1990s affected the way in which the new Macedonian state initially approached its relations with non-majority communities, in particular the Albanians (Engström 2002b: 6). Existential concerns manifested themselves particularly strongly in questions that threatened the territorial integrity of the state, made federalism a taboo subject and profoundly influenced Macedonia's eventual model of decentralisation.

Horizontal inequalities and the structural causes of ethnic conflict

Inequalities between ethnic groups, real or perceived, matter to the likely emergence of ethno-political conflict. Relative deprivation theorists such as Ted Robert Gurr (1970) and Susan Woodward (1995a) attribute violence to the discrepancy between ethnic groups' perceptions of what they think deserve in society and what they are capable of getting. Those conscious of relative deprivation feel disadvantaged and it is this feeling of injustice, and the resulting frustration, which may cause violent group mobilisation along ethnic lines. By contrast, Donald Horowitz locates the possible causes of conflict in rivalrous comparisons of group worth; he observes how, 'like individual self-esteem, collective self-esteem is achieved largely by social recognition .... Relative group worth and relative group legitimacy thus merge into a politics of ethnic entitlement' (Horowitz 2000: 185–6). The contest for group worth or status, he concludes, is the common denominator of ethnic conflict among unranked groups.[5] As intra-group loyalty strengthens, the prospect of confrontation increases. Deprivation and group entitlement theorists therefore believe that enhancing the political standing of certain ethnic groups, in addition to improving their socio-economic conditions, may reduce feelings of exclusion and with it, the likelihood and intensity of ethnic violence (Koktsidis 2012: 22).

While Gurr's early work focused on how disadvantaged groups mobilise, sometimes violently, researchers on horizontal inequalities recognise the role that both the deprived group and those in positions of power have in managing inter-group inequalities (Diprose 2008: 116). Frances Stewart (2004, 2008) refers to the discrepancies which exist between culturally defined groups as 'horizontal inequalities'. These can be based on political, cultural, social or economic status, and differ from inequalities between individuals or households, which she regards as 'vertical'. Political inequalities in the distribution of political opportunities and power among groups may occur at the levels of the presidency, cabinet, parliament, local government or civil service, among others. Political exclusion is likely to alienate group leaders and provide an incentive for group mobilisation (Stewart *et al.* 2008c: 306). Cultural inequalities include the extent to which a state recognises (or fails to recognise) a group's cultural practices, such as its language or religion, or its preferred self-designation. As Bikhu Parekh has observed (2000: 222), where a particular group has historically been dominant, claims to cultural 'neutrality' are often regarded as little more than the implicit privileging of that dominant culture. Cultural inequalities are particularly potent for group mobilisation because of their inherent link to group identity (Langer and Brown 2008: 51). Finally, social inequalities may include discrepancies in access to public services, such as education, and the allocation of state resources and infrastructure; while economic inequalities include differential access to state assets, employment opportunities and income levels (Stewart 2008: 13).

Inequalities are frequently multi-dimensional, and reinforcing, and may explain the persistence of group-based deprivation in many countries. A lack of access to education may lead to low incomes, and both may be responsible for and also caused by a lack of political power (Stewart *et al.* 2008a: 55). Similarly, the adoption of an official language not only increases the political and cultural status of its mother-tongue speakers, but can also bring direct material benefits to that group in increased access to employment and promotion (Langer and Brown 2008: 46). Policies to address inter-group inequalities can take either a direct or indirect approach. Ethnic quotas in public administration, for example, represent a direct approach, while regional redistributive policies or the decentralisation of power fall into the second category (Stewart *et al.* 2008c: 303). Direct policies unavoidably increase the saliency of identity differences, whereas indirect policies are (or may be seen to be) broadly ethnically neutral and perhaps therefore can contribute to the integration of different ethnic groups over time.

While the presence of severe inter-group inequalities may be a necessary motive for political or even violent mobilisation, conflict is not inevitable where such inequalities exist (Stewart 2008: 11). What makes violent conflict more likely, argues Stewart, is when political, cultural, social and economic inequalities coincide, and where the same group is deprived across every dimension (Stewart 2008: 11; Langer *et al.* 2012: 7). The existence of inter-group inequalities is insufficient to explain whether group grievances become a political issue at the state level: that requires that inequalities are jointly experienced and prioritised by group leaders and their followers. Even with the presence of severe socio-economic inequalities at the mass level, the absence of political inequalities among elites may reduce the risk of violent group mobilisation because group leaders lack the incentives to mobilise their constituents for violent conflict (Langer 2008: 164). This may also be the case when group leaders are politically included but are not dominant, since they can still enjoy the 'perks' of office, such as opportunities for personal enrichment and the dispensing of patronage (Stewart *et al.* 2008b: 289–90). The motives shaping a group's potential leaders are particularly important because they may have access to more resources and can arouse support by accentuating common identities or increasing perceptions of inter-group inequalities (Stewart *et al.* 2008b: 289).

Advocates of grievance-based accounts of conflict have been criticised for understating alternative economic explanations for conflict, such as the existence of organised criminal networks and war entrepreneurs. Predation or greed theorists such as Paul Collier and Anke Hoeffler (2004), for example, have argued that violent conflicts may be driven by private material gains and not by genuine grievances, and when grievances do exist, they are manipulated by militant opportunists as pretexts for revolt.[6] Such an interpretation has not been without its critics.[7] Regardless of whether group-based grievances are genuine or have been subject to political manipulation, as researchers of Macedonia's 2001 conflict such as Hislope (2001), Latifi (2001), Daskalovski (2006), Vankovska (2006) and Neofotistos (2012) have argued, sensible deprivation and predation theorists agree that within post-conflict situations, the only way to construct sustainable peace is to promote principles of good governance, such as equality of opportunity and the impartial rule of law.

The Republic of Macedonia

The Republic of Macedonia became an independent state in September 1991. The most southerly located of the former Yugoslav republics, Macedonia shares borders with Albania, Bulgaria, Greece, Kosovo and Serbia, and its ethnically diverse population, although totalling a mere 2 million, reflects the cultural diversity of the region and a legacy of shifting borders and empirical conquests. The most recent census in 2002 found Macedonia's ethnic breakdown to be 64.2 per cent Macedonian, 25.2 per cent Albanian, with the remaining population made up of Turks, Roma, Serbs, Bošniaks, Vlach and those that declared themselves 'Other'.

Macedonia's declaration of independence from Yugoslavia in September 1991 signified the first time that 'Macedonians' had had an independent state of their own in modern times. Famous in antiquity under Philip and his son

Table 1.1 Population of the Republic of Macedonia according to ethnic affiliation, 2002

Ethnic affiliation	Percentage of total population
Macedonian	64.2
Albanian	25.2
Turkish	3.9
Roma	2.7
Serbs	1.8
Bošniak	0.8
Vlach	0.5
Other	1.0

Source: SSO (2003: 19)

Alexander of Macedon, no state since the Roman conquest of Macedonia in 168 BC had borne the name 'Macedonia' (Rossos 2008: 213). Whether ancient Macedonia had been Greek or not had been contentious, and controversies over the genealogical lineages, real or alleged, between Slavs and Hellenes continue to this day. Between the Roman Republic and 1912 the territory belonged successively to the Byzantine, medieval Bulgarian and Serbian, and Ottoman empires (Barker 2001: 4). As 'Vardar Macedonia', incorporated within Serbia in the First Balkan War, it became part of the Kingdom of Yugoslavia, but without distinctive self-government. It was only in 1944 that Josip Broz Tito, then General Secretary of the League of Communists of Yugoslavia, recognised Macedonia as a separate republic within the prom-ised Yugoslav federation and as having a distinct Macedonian identity and national language (Shoup 1968: 144–7, 178–9).

Before the creation of the People's Republic of Macedonia in 1944, the experience of those living there and in its immediate neighbourhood was of repeated partition of the various territories called by that name between neighbouring states, and denial of the existence of a distinct Macedonian identity that was not merely a local variant on one of its neighbours. While a victorious union between Serbia, Montenegro, Bulgaria and Greece may have liberated the Macedonian region from centuries-long Ottoman rule during the First Balkan War of 1912–13, competing claims to Macedonia by the victors, among other matters, led to the Second Balkan War in 1913. The outcome was the Treaty of Bucharest, concluded in August 1913, which, notes Loring Danforth (1997: 51), was 'a great tragedy' for the Macedonian people, since, instead of becoming an independent country, the geographic and ethnographic unity of Macedonia was carved up by its neighbours. The treaty awarded Bulgaria approximately one tenth of Macedonian ter-ritory (known as Pirin Macedonia), Greece one half (Aegean Macedonia) and Serbia the remaining two-fifths (Vardar Macedonia, the geographical unit that is now the Republic of Macedonia) (Ackermann 2000: 55). Serbia

Figure 1.1 Macedonia and its partition between Greece, Serbia and Bulgaria in 1913

Source: Map first cited in Wilkinson (1951: 186)

Note: The references in the key are as follows: (1) limits of territory disputed by Serbia and Bulgaria in the Secret Annex of their Treaty of 1912; (2) new boundaries under the terms of the Treaty of Bucharest (1913) and the Conference of London (1913); (3) Boundaries in 1912; (4) Bulgaro-Turkish boundary under the terms of the Treaty of London (1913); (5) Romanian gains as a result of the Balkan Wars; (6) Serbian and Montenegrin gains; (7) Greek gains; (8) Bulgarian gains.

proclaimed Vardar Macedonia to be 'South Serbia', the language spoken there was considered a dialect of Serbian and its inhabitants were regarded as 'South Serbs' (Danforth 1997: 65; Rossos 2008: 131).

Although occupied by Serbia, Vardar Macedonia's experience with partition and conquest did not end in 1913. Driven by the project of a Greater Bulgaria, which had been achieved briefly under the Treaty of San Stefano of March 1878, Bulgaria's army successfully occupied Vardar Macedonia during World War I. However, its claims to the territory were rejected at the Peace of Neuilly in November 1919, under which Vardar Macedonia became an integral part of the Kingdom of Serbs, Croats and Slovenes, or what would be known as the Kingdom of Yugoslavia ('South Slavia') after 1929.[8] The region of Macedonia was once again occupied during World War II, this time by German, Italian and Hungarian forces, with Bulgaria and Italy dividing Vardar Macedonia between 1941 and 1944. The Italian occupation of western Macedonia, Kosovo, parts of southern Montenegro and Albania proper was the first and only time that Albanian-dominated lands had been united in a 'Greater Albania'.[9] Albania's borders, drawn up by the Great Powers at the London Conference in 1913, largely ignored the demographic realities of the time and left a substantial number of Albanians living outside the boundaries of the new state.[10] This short-lived period of national unity, a dream of

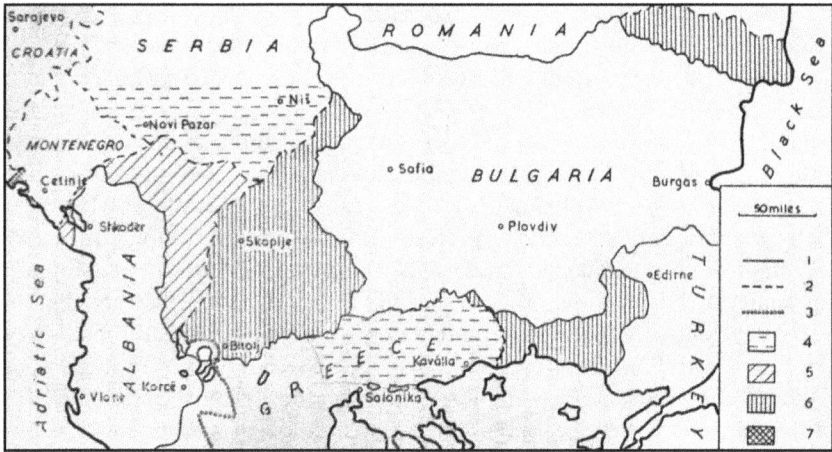

Figure 1.2 Boundary changes, 1941–1943

Source: Map first cited in Wilkinson (1951: 302)

Note: The references in the key are as follows: (1) boundaries in 1938; (2) boundary modifications, 1941–43; (3) extension of Albanian boundaries contemplated in 1941; (4) parts of Serbia and Greece under Bulgarian occupation; (5) Albanian gains; (6) Bulgarian gains; (7) Italian gains.

Albanian nationalists since the League of Prizren in 1878, has remained in the minds of Albanians and Macedonians ever since.[11]

Between the conclusion of the Second Balkan War in 1913 until the end of World War II, the peoples in all three regions of Macedonia (Vardar, Pirin and the Aegean) were subject to violent campaigns of assimilation on the part of their occupiers, whose aim was to convince them that they were actually Serbs, Bulgarians or Greeks respectively (Banac 1984: 317; Danforth 1997: 51). For example, in Vardar Macedonia the policy of forced Serbianisation began initially during the first Serbian occupation (1913–15) and only ended in September 1915 when Bulgaria entered World War I, occupied Vardar Macedonia and introduced its own forced assimilation policy. Vardar Macedonians experienced their third 'baptism by fire' in six years, however, when Serbia resumed its occupation after 1919 (Rossos 2008: 137). Macedonia's occupiers continued to deny the existence of a distinct Macedonian identity, because to do otherwise would have threatened their past territorial gains and/or future aspirations (Rossos 2008: 283).

The denial of a distinct Macedonian identity in Vardar Macedonia initially persisted until Tito's partisans and the leaders of the Yugoslav Communist Party adopted a new policy toward those to whom the socialists referred as the 'Slavs' of Macedonia at the first session of the Antifascist Assembly for the National Liberation of Macedonia (known as ASNOM) on 2 August 1944. Later, Tito established the People's Republic of Macedonia as a federal state within the new Democratic Federation of Yugoslavia and in doing so, undermined not only Bulgarian irredentist claims to Macedonia, but also Serbian nationalists' ambitions to make Macedonia once again part of a Greater Serbia (Shoup 1968: 144–7; Banac 1984: 328). Another motive behind the Communist Party of Yugoslavia's decision to recognise the existence of a separate Macedonian nation may have been the intention to also extend Yugoslav control over Bulgarian and Greek Macedonia (Danforth 1997: 66).[12] Significantly, a special resolution making Macedonian the official language of the federal state was also adopted by ASNOM, and linguists subsequently began the process of codification and standardisation that led to the development of the Macedonian literary language (Shoup 1968: 178–9; Poulton 2000: 52). One further step in the development of Macedonian national consciousness was the restoration of the Archbishopric of Ohrid, previously known as the Bulgarian Archbishopric of Ohrid, in 1958 and the establishment of an independent autocephalous Macedonian Orthodox Church in 1967, exactly 200 years after the Archbishopric of Ohrid had been abolished (Danforth 1997: 53).[13]

Between 1944 and September 1991, when the Republic of Macedonia declared independence from Yugoslavia, the old 'Macedonian question', i.e. whether a distinct Macedonian nation existed, was effectively frozen. The military discipline maintained between East and West during the Cold War, along with the presence of a relatively strong Yugoslav state and army, prevented the emergence of potential irredentist aspirations towards Vardar Macedonia (Reuter 2001: 30). However, the Macedonian 'question' was reopened after 1991 when the Republic became an independent state for the first time and, to varying degrees, the 'four wolves', as Macedonia's neighbours Greece, Serbia, Bulgaria and Albania have often been referred to, began once again to openly challenge the existence of the Republic, along with the Macedonian national identity and language. In so doing, they undermined the legitimacy of the fledgling state and its attempts to gain international recognition of its existence.

While Bulgaria was the first government to recognise the newly independent Republic of Macedonia in 1992, it continued to officially consider the Macedonian nation and language as belonging to 'western Bulgaria' (Neofotistos 2011: 296). In doing so, it openly undermined the state's most fundamental reason for existence: the justification of a separate Macedonian nation (Phillips 2004: 59; Koktsidis 2012: 126). Bulgaria continued to regard the Republic as a nation-building 'test tube', an artificial creation of Tito (Troebst 2001: 61; Rossos 2008: 268). It was not until February 1999, and in response to the Republic of Macedonia renouncing any claim on Pirin Macedonia, that Bulgaria recognised the existence of a Macedonian language, culture and nation separate from Bulgaria (Phillips 2004: 60).

Serbia also continued to regard the Republic as an artificial creation of Tito. Moreover, it maintained its rejection of the autocephalous Macedonian

Church as an independent Orthodox Church following its formation in 1967 (Neofotistos 2011: 296). Alarmingly for the new Republic, Serbia failed to establish diplomatic relations with it until 1996, and until that time implied that the territory was historically part of Serbia (Dobrković 2001: 80). During the early 1990s the leader of the Serbian far right, Vojislav Šešilj, spoke in favour of partitioning Macedonia between Bulgaria, Serbia and Albania, and according to Andrew Rossos (2008: 271), 'reliable reports and unconfirmed rumours' suggest that talks took place between Serbian President Slobodan Milošević and Greek Prime Minister Konstantinos Mitsotakis during 1992 and 1993 regarding the possible partition of Macedonia and the formation of a Serbian–Greek confederation.[14] The behaviour of Yugoslav troops along Macedonia's border, in contempt of the UN's preventive force mission during the early 1990s, further exacerbated the perception of persisting Serbian territorial aspirations.[15]

It was, however, Greek denial of the existence of a distinct Macedonian national identity, along with the Republic's choice of state name and symbols, which had and continues to have the most damaging impact on the Republic of Macedonia. There are three aspects to the name dispute between Greece and the Republic of Macedonia: the name of the country, the scope of its usage and the adjectives for nationality and language. The quarrel, concludes Danforth, is ultimately a dispute over which group has the rights to everything associated with the name 'Macedonia' – its culture, its history, its symbols and, ultimately, its territory (Danforth 1997: 154). Greece has argued that use of the name 'Macedonia' is not only a theft of a Greek birthright, to which Greece claims exclusive ownership, but also amounts to staking a future territorial claim to Greek Macedonia (Danforth 1997: 36; Perry 1997: 269).[16] For Macedonians, the choice of their name is more than a basic human right: it is about their very existence as a separate people. Calling into question their identity is linked to the very survival of the state, since Macedonians regard their identity as being inseparable from their name (Rossos 2008: 269). As the then Macedonian President Kiro Gligorov told European Commission foreign ministers in the early years of Macedonian independence: 'To comply with the Greek demand that Macedonia change its name would mean that the people of that republic would also lose their name, from which it would further stem that this people have no right to a state at all' (cited in Rossos 2008: 269). Macedonian heritage is only one part of the Greek identity, while for Macedonians (Slavs or classical Greeks) there is no other. Letting the name dispute fester while continuing to use the provisional name 'Former Yugoslav Republic of Macedonia' was not only a humiliation for the Republic, but also implied only a provisional acceptance of the state.[17] While disputes with Greece over the initial design of the Republic's flag and parts of its Constitution were resolved in an Interim Agreement signed in September 1995, disagreement over use of the name 'Macedonia' remains unresolved at the time of writing.[18]

Finally, although the Republic of Albania is considered one of the 'four wolves', it is Macedonia's Albanian community which is perceived to be a greater threat to the territorial integrity of Macedonia than its western neighbour. Albania was one of the first states to recognise Macedonia (without reservations) by its constitutional name. Although there have been instances when Albania has been associated with calls for the creation of a 'Greater Albania', because of its preoccupation with its own political crises and reliance on international support, Macedonia's neighbour has largely avoided becoming embroiled in the country's domestic affairs.[19] Albania's interest in the human rights issues of Albanians in neighbouring states was also dominated by the difficult conditions endured by Albanians in Serbian-ruled Kosovo during the 1990s and, as a result, it did not pursue the concerns of the Albanian minority in Macedonia very energetically during this period (Pettifer 2001a: 21; Kola 2003: 394–5).

The Republic of Macedonia's Albanian community

While officially constituting a quarter of the new state's population, the Albanian community represents a demographic majority in certain parts of the Republic of Macedonia.[20] As Figure 0.1 demonstrates, Albanians reside mainly in compact areas in the north and west of the country, along the borders with the Republic of Albania and the Republic of Kosovo. The population of the Polog planning region, situated in the north-west of the country, for example, has a majority of 73 per cent Albanians and within this region some municipalities are overwhelming dominated by Albanians.[21] For instance, Tearce municipality has a local Albanian population of 84.4 per cent, while Zajac and Želino municipalities have local Albanian populations of 97.4 and 99.2 per cent respectively (SSO 2003: 24–5). Significantly, however, sizable Albanian communities also reside in the capital city, Skopje, and in the north-east of the country around the Kumanovo valley (see Table 1.3). In contrast, the smaller Turkish, Roma, Serbian, Bošniak and Vlach communities are dispersed throughout the country and rarely constitute a majority locally.

Table 1.2 Population changes in the Socialist Republic and Republic of Macedonia, 1948–2002

Ethnic group	Population census							
	1948	1953	1961	1971	1981	1991	1994	2002
Macedonians	68.5	66.0	71.2	69.3	67.0	65.3	66.6	64.2
Albanians	17.1	12.5	13.0	17.0	19.8	21.7	22.7	25.2
Turks	8.3	15.6	9.4	6.6	4.5	3.8	4.0	3.9
Roma	1.7	1.6	1.5	1.5	2.3	2.6	2.2	2.7

Source: SSO (2003: 19)

Table 1.3 Degree of ethnic heterogeneity in selected municipalities, 2002

Municipality[a]	Local population	Macedonian (%)	Albanian (%)	Turkish (%)
City of Skopje	506,926	66.8	20.5	1.7
Kumanovo	105,484	60.4	25.9	0.3
Tetovo	86,580	23.1	70.3	2.2
Gostivar	81,042	19.6	66.7	9.9
Kičevo	30,138	53.6	30.5	8.1
Struga	63,376	32.1	56.9	5.7

Source: SSO (2006: 20–5)

Note

a These six municipalities were selected because of their significant population size and location in the north and west of the country. Data based on the enlarged (post-2004 territorial reorganisation) municipal boundaries.

(See Appendix B for maps illustrating the pattern of territorial distribution of Turkish and Roma communities in the country.)

Ethnic demographics are a contentious issue in Macedonia, given the higher fertility rates of Albanian, Turkish and Roma communities. The data in Table 1.2 demonstrates that the Albanian (as well as Roma) population has increased steadily in recent decades at the expense of the majority Macedonian population.[22] As a result of the higher birth rates and migration from Kosovo, the number of Albanians recorded in the 2002 census was 25.2 per cent, up from 11.7 per cent in 1953 (Brunnbauer 2004: 568–75; SSO 2003; Daskalovski 2006: 80). In the eyes of many Macedonians, this 'demographic expansion' of the Albanian community was a deliberate political strategy for increasing their influence in the state (Poulton 2000: 128; Brunnbauer 2004: 576).

Despite the Albanian community's (increasing) dominance in many parts of the north and west of Macedonia, these areas remain ethnically heterogeneous. The data in Table 1.3 illustrates how the six largest municipalities in the north and west of the country, in addition to the City of Skopje, continue to have sizable local minority communities. This demographic reality has significant implications for the design of local government institutions in Macedonia and, in particular, the need to incorporate local power-sharing mechanisms.

Even though Macedonians still constitute a majority in the state, they are outnumbered by Albanians in the region and are 'acutely aware' that many Albanians in Macedonia express a greater sense of solidarity with Albanians in Kosovo than with their Macedonian fellow citizens (Brown 2003: 246). Memories of Fascist Italy's annexation of western Macedonia during World War II, making a Greater Albania a reality for the first time, remain firmly imprinted on the Macedonian consciousness (Balalovska 2001: 4). So do the various demonstrations held by Macedonian Albanians throughout the Yugoslav period, during which they demanded equal rights with Yugoslavia's six constituent nations (the Bosnians, Croats, Macedonians, Montenegrins,

Serbs and Slovenes).[23] The most notable demonstrations took place in 1968, 1981 and 1990, when protestors in the Albanian-majority city of Tetovo repeatedly demanded the creation of a seventh Yugoslav republic through the unification of Kosovo with Albanian-majority areas of western and northern Macedonia, in addition to greater education and language rights (Palmer and King 1971: 181; Poulton 2000: 126). However, notes Koinova (2013: 35), protests mainly echoed those in Kosovo and, because of increasing state repression, never developed a significant dynamic of their own.

It was, however, the behaviour of the two Albanian political parties that gained power during Macedonia's first multi-party elections in November and December 1990, namely, the Party for Democratic Prosperity (PDP-*Partia për Prosperitet Demokratik*) and the People's Democratic Party (NDP-*Partia Demokratike Popullore*, commonly known by its name in Macedonian Народна демократска партија), that caused particular concern for the inexperienced new Republic during the early 1990s. The first incident that implied Macedonia's Albanian community's lack of commitment to the survival of the new state was the PDP's and NDP's successful call to boycott Macedonia's referendum on independence on 8 September 1991. The reason given for the boycott was Albanian disapproval of the wording of the referendum question, which included the option of rejoining a new Yugoslav federation (Phillips 2004: 50). However, the boycott, along with PDP and NDP deputies' refusal to participate in a subsequent parliamentary vote on the new Constitution later that same year, in protest over the wording of its Preamble (discussed below), also reflected a broader concern among Albanians in Macedonia over their status as a minority in an independent Macedonia. Instead, both parties held their own referendum on political and territorial autonomy for Albanians in Macedonia in January 1992, where 74 per cent of approximately 280,000 Albanians (92 per cent of eligible voters) favoured autonomy (Danforth 1997: 145; Ackermann 2000: 61). Fearing the referendum represented a first step towards secession, the Macedonian Government subsequently declared the referendum on autonomy illegal. The Albanian community also boycotted the population census that was held in April 1991 and 'vigorously' lobbied against international recognition of Macedonia by the United Nations and the European Union until the political rights of the Albanian community were improved (Ackermann 2000: 106; Poulton 2000: 195). Such actions were regarded by Macedonians as a 'stab in the back', particularly given the significant external challenges the Republic was facing with neighbouring states at that time.

Political inequalities

According to Kevin Adamson and Dejan Jović (2004: 303), ethnic disputes in Macedonia are not the result of ancient hatreds, as some observers would have us believe. Rather, they are a consequence of political responses to the task of recasting both Macedonian and Albanian post-Yugoslav identities. The formation of an independent Macedonian state in 1991 represents one such circumstance, since a consequence of this process was that Macedonia's different ethnic communities had to renegotiate their status and the protection granted to them within the new state. Maria Koinova (2013: 38) refers to such episodes as a 'critical juncture'; that is, a short period of time before group relationships become formally institutionalised and where 'chance matters, volatility is high, and political agents have substantially heightened freedom to affect the outcome of interest'. The declaration of independence and subsequent drafting of a new Constitution in 1991, based on previous amendments made in 1989, gave rise to very different concepts regarding the nature of the state and the status of Macedonia's ethnic communities living within it. Jenny Engström suggests the Macedonian–Albanian conflict is not merely over rights but, more fundamentally, about who controls the state and what kind of state Macedonia should be: 'Ultimately, then, the conflict between Macedonians and Albanians boils down to the question of who holds the power' (Engström 2002a: 6). A senior politician, speaking in 2004, validated this interpretation in the following remark:

[E]ach side holds a different view of the ownership of ... the country: is it a country with one principal nationality plus large ethnic minorities whose rights are protected and guaranteed, or is it a multi-ethnic country belonging to several ethnic groups?

(PER 2004: 15)

The Preamble to the 1991 Constitution demonstrates how, during the 1990s, Macedonian leaders perceived the newly independent state as belonging primarily to the majority Macedonian community, with the other ethnic groups representing 'junior partners' or mere 'tenants' (Perry 2000: 277; Engström 2002b: 15). It declared:

Taking as the points of departure the ... heritage of the Macedonian people and their struggle over centuries for national and social freedom as well as for the creation of their own state ... Macedonia is established as a national state of the Macedonian people in which full equality as citizens and permanent co-existence with the Macedonian people is provided for Albanians, Turks, Vlachs, Romanies and other nationalities living in the Republic of Macedonia.

(Official Gazette 2001a)

The sense of state ownership and entitlement is particularly noticeable when the text is examined alongside an earlier (1974) version of the Preamble, which declared the Socialist Republic of Macedonia to be 'a national state of the Macedonian people and as a state of the Albanian and Turkish nationalities in it' (Caca 1980: 92; Poulton 2000: 133). According to Gjorgji Caca (1980: 93–4), nationalities living in the Socialist Republic of Macedonia during the Yugoslav period were considered not just citizens, but 'an elemental factor of the self-managing socialist community' and 'equal holders of the sovereignty of the people'. The constituent elements of Macedonian statehood under socialism were therefore the Macedonian nation and the Albanian and Turkish nationalities.

While Macedonian nationalists recognised the existence and rights of the communities, including the Albanians, in the 1991 Constitution, they did not agree that Albanians should be granted the same status as Macedonians within the Republic (Adamson and Jović 2004: 305). From an Albanian perspective, however, being regarded as a mere 'minority' effectively downgraded the Albanian community to the rank of second-class citizens.[24] It also placed them on a par with other numerically inferior ethnic groups, such as the Turks and Roma. For this reason, Albanian politicians during the 1990s, and later the NLA insurgents in 2001, demanded the recognition of their community as an equal partner in the state.[25] In support of their claim that they constituted not a minority but a rather 'constituent people', Albanian politicians emphasised their relative size in relation to the other non-majority communities (Sokalski 2003: 76). Arben Xhaferi, leader of the largest Albanian political party in government at that time, declared in 1998: 'the presumption that Albanians are a "minority" in the Balkans flies in the face of historical fact: Albanians are the third largest ethnic group in the region .... They are a majority that was divided by force' (Xhaferi 1998). He was of course referring to the demarcation of Albania's borders by the Great Powers in 1913, which left a substantial number of Albanians living outside the boundaries of the new state. Interestingly, as Duncan Perry and others have noted, the Albanians made no similar demand on behalf of Macedonia's other ethnic groups. None of the smaller communities, with the exception of the Serbs, actively pursued constitutional change during this time (Perry 1997: 253; Mandaci 2007: 10).

A second key political grievance voiced by the Albanians during the 1990s was the fact that, in an effort to underline the civic character of the state, the 1991 Constitution put a greater emphasis on individual rights and freedoms of citizens, as opposed to the collective rights of national minorities advocated in earlier (socialist) versions (Marko 2004/5: 698).[26] As a consequence, the new Constitution removed the collective rights granted to Macedonia's non-majority communities in terms of proportional representation by quota on public bodies, language rights and the right to fly national flags on specific public occasions (Sokalski 2003: 80). Slavko Milosavlevski (2003) suggested that, at the time, it was assumed that the development of democracy would by itself decrease the importance of collective rights at the expense of the rights of the individual. The composition of a state's civil service is, of course, an important indicator of who owns the country, as well as of how groups are doing in their struggle for group worth (Horowitz 2000: 226). According to an International Labour Organization report examining the representation of minorities in Macedonia's public administration, Albanians constituted only 2.5 per cent of all public employees in 1991. While their representation in the public administration increased to 10.2 per cent by 2001, it remained well below the Albanians' estimated population size of 25 per cent (Daskalovski 2006: 195). Equitable representation for the Albanian community in the public administration, as well as the police, army and judiciary therefore became another significant political demand.[27]

A further political demand of Albanian politicians, and later the NLA, was the decentralisation of additional responsibilities to the municipalities.[28] According to Ugo Amoretti and Nancy Bermeo (2004: 2), demands for enhanced territorial self-government are particularly common when groups are territorially concentrated. As Figure 0.1 illustrates, this is the case for Albanians in the north and west of the country. Before Macedonia's independence in 1991, the Socialist Federal Republic of Macedonia had been heavily decentralised and municipalities had enjoyed a broad range of government competences, including economic regulation, national defence and almost complete financial autonomy (Horvat 1976: 244–7; Caca 1980: 107). However, the 1991 Constitution, which was developed under the pressure of unfavourable domestic and external circumstances, such as persistent existential challenges to the Macedonian nation and state and war in Slovenia and Croatia, reduced the powers of the municipalities considerably, and established a strongly centralised system of government. This process was consolidated in 1995 by a new Law on Local Self-Government (Official Gazette 1995).

The recentralisation of the state during the 1990s was of particular concern to the Albanian community, who claimed that the consolidation of a centralised, unitary state was performed largely at their expense (Xhaferi 1998; Ragaru 2005: 7). The accompanying process of redistricting municipal boundaries in 1996 was widely interpreted among the Albanian community as intended to break up local Albanian majorities within municipalities, with a view to opposing possible demands for autonomy (Ragaru 2008: 6). An official statement issued by the Albanian-majority municipal council of Tetovo in May 1996 condemned the process of redrawing administrative boundaries, which meant that the largest, most developed municipalities of western Macedonia would have fewer Albanians. One Albanian opposition figure lamented at the time that the Albanians of Macedonia had lost the state in 1991 and the municipality in 1996 (Friedman 2009: 215).

It is important to stress that, despite some calls for greater autonomy and even independence by Albanian-dominated areas during the early 1990s, by 2001 the demands of mainstream Albanian politicians and the NLA insurgents were for greater decentralisation rather than independence or the merger of territory with neighbouring Kosovo or Albania (Latifi 2001: 104). An important difference between Macedonia's conflict and others experienced in the former Yugoslav region is that the dispute was ultimately one of *internal*, as opposed to *external*, self-determination: it was not about competing state projects, but rather competing ideas concerning ownership of the state (Poulton 2000: 198). This observation is significant because it influenced the form the political settlement of territorial demands ultimately took and, suggests Florian Bieber (2008: 7), makes the prospect of peace more enduring.

Stefan Wolff and Marc Weller have suggested that ethnic minorities make territorial demands that reflect historic continuities and perceived contemporary opportunities (Wolff and Weller 2005: 5). Amid the uncertainties of Macedonia's first years of independence from Yugoslavia, Albanians organised a referendum on greater autonomy for western Macedonia in January 1992 and subsequently declared an 'Albanian Autonomous Republic of Ilirida' (*Republika e Iliridës* in Albanian) within a broader 'Federal Republic of Macedonia' in Struga two months later (Ackermann 2000: 61).[29] Further, the so-called 'weapons plot' of November 1993 led to several PDP officials, including the Deputy Minister for Defence, being implicated in the discovery of what the Macedonian media referred to at the time as an irredentist 'Albanian paramilitary organization' (Pettifer 2001b: 140). However, the international community's insistence on maintaining the territorial integrity of states during the wars in Croatia, Bosnia and Herzegovina and Kosovo during the 1990s led to a lessening of Albanian politicians' demands during the 1990s and later the NLA's in 2001 (Weller 2005: 71). Particularly influential in this respect was German diplomat Geert Ahrens, Chair of the Working Group on Ethnic and National Communities and Minorities of the International Conference on the Former Yugoslavia. This working group, which existed for nearly five years between October 1991 and January 1996, successfully mediated on a range of minority demands and dissuaded the Albanians from seeking territorial autonomy after 1992 (Ackermann 2000: 103). As a result, by 1996, even the more nationalist Albanian political leaders such as the Democratic Party of Albanians' Arben Xhaferi had retreated from their earlier positions on territorial autonomy and instead spoke of 'internal self-determination' for Macedonia's Albanian community, meaning some form of cultural as opposed to territorial autonomy (Ackermann 2000: 61).

Evidence also suggests there was little appetite among the war-weary Albanian community in Macedonia for border changes by 2001.[30] According to a nationally representative opinion poll commissioned by the US State Department's Office of Research in April/May 2001, while 69 per cent of Albanians admitted to being sympathetic to the NLA's demands, 87 per cent stated it was personally important to them that Macedonia remain united. In addition, a majority of Albanians (71 per cent) stated that they would prefer to live in an ethnically mixed Macedonia than an enlarged Albanian state (Daftary and Friedman 2008: 268).

Interestingly, not all calls for territorial autonomy for Albanian-dominated regions have come from Macedonia's Albanian community.[31] Most controversial was a proposal for partition of the country offered by the Macedonian Academy of Sciences and Arts (MANU) in May 2001. According to this plan, proposed exchanges of population were designed to turn western Macedonia into a homogeneous Albanian enclave, ready for eventual cession to Albania. In return, Albania was expected to yield to Macedonia a small area of land

populated primarily by Macedonians (Phillips 2004: 123). A copy of the proposal, published in the Macedonian-language newspaper *Dnevnik*, can be
found at Appendix D. While attracting limited support in some Macedonian
political circles, the proposal was rejected by Albanian politicians and the
NLA (Latifi 2001: 102).[32] The Albanian community in Macedonia, it has
been suggested, rejected the proposal not necessarily because they were
against the idea of partition, but rather because it was 'the wrong map'.[33]
The MANU proposal ignored the needs of approximately half the country's Albanian community living in Skopje and the areas east of the capital,
including the Kumanovo valley. Former President of the Democratic Party of
Albanians (DPA) Arben Xhaferi remarked that, given the geographic dispersal of Albanians in Macedonia, partition, federalism or even regional autonomy can only be a viable option if territory is forcibly cleansed.[34]

To summarise, Albanian politicians during the 1990s, and later the NLA in
2001, demanded the recognition of their community as a 'constituent people',
equitable representation in the public administration and other public bodies,
the reinstatement of group rights such as the right to use community flags
and symbols, and greater decentralisation of powers to local government as
a means of correcting the perceived political inequalities that existed between
Albanians and the majority Macedonian community.

Cultural inequalities

The greater emphasis placed on individual as opposed to collective rights in the
1991 Constitution also adversely affected the cultural status of Macedonia's
non-majority groups; particularly in the eyes of the Albanian community.
The new Constitution declared the Macedonian language and its Cyrillic
alphabet to be the Republic's only official language and made no reference
to the use of Albanian in Parliament. While the Constitution did permit the
use of community languages alongside Macedonian in municipalities where
the majority of inhabitants belonged to a non-majority community, this right
was rarely respected and was indeed annulled by the Constitutional Court in
1994 (Official Gazette 1991: Art. 7; Caca 2001: 152).

The reduction in language rights prompted Albanian politicians, and later
the NLA, to request that Albanian be granted the status of a second official language. On a practical level, this would mean that the Albanian language could be used in Parliament, in communications with representatives
of central government branch offices and at all levels of the education system
(including tertiary). They also demanded reinstatement of the right of communities to use their language locally in municipalities where they live in substantial numbers. Clearly, restrictions on the official use of one's language
represent both a political and cultural status inequality. Language is the
quintessential entitlement issue, as well as a symbol of domination: 'As the
demand for a single official language reflects the desire for a tangible demon-
stration of pre-eminence, so linguistic parity is transparent code for equality

more generally' (Horowitz 2000: 220). Restrictions placed on the use of one's language by the state also represent an important socio-economic inequality, since it may affect a community's ability to participate equally in the education system and labour force.

Two further culture-related grievances created by the rewording of the Constitution in 1991 were the right of Macedonia's communities to fly their flags in front of local public buildings and the official status of Islam in the country. Article 8 of the new Constitution maintained Yugoslavia's legacy of guaranteeing non-majority communities the right to self-expression, including the use of national symbols such as flags. However, during Yugoslav times, these community flags had been distinguished from those of their titular countries by the inclusion of a red five-pointed star. When these stars were removed from the flags after Macedonia's independence, they became identical to their titular state flags. Disagreement over Gostivar and Tetovo municipalities' right to fly 'flags of foreign states', in recognition of sizable local Albanian and Turkish communities, led to the flags' removal by special police forces in July 1997, the arrest of both mayors and riots which resulted in three civilians dead and up to 400 injured (Poulton 2000: 189).[35] Legislation on the use of community flags was repealed by the Constitutional Court in November 1998, and the right to use them subsequently became a key political demand (Helsinki Committee 1999). Finally, Article 19 of the Constitution referred to the legal status of 'the Macedonian Orthodox Church and other religious communities and groups'. The symbolic ranking of the Macedonian Orthodox Church over 'other' religious communities further aggravated the (predominantly Muslim) Albanian community's sense of cultural injustice (Daskalovski 2006: 66, 161).

Albanian politicians, and later the NLA, therefore called for Albanian to be granted the status of a second official language and for its broader use at the local level, greater use of community flags and symbols and for Islam to be granted constitutional equality with other religions, to correct perceived cultural inequalities between the Albanian and Macedonian communities.

Social inequalities

One important area often overlooked in assessments of the factors that exacerbated ethnic tensions during the 1990s is equitable access to Albanian-medium education at primary and secondary levels.[36] Demands for the establishment of an Albanian-language university in Macedonia dominated the political discourse during this period and, arguably, its subsequent analysis.[37] Dissatisfaction over the availability and quality of Albanian as well as Turkish-medium education increased tensions between the different ethnic groups, and Albanian politicians considered improving standards as a crucial way of achieving social and economic parity with the majority Macedonian community (Myhrvold 2005: 6).

According to Frances Stewart, persistent differences in the learning achievements of students across groups may be caused by language issues and by differences in the quality of education because of inequalities in the quality of infrastructure across locations (Stewart 2004: 66). With regard to the former, although Article 48 of the new Constitution granted citizens the right to education in their mother tongue at primary and secondary levels of education, the reality before 2001, particularly with regard to secondary education, was very different (Official Gazette 1991: Art. 48). A 1985 law on secondary school education, which permitted the establishment of Albanian-medium classes only if there were at least 30 students enrolled and enough qualified teachers, was more strictly enforced in the years preceding Macedonia's independence in 1991. The result was the closure of classes with insufficient Albanian students, and some Albanians were therefore forced to attend mixed classes with instruction in the Macedonian language. While 8,200 students had attended Albanian-language secondary schools in 1981, the figure had fallen to 4,221 by 1989 (Poulton 2000: 129). Further, while ten secondary schools had offered Albanian-medium classes during the Yugoslav period, by mid-1993 only one such school remained (Poulton 2000: 185). According to official data, only 31 per cent of Albanian students who received primary education in their mother tongue continued their studies in Albanian-medium secondary schools in 1994.[38] While numbers did improve during the second half of the decade, the proportion of non-majority students receiving secondary education in their mother tongue remained at only 14 per cent in 1998 (Koktsidis 2012: 82). Resentment towards the new system of increased compulsory tuition in Macedonian was so strong that a significant number of Albanian students boycotted classes and staged protests in Kumanovo and Gostivar during 1997 and 1998 (Koktsidis 2012: 130).[39]

Restrictions on the availability of Albanian-medium education also affected the number of Albanian teachers employed, and many Albanian-medium teachers who refused to accept these changes were removed from their positions (Myhrvold 2005: 25). According to Miranda Vickers and James Pettifer (1997: 173), the number of Albanian teachers employed by the state decreased substantially after independence. By 1994, only 400 teachers remained, compared to nearly 2,500 in the autumn of 1991. The closure of Albanian language courses at Pristina University in Kosovo during 1991 following the removal of the province's autonomous status by Serbian President Milošević also meant that access to teacher training for Albanian-medium teachers was severely restricted, and this led to a shortage of qualified Albanian teachers. In response, Albanian politicians demanded that Albanian-language instruction at the two-year Pedagogical Academy be reinstated in Macedonia, and the Academy be upgraded to a four-year Pedagogical Faculty (Myhrvold 2005: 26).[40] Legislation was eventually passed in 1997 which reinstated Albanian-language instruction at the Pedagogical Academy. However, the Academy was not upgraded to a full Faculty and this meant teacher training remained available only at pre-school and primary school levels and not at the secondary level (Myhrvold 2005: 20).

Finally, considerable discrepancies in the location of educational facilities (particularly secondary schools) and their physical condition, in addition to the distribution of educational funds, meant that Macedonia's Albanian community correctly perceived the quality and availability of the education they received to be inferior (Risteska 2013b: 201). Most primary and secondary schools were built during the 1960s and 1970s and the school network reflected the demographic situation of this period. As the analyses in Chapters 3 and 5 demonstrate, given socialist planning's tendency to concentrate infrastructure in urban areas, secondary schools were located in towns and cities and were therefore frequently inaccessible to the Albanian and Turkish communities that resided in rural areas. This reality also affected rural communities' access to other basic services, for example healthcare and public utilities such as water supply.[41] Secondary school enrolment rates among Albanians were therefore particularly low. While constituting 30.2 per cent of primary school students in 1998/9, Albanians represented only 15.6 per cent of secondary school students (and only 5.5 per cent of university students) (Novkovska 2001: 11). Further, uneven demographic growth between Macedonia's ethnic communities meant that larger class sizes and overcrowding were common in areas inhabited by Albanians. The fact that municipal responsibility for the delivery of education and its funding was recentralised during the 1990s meant that decisions over spending became less transparent and vulnerable to political manipulation. This exacerbated the perception that funding decisions taken in the capital were being made at the expense of non-majority communities.

In response to these social and cultural inequalities Albanian politicians, and later the NLA, demanded greater access to Albanian-medium education at all levels, in addition to increased local control over the provision of key basic services such as education, healthcare and social welfare. Acquiring greater local administrative and financial responsibility for the provision of these services, it was assumed, would reduce perceived inequalities in their quality and availability.

Economic inequalities

Macedonia had always been among the poorest Yugoslav Republics; experiencing high rates of unemployment, particularly among its young people (Horvat 1976: 60; Fox and Wallich 2007: 400). Registered unemployment had been on the rise since the early 1960s, surpassing 20 per cent in the early 1990s (Table 1.5). Macedonia's transition to a market-orientated economy therefore began under very difficult economic circumstances. The industrial sector had been in decline since the 1980s, triggered by the loss of federal subsidies to its companies and the crisis of the socialist banking sector (ESI 2002b: 7). Macroeconomic conditions inherited from Yugoslavia were extremely unfavourable, and the country's economy experienced negative growth rates, high inflation and relatively high levels of domestic and foreign debt (UNDP 2006: 13).

As a small landlocked country, Macedonia is heavily dependent on its neighbours for trade and the transit of its goods to markets elsewhere. Its location therefore makes it vulnerable to the effects of external shocks and regional political events. Three events in particular had a significant impact on Macedonia's already fragile economy and greatly increased the pain of economic transition. First, the disintegration of the protected Yugoslav market, in addition to sanctions imposed on the Federal Republic of Yugoslavia by the United Nations between 1992 and 1995, meant that Macedonia lost its principal trading partner. Access to its overland corridor to markets in Western Europe was also blocked as a result. Official estimates suggest that the trade embargo against the Federal Republic of Yugoslavia may have cost Macedonia US$3 billion in total lost trade (Liotta and Jebb 2004: 76).

Second, the imposition of a unilateral trade embargo by Greece during the same period because of the name dispute cut Macedonia's access to the sea port of Thessaloniki. This further affected the country's economy and led to a real sense of international alienation. The United Nations Development Programme (UNDP) estimated that extended transport routes, additional loading and unloading costs, and more customs inspections increased export transportation costs by as much as 20 per cent during 1992 and 1995 (UNDP 2001: 44). The Greek blockade may have cost Macedonia a further US$1.5 billion in lost trade (Rossos 2008: 276). Lastly, war in neighbouring Kosovo during 1999, along with the burden of having to cope with the influx of over 200,000 refugees (almost a tenth of the country's population), also took its toll on Macedonia's fragile economy (Poulton 2000: 201). One estimate placed the cost at US$630 million in lost exports for the three months of the Kosovo conflict (Phillips 2004: 75). Prolonged regional instability meant that Macedonia could not attract any sizeable direct foreign investment during its first decade of independence. Gross Domestic Product (GDP) fell by 41 per cent between 1989 and 1995, leading the International Crisis Group (ICG) to predict in May

Table 1.4 Indices of nominal and real salaries and costs of living, 1990–1997 (percentages)

Year	Nominal net salaries	Cost of living	Indices of real salaries
1990	100.0	100.0	100.0
1991	184.4	210.8	87.5
1992	1,984.4	3,396.6	58.4
1993	11,818.8	15,692.4	75.3
1994	24,231.3	35,825.7	67.6
1995	26,815.6	41,450.3	64.7
1996	27,553.1	42,403.7	65.0
1997	28,321.8	43,506.2	65.1

Source: UNDP (2001: 80)

Table 1.5 Unemployment as a percentage of the labour force, 1991–2000

Year	1991	1992	1993	1994	1995	1996	1997	1998	1999	2000
Unemployment rate (%)[a]	19.2	19.8	28.3	31.4	37.7	31.9	36.0	34.5	32.4	32.2

Sources: UNDP (1999: 39; 2001: 23)

Note

a These figures do not reflect so-called 'latent unemployment', which refers to a large number of employed persons whose remuneration arrives late, is received irregularly, or not received at all (UNDP 2001: 24).

Table 1.6 Labour market indicators of selected groups, according to ethnic affiliation, 2002 (percentages)

	Average	Macedonians	Albanians	Turks	Roma
Employment rate	61.9	68.0	38.8	41.8	21.5
Unemployment rate[a]	38.1	32.0	61.2	58.2	78.5
Non-activity rate	52.8	46.5	70.7	61.9	52.4

Source: UNDP (2004b: 50)

Note

a High non-activity rates among the Albanian and Turkish communities will inflate their respective unemployment rates.

1999 that 'if the economy continues its downward slide, many people can be expected to turn against the government' (ICG 1999: 10; Rossos 2008: 276).

According to the think-tank European Stability Initiative (ESI), economic insecurities, diminishing resources, and collapsing lifestyles during the 1990s represent the 'other Macedonian conflict', often overlooked by international observers.[42] A restrictive monetary and fiscal policy resulted in only partial macroeconomic stability, and Macedonians experienced high inflation and a significant decline in living standards (see Table 1.4) (UNDP 2004b: 41). Survey data published in the UNDP's National Human Development Report for Macedonia in 2001 suggested that the principal cause of economic insecurity among citizens was unemployment, followed by low or irregular remuneration, and inadequate social assistance (UNDP 2001: 11). As Table 1.5 illustrates, unemployment rose significantly during the 1990s and disproportionately affected the young.[43] While unemployment affected all ethnic communities, and the closure of publicly owned enterprises undoubtedly affected the majority Macedonian community the most, rates of unemployment were unequally distributed across the country, as well as between the different ethnic groups (Table 1.6) (World Bank 2003a: 34; UNDP 2004b, 46).[44] For example, the unemployment rate of Albanians was twice that of Macedonians, and a clear majority of Albanians, Turks and Roma were unemployed. Combined with the effects of chronic rural under-development, ESI observed how numerous Albanians were 'trapped in a cycle of persistent poverty and high unemployment, which provides fertile ground for social and political instability' (ESI 2002a: 3).

To summarise, diminishing public resources, high levels of unemployment – which disproportionately affected non-majority communities – and a general decline in living standards formed the backdrop to Albanian politicians' demands during the 1990s. The inability of mainstream Macedonian politicians to adequately address the political, cultural, social and economic grievances of the Albanian community during the 1990s led to an erosion of trust in the political class. This created an opportunity for new agents and organisations, such as the NLA, who were prepared to pursue Albanian interests outside the discredited political process, to seek to address these demands through other means.

A nation under threat: the state's response to Albanian grievances

Existential insecurity had a significant impact on the way in which the Macedonian dominated-state approached its relations with non-majority communities, particularly the Albanians, during the 1990s and since (Engström 2002b: 4). Not only did persistent identity disputes with neighbouring states during the 1990s mean that the Government was too preoccupied to pay sufficient attention to growing domestic concerns, feelings of insecurity and lingering threat perceptions contributed to the majority's reluctance to acknowledge Albanian demands for greater rights (Engström 2009: 125). Clearly, a state that is self-confident and strong can be more accommodating of minority demands than one which is afflicted by political and/or economic weaknesses (Safran 2000: 32). The legitimacy of the new state progressively eroded among Macedonia's Albanian community and encouraged them to question the (ethnic) Macedonian people's right of exclusivity over the country (Koktsidis 2012: 126). Rogers Brubaker has claimed that one development after a titular nationality gains independence is fear of losing its newly acquired statehood, one that can easily develop into paranoia about perceived security threats (Brubaker 1996: 27). These possibilities were always likely in Macedonia, observes Kristina Balalovska (2001: 9), because of the long history of denial of the existence of the Macedonian nation and political entity, as well as the precarious existence of the state during the 1990s.

For the Macedonian political elite and community, yielding to demands that the Albanians be recognised as a constituent nation or that Albanian become a second official language was considered zero-sum politics. Concessions would dilute the sovereignty or the unitary nature of the state and ultimately threaten the precarious survival of the Macedonian national identity. Elevating the status of Albanians from a minority to a constitutive people, with 'its Titoist echo', generated the fear that Albanians would later demand self-determination and eventually the right of secession (Liotta and Jebb 2004: 67). The demand for republic-wide use of Albanian provoked concern that the Macedonian people would become marginalised in their own country. Macedonians feared Albanians would refuse to communicate in Macedonian and that bilingualism would make them no longer eligible for public sector jobs.[45] Within an environment of diminishing public resources, the otherwise plainly dominant Macedonians felt under siege, both socially and economically (ESI 2002a: i). Albanian demands for proportional representation in public administration could only be achieved at the expense of Macedonian workers, and therefore such requests were met with denial and trepidation.

These threat perceptions affected Macedonian attitudes towards decentralisation. As is the case in most former Communist countries, the concepts of 'federalism' and 'autonomy' are considered anathema.[46] Their long and bitter experience of occupation and partition means that they over-invested in the territorial integrity of the state, which they associate with the preservation and consolidation of their national identity (Engström 2002b: 13). Recentralisation during the 1990s, and resistance to decentralising power after 2001, was driven by fear that devolving further political power to the municipalities, particularly those dominated by Albanian communities, would threaten the state's existence (Latifi 2001: 179; IRIS 2006: 4). Decentralisation was often regarded as 'a step towards federalism' and '*de facto* partitioning of the country', which would make it increasingly possible for Albanian-dominated communities to secede (Ragaru 2005: 18). In an interview for the Belgrade weekly *Ekonomiska Politcia*, published soon after the Gostivar flag protests of July 1997, the then Macedonian President Gligorov remarked, 'what is at issue here is to turn part of Macedonia's territory into an autonomous region to approach the ultimate goal of independence and secession from our state' (Gligorov 2001: 99). And any Albanian secessionist attempt would carry the risk of the country's remaining 'rump' falling prey to its historically predatory neighbours (Poulton 2000: 126).

The majority Macedonian population (and some among the micro-minorities) also feared becoming marginalised in Albanian-dominated municipalities (the 'minorities within minorities' phenomenon) (Bieber 2005a: 118).[47] The fear was that they would become 'foreigners in their own country', because of the extensive use of the Albanian language in these municipalities (Brunnbauer 2002: 17). Daskalovski suggests Macedonians were also anxious that they would be denied access to public resources and employment, and recalls events in 1991, when the Albanian community took power in Tetovo municipality and promptly replaced all Macedonians in charge of the public enterprises with Albanians (Daskalovski 2006: 212). The fact that ethnic communities in Macedonia regard the decentralisation of power to municipalities as a zero-sum game, where one community gains control at the expense of the other, exacerbated such concerns (Brunnbauer 2002: 16). As Nadège Ragaru candidly observed:

[T]he moment one community comprises above 50 per cent of the total population in any given unit of government, that unit becomes 'hers' .... Minority rights might be respected, yet community preference will be the rule rather than the exception. In this respect, 'minorities' (nationally) do not 'behave' better than the 'majority' when they are locally dominant.

(Ragaru 2008: 25)

The design of decentralisation within the Ohrid Framework Agreement

Between late January and mid-August 2001 the NLA organised an armed insurrection against the Macedonian Government. At the start of the conflict, the organisation's goals were unclear. Its early communiqués claimed it was fighting against 'Slavo-Macedonian oppressors' and would 'fight until Macedonia constitutionally becomes a Macedonian-Albanian or Albanian-Macedonian state'. However, the NLA later changed its rhetoric and argued that it was fighting for the human rights of Albanians in Macedonia and for constitutional reforms (Daskalovski 2006: 89). The NLA's origins were just as murky. While analysts agree that many of the fighters were Kosovo Liberation Army veterans from the war against Serbia in 1999, NLA members claimed that the rebel force comprised several thousand men coming from Macedonia.[48] For the first few months of the armed insurrection, hostilities were concentrated in the north and west of the country, close to the border with Kosovo and the Albanian-majority city of Tetovo. However, after the NLA threatened to attack the capital Skopje and bomb the nearby oil refinery and international airport in June, the conflict entered a new stage. Diplomatic efforts to reach a political rather than military solution intensified and the internationally sponsored Ohrid Framework Agreement, which brought an end to the fighting, was signed in Skopje on 13 August. Parliament was to adopt constitutional amendments and other reform legislation within 45 days, while the NLA was to disarm itself under NATO supervision.

The role of the European Union (EU), in particular its Common Foreign and Security Policy High Representative Javier Solana, the United States and NATO was instrumental in getting the conflicting parties to reach a political solution. Fearing a descent into full-scale civil war that would threaten regional stability and endanger the NATO mission in neighbouring Kosovo, Western diplomats intervened first to facilitate dialogue between the main political parties and later to broker a peace agreement. As early as April, international actors sponsored the creation of a 'Government of National Unity', involving the four largest parties: VMRO-DPMNE, SDSM, DPA and PDP.[49] Somewhat reluctantly, the coalition was eventually formed in May and negotiations began on constitutional reforms to address inter-ethnic issues (Phillips 2004: 117). The efforts of Western diplomats, in particular EU special envoy François Léotard and US diplomat James Pardew, were crucial in moving Macedonian politicians towards a negotiated conflict settlement. Solana and NATO political envoy Pieter Feith have also been praised for persuading the Government not to declare a state of war during the seven-month insurgency, and for maintaining pressure on Skopje to uphold various ceasefire agreements (Daskalovski 2006: 109–10).

Throughout the conflict, the EU successfully used political incentives to convince Macedonian politicians to take a specific course of action. As the DPA leader Arben Xhaferi observed at the time: 'troops and weapons did not stop violence. What did was the hope provided by the EU that it would intervene in starting political negotiations' (cited in Daskalovski 2006: 107).[50] On 5 April the European Commission granted Macedonia the most favoured national status and four days later the country became the first in the region to (somewhat prematurely, some would argue) conclude a Stabilisation and Association Agreement.[51] The EU also pledged an aid package of €40 million for 2001 through its CARDS programme for the Western Balkans, while the International Monetary Fund promised a further €50 million in macro-financial grants and loans. All funds were dependent on the Macedonian political parties reaching a political settlement to the conflict (Daskalovski 2006: 108–9).

Although international actors condemned the NLA's violent tactics, their insistence on restraint and a proportional use of force by the Macedonian security units frustrated many Macedonians and gave rise to anti-Western sentiment. According to the British journalist John Phillips, virtually all international actors in Macedonia were accused of pro-Albanian bias by Government officials.[52] Macedonians also criticised Western diplomats' change of rhetoric towards the NLA. For example, at the onset of the crisis, the NLA fighters were regarded as 'terrorists' and 'murderers', but later the international community moderated its tone and referred to them as 'rebels'. The reason for this change in terminology, claims Daskalovski (2006: 138), is not difficult to find: once Western diplomats favoured a political solution to the crisis, they needed the NLA's approval to stop the fighting. The reluctance of some Macedonian politicians to stand by the Framework Agreement, once signed, was clear from the delays experienced during its passage through Parliament. The Agreement and constitutional changes were eventually ratified on 17 November – more than six weeks late – and only after strong pressure from the EU and NATO. The Law on Local Self-Government, also due to be adopted within 45 days from the signing of the Agreement, was finally approved on 24 January 2002.[53]

The ultimate goal of the Framework Agreement was to accommodate the grievances of the Albanian community, while at the same time address the insecurities of the Macedonians by preserving the territorial integrity of the state. The Agreement's Basic Principles declared: 'Macedonia's sovereignty and territorial integrity, and the unitary character of the State are inviolable and must be preserved. There are no territorial solutions to ethnic issues' (Official Gazette 2001b: Art. 1.2). Its aim was to achieve peace through a process of integration, institutional bargaining and compromise at both the local and state level, rather than through territorial division (Ordanoski and Matovski 2007: 1). Unlike Bosnia's Dayton Agreement, Macedonia's Framework Agreement sought to strike a balance between consociational, centripetalist and integrative approaches to peace building and in doing so, 'square a circle' between the existence of a unitary state and institutional recognition of ethnic diversity (Ragaru 2008: 21).

Contrary to widespread misperceptions, Albanian politicians did not achieve all of their demands at Ohrid. For example, in the domain of executive power-sharing, the creation of the post of Vice-President with veto powers, which would be filled by an Albanian, and the demand for municipal control of local police forces, were not accepted (Daftary and Friedman 2008: 278). Also lost were elevating the constitutional status of the Albanian community to a constituent people, making Albanian an official language state-wide and the creation of a second parliamentary chamber (Ilievski 2008: 27).

In its Basic Principles, the Framework Agreement declared: 'The development of local self-government is essential for encouraging the participation of citizens in democratic life, and for promoting respect for the identity of communities' (Official Gazette 2001b: Art. 1.5). Certainly, the Agreement called for the transfer of 11 new municipal competences, along with a revised law on local government financing to ensure sufficient resources and fiscal autonomy; 'a cure against federalisation' remarked one Albanian politician at the time (PER 2003: 11).[54] However, the municipalities were not awarded any legislative functions, and many of the devolved competences remain limited and are not held exclusively by them.[55] The municipalities remain ultimately subordinate to the authority of central government even though, significantly, their right to the devolved competences is constitutionally entrenched (Official Gazette 2001a: Art. 115).[56] Residual powers remain at the central level. The municipalities are also not directly represented at the central level, as federal units would be in a bicameral system. The only mechanism available to the municipalities for influencing central government policy – aside from informal political party channels – is the municipal association, known by its Macedonian acronym 'ZELS'.[57]

Despite common perceptions suggesting the contrary, decentralisation was framed to conform with the Council of Europe's European Charter of Local Self-Government and the principle of subsidiarity, rather than granting fully-fledged self-government to the Albanian community.[58] Ermira Mehmeti, then spokeswoman for the Albanian party Democratic Union for Integration (DUI), led by former head of the NLA, Ali Ahmeti, remarked how Arend Lijphart's models of non-territorial corporate autonomy and segmental autonomy along ethnic lines were abandoned during negotiations because of the Government's insistence on preserving the unitary character of the state (Mehmeti 2008: 73).[59] Unlike examples of territorial autonomy, the ethnic nature of Macedonia's municipalities is not explicitly recognised. In contrast to neighbouring Kosovo, Macedonian municipalities comprising a significant non-majority community do not enjoy any special asymmetrical status (UNSC 2007: Art. 4; Sulejmani 2008: 152). All have been granted the same

competences, regardless of local demographics. Finally, Macedonian municipalities are not permitted to merge with neighbouring jurisdictions, though
they are allowed to co-operate with one another and form joint public institutions (Official Gazette 2002: Art. 14). Given the territorial concentration
of Albanians in the north and west of the country, it is no surprise that the
government adopted reforms to disperse limited and conditional authority to
more than 80 non-ethnically defined local units. This would not have been the
outcome had the state endorsed the creation of regional units or indeed an
autonomous region.

Under the terms of the Framework Agreement and subsequent Law on the
Use of Languages, Macedonian remains the only official language throughout
the country and which can be used at the international level (Official Gazette
2001b, 2008b). However, any other language spoken by at least 20 per cent of
the population locally is also recognised as an official language within municipalities and can be used in communication with regional units of ministries
(Official Gazette 2001b: Art. 6.6). Regarding languages spoken by less than 20
per cent of the population within a municipality, the Agreement also allows
the possibility for their use as an official language, but the decision to do so
remains at the discretion of the municipality. The recognition of community
languages comes as a function of demographics, rather than through symbolic
recognition of their equal status with the Macedonian language. Nowhere in
the Framework Agreement or subsequent legislation is use of the 'Albanian'
language, for example, specifically mentioned. Such an arrangement risks
causing friction in the future if a situation arises where local demographic
changes mean a particular community no longer meets the required 20 per
cent threshold. Even at the local level, community languages are not in autonomous official use and can only be used alongside Macedonian (Sulejmani
2008: 144). The Agreement and subsequent Law on the Use of the Flags of
the Communities also regulates the use of community emblems, such as the
flying of community flags in front of local public buildings, if that community
constitutes a majority within a municipality (Official Gazette 2001b, 2005).

Lastly, given the heterogeneity of many local areas, and to protect against
the marginalisation of non-majority communities within municipalities,
Macedonia's decentralisation design incorporates both consociational and
integrative power-sharing provisions. The combination of local power-sharing
mechanisms with territorial self-government in this way, in addition to decentralisation's place within the wider Framework Agreement, represents an
example of the emerging practice of complex power-sharing.[60] Proportionality
within municipal administrations, councils, committees and local public
administration was envisaged, although the Framework Agreement does not
call for strict ethnic quotas. This is in contrast to other consociation-inspired
political settlements, such as Bosnia's Dayton Agreement (OHR 1995).
Qualified voting procedures in Macedonia were foreseen to ensure greater
consensus in decision-making within municipal councils. They operate along
similar lines to Arend Lijphart's concept of minority veto; however, the right

to use them is not given to a particular ethnic community.[61] Committees for Inter-Community Relations were also envisaged in ethnically mixed municipalities to facilitate institutional dialogue locally between different ethnic communities. Finally, two-round, run-off elections for mayors provide an opportunity for 'voter pooling' across ethnic divides, while the revision of municipal boundaries based on non-ethnic criteria was envisaged to proliferate points of power and to emphasise non-ethnic cleavages.[62] The way in which the institutional design of decentralisation combines consociational and integrative power-sharing mechanisms to simultaneously accommodate and integrate ethnic diversity at the local level is illustrated in Table 1.7.

According to proponents of complex power-sharing, forms of territorial autonomy (which may also include decentralisation) will only contribute

Table 1.7 The accommodation and integration of ethnic difference through decentralisation

Accommodation of ethnic difference	*Integration of ethnic difference*
'The multi-ethnic character of Macedonia's society must be preserved and reflected in public life.' 'The development of local self-government is essential for ... promoting respect for the identity of communities.'[a]	'Macedonia's sovereignty and territorial integrity, and the unitary character of the State are inviolable and must be preserved.'[b]
Enhanced municipal competences	Municipalities remain ultimately subordinate to central government authority
	Municipalities have no legislative functions
Increased language rights for non-majority communities	Competences remain limited and are not exclusive
Recognition and use of community emblems (flags, etc.)	Municipalities are not directly represented at the central level
Consociational arrangements locally: • proportional elections to municipal councils / committees • equitable representation in municipal and local public administration • qualified voting procedures • Committees for Inter-Community Relations	Municipalities participate in institutions of the common state Symmetrical decentralisation: municipalities comprising a significant minority ethnic community do not enjoy special status No formal recognition of the ethnic character of municipalities No explicit recognition of communities benefiting from language rights Relatively large number of municipalities (proliferating points of power) and no regional level of government Majority run-off system: election of a common mayor

Notes

a Official Gazette (2001b: Art. 1.3 and Art. 1.5).

b Official Gazette (2001b: Art. 1.2).

to the management of self-determination conflicts if they are applied in the context of an overall institutional design that gives regionally concentrated groups a strong stake in the centre (Weller and Wolff 2005; Weller *et al.* 2008; Wolff 2009). Accordingly, local populations and their representatives are incentivised to remain part of the larger state. The need to combine decentralisation with additional power-sharing mechanisms at the central level is particularly critical in Macedonia, given the demographic strength of the Albanian population (25 per cent of the population). The significance of the territory dominated by the Albanian community relative to the rest of the state (Albanian-majority areas constitute approximately one third of the country) is an additional factor which makes power-sharing at the centre essential (Wolff 2009: 33). For this reason, the broader Framework Agreement included further soft power-sharing mechanisms designed to integrate the Albanian community into wider state structures. For example, the equitable representation of all communities in the national civil service and public administration, police and Constitutional Court was envisaged. Consociational techniques, such as qualified voting in Parliament and the re-establishment of a parliamentary Committee for Inter-Community Relations, was also foreseen. While the Framework Agreement includes no formal requirements for multi-ethnic coalitions in government, the country's demographic balances, coupled with the use of proportional representation in parliamentary elections, makes Albanian political parties' participation in coalition governments likely (Bieber 2008: 27; Wolff 2008: 432–4).[63]

Decentralisation and its ability to address inter-group inequalities

Macedonia's decentralisation seems *directly* to address many (but not all) of the political, cultural status, social and economic inequalities experienced by the Albanian community during the decade after the Republic's independence in 1991. For example, widening political participation at the local level creates alternative sites of power and patronage for local elites and may help legitimise government institutions in the eyes of previously marginalised, disenchanted communities. Additionally, devolving the management of controversial issues such as the use of community languages and symbols to the municipal level goes some way both to accommodating and to diluting Albanian cultural demands (discussed in more detail in Chapter 2). Finally, enhancing municipal responsibility over the provision of public services such as education should lead to a more equitable distribution of state resources, in addition to more culturally responsive services. This argument will be assessed in what follows. In principle, it seems that decentralisation has the potential to address the grievances of both Albanian political elites and the masses, while remaining sensitive to the insecurities of the Macedonian majority.

Decentralisation may also contribute *indirectly* to addressing underlying sources of insecurity, such as socio-economic inequalities, that make Macedonia prone to group-based conflict. The Framework Agreement does not include any direct provisions designed to address the economic inequalities experienced by the Albanian community in Macedonia, an area often neglected in peace processes and agreements.[64] However, advocates of decentralisation suggest that devolving responsibility for local economic development and public service delivery to municipalities may promote economic growth through increased public sector efficiency, in addition to reducing poverty through the design of basic services that more effectively meet local needs (Oates 1972: 11–13; Crawford and Hartmann 2008: 18–21). Decentralisation is also perceived to address rural under-development by promoting a more equitable distribution of state resources locally and by uniting poor areas with more affluent ones (Ahmad and Brosio 2009: 11). This argument will also be examined below. The extent to which decentralisation has the potential to address the material and cultural inequalities that existed between the Macedonian and Albanian communities in the 1990s, while also recognising the concerns of the majority, is summarised in Table 1.8.

Conclusion

Multiple structural inequalities in the political, cultural, social and economic domains existed between Macedonians and Albanians in the new Macedonian state. These inequalities coincided, making them more persistent. They also existed simultaneously at the elite and mass levels, and this made the risk of inter-ethnic conflict more likely.

A long legacy of occupation and partition, along with persistent identity disputes with its neighbours during the 1990s, has affected the way in which the Macedonian majority approached its relations with non-majority communities, in particular the Albanians. Challenges to the Macedonian national identity contributed to the majority's reluctance to acknowledge Albanian demands for greater rights and undermined the legitimacy of the state among Albanian community, and encouraged them to question the Macedonian people's right of exclusivity over the country. Macedonian threat perceptions also affected the state's attitude towards decentralisation and influenced the institutional design the reform ultimately took. Despite granting local communities enhanced autonomy over the management of their own affairs and resources, decentralisation ultimately represents an attempt to integrate non-majority communities (particularly the Albanians) into unitary state structures. It tries to do so by ensuring that the municipalities remain ultimately subordinate to central government, have no explicit ethnic identity and are sufficiently numerous to fragment the power base of non-majority communities across multiple local units. The pre-eminence of the Macedonian language, which remains an official language in municipalities dominated by non-majority communities, in addition to decentralisation's combined use of consociational techniques locally, also reflects a desire to ensure local minorities are not marginalised at the municipal level.

Table 1.8 How decentralisation in Macedonia may address inequalities

Inequalities	Albanian demands	Macedonian insecurities in relation to Albanian demands	Addressed by decentralisation?
Political participation			
Constitutional status	Recognition as a constituent people	Equates to a denial of the right of Macedonians to have their own nation-state Fear of right to self-determination and secession	No – partially addressed in the Agreement (OFA) and constitutional amendments
Collective/group rights	Restoration of collective rights, e.g. proportional representation in the public administration, police, army, judiciary, etc.	Concern PR would be achieved at the expense of Macedonian workers	Partially – new jobs created in municipal administrations and in OFA
Local government	Restoration of competences and fiscal autonomy/widen political participation by creating alternative sites of power	Fear of threats to the territorial integrity of the state Threat of being marginalised in Albanian-dominated areas	Yes – directly by widening political participation Inclusion of power-sharing mechanisms
Cultural status			
Use of language	Albanian as a second official language state-wide	Poses a threat to the survival of the Macedonian national identity Fear of bilingualism in the public administration	No – not addressed in OFA
Use of language	Right to use Albanian at the municipal level	Fear of marginalisation in Albanian-dominated areas	Yes – directly. In certain municipalities, alongside the use of Macedonian

Flags and symbols	Right to fly community flags in front of local public buildings	Fear of secession	Yes – directly
Constitutional status of Islam	Equal status with Macedonian Orthodox Church	Equates to a denial of the right of Macedonians to have and control their own nation-state/'homeland'	No – addressed in OFA and constitutional amendments

Social aspects

Primary/secondary education	Access to education in mother tongue	Threat to the superiority of the Macedonian language	Yes – directly
Primary/secondary education	Equitable and transparent allocation of educational funds and infrastructure	Threat to the superiority of the Macedonian language	Yes – directly
Primary/secondary education	Teacher-training for all Albanian-instruction teachers	Threat to the superiority of the Macedonian language	No – addressed in OFA
Tertiary education	Establishment of an Albanian-medium university	Threat to the superiority of the Macedonian language	No – addressed in OFA
Equitable access to basic services	Improve infrastructure in rural areas	Struggle for control over diminishing state resources	Yes – directly

Economic aspects

Employment and income levels	Improve access to public employment at all levels	Concern PR would be achieved at the expense of Macedonian workers	Partially and indirectly – new jobs created in local administrations
Rural under-development and equitable access to basic public services	Equitable distribution of state resources; Improve infrastructure in rural areas	Struggle for control over diminishing state resources	Yes – indirectly by equitable distribution of state resources, and by uniting under-developed rural areas with urban ones

While decentralisation may unable to address all of the grievances raised by Albanian politicians and the NLA, when placed within the broader context of the Framework Agreement, the reform has the potential to directly address many of the inequalities that were responsible for raising tensions between the Macedonian and Albanian communities during the 1990s. Importantly, the inequalities that decentralisation seeks to address are experienced by both the Albanian political elites and the masses, and their resolution should therefore make violent group mobilisation less likely in the future. Decentralisation may also contribute indirectly to reducing socio-economic inequalities; an important underlying structural source of insecurity. The following chapters examine the extent to which the implementation of decentralisation in Macedonia between 2005 and 2012 has reduced the political, cultural, social and economic inequalities experienced by Macedonia's Albanian community.

Notes

1 See Pettifer (2001a).
2 For an analysis of the perceived 'spill-over effects' of the war in Kosovo during 1999 and political instability in the Preševo Valley, southern Serbia, during 2001 see Hislope (2003), Vankovska (2006) and Neofotistos (2012). For an assessment of how organised criminal networks and state corruption contributed to political instability in Macedonia see Hislope (2001).
3 Integration and consociation represent two contrasting approaches to managing ethnic difference. Integrationists reject the idea that ethnic difference should necessarily translate into political differences and support constitutional strategies which promote a common public identity which transcends, cross-cuts and minimises ethnic cleavages without (importantly) demanding ethnocultural uniformity in the private sphere. Examples include common state institutions, the promotion of individual rather than communal rights, the design of mixed or non-ethnic territorial entities and electoral systems which encourage the formation of pre-election coalitions across ethnic divides. In contrast, advocates of consociationalism, such as Arend Lijphart, John McGarry and Brendan O'Leary, promote the accommodation of dual or multiple public identities and institutional respect for difference. Consociational strategies include executive power sharing, proportionality in the public administration, minority vetoes and segmental autonomy (territorial or corporate) along ethnic lines. For further details see McGarry *et al.* (2008: 41–2, 58–63) and McGarry and O'Leary (2008: 369–70). See also Lijphart (1977, 2008).
4 Referring to the country's majority Macedonian population as 'Slav Macedonians' or as 'the Slavic majority' is disputed. Nationalist politicians contest the Slavic origin of Macedonians (a theory advocated by the former socialist regime) and instead claim that the population originate from ancient Macedonians, whose European heritage dates back to the eighth century BC (Neofotistos 2011: 302). Its use here is to differentiate the community from Macedonia's other ethnic groups, for example Turks, Roma, Serbs, etc.
5 According to Horowitz (2000: 21–36), relations between ethnic groups entail clearly understood conceptions of superordinate and subordinate status. In unranked systems, parallel ethnic groups coexist and each group is internally stratified with its own legitimately recognised elite. Ethnic groups do not therefore stand in a generalised hierarchical relation to each other. In ranked systems, ethnic groups are

ascriptively defined components of a single society. Elite status is only possible for members of a subordinate group if they are willing and able to renounce their origins by passing into the superordinate group. Within the Macedonian context, Albanians would argue that their relations with Macedonian Slavs were ranked; Macedonians that they were unranked.

6 According to Collier (2006: 2): 'A rebel organization simply cannot afford to be regarded as criminal: it is not good publicity and it is not sufficiently motivating. Rebel organizations have to develop a discourse of grievance in order to function. Grievance is to a rebel organization what image is to a business.'

7 See for example Keen (1996, 1998, 2001), Cramer (2006) and contributions to Berdal and Malone (2000) and Heiberg *et al.* (2007).

8 The treaty was superseded four months later by the Treaty of Berlin, following the Congress of the same name, when Germany and the Concert of Great Powers forced Bulgaria to reduce its claims (Ackermann 2000: 55; Phillips 2004: 25).

9 Italy's occupation of western Macedonia incorporated the Albanian-dominated towns of Tetovo, Gostivar, Debar and Struga into a 'Greater Albania' (Kola 2003: 22–3).

10 The Republic of Albania constitutes roughly half the territories inhabited by Albanians in the Balkans (Kola 2003: 384).

11 The League of Prizren was established on 10 June 1878 in the Ottoman Vilayet of Kosovo. While emphasising their commitment to preserving the Ottoman Empire in the Balkans, Albanian leaders called for a single Albanian vilayet with a centre in the middle of Albania, Albanian language rights and greater local autonomy. The Ottomans refused the League's demands and crushed it soon after (Kola 2003: 8–10; Malcolm 1998: 221–7).

12 A proclamation of 4 August 1944 stated: 'With the participation of the entire Macedonian nation in the struggle against the Fascist occupiers of Yugoslavia, Bulgaria and Greece you will achieve unification of all parts of Macedonia, divided in 1915 and 1918 by Balkan imperialists' (Poulton 2000: 106).

13 Founded in 893, the Archbishopric of Ohrid was an autonomous Orthodox Church under the tutelage of the Ecumenical Patriarch of Constantinople. It became one of the most important centres of Slavic culture in the Balkans and was respected during Byzantine, Bulgarian, Serbian and Ottoman rule until it was abolished by the Ottoman Sultan and Patriarch of Constantinople in 1767 (Rossos 2008: 35–6, 45).

14 During a debate on the former Yugoslavia in the UK House of Commons in November 1992, David Trimble MP said: 'Before war broke out in Bosnia, Milošević clearly signalled his desire to do a deal with his neighbours to carve up Bosnia. Now he is signalling his desire to do the same with Macedonia .... What concerns us now is Greek ambition, together with Serb and, perhaps, Bulgarian ambition ... we should make it abundantly clear that we will not tolerate any forcible intervention by other parties in Macedonia. We should make our feelings very clear to the Greeks.' HC Debates 16 November 1992, vol. 214, c. 100.

15 According to Lund (2000: 178), despite the preventive deployment of UN peacekeepers along the Macedonian–Serbian border from December 1992, small contingents of the Serbian army would penetrate across, occupy an area and eventually retreat, but only after tensions arose and negotiations were required. See also Sokalski (2003: 54).

16 Such fears may seem improbable, given Greece's membership of NATO. Nonetheless, they are deeply rooted in historical experience as recent as the Greek Civil War (1946–9), when the territorial integrity of Greece was threatened by Bulgarian and Yugoslav claims to parts of Greek Macedonia.

17 The 'Former Yugoslav Republic of Macedonia' (FYROM) is a provisional reference created in 1993 for the specific use of the UN, pending resolution of the dispute. It has since been used by other international organisations, such as the European Union, Council of Europe and World Bank.

18 The initial design of the Republic's flag included the Vergina sun, a symbol of the ancient Macedonian kings, which adorned the tomb of Philip of Macedon. The flag was redesigned in 1995, 19 months after Greece imposed a trade embargo on Macedonia in protest, to depict a yellow sun on a red field with eight rays extending to the edge of the field. The Greek government also objected to Article 3 of the Constitution, which declared 'the borders of the Republic of Macedonia may be changed only in accordance with the constitution', and Article 49, which stated that the Republic 'cares for the status and rights of those persons belonging to the Macedonian people in neighbouring countries [and] assists their cultural development and promotes links with them' (Official Gazette 1991; Neofotistos 2011: 297; Vankovska 2013: 96).

19 According to Paulin Kola (2003: 394), if Albanian nationalism ever existed, it was rooted more outside Albania than within: 'The creation of "Greater Albania" has never been official policy in Tirana, and Albanian Communist governments have successfully inculcated in the people that sense of alienation from the rest of the nation through … progressive impoverishment … and an information blackout on news surrounding Albanians beyond the borders of the country.'

20 However, Albanian politicians frequently claim that the size of the Albanian community in Macedonia is much greater than official figures suggest. Interview with Arben Xhaferi: 23 June 2010, Tetovo.

21 See also Appendix L for a map of Macedonia's planning regions.

22 Fluctuations in the Albanian and Turkish populations during the 1953 and 1961 censuses may have been caused by the migration of a significant number of Yugoslav Turks (and of Albanians claiming to be Turkish) to Turkey during this period, and by the efforts of Yugoslav governments to reclassify Albanians as Turks (Poulton 2000: 138).

23 Albanians in Yugoslavia had the official legal status of 'minority' (*narodnost*), rather than the more highly esteemed status of constituent 'nation' (*narod*). This distinction exposed Albanians to discrimination and negative stereotyping throughout the Yugoslav period. According to Vasilev (2013: 697), Albanian demands for group rights in Macedonia after 1991 represent a continuation of this Yugoslav-era struggle for greater political and cultural recognition. See also Varady (1997) for details on the distinction between *narodi* and *narodnosti*.

24 For Albanians, the former Yugoslav category of *narodnost* (minority) had negative consequences. Interview with senior NGO official: 13 November 2009, Gostivar.

25 A letter, attributed to the NLA's commander Ali Ahmeti in April 2001, demanded that the Constitution be amended to read: 'FYROM will be a state of two peoples: a Macedonian-Albanian state or an Albanian-Macedonian state' (Pettifer 2004b: 2).

26 Chapter 11 of the 1974 Constitution entitled 'Equality of Nationalities' stated: 'Municipalities and the Republic ensure that nationalities be proportionately represented in the municipal assemblies and the assembly of the Socialist Republic of Macedonia, and be adequately represented in their bodies' (Caca 2001: 151).

27 Police brutality against the Albanian community was also a regular occurrence. Clashes with the police in the Albanian-dominated Bit Pazar neighbourhood of Skopje left four dead in November 1992; the forced closure of the Albanian-language university in Tetovo left one dead in February 1995; and

demonstrations in Gostivar during July 1997 left three dead (Human Rights Watch 1996: 32).

28 Additional political demands were the creation of the post of Vice-President, which would be filled by an Albanian, local control over the police, amendments to the Citizenship Law (which included a stringent 15-year residency requirement that disproportionately affected Albanians), organisation of a new population census and changes to the Election Law in order to prevent gerrymandering.

29 A map illustrating the proposed 'Republic of Ilirida', constituting 36 per cent of state territory, can be found at Appendix C.

30 According to journalist Tim Judah (2001: 35), none of the Albanian Macedonians he spoke to in villages surrounding Tetovo seemed interested in a 'Greater Albania': 'The more we talked to the villagers the more it was clear that they were ambivalent in their support for the NLA.'

31 Eben Friedman has traced the first Macedonian call for partition to Saško Tororovski, a career diplomat, in a magazine article published in July 1992 (Friedman 2009: 211).

32 Then-Prime Minister Ljubčo Georgievski (VMRO-DPMNE) did not denounce the proposal and referred approvingly to the MANU plan while proposing his own partition scheme ('Theses for the survival of the Macedonian nation and state') while in Opposition and politically marginalised in 2003 (Friedman 2009: 213–14).

33 An alternative map, along the lines offered by the 'Republic of Ilirida' (at Appendix C), may have generated greater support. Interview with senior NGO official: 13 November 2009, Gostivar.

34 Arben Xhaferi did not endorse such steps. Interview with Arben Xhaferi: 23 June 2010, Tetovo.

35 A law passed the previous month had stated that community flags could only be flown on public buildings on certain holidays and alongside the Macedonian flag, but both mayors had rejected this law (Daskalovski 2006: 73).

36 Restrictions on a group's access to education in its mother tongue can be considered both a cultural and a social inequality.

37 For details of the establishment of an 'illegal' Albanian-language university in Mala Recica, Tetovo in 1994 and its treatment by the state see Ackermann (2000: 142–4) and Vetterlein (2006: 10–12).

38 Koktsidis 2012: 82.

39 In August 1998 at least 128 Albanian protesters in Kumanovo were detained for up to 60 days and the organisers were arrested and some later imprisoned.

40 The Academy had prepared teachers for first- to fourth-grade classrooms only (primary education), whereas a Faculty would train teachers for fifth- to eighth-grade subjects (secondary education).

41 An opinion poll completed by UNDP in 2001 found that most people believed villages in the hills and mountains have too little access to services from medical institutions (88.6 per cent), secondary schools (87 per cent), social welfare and local government (68.7 per cent) and cultural institutions (90.1 per cent) (UNDP 2001: 64).

42 See ESI (2002a) for detailed analysis.

43 Almost half of all persons registered unemployed in 2000 were under 30 years old (ESI 2002a: 25).

44 See also Dimova (2010) for an exploration of how economic changes affected interactions between Albanians and Macedonians in the northern city of Kumanovo after 1991.

45 An estimated 90 per cent of the Albanian community are proficient in Macedonian, whereas less than 2 per cent of Macedonians can speak Albanian (ICG 2001: 6).

46 Francesco Palermo (2012: 80, 84) observed that 'in post-communist societies autonomy is, "by default", linked to ethnic claims, and these are automatically associated with a threat to the territorial integrity of the state'.

47 In such circumstances, dominant ethnic groups often build alliances with micro-minorities against the largest minority.

48 According to Židas Daskalovski (2006: 96): 'Macedonian officials criticised NATO for not doing enough to disarm the Kosovo rebel forces, discourage their encampment in the buffer Ground Safety Zone separating Kosovo from Serbia, and prevent their entry in Macedonia.' See also Koktsidis (2012: 161–7) for more information on the origins of the NLA.

49 Right-wing VMRO-DPMNE (Внатрешна македонска революционерна организација – Демократска партија за македонско национално единство) had been in a coalition government with its junior partner, the DPA and another smaller Macedonian party (Democratic Alternative – Демократска алтернатива or ДА in Macedonian) since November 1998. The Social Democratic Union of Macedonia (SDSM – Социјалдемократски сојуз на Македонија) and PDP had been in opposition.

50 According to James Pettifer (2001b: 141), 'As the FYROM government is wholly dependent on external funds from these countries for survival, it is usually possible for Skopje policy to be manipulated in any direction the foreign ambassadors see fit.'

51 A Stabilisation and Association Agreement constitutes the framework of relations between the EU and individual western Balkan countries. Within the context of accession to the EU, the Agreement sets out common political and economic goals and serves as the basis for implementation of the accession process.

52 Nationalist mobs attacked the American, British and German embassies in July 2001, as well as many foreign businesses (Phillips 2004: 131–3).

53 Delays to the adoption of the Law on Local Self-Government were caused when Albanian politicians walked out of the parliamentary session in protest against government tabled amendments to the draft law. They considered the amendments a breach of the preliminary deal (Latifi 2001: 175–82). According to a BBC news report on 7 December 2001, a spokesman for the European Union in Skopje warned that a planned donor conference was in doubt unless the law was passed within the next few days.

54 Those specifically referenced in the Framework Agreement were: areas of public services, urban and rural planning, environmental protection, local economic development, culture, local finances, primary and secondary education, social welfare and healthcare. Official Gazette (2001b; 2002: Art. 22).

55 As shown in Chapter 3 below, municipalities only have responsibility for the maintenance of primary and secondary school buildings, their networks, and the payment of staff salaries, rather than an ability to set policy or influence the development of curricula (Official Gazette 2002: Art. 22.8).

56 The Law on Local Self-Government (Official Gazette 2002: Articles 51, 71, 87) also states that disputes between the different tiers of government will be resolved impartially by the Constitutional Court.

57 'Заедница на Единиците на Локалната Самоуправа на Република Македонија' – ЗЕЛС (Association of the Units of Local Self-Government of the Republic of Macedonia).

58 Article 3.1 of the Framework Agreement states: 'A revised Law on Local Self-Government will be adopted that reinforces the powers of elected local officials and enlarges substantially their competencies in conformity with the Constitution ... and the European Charter on Local Self-Government, and reflecting the principle of subsidiarity in effect in the European Union' (Official Gazette

2001b). Article 4.3 of the European Charter states: 'Public responsibilities shall generally be exercised, in preference, by those authorities which are closest to the citizen' (Council of Europe 1985).

59 See also Lijphart (1977: 43; 2002: 51). The DUI (*Bashkimi Demokratik për Integrim – BDI* – in Albanian) is the largest Albanian political party. It has been a junior member of the national governing coalition with the (Macedonian) VMRO-DPMNE (*Внатрешна македонска револуционерна организација – Демократска партија за македонско национално единство – ВМРО-ДПМНЕ*) since 2008.

60 An early study into the theory and practice of complex power-sharing defined these settlements to be: 'those that concurrently deploy autonomy, governmental, and executive power-sharing, veto and voting mechanisms, human and minority rights regimes, dispute settlement mechanisms, and the involvement of a layer of international involvement or even international governance' (Weller *et al.* 2008: ix–x). While the Framework Agreement combines territorial self-governance with a range of power-sharing mechanisms at both the central and local level, other complex power-sharing settlements, for example in Northern Ireland, also have elements of co-sovereignty in its arrangements and oversight agreed between its patron states. See O'Leary (2008b) for a more detailed analysis of the Belfast or Good Friday Agreement and the British–Irish Agreement.

61 This is an example of what John McGarry and Brendan O'Leary call 'liberal consociation'. A liberal or self-determined consociation rewards whatever salient political identities emerge in democratic elections, whether these are based on ethnicity or religion, or on subgroup or trans-group identities. In contrast, corporate or predetermined consociations accommodate groups according to ascriptive criteria on the assumption that group identities are fixed and that groups are both internally homogeneous and externally bounded (McGarry and O'Leary 2007: 675–6).

62 'Voter pooling' is a practice advocated by centripetalists such as Donald Horowitz which encourages vote-seeking politicians to reach out to attract votes from ethnic groups other than their own (Horowitz 1991: 226; 2000: 598).

63 A general (voluntary) practice of appointing deputy ministers from a different ethnic group to the Minister across Government is also observed. For a more detailed analysis of the wider Framework Agreement and its proposed constitutional amendments, which clarified the legal status of Macedonia's ethnic communities, their languages and religions, see Bieber (2005a, 2005b), Daskalovski (2006) and Daftary and Friedman (2008).

64 See Hoddie and Hartzell (2005: 90–1) and Stewart *et al.* (2008c: 323). The exception is the requirement of equitable representation for the communities in the public sector. However, this is likely to benefit only those individuals with sufficient qualifications and political connections.

2 Has decentralisation enhanced local democracy?

Introduction

This chapter considers whether the decentralisation process in Macedonia has contributed to widening effective political participation and strengthening democracy at the local level, and has thereby also contributed to addressing a significant political grievance of the Albanian community during the 1990s. While the creation of sub-central tiers of government increases the possibilities for diverse communities to participate in political structures, the intrinsic value of local democracy should not be overlooked. Indeed, local government represents state structures that are closest to the citizens and where the right to participate in public affairs can be most directly exercised. Constituting 'the main foundations of any democratic regime', municipalities may (or may not) represent the ideal medium through which the democratic principles of participation, equity, transparency and accountability can be realised (Council of Europe 1985). It is surprising, given the fact that a significant proportion of the minority protection mechanisms envisaged in the Framework Agreement are at the local level, that those monitoring the realisation of these rights remained preoccupied with their implementation at the national level.

This review begins by demonstrating the theoretical debate regarding political decentralisation and its ability to mitigate ethnic conflict by facilitating the effective participation of national minorities in local institutions. It will then determine whether decentralisation in Macedonia has contributed to reducing political inequalities by: improving the political representation of diverse groups in local decision-making processes; deepening local democracy by providing opportunities for local residents to participate in local governance; and enhancing the transparency, accountability and responsiveness of municipal governments. Finally, the opportunities Macedonian citizens had for participating directly in local decision-making processes will be evaluated. Municipal government, notes Timothy Sisk (2001: 12), is only one part of the equation; albeit an important one. The notion of citizens' participation is also central to the concept of local governance.

This chapter does not intend to assess the claims of some smaller ethnic communities that the gerrymandering of municipal boundaries in 2004 led to their effective political exclusion in some municipalities.[1] Nor does it seek to evaluate the participation of the municipalities in central decision-making processes. As previous sections have explained, as a unitary state, Macedonia does not have a bicameral system where the local level is represented centrally. The views of municipalities are only represented formally through the municipal association, ZELS, or informally through political party structures. Instead the chapter argues that while decentralisation has expanded the potential space available for citizens to participate in local governance, it has not sufficiently guaranteed the participation of local communities, or that their participation is both equitable and effective. This chapter also suggests that advocates of the decentralisation process in Macedonia have failed to sufficiently appreciate the extent to which the over-dominance of some political parties, which lack democracy in their internal management structures and decision-making processes, and the pervasiveness of patronage-based politics in daily life has undermined its potential benefits.[2]

Decentralised governance and conflict management

The creation or enhancement of sub-central units allows groups which may be a minority at the state level, but which constitute a majority locally, to exercise governmental power in ways that would otherwise be foreclosed if the whole country was one undifferentiated territory (Horowitz 2007: 958). Importantly, it does so while maintaining the territorial integrity of the state. Increasing the number of arenas in which there are political prizes to be won can also have the important distributive side-effect of creating employment opportunities within the new bureaucracies and service sectors (Horowitz 2000: 605). By making government more representative of society, decentralisation may help legitimise government institutions in the eyes of previously marginalised, disenchanted communities, and thus encourage greater loyalty towards state structures. While the authority of central government is reduced as a result of decentralisation, concedes Walter Kälin (1999: 49), the legitimacy of the state as a whole can be enhanced.

Decentralisation's potential for strengthening local democracy is an argument long advocated by development agencies such as UNDP and the United States Agency for International Development (USAID) (Shah and Thompson 2004; USAID 2009). Attempts to strengthen democracy at the local level are of particular concern in post-conflict and multi-ethnic environments such as Macedonia and complement the democratic peace proposition that democracies are inherently more peaceful than non-democratic regimes. A healthy system of local democracy, in which all groups feel represented and can influence the institutions and policy decisions of governance, can help prevent feelings of alienation and frustration with the state (Sisk 2001: 74). Such institutions may prevent conflict by providing outlets for grievances and creating opportunities for consensual (rather than conflictual) problem-solving.

As a system for bargaining and negotiation, democracy can also help manage conflict constructively by keeping disputes within the boundaries of political dialogue rather than allowing them to escalate into violence (Sisk 2001: 76). Such 'learning laboratories', notes Zoë Scott (2009: 16), may facilitate local politicians to build trust among groups and acquire political and conflict resolution skills that can be used in different social arenas. Training in compromise is essential in ethnically divided societies, particularly before local politicians rise to the central level where more complex and delicate issues of state policy may need to be resolved (Manor 1999: 49; Horowitz 2007: 960). Finally, local government may serve as an incubator for small ethnic parties that choose to form inter- and trans-ethnic alliances (Treisman 2007: 245). If, as Dawn Brancati suggests, decentralisation helps proliferate regional and ethnic political parties, it may be difficult for one group to dominate locally and incentives for the formation of inter-ethnic coalitions may therefore be enhanced (Brancati 2006; Horowitz 2007).

Although decentralisation already contributes to the widening of civic participation through the creation of alternative sites of power and patronage, development agencies advocate supplementing periodic local elections with activities that facilitate the continuous involvement of citizens in decision-making processes. For people to participate fully in their local community, 'the vote needs to be reinforced by the "voice"' (Kauzya 2005: 7). Citizens' participation follows the school of thought historically associated with Rousseau's concept of democracy being the direct engagement by citizens on virtually all community matters (Sisk 2001: 13; Crook 2002: 308). Such activities may take the form of frequent public consultations, participatory planning and budgeting, and can successfully empower ethnic minorities, women and those less educated to become involved in local affairs (Manor 1999: 97; Crook 2002: 308). Direct democracy promotes inter-ethnic dialogue and may avert ethnic conflicts born out of misunderstanding or ignorance (Ghai 2001: 6). It can also promote greater transparency and accountability in local governance, resulting in the increased responsiveness of municipal institutions to local needs and the curbing of corrupt practices (Kälin 1999: 50; Treisman 2007: 12). One further important outcome of citizen participation is the creation of what the political scientist Robert Putnam (1993) refers to as 'social capital'. Social capital is the basis of legitimacy for government institutions and is necessary for effective and efficient governance. Without it, when trust and confidence are lacking, communities are dysfunctional and in the worst case scenarios violence among contending social forces may erupt (Sisk 2001: 147). Significantly, however, enhanced citizen voice can only be effective if municipal governments are ready to listen and citizens have sufficient capacity to stimulate change (Crook 2002: 319; Barter 2008: 2).

Decentralisation and the creation of local tyrannies

Despite the prevalence of reforms worldwide, the academic community and more recently donor agencies have become increasingly sceptical of decentralisation's performance as a panacea for culturally diverse unitary states. For example, writing on behalf of the United Nations in 2005, John-Mary Kauzya surprisingly concluded: 'as a process, it does not possess intrinsic or natural predisposition to peace, democracy or development' (Kauzya 2005: 15). Many authors have warned that the promotion of decentralised governance in ethnically divided societies is not devoid of risk and its success cannot be guaranteed. Its implementation may even have unwanted effects which can inadvertently exacerbate the causes of conflict (Schou and Haug 2005; Braathen and Bjerkreim Hellevik 2008; Grasa and Camps 2009). Policy makers, notes Scott (2009: 18), should understand that while decentralisation alters conflict dynamics, it does not necessarily exacerbate or remove them. Devolving contentious issues to the local level may quarantine conflict, but weak, nascent local institutions may be ill-equipped or unwilling to manage the conflicts that arise (Braathen and Bjerkreim Hellevik 2008: 21; Diprose 2008: 395). Once central government has relinquished the management of potentially sensitive identity issues to local entities, they may no longer be able to act as arbitrators and to take steps to prevent discriminatory behaviour (GTZ 2006: 7).

The creation of newly defined local units, together with the entrenchment of ethnicity locally, may lead to the creation of 'local tyrannies' and exacerbate discrimination against small ethnic communities (Nordlinger 1972: 31; Coakley 2001: 312; Treisman 2007: 239). In this respect, decentralisation may not only freeze – as opposed to reduce – instances of ethnic conflict, it may also relocate them from the central to local level and cause them to become more intense. Unless there is complete homogeneity in each local area, the system will create new 'minorities within minorities', who may be subjected to domination by local elites who capture power by 'democratic' means (Crook 2002: 305). As Chapter 1 has explained, anxiety over becoming 'foreigners in their own country' was a particular fear held by the majority Macedonian community during the 1990s and which hindered the implementation of decentralisation reforms to 2001. Ethnic minorities that have just 'won' greater autonomy from central government may resent having to share power with other ethnic groups locally (Weller and Wolff 2005: 268). Resentment may be particularly intense when local minorities are members of the dominant group at the state level, and if the creation of new boundaries has altered the majority/minority status of local ethnic groups (Green 2008: 446). A possible consequence might be politics which may favour local majorities and encourage discrimination against local minorities in the development of public policy and investment programmes, service delivery, procurement and public employment (Choudhry 2008b: 153). Discriminatory tactics may also adversely affect women and those who do not share such ethnocentric worldviews (Rebouche and Fearton 2005; Beall 2006). Where rigid employment quotas do exist, notes Florian Bieber (2004: 20), the inclusion of smaller ethnic communities in decentralised institutions may only represent tokenism, with real decision-making power being monopolised by the dominant ethnic group.

Another possible negative consequence resulting from the reduction in central government influence locally is an increase in elite capture, with resources designated to benefit the larger population usurped by a few, corruption and rent-seeking behaviour and the entrenchment of patronage or clientelistic politics. These can undermine the benefits associated with decentralisation (Blunt and Turner 2005: 79; Devas and Delay 2006: 692). Where hierarchical chains of patron–client relationships are already dominant in politics, devolving political power and resources to local governments may simply shift the locus of clientelism and corruption (Diamond 1999: 12). This process may even make these problems more difficult to control, because disciplined party structures and countervailing interests, often found at the central level, are absent. Elite capture and patronage politics may also be more acute at lower levels of government because the fixed costs of organising make it harder for smaller groups of people to establish resistance groups (Jeram 2008: 18). Clientelistic promises can be easier to make and fulfil at more local levels, due to the closer social relations between elected representatives and their clients (Keefer 2005: 7). As a consequence, even the strongest advocates of decentralisation argue that effective devolution should be accompanied by corresponding mechanisms to ensure accountability of local actors involved in allocating resources and influencing local political decisions (Kauzya 2005: 15; Cheema 2007: 170).

Representative democracy: the design of municipal power-sharing mechanisms

Given the significant risks associated with decentralisation, experts are increasingly of the opinion that forms of territorial self-government should be combined with other conflict management mechanisms such as power-sharing to reassure groups in deeply divided societies of their ability to participate meaningfully in local decision-making processes (Bunce and Watts 2005: 139; Weller and Wolff 2005: 4). Under majoritarian systems, warns Arend Lijphart (1999: 32–3), governments may constitute a 'majority dictatorship' and there may be 'civil strife rather than democracy'. Power-sharing arrangements, in contrast, embrace joint or consensus decision-making by all major mobilised groups in society, thereby offering a viable alternative to destabilising, 'zero-sum' democracy (Sisk 2001: 74; Norris 2008: 223).

The emerging practice of complex power-sharing represents an attempt to move beyond what Stefan Wolff regards as 'the rigid theoretical divisions between consociational (and integrationist) power sharing and power dividing' (Wolff 2007: 375). This hybrid model of conflict management, increasingly advocated by scholars and practitioners alike, endeavours to address complex self-determination disputes by retaining self-government at its heart, but combining it with additional mechanisms for accommodating diversity, especially forms of power-sharing (Wolff 2009: 38). As Chapter 1 has demonstrated, the Framework Agreement is an example of complex power-sharing.

The decentralisation process, for example, forms part of a wider package of reforms which also include proportionality throughout the state election system and public administration, qualified voting procedures to ensure consensus in decision-making, the re-establishment of a state Parliamentary Committee for Inter-Community Relations and enhanced recognition of community languages and symbols. Significantly, these predominantly consociational power-sharing mechanisms are also envisaged at the municipal level.

Proportionality within municipal councils, committees and the local public administration represents an essential mechanism for assuring the participation of different ethnic groups in both elected and administrative bodies. While the equitable representation of Macedonia's communities in the public administration had long been a state objective, and was indeed enshrined in the 1974 Constitution of the Social Republic of Macedonia, as Chapter 1 has discussed, the reality during the 1990s had been very different.[3] The 1991 Constitution removed the collective rights previously granted to Macedonia's communities, including proportional representation by quota on public bodies. Consequently, Albanians constituted only 2.5 per cent of all public employees at the state level in 1991, a proportion which had only increased to 10.19 per cent by 2001 (Daskalovski 2006: 195). However, almost ten years after the 2001 conflict, and the reinstatement of group rights by the Framework Agreement, the proportion of Albanians employed in the civil service at the state level remained at 16.9 per cent in 2010, despite constituting 25.17 per cent of the population (Ombudsman of the Republic of Macedonia 2011: 33).[4] It is important to note that the Framework Agreement and subsequent legislation does not call for strict ethnic quotas in Macedonia's civil service and public administration. Municipalities are not legally obliged to employ a certain percentage of different ethnic groups. Municipal councillors are also elected by a proportional representation system and are appointed to council committees on the same basis. In contrast, mayoral candidates are elected according to a two-round, majority run-off system, which represents a more integrative approach to power-sharing because it seeks to encourage 'vote-pooling' across ethnic lines (Horowitz 2000: 601–52; McGary *et al.* 2008: 55).

Qualified voting procedures, sometimes referred to as 'double-majority' or 'Badinter-majority' voting, are also envisaged to ensure greater consensus in decision-making within municipal councils.[5] They operate along similar lines to Arend Lijphart's concept of minority veto; however, they differ in that the right to use them is not given to one particular community. Instead, certain issues debated in municipal councils cannot be approved without 'the majority of votes of the present council members, within which there must be a majority of votes ... belonging to the communities which are not the majority of [the] population in the municipality' (Official Gazette 2002: Art. 41.3). While offering protection to minority communities against the strength of the majority in municipal decision-making, the procedure does not constitute full veto power, and Joseph Marko has noted that it represents a much weaker mechanism than comparable provisions in other ex-Yugoslav republics (Marko 2004/5: 709). One reason for this is the fact that use of 'double majority' voting in Macedonia is restricted to the following areas of municipal decision-making: culture, use of languages and alphabets and determining the use of the municipal coat of arms and flag (Official Gazette 2002: Art. 41.3). In all other areas, minority support is not required to approve decisions. The advantage of this relatively restrictive procedure, observes Florian Bieber, is that it can help prevent blockage of the entire decision-making process, as is the case Bosnia and Herzegovina (Bieber 2005a: 111). Nevertheless, such limitations on use, Bieber concludes, contain an inherent danger that decisions which may have a profound impact on minorities, such as education or economic policy, are beyond the reach of the minorities' veto.

The Law on Local Self-Government also obliges municipalities where a minority group represents more than 20 per cent of the local population to establish Committees for Inter-Community Relations (Official Gazette 2002: Art. 55). Municipalities with local minority communities comprising less than 20 per cent are also permitted to establish such Committees, however the decision to do so is at the discretion of the municipal council. The Committee's membership should reflect the ethnic structure of the local population and each ethnic community should be represented equally. Comparable to Lijphart's consociational notion of arbitration mechanisms, the role of these Committees is to enable institutional dialogue between municipal councils and different local minority communities that may not otherwise be adequately represented in the municipal council. Their task involves reviewing issues pertinent to local inter-ethnic relations, for example those requiring the use of qualified voting procedures, and providing opinions and solutions on them. Municipal councils are obliged to consider the Committee's appraisals and to make decisions regarding them.

One final consociational principle reflected in post-2001 municipal governance is the enhanced use of community languages, flags and symbols locally. As Chapter 1 has discussed, the inability of Macedonia's non-majority communities to use their languages and flags locally represented a significant cultural inequality during the 1990s. According to the Law on Local Self-Government and subsequent Law on Use of Languages, the Macedonian language remains the official language in the municipalities; however, any other language spoken by at least 20 per cent of the population locally is also recognised as an official language (Official Gazette 2002, 2008b). With regard to languages spoken by less than 20 per cent of the local population, the Law also allows the possibility for their use as an official language, but the decision to do so remains at the discretion of the municipality. Formally recognising a community language means it can be used in municipal council sessions and citizens are permitted to submit applications to municipal bodies in their mother tongue. Municipalities are also obliged to correspond with citizens in their own language if requested by the citizen. In such instances, the citizen will receive a response from the municipality in both Macedonian and the community language requested (Common Values 2009: 53). The Framework Agreement and subsequent Law on the Use of the Flags of the Communities also regulates the use of community emblems, such as the flying of community flags in front of local public buildings if that community constitutes a majority within the municipality (Official Gazette 2001b, 2005).

The effectiveness of consociational power-sharing mechanisms locally

Proportionality

Analyses of the equitable representation process have consistently emphasised how the recruitment of both majority and non-majority employees has been 'highjacked' by political parties and shows little regard for the candidates' skills and experience (European Commission 2008: 11; 2009: 13; 2010: 10; 2011b: 10; Risteska 2013a). Indeed, local interlocutors told the ICG in 2011 that a job in the public administration requires a DUI or VMRO-DPMNE party card and several thousand euros (ICG 2011: 10). In particular, it has been claimed that DUI see equitable representation as an opportunity to 'take care' of former NLA combatants and their families. Allegedly, every third new recruit must be related to a former NLA member (Taleski 2011: 15). The Helsinki Human Rights Committee has claimed that party discrimination is particularly prevalent in municipal administrations (ICG 2011: 10). Employment data from a selection of 12 multi-ethnic municipalities displayed in Appendix E confirms the hypothesis that representation of a particular local community in the local administration is more likely to improve when the mayor is from the same ethnic group. This implies that mayors are regularly favouring their own (ethnic) party supporters in the recruitment of new employees. Albanian mayors in the municipalities of Brevnica, Čair, Struga and Vrapčište, for example, have succeeded in improving the representation of their community in the municipal administration. In contrast, communities constituting more than 20 per cent in a given municipality, but less than 50 per cent (implying the mayor is of another ethnicity), have been less successful (see data for Albanians in Dolneni, Petrovec and Zelenikovo). Such practices also impact negatively on the representation of smaller ethnic communities which are often dispersed between municipalities and only constitute a majority in a handful of them.[6]

Reports of 'large-scale dismissals' in the wake of local elections are further evidence of the politicisation of municipal administrations (ICG 2011: 10). While employed at South East European University, Tetovo, during the March 2005 municipal elections, the author witnessed at first hand the political pressure placed on the Dean of Public Administration to employ individuals who had recently lost their job in neighbouring Gostivar municipality.[7] Little has changed in recent years, prompting the European Commission to remark in its 2010 Progress Report on Macedonia how the number of complaints submitted to the Civil Service Agency regarding the replacement or dismissal of municipal civil servants increased following the 2009 municipal elections (European Commission 2010: 10; Boskovska 2010: 94). It is important to emphasise that, as the political party governing the largest number of Albanian-dominated municipalities since 2005, DUI has equally disenfranchised Albanians who are not party members from potential positions in the local civil service and public administration.[8]

No doubt influenced by a desire to conceal blatant political bias in the selection of non-majority candidates, the process of equitable representation remains shrouded in secrecy. The Secretariat for the Implementation of the Ohrid Framework Agreement (SIOFA) led by the Albanian party DUI, for example, has failed to publish any reports on equitable representation in the ten years since the Agreement was signed, although the Ombudsman's Office does publish some data in its annual reports.[9] SIOFA also remains without a database to monitor equitable representation, despite expressing its intention to do so in 2010.[10] According to leading development experts, the extent to which governments adopt mechanisms to regularly monitor the progress of reforms represents a litmus test for assessing its true commitment to its outcomes (Eaton *et al.* 2010: 64). This therefore prompts scepticism regarding DUI's commitment to the Framework Agreement's principles, especially as it presents itself as the only true guardian of the Agreement's implementation.

Where there is data on equitable representation, it is important to note that it refers largely to progress made in the recruitment of civil servants in the municipal administration, as opposed to members of the public administration (those employed in schools, health centres, public enterprises, etc.). According to 2009 statistics, approximately 105,500 persons are employed at the state level in the public sector, with only 9,700 (less than 10 per cent) comprising civil servants (Emurli 2010: 15). This means no reliable data currently exists for roughly 40,000 persons employed in the public administration locally, not to mention the significant number of individuals employed on temporary contracts who are considered neither civil servants or members of the public administration for statistical purposes. One senior DUI official estimated that only 7 per cent of the public administration was Albanian in December 2009 (ICG 2011: 15). There is currently no way, however, of verifying this claim.

Progress in the promotion of equitable representation in municipal administrations is also hampered by practical considerations rather than a lack of political will. 'Often', observed the OSCE in its 2009 Decentralization Survey, 'the municipal leadership is willing to implement the principle of equitable representation but possesses only limited resources to do so' (ICG 2011: 15). Respondents to the Survey indicated that the following factors obstruct municipalities' ability to achieve a representative workforce: the lack of qualified candidates from non-majority communities, political pressures to employ staff, existing over-employment in the municipality and the lack of any legal obligation to do so. Indeed, considering that the post-2001 non-majority recruitment drive began at a time when state agencies were under increasing pressure to downsize by international agencies such as the World Bank and when public enterprises were scheduled for restructuring, privatisation and often closure, equitable representation has frequently been regarded as one of the most sensitive elements of the Framework Agreement (Brown *et al.* 2002: 16; Ragaru 2008: 14). Given the lack of enforcement mechanisms within the regulatory framework to ensure public institutions meet recruitment targets for non-majority communities, it is understandable that progress at the municipal level has been slow.

Qualified voting procedures

With regard to the use of the Badinter/'double-majority' voting procedures designed to ensure greater consensus in municipal council decision-making, research undertaken by both the Institute for Regional and International Studies and the Association for Democratic Initiatives (ADI) suggests this practice is 'rarely respected at the local level' (ADI 2006: 19; IRIS 2006: 14). ADI's interviews with representatives from the multi-ethnic municipalities of Gostivar, Kičevo, Struga and Debar during 2006 found that in many instances local councillors were unaware of the compulsory nature of the qualified voting procedures for specific topics. The councillors also felt its use unnecessary, because issues requiring a double majority had not featured on the agenda of municipal councils (ADI 2006: 17, 64). Other councillors interviewed were opposed to the procedure's application outright, suggesting its use would be perceived as an indication of poor community relations and should therefore be avoided (ADI 2006: 72, 82).

Fieldwork undertaken by the author in selected multi-ethnic municipalities during June 2010 found that attitudes towards the use of qualified voting procedures have not changed significantly.[11] In most cases, political deals between the major parties concerning sensitive local issues are made 'behind closed doors' and long before the issue is debated in municipal councils.[12] This practice, which Lijphart refers to as summit diplomacy, may be beneficial in divided societies where strong and decisive leadership is essential. It has been criticised, however, by opponents of consociationalism for being incompatible with concepts of modern participatory democracy, especially since smaller ethnic communities (with fewer elected representatives) are usually marginalised from the process (Lijphart 1977: 40; Roeder and Rothchild 2005: 328; Weller *et al.* 2008: 707). In Macedonia's case, it makes local minority protection mechanisms, such as qualified voting procedures and Committees for Inter-Community Relations, irrelevant. Given the restricted use of qualified voting procedures, along with the narrow interpretation of their use by many municipal councils, ADI has recommended its application be broadened to apply more flexibly to other issues affecting the lives of non-majority communities, such as local education policy and adoption of the municipal work programme and budget (Rahić and Haziri 2010: 42). Kenan Hasipi, a prominent Turkish Member of Parliament, has also suggested introducing a 'triple-majority' procedure to ensure smaller communities represented by fewer councillors locally are not marginalised when it is applied (Klekovski 2011: 53).

Mediation processes: municipal Committees for Inter-Community Relations

The effectiveness of veto rights, notes Florian Bieber (2004: 21), depends not only on their scope of application; the effectiveness of mediation processes activated once a veto is invoked is also crucial. In accordance with the law, the 20 multi-ethnic municipalities legally required to establish Committees for Inter-Community Relations had done so by 2010. According to data collated by the municipal association, by the end of 2010 a further 12 municipalities had also established Committees on a voluntarily basis.[13] It is admirable that so many municipalities have recognised the benefit of establishing these Committees, even though they are not all obliged to do so and receive no additional funding from Government as a result. However, upon closer examination, an increasing number of research reports have questioned the effectiveness of these Committees (CDI 2007; Forum 2008; OSCE 2009; Rahić and Haziri 2010). Such criticism led a prominent UN programme in Macedonia to conclude at the end of 2010 that the Committees are 'generally found to convene for the sake of demonstrating that they have done so, and they rarely provide advisory, preventive or reactive recommendations' (UN 2010: 5).

One of the criticisms frequently directed against the municipal Committees, most notably in the European Commission's Progress Report on Macedonia in 2010, is that 'their role is still largely unknown by the public' (CDI 2007: 9; European Commission 2010: 21). The OSCE's decentralisation survey for 2009 corroborates this conclusion, finding that only 19 per cent of respondents were aware of their existence, while 58 per cent of survey respondents did not know whether their municipality had established one (OSCE 2009: 62). The European Commission has also observed how the Committees' effectiveness continues to be limited by 'poor operational capacity', 'unclear competences', a 'lack of resources' and that their 'recommendations are often disregarded' by municipal councils (European Commission 2010: 21; 2011b: 20). Unlike municipal Equal Opportunities Commissions, these Committees are not permanent bodies of the municipal council, their members' expenses are not reimbursed and they are not supported administratively by a dedicated municipal employee responsible for mainstreaming race equality throughout municipal policies and practices. Despite various capacity-building projects during 2008–11 and the creation of guidance manuals recommending the contrary, municipalities generally remain unable or unwilling to provide Committee members with the necessary administrative and financial support, along with appropriate working conditions to conduct meetings in (Forum 2008: 8–9; UN 2010: 20; Metamorphosis and Common Values 2011: 22; ZELS 2009: 1).

Membership of the Committees has also been the subject of much criticism, in particular the method by which members are selected. Since members are generally not elected by local citizens, but rather are appointed by the municipality, ensuring their legitimacy and accountability to the communities they represent remains a challenge. The local non-governmental organisation 'Forum' has highlighted the substantial role political parties continue to play in the nomination and selection of Committee members. Where municipal Nomination Committees exist, Forum's research has observed, mayors commonly appoint Committee members and consequently 'the possible political influence and possible pressure on external Committee members is very high' (Forum 2008: 12). Very often the four-year mandate of Committee members corresponds with that of municipal councils and this also represents 'a source of undue political influence' (UN 2010: 39). The frequency with which members are also municipal councillors is illustrated in the membership data of 32 municipal Committees in Appendix F. Being both a municipal councillor and a member of a Committee is not necessarily problematic, because councillors are at least elected by the local community and their involvement in the Committee may help raise its profile and integrate it further into municipal structures. Committees comprising municipal councillors may also have greater capacity to advocate community interests and be better placed to ensure its recommendations are adopted by the municipal council (UN 2010: 40).

The frequency with which the composition of municipal Committees fails to equitably reflect the ethnic structure of the local population is also illustrated by the membership data in Appendix F. This data demonstrates how smaller communities, particularly the Roma, are often not represented in their local Committees. Interestingly, a Macedonian Muslim (or Torbeš) councillor from Struga municipality complained how membership of his local Committee was restricted to those ethnic groups recognised by the Constitution.[14] His community is therefore not directly represented in the Committee and relies on the efforts of a local Egyptian, appointed to represent the 'Others' (Official Gazette 2001a). The data in Appendix F also suggests that, when smaller communities are represented, they are frequently outnumbered by the representatives of other, larger local communities, notably Macedonians and Albanians. The significant under-representation of women in the membership of these Committees is another development which undoubtedly affects local communities' ability to represent their diverse needs effectively to the local administration. Since there are no consequences for municipalities when a particular local community is not represented or where that representation is unequal in the Committee, the NGO Forum doubts municipal leaders will attach a high priority towards resolving such breaches in the law (Forum 2008: 7).

Community languages and symbols

The enhanced use of community languages, flags and symbols in municipalities is the final consociational principle reflected in the decentralisation process and one which assists municipalities to become more responsive to local communities. Reducing the threshold for mandatory use of community languages from 50 to 20 per cent of the local population has meant that Albanian has acquired official status in 29 of the 85 municipalities (including, significantly, the capital Skopje), Turkish in four, Serbian in one and Romani also in one (Common Values 2009: 53). In addition, Kruševo has formally recognised the Vlach language, even though the local Vlach population constitutes only 10 per cent, Gostivar has recognised Turkish and Kumanovo has recognised both the Romani and Serbian languages (SSO 2003: 128).[15] It is worth emphasising that while official use of the Albanian language has become mandatory in more than a third of Macedonia's municipalities, use of community languages other than Albanian is obligatory in only six (approximately 7 per cent). The Law on Local Self-Government leaves the decision to recognise the languages of communities constituting less than 20 per cent locally at the discretion of municipalities dominated generally by Macedonian or Albanians. To date this option has only been considered by a handful, prompting the European Commission to conclude in its 2009 progress report on Macedonia that 'little progress can be reported regarding use of the languages of the smaller ethnic communities' (European Commission 2009: 20). The dispersal of the Turkish, Roma, Serbian and Vlach communities throughout Macedonia means that in most municipalities they fall well below the 20 per cent threshold required to benefit from the enhanced language rights introduced by decentralisation.

Even when a community language has been formally recognised, there is no guarantee that, however well intentioned the municipality's decision to do so, it will become a working language in practice. This is particularly the case in municipalities where a local community is not in the majority and the political strength of that community remains weak. Municipalities do not receive additional state resources to fund associated costs, such as the salaries of translators or interpreters. While larger municipalities can more easily meet the expense of hiring additional members of staff, smaller, less affluent municipalities, such as Kruševo where Albanian and Vlach have been recognised as additional official languages, cannot (Hasani 2010). In many instances, expensive simultaneous interpretation equipment donated to municipalities by international donors remains unused.[16] In addition, the quality of interpretation, given meagre municipal salaries and a shortage of sufficiently qualified candidates locally, even when translators are employed by municipalities, is often inadequate (European Commission 2011: 19).

An inter-ministerial working group, comprising SIOFA, ZELS and line ministries among others, was set up in June 2010 to assess the level of implementation of the Law on Use of Languages. The group concluded that smaller municipalities are reluctant or unable to fund translation, especially when large parts of the local population are bilingual. It also found that citizens' knowledge of their language rights is poor and there remains little political will locally to implement the law.[17] However, and as with equitable representation, no formal mechanism for monitoring language use in the municipalities has been established by the Government, including SIOFA, to date. This may be one reason why Macedonia had not ratified the European Charter for Regional and Minority Languages (1992), despite signing it in July 1996.[18] In addition, the efforts of the inter-ministerial working group to monitor progress were initially delayed for months as a result of SIOFA's reluctance to lead the initiative.[19] DUI's proposal to amend the law on language use in the wake of its parliamentary electoral success in June 2011, one year after the working group delivered its conclusions, also failed to include measures that would improve the realisation of citizens' language rights locally.[20]

Realisation of the enhanced use of community emblems has also been beset with problems. The Law on the Use of Flags of the Communities was originally adopted in 2005 when DUI was in coalition with the Social Democrats (SDSM). However, once in government, VMRO-DPMNE subsequently challenged the Law in the Constitutional Court and certain provisions were annulled in 2007 (European Commission 2008: 21). The situation was rectified when amendments to the Law were passed in July 2011. These amendments confirmed the right of communities constituting more than 50 per cent in a given municipality to display their flag alongside the state flag outside public and local buildings. However, the state flag must be one third larger in size than the community flags (IDIVIDI 2011).

Direct democracy: participatory mechanisms and how municipalities communicate with citizens

Advocates of deliberative democracy theory argue that the best way to resolve tensions between traditional cultural practices and liberal principles in socially plural democracies is to extend local deliberation processes beyond the limits of formal political processes (Deveaux 2005: 340; Mahajan 2005: 103). This requires local politicians to expand their understanding of democratic political activity and to increase the space available for continuous civic involvement in decision-making. Frequent public consultations, participatory planning and budgeting, for example, may enable different sections of the community, particularly those previously excluded or marginalised, to have a direct say in how local decisions are made. Open debate and dialogue will allow local citizens to interrogate existing practices and suggest improvements that may result in more appropriate and equitable public services (UNDP 2009a: 31). Citizens' participation will also empower local communities, allowing them to take ownership of decisions and make it less likely that they resist or withhold support for new initiatives (Sisk 2001: 150; Thede 2009: 117). While collective decision-making can be complicated, time-consuming and sometimes unattainable, observes Timothy Sisk (2001: 146), consensus-based decisions are generally more legitimate and widely accepted than decisions taken by elected officials acting independently. Importantly, those designing such activities should consider who commonly participates in these events and how meaningful their contribution is.

According to the Law on Local Self-Government, 'citizens shall directly participate in the decision-making process on issues of local importance through civil initiative, citizens' gatherings and referendum' (Official Gazette 2002: Art. 25). The Law also obliges municipalities to cover the cost of such activities. Since 2006 the OSCE's annual survey on decentralisation has monitored the degree to which the municipalities provide opportunities for citizens to participate directly in local decision-making processes (OSCE 2006a, 2007, 2008e, 2009, 2011). When asked what type of participatory planning activities the municipality organises, in 2011 the vast majority of survey respondents confirmed that they organised regular consultation hours during which citizens could discuss issues with the mayor (94.6 per cent of respondents) (OSCE 2011: 9). Other popular approaches cited by the municipalities were meetings with neighbourhood communities (89.2 per cent of respondents) and with groups of citizens to discuss a particular issue (77 per cent of respondents). This is an improvement on previous survey findings, when in 2008, for example, only 43 per cent of municipalities arranged regular office hours for citizens, 30 per cent consulted with neighbourhood communities and 27 per cent organised citizens' gatherings (OSCE 2008c: 45).[21]

Similarly, the 2011 survey found that the most popular means of communicating issues of local concern to citizens was during individual meetings with municipal employees (92 per cent of respondents) (OSCE 2011: 10). Other common forms of communication were by telephone (88 per cent) and during citizens' gatherings (68 per cent). More transparent, public forms of communication, such as web forums (23 per cent), announcements on municipal websites (4 per cent) and use of the local media (3 per cent), were less favoured. In his critique of local participatory democracy in Bosnia and Herzegovina, Edin Hodžic makes the following observation: '[It] is more ... a system of lobbying, advocating and pushing for a certain action through certain persons, which depends on personal contacts and connections within the municipality.' As such, the inclusion of citizens in local processes represents 'a chaotic web of lobbying and problem solving, rather than an institutionalised and meaningful mechanism of political participation, dialogue and co-decision making' (Hodžic 2011: 49). In Brazil, Baiocchi and Heller (2009) also found evidence of what they refer to as 'instituted participatory democracy', where the rules and processes for participation are carefully controlled by local political elites and are based on individual participation, rather than being organised spontaneously along civil society lines. Hodžic's and Baiocchi and Heller's insight holds resonance for participatory approaches in Macedonia. Such initiatives, Hodžic and others note, should be open, rather than hidden, which may increase the potential for corruption and the unfair resolution of local disputes (García-Guadilla and Pérez 2002: 101; UNDP 2009a: 84).

One initiative in Macedonia that seeks to demonstrate the benefits of participatory mechanisms to both municipalities and citizens is the 'Community Forums' project sponsored by the Swiss Agency for Development and Co-operation (SDC). According to the project's manager, its purpose is to build the capacities of municipalities to organise transparent and inclusive decision-making practices as well as encourage local citizens to develop a sense of responsibility in spending municipal funds.[22] Through participating in structured discussions open to all, citizens become better acquainted with how the municipality's budget is spent and, consequently, more appreciative of the fact that it is impossible to meet the needs of all citizens when funding is limited. Since 2006, 25 municipalities have participated in the project, with a further 18 municipalities participating in its third phase, which began in September 2011.[23] Significantly, the municipalities do not just consult Community Forum members on local priorities. Participants decide which local needs should be prioritised, in accordance with the municipality's strategic and/or local economic development plans, and municipal representatives are granted the same voting rights as other members. Realised projects are therefore varied and have addressed local needs, such as infrastructure, economic development, water supply and waste water and environmental protection. Municipal budget forums have also been initiated since September 2011.

When asked whether those municipalities that had already participated in the project had welcomed the opportunity to involve citizens more actively in local affairs, the project manager's response was mixed. In some cases she believed the municipalities had been genuinely appreciative of the opportunity to 'share the burden' of local decision-making, while in others they were clearly taking part in the project only to receive additional funds.[24] It is too early to say whether this process will be sustainable. However, by June 2011 38 municipalities had amended their Statutes to include Community Forums as a mechanism for involving citizens. This means they were now legally obliged to initiate such practices in the future.[25]

While the OSCE's annual decentralisation survey measures municipal perceptions on a range of local governance issues, UNDP's 'People Centered Analyses' reports, in contrast, are based on large-scale, nationally representative opinion polls (UNDP 2008, 2009b, 2010a). As a result, their research findings paint a very different picture of the municipalities' success at reaching out to local citizens. Table 2.1, for example, illustrates the extent to which respondents to the 2010 UNDP survey were active in local affairs. The low proportion of citizens that had either participated in municipal activities or intended to do so in the future suggests citizens were generally not interested in exercising their voice (UNDP 2010a: 91). The previous year's survey also found that, when asked whether they had contacted a municipal representative for assistance in the preceding six months, relatively few respondents had done so. Only 7 per cent of respondents, for example, had reported an issue to their municipal council and 8 per cent had contacted their mayor to solve a problem, with only a third of these having their problem resolved

Table 2.1 Levels of citizens' participation at the municipal level, 2010

Proportion of respondents who in the past 12 months have:	Proportion (%)	Respondents with a future interest (%)
Participated in meetings	6	29
Made a telephone call	6	27
Signed a petition	4	22
Filled in a questionnaire	11	33
Participated in a focus group/telephone interview	4	18
Written a letter/sent an email	3	19

Source: UNDP (2010a: 92)

in this way (UNDP 2009b: 84). Overall, 80 per cent of respondents in 2009 believed they had no influence over the decisions made in their municipality (UNDP 2009b: 81). While the UNDP reports do not include data disaggregated according to ethnicity, the analysis for 2010 confirms that no significant differences across ethnic groups were found, although Roma citizens were least likely to engage with their municipality (UNDP 2010a: 92).

Subsequent research confirms that this 'culture of passivity' among citizens remains as significant a challenge to the success of participatory practices as the reluctance and capacities of municipalities to share power (Forum 2011; OSCE 2011). This phenomenon is not unique to Macedonia, because studies of local governance in Serbia and Bosnia-Herzegovina have also documented low rates of civic participation (Mitchell Group 2008; Pickering 2012). Such inertia may be because the average citizen is either apathetic or unwilling to participate in local affairs, especially if local mechanisms for participation are not transparent or have become politicised, or simply that they are satisfied with their current level of involvement and quality of service provision. However, some have claimed that the political culture of former Communist societies has left an indelible mark on the socialisation process of citizens (Illner 1998: 30; Bunce and Watts 2005: 137). If democracy is to be successful in these transition countries, it needs to change how people perceive their role as citizens, and to empower them with a sense that they can and need to participate in society (Mavrikos-Adamou 2010: 517). This realisation is essential because the existence of a vibrant civil society represents an important precondition for successful decentralisation (Tranchant 2007: 3; Barter 2008: 3).

Internal political party democracy and discipline

Although in theory, the introduction of local elections is perceived to enhance the responsiveness and accountability of municipal governments to their constituencies, the extent to which this change actually takes place depends on how power is distributed within the political parties. The structure of parties is therefore a crucial factor in determining the autonomy of local politicians and their ability to respond to diverse local needs effectively (Coppedge 1994: 164; Bahl 1999: 5; Burki *et al.* 1999: 15; Willis *et al.* 1999: 48; Montero 2005: 64). Political parties in decentralised governance systems, remarks Pieter van Houten, should ideally be relatively decentralised in their own organisational structures. If not, the promise of enhanced local autonomy and responsive governance will remain unfilled (Manor 1999: 35; van Houten 2004: 11). Strong and disciplined parties can 'make a mockery' of decentralisation (Eaton and Connerley 2010: 5).

In his seminal work on federalism, William H. Riker observed how the federal relationship may be centralised according to the degree to which: '(1) … one party controls both levels of government; and (2) … each potential governing party at the central level controls its partisan associates at the level of constituent governments' (Riker 1964: 131). Others have since operationalised Riker's theory by focusing on the following elements of national party organisation and discipline: the nomination, approval and funding processes of candidates for public office, enforcement of the party line in political decision-making, the arbitrary removal of local politicians from office and the existence of clientelistic relationships within parties. Central control over the selection and financing of local candidates, for example, means local officials may remain beholden to their central government sponsors rather than local constituents, since the success of their careers will depend largely on respecting the party leadership (Eaton 2001: 106; Hopkin 2003: 231; Bland 2010: 51). The use of closed lists in electoral systems based on proportional representation has also been identified as a particularly effective tool for allowing party leaders more discretion over the selection and control of local candidates (Coppedge 1994: 22; Sisk 2001: 130; Montero 2005: 66). Strong, centralised party discipline is not necessary negative. What is bad for democracy, concedes Michael Coppedge (1994: 37), may actually be good for stability. However, the experience of Venezuelan politics during the 1980s demonstrates that, although in the short term strong parties may make a regime more resilient, in the long term they undermine the quality of democracy, ultimately making the regime less stable (Coppedge 1994: 9).

Based on Riker's first observation, the dominance of political parties VMRO-DPMNE, led by Prime Minister Nikola Gruevski, and DUI, led by the former head of the NLA, Ali Ahmeti, at both municipal and parliamentary levels in Macedonia suggests the potential for state parties to exercise control over local counterparts at the expense of responsive and accountable municipal government is considerable. Since 2009, VMRO-DPMNE has controlled 56 (including the City of Skopje) out of a possible 85 municipalities, whereas their coalition partners DUI control a further 14 (ODIHR 2000, 2005, 2009). This means that between them the central governing coalition controlled over 80 per cent of all municipalities. Similarly, since 2009 the four largest national parties[26] have controlled 77 municipalities (over 90 per cent), while the number of independent mayors has declined steadily since the start of decentralisation in 2004.[27] This leaves little room for dissent between local and central level political priorities. As an NGO critic remarked: 'You cannot count on the Mayors coming from the ruling coalition to push decentralisation too far ... they are not in a position to stand up as they will lose the support they have been getting until now.'[28] Another expert continued: 'The Mayors respect the party line and are silenced by additional sources of funding.'[29] The fact that membership of the municipal association has become increasingly dominated by government-aligned municipalities, and its president is a VMRO-DPMNE mayor for the influential City of Skopje, furthers this impression. According to the ICG (2011: 20), ZELS has 'fallen under the patronage of the ruling parties' and international donors are no longer 'happy about how it is run'. Observers have noted how, during the 2009 municipal elections, VMRO-DPMNE campaign posters featured images of Prime Minister Gruevski beside individual mayoral candidates proclaiming 'together we can do more'. Similar posters were prepared for DUI mayoral candidates. Such images 'run counter to decentralisation logic' and suggest the parties 'treat the municipalities like an extended hand of the government'.[30]

High levels of central control and member discipline within all Macedonian political parties (Riker's second condition) also imply the subordination of local politicians in party structures at the expense of local democracy. In a 2011 report appraising the ten years since the adoption of the Framework Agreement, the ICG questioned whether 'non-democratic parties, operating within a non-democratic structure' can 'bring democracy to Macedonia' (ICG 2011: 9). The report described Macedonian political parties as being

> highly centralised and ethnically based. Policy-making capacity is poor, and rank and file have little opportunity to participate in decisions. An ex-parliament speaker argued: 'Every party is conquered by one man and a small group around him. MPs get direct orders' .... The popular wisdom in Macedonia calls political parties with incumbent leaders 'sultan' parties.
>
> (ICG 2011: 8)

Gordana Siljanovska-Davkova, Professor of Law at SS Cyril and Methodius University in Skopje, believes most parties in Macedonia continue to operate under organisational principles inherited from the League of Communists. Her research emphasises the role central party presidencies (supported by a closed list system), rather than local party organisations, play in nominating office holders, and notes how 'the leadership selects/elects obedient party friends rather than persons with integrity, who can properly represent the electorate' (Siljanovska-Davkova 2005: 49).[31] Tight party discipline, concludes Siljanovska-Davkova, ensures party factions or critics are banned, members lack the courage to speak up for fear of being considered a 'traitor', and a general lack of transparency prevails, where decisions are not taken openly or with consensus (Siljanovska-Davkova 2005: 41).

A review of internal party democracy in Macedonia by the Center for Research and Policy Making in 2013 found no evidence to suggest that the management and functioning of one particular party was significantly less democratic than another, or that transparency in internal party decision-making processes has either improved or declined in recent years (CRPM 2013). However, increases in the proportion of municipalities politically aligned to governing parties after 2009 may have exacerbated the impact of limited internal party democracy on municipal political autonomy vis-à-vis the government. What may appear to be representative local governments, responsive to the needs of local citizens, may in reality be only a deconcentration of central government.

The pervasiveness of patronage politics

One significant factor deterring citizens from participating in local affairs is the pervasiveness of patronage politics or clientelism in Macedonia. Research suggests that, as a post-Communist country, Macedonia may be particularly predisposed to patronage-based party–voter linkages. Martin Shefter, for example, has argued that if democratisation occurs within the context of an unconsolidated state, strong pressures are created for patronage politics (cited in O'Dwyer 2006: 193). This is particularly true in ethnically diverse democracies, where intra-ethnic party competition may act as a powerful catalyst for intensifying clientelism (Kitshelt and Wilkinson 2007: 32). Conor O'Dwyer has gone further by suggesting the presence of robust and institutionalised party competition determines whether the *predisposition* to patronage politics becomes the *practice* of patronage politics (O'Dwyer 2006: 8). Failure to establish coherent governments and credible oppositions, both composed of stable programmatically defined parties, leaves voters unable to discipline governing parties (O'Dwyer 2006: 19, 192). Others have suggested the level of economic development of a state is the most commonly confirmed predictor of differential modes of democratic accountability, because programmatic parties are only attractive to voters with sufficient assets to become indifferent to clientelistic-targeted goods (Kitshelt and Wilkinson 2007: 24). Finally, O'Dwyer and others have suggested the Communist Party's *nomenklatura* system, through which the Party carefully vetted applicants to administrative positions and used them as rewards for the party faithful, has left a lasting legacy in post-Communist states (O'Dwyer 2006: 13; Hale 2007: 247).[32] While the fall of Communism may have formally ended the *nomenklatura* system, in practice there have been few effective constraints on the continuation of these appointments by governing parties.

The prevalence of clientelism at both the central and local levels in Macedonia is not without consequences, most of which can undermine the potential benefits of decentralisation this chapter has sought to evaluate. The capture of local institutions by the political parties, for example, weakens the ability of decentralised governance to promote the representation of diverse groups in decision-making processes. As this chapter has already demonstrated, closed candidate lists that are generally tightly controlled by national parties has done little to facilitate independent candidates and local party representatives from entering public life. The immense resources required to satisfy horizontal clientelistic relationships, between political parties and citizens, reduce the competitiveness of democracy by making it very difficult for challengers (either independent or opposition candidates) to establish credibility as a potential alternative source of benefits (Kitshelt and Wilkinson 2007: 13; Van de Walle 2007: 64).

This chapter has also demonstrated how patronage politics has dominated the recruitment of municipal civil servants, and no doubt the more extensive public administration at the expense of transparent merit-based criteria. It is also the cause of what Conor O'Dwyer refers to as 'runaway state-building': the rapid expansion in the size of state administrations without a commensurate increase in its professionalism and effectiveness (O'Dwyer 2006: 28). In 2011 the ICG estimated in that the Macedonian public administration had grown by 40,000 in three years and was 'over-staffed, [where] old employees have been pushed aside and are still getting paid, while party loyalists were hired and now make most decisions' (ICG 2011: 10). Appendix E shows the rate of expansion in municipal administrations between 2006 and 2010. Patronage-based recruitment not only means that local communities are denied equal access to state employment. Unchecked patronage-based expansion limits the effectiveness of municipal administrations, makes them less accountable and may even weaken the legitimacy of the new democratic order itself (O'Dwyer 2006: 192).

Pervasive patronage politics may also undermine decentralisation's ability to deepen local democracy, and the relationship between patronage and weak social capital is cyclical. Disenchantment in local political processes increases the likelihood of patronage-based party–voter linkages, because the parties have no other effective way of attracting and holding on to voters. The absence a vibrant civil society serving as public watchdogs and checks on the exercise of state power may also encourage clientelism since the risks associated with political strategies based on the distribution of patronage are reduced (O'Dwyer 2006: 22; Van de Walle 2007: 67). In turn, patronage fuels voter apathy and deters local residents from becoming active in municipal affairs. One could therefore argue that the introduction or extension of democratic party politics in local environments where levels of civic engagement is low may in fact lead to the expansion of patronage politics (García-Guadilla and Pérez 2002: 105; O'Dwyer 2006: 170).

Finally, the existence of *horizontal* clientelistic relationships between political parties and voters and *vertical* patronage-based relations within parties, reinforced by undemocratic party structures, undermines decentralisation's ability to enhance the accountability and responsiveness of municipal governments. Democratic accountability in systems dependent on clientelistic exchange between parties and voters does not derive from local politicians' success in delivering collective benefits, such as improvements to public services. Instead, the voting preferences of citizens are frequently influenced by the promise (or loss) of a job or financial reward (Kitshelt and Wilkinson 2007: 2).

For example, according to international monitoring reports of the March 2013 municipal elections, the government announced multiple vacancy notices as well as increases in pensions, welfare benefits and state support for agricultural products during the campaign (ODIHR 2013: 11). The same report also noted how 'allegations of intimidation of voters, especially public sector employees, persisted throughout the campaign period', and concluded: 'regardless of the veracity of such accusations, their pervasiveness diminished confidence in the fairness of the electoral process and raised concerns about voters' ability to cast their vote free of fear of retribution' (ODIHR 2013: 11). In such environments, there is little incentive for politicians to abide by electoral promises of policy change, because voters will generally not reward them for doing so. Similarly, the existence of vertical clientelistic dependencies between local politicians and the central leadership within parties also frustrates decentralisation's perceived ability to promote responsive local governance. Such relations allow party leaders to maintain control over political decisions as well as state resources by nominating loyal, subservient 'clients' at the sub-central level.

Summary

This chapter has examined whether decentralisation in Macedonia, including its combined use of local power-sharing mechanisms, has facilitated the effective participation of diverse communities in municipal governance. Specifically, it asked whether decentralisation has contributed to: improving the political representation of diverse groups in local decision-making processes; deepening local democracy by providing opportunities for local residents to participate in local governance; and enhancing the transparency, accountability and responsiveness of municipal governments.

While decentralisation has undoubtedly expanded the potential space available for citizens to participate in local governance – either directly or through elected representatives, it has not guaranteed that this participation is both equitable and effective. Implementation of the largely consociational power-sharing mechanisms envisaged locally, which are designed to facilitate inclusive decision-making, remains in its infancy and is vulnerable to being highjacked by the political parties or ethnic groups constituting a majority locally. For example, the process of promoting equitable representation among civil servants employed in municipalities (and possibly also the local public administration) has become overly politicised and favours local majority ethnic communities at the expense of others. Qualified voting procedures are rarely respected by municipal councils, and in most cases political deals between major parties are made 'behind closed doors' and long before issues can be debated openly in municipal councils. Further, municipal Committees for Inter-Community Relations, tasked with representing local communities that may not otherwise be adequately represented in the municipal council, do not function effectively, if at all. Macedonia's smaller ethnic communities, living scattered throughout the country, fail to reach the thresholds required to benefit from these minority protection mechanisms and have been marginalised in the decentralisation process, which benefits only territorially concentrated communities. Macedonians and Albanians residing in small numbers in municipalities where another ethnic community is in the majority are subject to a similar fate. Finally, there is a danger local consociational mechanisms will continue to advance multiculturalism, or at least bi-nationalism, at the expense of broader intra-ethnic relations, i.e. between members of different political parties.

Concerning the deepening of local democracy, decentralisation since 2005 has brought local governance closer to citizens and has consequently increased opportunities for local residents to participate in local decision-making processes. Such initiatives, encouraged by new legislation, include civil initiatives, citizens' gatherings and referendums and are aimed at enhancing the transparency, accountability and responsiveness of municipal governments. However, successful decentralisation requires a context in which dominant political values include a commitment to popular participation and support for bottom-up decision-making. While the emphasis power-sharing techniques place on the empowerment of political elites and summit diplomacy may be beneficial in ethnically divided societies, evidence suggests such practices may operate at the expense of local participatory democracy. Evidence of instituted participatory democracy, where the rules of participation remain controlled by local political elites and is mostly limited to participation on an individual basis, has also restricted the potential for citizens to participate meaningfully in local decision-making processes. Further, a culture of passivity among local citizens, potentially fuelled by pervasive patronage networks and an overly politicised local administration, remains as significant a challenge to the success of participatory practices as the reluctance and capacities of municipalities to share power.

The existence of *horizontal* clientelistic relationships between political parties and voters also undermines decentralisation's ability to enhance the transparency, accountability and responsiveness of municipal governments to local citizens. In such environments, there is little incentive for local politicians to abide by electoral promises, because voters will generally not reward them for doing so. Similarly, *vertical* patronage-based relations within parties, reinforced by undemocratic party structures, frustrate decentralisation's perceived ability to promote responsive local governance. Unchecked patronage-based employment also limits the effectiveness of municipal administrations, makes them less accountable and may even weaken the legitimacy of the new democratic order itself. Attempts to improve local governance and transparency in Macedonia through decentralisation will fail unless greater consideration is given to the often directly opposing incentives facing politicians charged with implementing reforms in patronage-based environments.

Notes

1 For more information on this and other examples of how implementation of the Framework Agreement has favoured Albanians at the expense of other smaller ethnic communities see Mandaci (2007).
2 Part of this analysis is also available in Lyon (2015).
3 Chapter 11 of the 1974 Constitution of the Socialist Republic of Macedonia, entitled 'Equality of Nationalities' stated: 'Municipalities and the Republic ensure that nationalities be proportionately represented in the municipal assemblies … and be adequately represented in their bodies' (Caca 2001: 151).
4 Many Macedonians would argue that there are not enough sufficiently qualified Albanians to reach this target. Interview with OSCE official: 24 March 2009, Skopje.
5 Named after the French judge Robert Badinter.
6 See Appendix E and Risteska (2013a). In particular, the Serbs in Kumanovo, the Roma in Kičevo and the Bošniak community in Petrovec. It is important to note that Serbs in Čučer-Sandevo and Staro Nagoričane are in fact over-represented in the municipal administrations. However, staffing numbers are small in both municipalities, which may make the proportional analysis less accurate.
7 The incumbent Democratic Party of Albanians (DPA) lost control of Gostivar municipality to its bitter rival DUI in March 2005.
8 DUI controlled 15 municipalities compared to DPA's two as a result of the 2005 elections, and 14 compared to 1 DPA-led municipality since subsequent elections in March 2009.
9 However, the Ombudsman's Office annual reports focus primarily on equitable representation in central government institutions rather than in the municipalities.
10 Interview with a senior representative of SIOFA: 27 June 2010, Tetovo.
11 Interview with municipal councillor in Struga municipality: 2 June 2011, Struga.
12 Interview with Aleksandra Bojadzieva, NGO representative and member of the Council of Europe's Advisory Committee on the Framework Convention on National Minorities: 21 June 2010, Skopje.
13 See data in Appendix F. However, missing membership data for half of these 20 municipalities suggests the Committees may not be as active as first thought.
14 Interview with municipal councillor in Struga municipality: 2 June 2011, Struga. The Preamble to the Constitution, amended in 2001, refers to 'the Macedonian people, as well as … the Albanian people, the Turkish people, the Vlach people, the Serbian people, the Romany people, the Bosnian people and others'.
15 Interviews with: the president of the municipal council in Kruševo municipality: 4 June 2010, Kruševo; a municipal councillor in Gostivar municipality: 27 May 2010, Gostivar; and an OSCE official: 4 April 2011, Skopje. The Roma community represent 4.03 per cent of the local population in Kumanovo municipality, while the Serbian community represent 8.59 per cent.
16 Interview with Albanian municipal councillor in Kruševo municipality: 4 June 2010, Kruševo.
17 Interview with an OSCE official: 4 April 2011, Skopje.
18 Data regarding states that have signed and ratified the European Charter for Regional and Minority Languages is available at: http://conventions.coe.int/Treaty/Commun/ChercheSig.asp?NT=148&CM=8&DF=&CL=ENG (accessed: 7 November 2011).

19 According to an internal OSCE report, 'due to the lack of interest of its members and a lack of support by the Government, the working group held only three meetings before finally being dissolved in October 2010. Email correspondence with a senior OSCE official: 14 March 2012.

20 The amendment proposed by DUI included only one change in Article 3, paragraph 2 of the Law: 'A member of the Parliament, **appointed or elected functionary**, who speaks a language other than the Macedonian language spoken by at least 20 per cent the citizens in the Republic of Macedonia, is eligible to use the respective language in the sessions of the Parliament and in the sessions of the respective body.' The amendment (in bold text) was adopted on 15 July 2011. Email correspondence with an OSCE official: 15 November 2011.

21 The Law on Local Self-Government permits municipalities to establish urban or neighbourhood communities. Their competences are to 'review issues, take positions and prepare proposals for issues of direct and everyday importance for the life and work of the inhabitants of that territory' (Official Gazette 2002: Articles 82–6).

22 Interview with Community Forums project manager: 23 March 2009, Skopje.

23 Interview with Community Forums project manager: 16 June 2011, Skopje.

24 The municipalities must contribute at least 50 per cent of the project funds, with the SDC providing match funds. Initially municipal contributions ranged from 19 per cent to 48 per cent, but a requirement of 50 per cent was imposed in 2011. Interview with Community Forums project manager: 16 June 2011, Skopje.

25 Interview with Community Forums project manager: 16 June 2011, Skopje.

26 VMRO-DPMNE, SDSM, DUI and DPA.

27 During the 2005 municipal elections there were 90 independent candidates for mayor (in only 24 municipalities), of which 7 were elected. In the 2009 municipal elections, there were 52 independent candidates for mayor (in 12 municipalities) and only 2 were elected (ODIHR 2005, 2009).

28 Interview with Foundation Open Society Macedonia official: 27 June 2011, Skopje.

29 Interview with USAID project official: 14 June 2010, Skopje.

30 Interviews with Foundation Open Society Macedonia official: 27 June 2011, Skopje; and Westminster Foundation for Democracy project official: 24 June 2010, Skopje.

31 See also Siljanovska-Davkova (2009).

32 The term *nomenklatura* derives from the Latin *'nomenclatura'*, meaning a list of names. It referred to the Communist Party's authority to make appointments to key government positions, as well as throughout the party's own hierarchy (Georgiev 2008: 70).

3   Making local services more responsive to diverse needs

Introduction

This chapter examines whether devolving responsibility for the provision of public services can satisfy the demands of non-majority groups for greater autonomy over their own affairs. While responsibility for a range of public services was decentralised to the municipalities in Macedonia, I have chosen to concentrate this assessment on primary and secondary education for a variety of reasons.[1] First, primary and secondary education was one of the first competences to be devolved to municipalities in July 2005. Expenditure on education constitutes almost half of all government transfers to municipalities and 'the success of the entire decentralisation process is now in large measure dependent on what happens in primary and secondary education' (Levitas 2009: 5). Second, how education systems are designed and delivered is of particular importance to minority ethnic communities, since education is crucial for reproducing (and re-creating) the identity of a group (Bieber 2007: 17). Without the transmission of the aspects of their identity through education, observes Florian Bieber, non-majority cultures may disappear. Third, as one of the basic factors of human development, education is an important means of improving life chances, reducing poverty and promoting social inclusion. It therefore represents a significant mechanism for addressing economic inequalities, an underlying cause of conflict between different ethnic groups (UNDP 2004b, 2010a). Finally, and as Chapter 1 has demonstrated, given the various education-related disputes that had undermined community relations during the 1990s, education was and remains a highly contested political issue in Macedonia (Poulton 2000; Petroska-Beška and Najčevska 2004; Myhrvold 2005; Vetterlein 2006). Its delivery, notes UNDP (2009b: 43), can either promote or block reconciliation, depending on the education policies adopted and the way they are implemented.

This review begins with the principal arguments in favour of and against devolving responsibility for the provision of education to local communities. An assessment of the Macedonian education system before decentralisation will follow, accompanied by a discussion of the reforms introduced in 2005. Three key theoretical arguments will then be considered within the

Macedonian context: whether decentralisation facilitates the provision of heterogeneous local public services; decentralisation's ability to enhance participation and transparency in decision-making regarding the delivery of services; and whether decentralisation ensures a more equitable and transparent distribution of public resources. This chapter does not intend to assess whether decentralisation has improved educational outcomes in Macedonia. Measuring the quality of education is problematic as a result of a lack of reliable data. Educational standards are also affected by additional factors unrelated to decentralisation, such as teacher training, which cannot be easily isolated. Nor does it evaluate the impact of the state's ongoing nation-building agenda on non-majority communities (see Chapter 5 for more details), although such efforts have certainly been responsible for raising tensions between Macedonia' different communities and have affected the delivery of education policies and minority standards more generally. Instead, it argues that the decentralisation of primary and secondary education to municipalities has enabled local communities to more effectively meet the diverse needs of citizens. Persistent challenges, such as the politicised nature of the education system, increasing ethnic segregation in schools and the limited capacity of local stakeholders, unless adequately addressed, may, however, undermine the benefits of reform in the longer term.[2]

Decentralised public services and conflict mitigation

One of the most frequently cited theoretical arguments which promote decentralisation as a tool for managing ethnopolitical conflict is its ability to offer spatially concentrated groups greater control over their own affairs, thereby providing greater scope for the protection of their cultural identity (Kälin 1999: 307; Horowitz 2000: 217–20; Safran and Máiz 2000: 259). By granting non-majority groups greater control over their own destinies, decentralisation is believed to instil a greater sense of security within these groups so that they will not be subject to discriminatory practices and unwanted intrusions in the future (Manor 1999: 97; Jeram 2008: 9). Having greater decision-making power over local affairs may also allow different ethnic groups to better meet the diverse needs of their communities. The ability to differentiate policy for heterogeneous tastes can allow locally elected representatives to proactively address possible tensions before conflict situations arise (Lake and Rothchild 2005: 121; Siegle and O'Mahoney 2007: 1). The remoteness of central governments to citizens often leads to insufficient information regarding local needs and problems (Kälin 1999: 47). Bringing government 'closer to the citizen' (the subsidiarity principle) can therefore allow local communities the opportunity to more effectively express their preferences for public services and to participate in their design. Local administrations, concludes Walter Kälin (2004: 304), can be more physically accessible to the average person and thus more 'human' than a very distant and mighty central administration.

The proliferation of self-government units, coupled with a greater degree of fiscal decentralisation, may also have a moderating effect on another principal cause of conflict: the allocation and distribution of public resources. Feelings of grievance regarding obvious relative deprivation, note Grasa and Camps (2009: 32), often become the source of potential conflict. As Chapter 1 has discussed, this was certainly the case with regard to the allocation of education funding in Macedonia during the 1990s. Decentralisation may, according to Manor (1999: 104), alleviate inter-regional disparities by promoting a more equitable distribution of state resources by giving remote, poor and previously under-represented areas greater access to resources and influence. Decentralisation can also promote 'political realism', because a municipality's daily interactions – and frustrations – with central institutions will make them more aware of budgetary constraints and generate a more realistic understanding of what is and is not possible from the public purse (Manor 1999: 104). This realisation, concludes Manor, should promote political stability, since it will protect the political system from the backlashes which can occur when expectations are inflated and feelings of deprivation exist (Manor 1999: 48–9).

Arguments that favour devolving responsibility for education to the local level as a means of easing ethnic tensions are particularly relevant in multi-ethnic and multilingual societies such as Macedonia. The significance of being able to differentiate the delivery of public services for heterogeneous tastes, for example providing education in a community's mother tongue, cannot be underestimated. As Chapter 1 illustrates, many of the education-related conflicts that arose in Macedonia during the 1990s, for example, developed out of a widespread dissatisfaction with the quality and availability of Albanian and Turkish-medium education (Vetterlein 2006: 8). Devolving management responsibilities to representative local bodies, such as municipal and school councils, enables greater participation from local communities in decision-making processes and can allow citizens to more effectively express their preferences. Enhanced participation may also improve community empowerment, accountability, transparency and institutional responsiveness to local needs, because local communities will possess better knowledge of local conditions than a distant central government (the asymmetric information argument) (Cohen 2004: 5; Barrera-Osorio *et al.* 2009: 34). Involving local, diverse communities in the management of schools will therefore increase the legitimacy of the decisions that are made and possibly the education system more generally (McGinn and Welsh 1999: 31; Poiana 2011: 436). The problem of 'legitimacy crisis', notes Péter Radó (2010: 77), together with an inability of central governments to implement decisions locally, is often cited as the reason why governments devolve education responsibilities to local communities. Devolving education can therefore contribute to correcting the deficiencies associated with overly centralised systems.

Striking a balance between centralised and decentralised education systems

Despite the prevalence of decentralised education reforms worldwide, the academic community and more recently donor agencies have become increasingly doubtful of the reform's ability to improve the delivery of education locally. Such scepticism stems from both a lack of empirical evidence to validate theoretical claims and the existence of negative consequences associated with decentralisation that could potentially dilute the benefits of reform. Researchers warn, for example, that reducing a central government's ability to act against capture by local elites may lead to the entrenchment of patronage politics under decentralisation. As the previous chapter has shown, this risk is particularly great in Macedonia. If the capture of political processes by interest groups is easier at the local level, decentralisation may favour those local groups disproportionately (Galiani *et al.* 2004: 4; Devas and Delay 2006: 692). As Chapter 5 will demonstrate, differences in fiscal and administrative capacities at the local level may also exacerbate disparities in spending and educational outcomes between municipalities (De Grauwe 2004: 3; Winkler and Yeo 2007: 1). In a paper entitled 'Helping the Good Get Better but Leaving the Rest Behind', Galiani, Schargrodsky and Gertler (2004) researched the effect of secondary school decentralisation on education quality in Argentina. Their results found that the higher the provincial fiscal deficit, the smaller the positive impact of decentralisation, and the effect of school decentralisation on test outcomes was in fact negative in provinces running significant fiscal deficits (Galiani *et al.* 2004: 28).

Given the risks associated with devolving education responsibilities to municipalities, it is no wonder that many countries maintain centralised systems. One argument in favour of centrally controlled education finances is based on egalitarian principles which regard central control as the key for reducing or eliminating disparities perceived to be unfair (Radó 2010: 13). Advocates claim that people (and especially those who are poorly educated), if left to their own devices, will invest less in education than is good for them individually (Levitas 2002: 6). Central government is thus obliged to take action to ensure that investment in education reaches socially desirable levels. This can be achieved by redistributing wealth through equalising grants or the direct provision of education services, although, observes fiscal decentralisation expert Tony Levitas (2002), this rarely results in the degree of equality sought. Another argument in favour of maintaining central control over education policy emphasises how decentralisation may weaken the education ministry's ability to implement necessary structural and curriculum reforms (World Bank 2002: 16; Winkler and Yeo 2007: 1). Given these conflicting – but entirely rational – arguments, it comes as no surprise that many educational systems not only combine central and local responsibilities, but are continually being fine-tuned in the search for the most socially acceptable, economically efficient and educationally productive balance (Levitas 2002: 7).

Education provision in the Republic of Macedonia before decentralisation

As Chapter 1 has explained, in response to economic and political instability in the wake of the break-up of Yugoslavia, newly independent Macedonia abandoned the Yugoslav tradition of extensive autonomy and financial independence for municipalities and initiated a policy of centralisation. This process, note Jan Herczyński *et al.* (2009) was particularly severe in the education sector. The MoES explained the damage centralisation did to the education system in its ten-year strategy, published on the eve of decentralisation:

> This situation has generated many problems such as an inflexible structure of the system, marginalisation of the idiosyncrasies which stem from the specific features of the environment or place ... the existence of complex bureaucratic procedures in reaching decisions, the inability of the system to adapt to dynamic changes .... The procedures for choosing teaching and management staff have been focused towards one power point – the Ministry, which has resulted in the domination of party political and ethnic and personal interests when implementing the procedure of selecting staff, and marginalisation of professional quality as a key criterion .... Moreover, the responsibility of the schools, parents and local community for efficient functioning, and the opportunities for designing and implementing school development plans have been limited by complex bureaucratic procedures and restricted opportunities for finding alternative sources of finance.
>
> (MoES 2005: 22)

As a result of the centralisation, schools' autonomy was retracted and they became directly responsible to the MoES. The powers of school boards were also revoked and transferred to the MoES. Although the boards formerly retained a limited advisory role, their voice was routinely disregarded by central authorities. This structure led to the undemocratic governance of schools and key stakeholders, such as parents and teachers, were neither consulted nor informed of government decisions (World Bank 2002: 3; Myhrvold 2005: 23). Centralisation also led to the politicisation of the process of nominating and dismissing school directors, since the decision was taken by the Minister himself (Herczyński *et al.* 2009: 108). Some schools, notes Merle Vetterlein (2006: 9), also received preferential treatment thanks to better contacts with those responsible in the Ministry. Centralised decision-making regarding staffing and the opening and closing of the schools seldom corresponded with local needs, particularly in remote and sparsely inhabited areas of the country (Kumanovo 2010: 8). A further consequence of the centralising tendencies of the MoES was that its burgeoning administrative load distracted it from performing crucial strategic functions effectively, such as policy formulation, long-term planning and standards-setting (World Bank 2002: 13; Myhrvold 2005: 22).

The financial dimension of the centralisation was no less extreme than the political one and was motivated by a desire to control spending in a period of fiscal constraints (Herczyński *et al.* 2009: 109). Between 1996 and 2004, the budgets of all schools were prepared by the MoES and all school expenditures (even minor ones, such as magazine subscriptions) were processed by the centralised treasury system operated by the Ministry of Finance. The system of allocation norms for salaries and material expenditures based on the number of eligible classes a school provides was supposed to ensure a basic level of equity of school funding and, concludes Herczyński, to a certain extent it succeeded. However, it also blocked any local initiatives in the system, failed to ensure efficiency and was unable to keep pace with shifting demographic patterns (Herczyński *et al.* 2009: 110). Population changes at the time were characterised by rapidly increasing growth rates in Albanian-dominated municipalities and declining student numbers in Macedonian-majority rural areas. The result was substantial disparities in education spending across municipalities, which to a large extent reflected lower spending per student in predominantly Albanian schools (World Bank 2008: 23; UNICEF 2009: 31).

Table 3.1 illustrates significant disparities in primary education spending across municipalities based on urban/rural and ethnic characteristics in 2003. A comparable analysis based on fiscal data for 2005 was prepared by the World Bank and its findings corroborate these conclusions (World Bank 2008: 24). The data shows that the average per-student expenditure for primary schools in 2003 was 20,459 Macedonian Denars (MKD). However, education expenditure varied considerably across municipalities from 16,117 MKD in the large cities, such as the predominantly Albanian municipality of Tetovo, to 27,573 MKD in rural, predominantly Macedonian municipalities. Such disparities were matched by variations in class size: 27 students per class in Tetovo and 18.3 students in the rural Macedonian municipalities (Herczyński *et al.* 2009: 127). Since rural Albanian communities have school networks with urban characteristics (large class sizes), per-student spending in rural Albanian-dominated municipalities, notes Herczyński, was also smaller than in rural Macedonian ones. The World Bank's analysis concludes that while spending disparities can be partially explained by different student–teacher ratios across municipalities, funding inequalities appear to reflect the practice of allocating resources to schools on the basis of number of classes rather than the number of students (World Bank 2008: 23). The World Bank's analysis also notes that these spending outcomes before decentralisation were similar at the secondary level.

A further consequence of economic stagnation and uneven demographic shifts before 2005 was that, since the government could no longer afford to invest sufficiently in education, the school infrastructure was unable to keep pace with the rapidly changing student population. The data in Table 3.2

Table 3.1 Class sizes and expenditures in primary education per type of municipality, 2003

Type of municipality	Data	Macedonian		Mixed	Albanian		Macedonia
		>95 per cent	70–95 per cent		70–95 per cent	>95 per cent	
Skopje	Municipalities	2	3	3	1	1	10
	Class size	27.3	26.0	26.9	23.3	23.2	26.2
	Cost/student (MKD)	18,806	19,005	17,372	22,098	20,415	18,527
Large cities	Municipalities	2	2	1	1	–	6
	Class size	23.2	23.7	24.9	27.0	–	24.52
	Cost/student (MKD)	20,752	21,514	18,364	16,117	–	19,286
Small cities	Municipalities	18	6	3	–	–	27
	Class size	21.9	22.4	23.6	–	–	27
	Cost/student (MKD)	23,067	21,545	18,501	–	–	21,271
Rural	Municipalities	16	9	7	3	6	41
	Class size	18.3	18.8	19.0	23.4	23.6	20.89
	Cost/student (MKD)	27,573	27,516	26,564	17,977	18,317	22,647
Macedonia	Municipalities	38	20	14	5	7	84
	Class size	22.39	23.17	23.92	25.39	23.55	23.35
	Cost/student (MKD)	22,366	21,496	19,255	17,005	18,784	20,459

Source: Herczyński *et al.* (2009: 127)

Table 3.2 Utilities and maintenance costs in primary education per student, 2003

Data	Macedonian		Mixed	Albanian		Macedonia
	>95 per cent	70–95 per cent		70–95 per cent	>95 per cent	
Municipalities	38	20	14	5	7	84
Heated space for students (m²)	4.97	4.42	3.63	2.19	2.20	3.95
Heating cost per student (MKD)	1,240	1,503	1,081	712	611	1,149
Maintenance per student (MKD)	2,786	2,818	1,787	854	708	2,139

Source: Herczyński *et al.* (2009: 129)

illustrates that the space per student in Macedonian-majority municipalities was significantly higher (more than double) than in predominantly Albanian municipalities. This suggests many more Albanian students were obliged to attend school in multiple shifts during this period (Herczyński *et al.* 2009: 106). Since funds for heating were calculated according to the size of heated space, in addition to the number of class shifts, heating costs per student also varied significantly across municipality and ethnic group. Finally, the data in Table 3.2 shows how maintenance costs per student during 2003 also varied significantly across municipality; much greater than the disparities in total per-student spending (Table 3.1) (Herczyński *et al.* 2009: 129). While both Jan Herczyński's and the World Bank's analysis concentrate on funding disparities between Albanian- and Macedonian-dominated municipalities, it is logical to assume the funding system would have created similar inequalities for other ethnic groups experiencing rapid birth rates and who were living in densely populated areas, for example Roma communities in Skopje.

The legacy of more than a decade of over-bureaucratic, centralised management and the insufficient funding of school infrastructure was an education system no longer able to meet the diverse needs of its citizens. This was particularly true for ethnic and linguistic communities, whose educational preferences differed from those of the majority, and those living in rapidly expanding urban areas. Undemocratic school governance structures and an increasingly politicised educational environment often led to tensions locally and resulted in the delegitimisation of educational reforms and possibly also of the government in the eyes of marginalised local communities. Dissatisfaction over unequal educational standards – whether real or perceived – also increased tensions between different ethnic groups. The next section examines the changes introduced as a result of the decentralisation process in 2005. It will be followed by a discussion of whether this process has been successful in addressing some of the negative legacies of the previous decade.

Changes to the education system as a result of decentralisation

The decentralisation process, which seeks to enable greater community involvement in educational matters either directly or indirectly through their municipal representatives, began on 1 July 2005. Table 3.3 summarises the division of key responsibilities between stakeholders at the central, municipal and school levels. Responsibility for primary and secondary education was transferred to municipalities and they became 'founders' of schools, assuming ownership over school buildings, responsibility for their maintenance and the payment of staff salaries. Municipalities acquired the task of organising transport for students living more than 2 kilometres from school, student dormitories and for taking decisions on the opening and closing of schools, based on pre-defined criteria and the approval of the MoES. Local influence over the appointment of school directors was also enhanced by granting mayors responsibility over their appointment and dismissal, based on proposals from school boards. It is important to point out that responsibilities crucial to the design of the education system, such as the development of curricula, the approval of textbooks, teacher training and ultimate approval of many local decisions remained at the central government level.[3]

Given the increase in responsibilities at the local level, municipalities were obliged to establish education units within their administrations, as well as appoint municipal education inspectors to supervise the provision of education locally. While the role of municipal education officers remained to be standardised, a project managed by the OSCE, in coordination with MoES, the municipal association and municipal education officers during 2009 sought to define their function more precisely. It was suggested that their key roles were to: supervise the start and end of the school year; compile school data on behalf of the MoES; monitor procedures for supplying heating materials to schools, transportation and food for students; liaise with schools and the MoES; and to mediate education-related disputes (OSCE 2008d: 9; 2009: 3). The role of municipal education inspectors, when appointed by mayors, also remained unclear.[4] However, it was assumed their task was to supervise the working conditions in schools, the enrolment of students and ensure satisfactory arrangements for transport, food and student accommodation (OSCE 2006b: 14).

Increasing the powers of school boards, the management body of schools, was another important element of decentralisation which aimed to promote greater democratic governance in schools. It represents an example of power-dividing, an approach to institutional design proposed by Philip Roeder and Donald Rothchild (2005). The boards were assigned significant powers, including the authority to propose the school's annual work plan and budget to municipal councils, adopt the school statutes and propose the selection and dismissal of school directors to the mayor. Membership of the school boards was also amended in 2005; with parents assuming a third of seats and municipalities about the same. Other school board members

Table 3.3 Responsibilities of stakeholders within the decentralised education system

Central government	Municipalities	Schools
Prepares legislation, curricula, standards and strategic policy	'Founder' of school and is responsible for the maintenance of school buildings and staff salaries	Adopts schools' statute
Adopts plans and programmes for schools	Establishes and/or closes down schools and decides on their location	Proposes annual work programme; reports on schools' performance to municipal council
Defines the conditions to be met for founding a school and establishing classes	Adopts school decision to open or close classes, including those in different languages of instruction	Proposes annual financial plan to municipality
Manages and partially finances the education system through transfers to municipalities	Appoints and/or dismisses school director, upon the proposal of school board	Proposes annual balance of accounts to municipality
Approves draft textbooks	Organises and pays for transport and/or accommodation for students living far from schools	Advertises for election of school director, conduct interviews and propose two candidates to mayor
Adopts policies, procedures and conditions for professional and pedagogical training	Manages spending of central government transfers and provides own-source finances	Provides opinion on appointment of teachers and professional associates to school director
Carries out external assessments of students' achievement (exams)	Appoints municipal representatives to school boards	Makes decisions regarding complaints and appeals by school employees, students and parents
Supervises legal compliance of school programmes and monitors quality and efficiency of system	Supervises working conditions in schools, enrolment, transport, food, accommodation of students, etc. (municipal inspector)	
Operates the information system of education (data collection)		

included teachers and professional associates, the MoES and, in the case of secondary schools, a representative of the local business community. The role of school directors was also strengthened in 2005. Key aspects of their job were to undertake measures for the implementation of the school's work plan, select staff and make decisions on their deployment and termination, and report on the implementation of the work plan to the MoES and municipality (OSCE 2006b: 18). In an attempt to further depoliticise their appointment, a state exam for school directors was introduced in 2009 (Official Gazette 2009b: Articles 128, 129). While not strictly a feature of the decentralisation process per se, steps to professionalise the school director's role should be regarded as a direct consequence of their enhanced responsibilities and could lead to the more effective management of education locally.[5]

The process of politically and administratively decentralising in the education sector was accompanied by fiscal decentralisation reforms, which were carried out gradually in two phases. The division into two stages, whereby progression into the second phase was permitted only when municipalities fulfilled certain legal criteria, was proposed by the International Monetary Fund (IMF) and was motivated by the fear that poor fiscal management on behalf of the municipalities could contribute to an excessive budget deficit (Herczyński *et al.* 2009: 131).[6] During the first phase, which commenced in July 2005 and continued for two years, municipalities received earmarked grants from central government to cover maintenance costs (heating, electricity, etc.), repairs and student transportation. Staff salaries, however, continued to be paid directly by the central government (Herczyński 2011: 8; Risteska 2013b: 199). In the second phase, which began in September 2007 for those municipalities that satisfied the criteria, municipalities were entrusted with the payment of staff salaries. The earmarked grants received from the Ministry of Finance during the first phase were transformed into block grants, and both these and the block grants received for salaries could not be smaller than the equivalent funds previously allocated to municipalities (Official Gazette 2002: Art. 12). While the receipt of block, as opposed to earmarked, grants allowed municipalities greater discretion over how they could assign funding locally, neither the categorical grants for school maintenance nor the grants for salaries could be used for purposes other than education (Herczyński 2011: 8).

Another crucial fiscal reform introduced as a result of the decentralisation process was the move to a weighted education funding allocation formula based on the numbers of students in schools located in the municipalities, rather than on historical costs. The significance of this formula for the funding of primary and secondary education cannot be overestimated, because a weighted per-student system of financing over the longer term is the only way of ensuring that funds flow to where they are needed, i.e. where students attend school (Levitas 2009: 24). Not only does the use of such an allocation formula seek to ensure greater equity of funding across different municipalities, it also aims to improve transparency within the allocation of resources and reduce the possibility of discretionary payments. Such an approach to funding therefore has the potential to resolve an important grievance raised by the Albanian community during the 1990s.

The formula introduced for allocating primary education categorical grants to municipalities consisted of the following three elements: a lump sum, allocated to each municipality irrespective of the number of students located in its territory; payment based on the number of students attending schools located in municipalities, which was weighted for schools located in municipalities with low population density; and lower and upper buffers used to protect municipalities from excessive changes to the previous year's allocation (Herczyński *et al.* 2009: 140). The role of the lump sum was to protect smaller municipalities with fewer students that still need to maintain schools for them. The role of the weights for students in municipalities with low population densities was to provide additional funds to the small schools with small classes, where maintenance costs per student are higher (Herczyński *et al.* 2009: 141). The formula for allocating secondary education categorical grants to municipalities was very similar to that for primary education, although it did not initially include a lump sum and used only one density threshold. This changed in 2008 when the density threshold was abandoned and a lump sum added (Herczyński 2011: 17). As with the categorical grants, the allocation formula for block grants for primary education, introduced in 2008 for those municipalities in the second phase, included a lump sum, weighted per-student payments based on population density and the use of lower and upper buffers. However, it also included two additional coefficients, for students with special needs and for subject teaching to reflect the higher costs of teaching in higher classes (Herczyński 2011: 19–20). In contrast, the allocation formula for block grants for secondary education was much simpler and includes only a lump sum and one coefficient for students of vocational education (Herczyński 2011: 21).

Decentralised education and the promotion of heterogeneous policy-making

Mother-tongue education provision

One of the most broadly acknowledged rights in international minority protection standards is the right of non-majority communities to receive education in their mother tongue. While various international treaties indicate such an approach, the key document for states aspiring to membership of the European Union is the Council of Europe's Framework Convention for the Protection of National Minorities (FCNM) (1995) and specifically Articles 12 and 14.[7] It is worth emphasising that Macedonia has maintained an impressive record of ratifying international minority rights treaties and incorporating them into state legislation, although it had not ratified the European Charter for Regional or Minority Languages by mid-2012.[8] Despite this, and as Chapter 1 has illustrated, the provision of education in non-majority languages such as Albanian and Turkish during the 1990s had been problematic. Two particular incidents before the start of decentralisation in 2005 demonstrated the extent to which the provision of education in languages other than Macedonian remained a contentious issue in some localities. In Bitola during May 2000, for example, several thousand teachers, students and parents took to the streets to express discontent with government plans to open Albanian-medium classes for students at the 'Josip Broz Tito' gymnasium (Myhrvold 2005: 36). Protests of a similar magnitude erupted at the school once again in September 2003 when for a second time the government tried to open Albanian-medium classes (Myhrvold 2005: 38). In the Skopje municipality of Čair, tensions also arose during September 2003 when the government transferred seven Albanian-medium classes to the secondary economics school 'Arseni Jovkov' (Myhrvold 2005: 31).

Despite such high-profile cases, data published by the State Statistical Office confirms that the vast majority of Albanian students had access to primary education in their mother tongue between 2006 and 2011 (Table 3.4). While the actual number of students learning in Albanian has been gradually declining for a variety of reasons (from 73,932 in 2004/5 to 65, 121 in 2010/11), the overall proportion of students attending Albanian-medium classes increased and in 2010/11 stood close to 100 per cent.[9] The proportion of Turkish students learning in their mother tongue is much lower (approximately 60 per cent in 2004/5, see Table 3.5); however, this too increased between 2004/5 and 2010/11. The official data verifies that the number of primary schools offering instruction in Albanian also increased from 280 to 288 between the academic years 2004/5 and 2010/11 (Appendix G). Further, primary schools offering Turkish-medium classes increased from 57 to 62 during this time. In contrast, the number of primary schools offering instruction in Macedonian and Serbian languages decreased from 764 to 731 and from 11 to 7 respectively. The number of primary school class sections available in the community languages reflects a similar trend, with classes in Albanian and Turkish increasing during this period from 3,087 to 3,403 and from 272 to 352 respectively, while classes in both Macedonian and Serbian languages decreased.

The data for secondary education, however, shows a slightly different picture. Here, the proportion of Albanian students attending classes in their mother tongue is lower, but remained over 90 per cent of all Albanian students (Table 3.6). Interestingly, while the number of Albanian students attending Albanian-medium classes has increased since 2006, particularly because secondary school attendance became compulsory in 2008, so too has the total number of Albanians attending secondary school generally. The result is that the proportion of Albanian students attending Albanian-medium classes actually fell between 2004/5 and 2009/10, but improved in 2010/11 when the proportion stood at 95.02 per cent. Surprisingly, this had not been the experience of Turkish students, who,

Table 3.4 Proportion of Albanian students learning in their mother tongue (regular primary and lower secondary schools), 2004/5–2010/11

Year	No. of students	No. of students learning in mother tongue	Students learning in mother tongue (%)
2004/5	75,491	73,932	97.93
2005/6	–	–	–
2006/7	78,467	76,718	97.77
2007/8	75,141	73,571	97.91
2008/9	72,570	71,091	97.97
2009/10	69,922	68,668	98.21
2010/11	66,156	65,121	98.44

Sources: SSO (2006, 2008, 2009, 2010a, 2011, 2012a)

Table 3.5 Proportion of Turkish students learning in their mother tongue (regular primary and lower secondary schools), 2004/5–2010/11

Year	No. of students	No. of students learning in mother tongue	Students learning in mother tongue (%)
2004/5	9,514	5,561	58.45
2005/6	–	–	–
2006/7	9,599	5,998	62.49
2007/8	9,451	5,977	63.24
2008/9	9,304	5,715	61.43
2009/10	9,161	6,038	65.90
2010/11	9,011	6,043	67.06

Sources: SSO (2006, 2008, 2009, 2010a, 2011, 2012a)

between 2004/5 and 2010/11, enjoyed secondary education in their mother tongue in increasing – if only moderately so – numbers (Table 3.7). The data does however show that the number of secondary schools offering instruction in Albanian increased impressively between the academic years 2003/4 and 2010/11 from 23 to 34, and the number of class sections from 521 to 912, even though the proportion of Albanians learning in their mother tongue had in fact fallen (Appendix H). Schools and class sections offering instruction in Turkish also increased significantly (more than doubled), as the student numbers would suggest.

The official data, corroborated in interviews with municipal education officers, suggest that since the decentralisation process began, it has become relatively easy for municipalities to open new classes where the language of instruction is either Albanian or Turkish. Indeed, in reviewing Macedonia's second State Report on the implementation of the FCNM, the Council of Europe's Advisory Committee noted how

Table 3.6 Proportion of Albanian students learning in their mother tongue (higher secondary schools), 2004/5–2010/11

Year	No. of students	No. of students learning in mother tongue	Students learning in mother tongue (%)
2004/5	20,409	19,352	94.82
2005/6	–	–	–
2006/7	23,282	21,835	93.78
2007/8	24,225	22,357	92.29
2008/9	25,857	23,914	92.49
2009/10	27,663	26,028	94.09
2010/11	27,955	26,563	95.02

Sources: SSO (2006, 2008, 2009, 2010a, 2011, 2012a)

Table 3.7 Approximate proportion of Turkish students learning in their mother tongue (higher secondary schools), 2004/5–2010/11

Year	No. of students	No. of students learning in mother tongue[a]	Approx. no. of students learning in mother tongue (%)
2004/5	2,378	1,090	45.84
2005/6	–	–	–
2006/7	2,632	1,216	46.20
2007/8	2,695	1,326	49.20
2008/9	2,845	1,465	51.50
2009/10	2,948	1,476	50.07
2010/11	3,071	1,542	50.21

Sources: SSO (2006, 2008, 2009, 2010a, 2011)

Note

a I have calculated the proportion of Turkish students studying in their mother tongue by dividing the total number of students learning through the medium of Turkish with the total number of Turkish students. There is a possibility that students from other ethnic backgrounds, such as Albanians, may have chosen to study in Turkish and this has therefore inflated the overall proportion.

efforts have been made to improve the situation of schools providing instruction in Albanian and experiencing problems because of increased demand .... The Advisory Committee notes that, although tensions arose several years ago between students and families from the Macedonian and Albanian communities concerning the introduction of Albanian-language classes and schools, these tensions have gradually eased.

(Council of Europe 2008: 28)

Despite clear progress, a few examples do exist which suggest the provision of mother-tongue education remained contentious in some municipalities. These challenges related to the minimum threshold of students required to establish new classes (24), resistance to employing additional Albanian- or Turkish-speaking teachers (at the expense of Macedonian-speaking teachers) and the fact that any initiative required final approval from the MoES, in addition to the Ministry of Finance if there were financial implications.[10] Persistent difficulties in the opening of Albanian-medium classes in Bitola had still not been resolved by mid-2012, and other cases in Ohrid, Prilep, Veles and the secondary school 'Cvetan Dimov' in Skopje were given frequent, high-profile coverage in Albanian-language newspapers such as *Koha* (Hasani 2010: 2; Papraniku 2011: 5). This undoubtedly provided (Albanian) readers with the perception that the challenges facing mother-tongue education provision are much greater than they actually are.

A particularly high-profile case, which remained unresolved in mid-2012, concerns the primary school 'Goce Delčev', located in the village of Podgorci, Struga municipality. Before the start of the academic year 2008/9 the school's board requested permission by the municipality to open Albanian-medium classes. Since the number of students (11) involved was below the legal threshold, the municipality agreed to pay the salaries of the three teachers required and submitted the request to the MoES. In the absence of any response from the MoES, the classes were formed in November 2008 after a two-month delay. The request eventually received approval from the (Albanian) Deputy Minister of Education and Science on 9 March 2010; only to be reversed three weeks later by the Minister himself (of Macedonian ethnicity). The Minister declared the classes illegal, because they lacked ministerial approval, and the parents of the students affected were fined and issued with a court summons. Questioning the level of Albanian-language proficiency of the 11 students, the MoES proposed to establish a commission in order to assess their right to 'mother tongue' education in Albanian.

This case is controversial because it involved Macedonian Muslims (Torbeš), vulnerable to the assimilationist tendencies of the local Albanian population. It also occurred in Struga, a municipality significantly affected by the territorial reorganisation of 2004 (discussed at length in Chapter 5), and where relations between (now majority) Albanian and (previous majority) Macedonian secondary school pupils are often fragile.[11] Parallels can be and have already been drawn with the forced closure of two private primary schools offering Turkish-medium classes in Centar Župa municipality by police in 1995. A subsequent Constitutional Court ruling, contrary to the principle of self-identification for national minorities, supported the government's decision to close the schools. It emphasised how the Turkish minority in the area 'did not speak sufficient Turkish' to claim the right to mother-tongue education for their children (Wilson 2002: 57).

Primary and secondary education in a student's mother tongue was only available to Albanian and Turkish students between 2005 and 2012, while a small proportion of Serbs (less than 1 per cent) attended classes in their mother tongue (Appendix I). As a consequence, other communities living in Macedonia, such as the Roma, Vlach, Bošniaks, in addition to most Serbs

Table 3.8 Proportion of students, according to ethnicity, learning in the Macedonian language (regular primary and lower secondary schools), 2006/7–2010/11

Ethnicity	2006/7	2007/8	2008/9	2009/10	2010/11
	(%)	(%)	(%)	(%)	(%)
Macedonian	100.0	100.0	100.0	100.0	100.0
Albanian	2.1	2.1	2.0	1.8	2.1
Turkish	37.3	36.4	38.4	34.0	33.3
Roma	97.1	96.9	97.1	96.7	96.6
Serbian	91.4	91.5	90.9	91.8	91.6
Vlach	100.0	100.0	100.0	100.0	100.0
Other	98.8	99.1	99.0	99.0	98.4

Sources: SSO (2006, 2008, 2009, 2010a, 2011, 2012a)

and many Turks, generally attended Macedonian-medium classes (Table 3.8). In response to recommendations from the Council of Europe's Advisory Committee on the FCNM that 'requisite attention is paid also to the needs of the smaller minorities', the MoES introduced a selection of elective classes ('the Language and Culture of Roma/Vlachs/Bošniaks') in 2008 (Council of Europe 2008: 29). These classes were offered once a week for third-grade students and twice a week for students attending grades four to nine (MoES 2010a: 24). As a method of promoting language proficiency for the smaller communities in their mother tongue, the elective classes were not offered to students of other ethnicities (i.e. Macedonians interested in learning Romany), nor were they available to Turkish and Serbian students unable to attend Turkish- or Serbian-medium classes locally (MoES 2010a: 86). Elective classes in the Albanian language were, however, available to all students from sixth grade upwards.

While the classes represent a central government initiative, it is the responsibility of schools and municipalities to offer these classes and to promote their availability to students and their parents. A survey carried out by the MoES in 2009 found that only a relatively small number of Roma and Bošniak students had signed up for these elective classes, although the numbers of Vlach students doing so was more impressive. The low participation rate, concluded the MoES, 'raises doubts about the procedures and manner in which the schools offer [the] subject to the students' (MoES 2010a: 25). The fact that at least 15 students are required to form an elective class represents an additional challenge to opening additional classes in the future.

Rationalisation of the school network

A second example of how decentralisation may enhance communities' ability to meet local needs more effectively is the devolution of responsibility for opening and closing schools to municipalities.[12] As previously discussed, the existing school network reflects the demographic situation of the 1960s and

1970s when most primary and secondary schools were built. This has resulted in considerable discrepancies in the location of educational facilities. As elsewhere in the post-Communist world, for example in Poland, Macedonia inherited a large number of rural primary schools; schools that were largely responsible for making literacy nearly universal during the socialist period and to which people understandably are deeply attached (Levitas and Herczyński 2002; Levitas 2002). However, continual demographic decline in rural areas which disproportionately affects Macedonian communities, combined with increasing migration from rural to urban areas, has left many of these rural schools with very few students. Approximately 30 per cent of all primary schools, for example, have fewer than twenty students and are increasingly costly to maintain (Appendix J). In contrast, population growth in urban areas, particularly those populated by Albanian and Roma communities in the north and west of the country, has resulted in significant overcrowding in schools (OSI 2007: 25). As Chapter 5 will examine in more detail, considerable urban/rural disparities also exist in the secondary school network. Socialist planning's tendency to concentrate investments largely in urban areas has meant that secondary schools are generally only located in the major towns and cities. Not only has uneven demographic growth resulted in significant overcrowding in many urban secondary schools, the lack of secondary schools in rural areas means students are required to travel long distances in order to attend classes. Any decision concerning the redistribution of resources from under-populated (predominantly Macedonia) areas in the east of the country to over-populated (predominantly Albanian) areas in the north and west is understandably a sensitive issue.

One example of how the inadequate school network manifests itself is the significant proportion of schools required to operate multiple shifts in order to accommodate students. As the data in Table 3.9 shows, over one third of primary schools in 2010/11 were obliged to operate two shifts, which usually ran from 07.30 to 12.00 and from 12.30 to 18.00 each day (OSCE 2008d: 23). While multiple school shifts is not a new phenomenon, it represented a persistent challenge to the provision of equitable educational standards and only limited progress has been made since 2005 to resolve it. The data in Table 3.9 also confirms that approximately 1 per cent of primary schools operated three shifts on a daily basis. During the academic year 2010/11 these schools were located in the municipalities of Šuto Orizari, Gjorce Petrov, Gostivar, Kičevo, Kumanovo and Strumica.[13] Operating multiple shifts not only requires lesson times to be shortened so that classes can be appropriately scheduled; it also limits the time and space available for extra-curricular activities or classes for students with additional support needs, such as language 'catch-up' classes. Interviews with municipal education officers and primary and secondary school directors in Šuto Orizari, Kumanovo and Gostivar municipalities verified that in such circumstances schools are compelled to shorten lessons to 30 minutes (Kumanovo 2010: 109).[14] Legally, the duration of lessons in primary schools must be 40 minutes and in secondary schools 45 minutes (Official Gazette 2008b: Art. 27; 2009b: Art. 39).

Table 3.9 Regular primary and lower secondary schools and students, according to the number and types of shifts, 2003/4–2010/11 (number of schools)

	2003/4	*2004/5*	*2005/6*	*2006/7*	*2007/8*	*2008/9*	*2009/10*	*2010/11*
One shift	601	598	–	591	583	586	597	616
Two shifts	399	402	–	390	401	394	383	366
Three shifts	12	10	–	19	3	11	10	8
Total	1,012	1,010	–	1,000	997	991	990	990

Sources: SSO (2006, 2008, 2009, 2010a, 2011, 2012a)

For secondary schools, the situation was more complicated because the schools function in multiple buildings and the shifts occur there.[15] Instead, the main source of complaints was overcrowding and reduced lesson time. Official data on either secondary school class sizes or the proportion of schools operating double or triple shifts is not publicly available. However, a 2008 report prepared by the World Bank estimated that as many as 87 per cent of secondary schools operate on a two-shift basis (World Bank 2008: 30). Secondary schools in the urban municipalities of Kumanovo, Gostivar and Tetovo – all with significant Albanian and Roma student profiles – are known to experience particularly acute spatial problems (Kumanovo 2011).[16] In a survey commissioned by UNDP in 2010, a quarter of interviewees complained of large classes, the proportion of which was higher among Albanian respondents because class sizes for this group are typically between 35 and 40 students (Sonce 2010: 15; UNDP 2010a: 98; Kumanovo 2011: 3). Not only is such practice illegal, because the maximum class size permitted in both primary and secondary schools is 34; it is also contrary to good pedagogical practice and has an impact on the quality of learning (Official Gazette 2008b: Art. 28; 2009b: Art. 41; World Bank 2008: 26).

There is evidence to suggest that the overcrowding experienced in secondary schools may have been exacerbated by two reforms introduced by the MoES to improve student participation rates (OSI 2007: 170). The first was the introduction of the 'class zero' in the academic year 2007/8, increasing the number of primary school years from eight to nine. The second reform was the decision to make secondary education compulsory from the academic year 2008/9. Clearly, the ensuing rise in student numbers at both primary and secondary schools will exacerbate existing spatial problems. It has been estimated that the changes to secondary education alone will result in a rise in students numbers of between 4 and 10 per cent until 2012 (OSCE 2008b: 4; UNDP 2008: 41). Such increases will understandably be greater in those areas where historically secondary school enrolment rates have been low (with significant Roma, Albanian and Turkish communities) (UNDP 2004b: 67). The result will be a disproportionate burden on those schools already significantly overcrowded (see Figure 3.1), unless substantial capital investments can be made to improve current facilities.

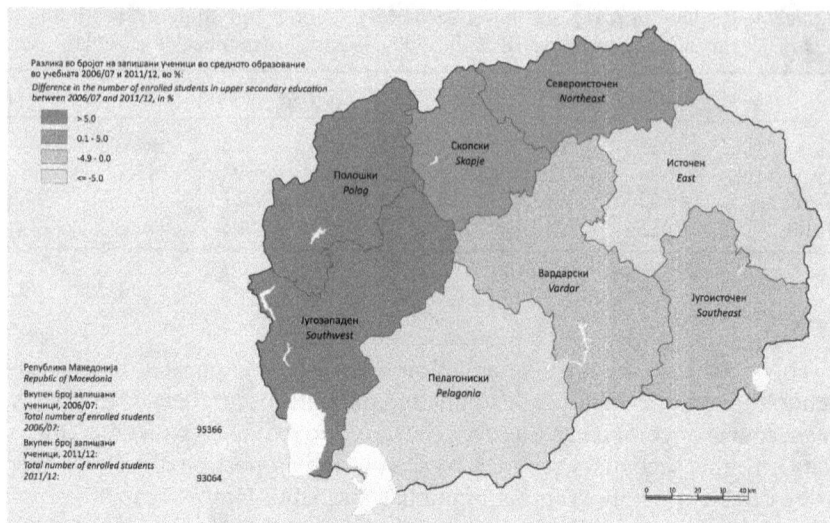

Figure 3.1 Map to show increases by region in the number of enrolled secondary
school students between 2003/4 and 2008/9

Source: SSO (2012b: 31)

Tables 3.10 and 3.11 show the attempts that have been made to rationalise both the primary and secondary school networks between 2002/3 and
2010/11. A monitoring report on the decentralisation process prepared by the
Center for Local Democracy Development found that initiatives to establish
new or close down existing primary schools were frequently raised by municipalities; however, their implementation is slow (CLDD 2011: 9). In 2008
for example, five of the twelve municipalities monitored by the Center raised
initiatives aimed at rationalising the school network; however only three of
which were successful. The record in 2009 was just as poor: from nine municipalities, only three initiatives were successful (CLDD 2011: 10). An important obstacle to rationalising the school network, notes the report, was the
MoES's delay in responding to applications, which took anything from one
to three years (CLDD 2011: 63). Other barriers to initiatives for rationalising
the school network, apart from the obvious challenge of accessing resources,
were unresolved property and tenure issues regarding school buildings, in addition to vague cadastral records (Bakiu 2010: 28; CLDD 2011: 10; Herczyński
2011: 8).

A dilemma exists regarding the building of additional secondary schools
in areas not already integrated into the existing network. A UNDP survey in
2008, for example, found that a significant proportion of secondary school
students (21.3 per cent) travelled more than 10 kilometres to attend classes
(UNDP 2008: 79). This is particularly evident in rural areas, where 47 per cent
of students travelled over 10 kilometres to the nearest secondary school. While

Table 3.10 Number of regular primary and lower
secondary schools, 2002/3–2010/11

Year	No. of schools
2002/3	1,020
2003/4	1,012
2004/5	1,010
2005/6	1,005
2006/7	1,000
2007/8	997
2008/9	991
2009/10	990
2010/11	990

Sources: SSO (2006, 2008, 2009, 2010a, 2011, 2012a)

Table 3.11 Number of regular upper secondary
school buildings, 2002/3–2010/11

Year	No. of schools
2002/3	96
2003/4	96
2004/5	100
2005/6	101
2006/7	104
2007/8	107
2008/9	110
2009/10	110
2010/11	114

Sources: SSO (2006, 2008, 2009, 2010a, 2011, 2012a)

shortening the distance students must travel to school will improve access
to education, there is a risk that building additional schools will 'ghettoise'
rural communities by cutting them off from urban centres and with it, the
prospect of integration into the wider (multicultural) society. Such dilemmas
have influenced debates on whether to build new secondary schools in the
predominantly Roma municipality of Šuto Orizari in Skopje, in Lipkovo and
in Struga (both predominantly Albanian municipalities).[17] Until discrepancies in the secondary school network are resolved, municipal transport for
students travelling long distances will remain vital.

The renaming of schools

The ability to change the name of a school so that it more closely reflects
local preferences is a further example of heterogeneous policy-making at
the local level. It is also another issue which caused controversy before 2005

and led the OSCE's High Commissioner on National Minorities to observe how 'decisions on renaming schools are currently taken by a simple majority and can have a polarising effect in multi-ethnic areas' (HCNM 2008: 4). An incident in 2003, for example, where Albanians in the village of Šemševo, Jegunovce municipality north-east of Tetovo, ignored procedures and renamed the primary school 'Dame Gruev' after the first Albanian teacher from the region ('Jumni Junuzi'), led Macedonian parents to withdraw their children from classes (NDC 2005: 3). In response, the High Commissioner recommended:

> Changing the procedure for decisions on school name changes to a more consensus-based procedure that includes all relevant stakeholders to ensure that the new name is perceived as legitimate and does not offend people with different cultural backgrounds. This could be achieved through involvement of consultative bodies such as school boards.
>
> (HCNM 2008: 5)

Observers have noted a trend in the years since decentralisation of renaming schools in order to better reflect the cultural and ethnic identity of local communities. For example, schools previously called after Macedonian heroes and dates of historical significance have been renamed with the names of Albanian or Turkish heroes and holidays (UNICEF 2009: 22). However, a review of school name changes initiated by the OSCE in 2011 found that, while some schools changed their names, it is inaccurate to conclude that a significant proportion had done so, or that school names were replaced with controversial choices.[18] Indeed, a comparative review of school names in 2006 and 2010 suggests only around 14 schools changed their name during that period, although there have been some additional cases since then and before 2006 (MCIC 2006, 2010). The OSCE's review did, however, find evidence of a handful of controversial cases. For example, schools were renamed after former NLA members in the municipalities of Lipkovo, Struga and Bogovinje and members of the Macedonian security forces killed in 2001 in Makedonska Kamenica and Zrnovci.[19] Another high-profile case arose in Gostivar when the name of a primary school *'Bratstvo i Edinstvo'* ('Brotherhood and Unity' in Macedonian) was replaced with the single word *'Bashkimi'*, meaning 'Unity' in Albanian. Macedonian students refused to accept their graduation certificates featuring the new school name for more than two years. However, a compromise was eventually found in 2009 and the school is known as *'Bashkimi/Edinstvo/Birlik'*, the word 'unity' in the Albanian, Macedonian and Turkish languages.[20]

Formal procedures for renaming schools do exist. Proposals for name changes must be initiated by the school board, which requires the consent of the municipal council before being submitted to the MoES for final evaluation and approval. However, a senior representative of the MoES conceded that problems can and do still arise locally, although such incidents have been less frequent since 2010 because most schools that have wanted to change their name have already done so.[21]

The role of school boards: enhancing participation and transparency in decision-making?

In a comprehensive review of school-based management processes on behalf of the World Bank, Barrera-Osorio *et al.* (2009) argue that greater community participation in school decision-making processes can improve accountability, transparency and responsiveness to local needs. However, they also observe how decentralisation does not necessarily give more power to the general public, because the powers devolved are susceptible to elite capture. The risk is greater, they note, in countries where local democracy and political accountability may be weak, where 'in some cases, the local community members [have] organised to take over one or more school councils and then used the councils for their own political ends rather than for the better education of children' (Barrera-Osorio *et al.* 2009: 35). Indeed, in his recommendations to the Minister of Education and Science during 2004, the High Commissioner on National Minorities warned how, 'in the extremely politicised environment, combined with a lack of an experience of democratic decision-making, it is unlikely that the situation [of governance in schools] would dramatically improve' (HCNM 2004: 4).

'It is often the case', observed the OSCE in 2008, 'that School Boards are politicised thus upholding their political party's interests … many Directors lobby among teachers and parents in order to get their preferred candidate elected' (OSCE 2008d: 16). While one OSCE official remarked how school boards often operate as 'mini municipal councils', with the appointment of representatives being highly politicised and discussions dominated by only a handful of members, experiences, the official also noted, are mixed and many boards do function well.[22] In her of review of participatory administrative reform in south-eastern European schools, Sinziana-Elena Poiana stressed the importance of further efforts to improve the capacity of board members and parents' awareness of their rights more generally in order that participatory school management becomes a reality (Poiana 2011: 450). A survey commissioned by UNDP in 2010, for example, found that as many as 80 per cent of parents indicated that they would not like to complain about the education their child receives, even if they had cause to do so (UNDP 2010a: 97). Relations between school boards, municipal education units and councils also needed improvement, because many boards considered their role has been marginalised by municipal management (OSCE 2008c: 13). Only a few municipalities have established mechanisms for regularly reporting school board decisions, with the majority of school boards reporting to municipal councils only once a year (OSCE 2008c: 15; CLDD 2011: 62).

A school board's ability to respond to heterogeneous needs, thus increasing the legitimacy of the decisions it makes, also depends on how well its membership reflects the diversity of the local community (Winkler and Yeo 2007: 2). Analysis of the membership of 60 primary school boards that applied to the USAID's Schools Renovations Project during 2010 confirms that over half (34 schools) did not fully represent the local student population they are supposed to serve.[23] Of these 34 school boards, Roma students were under- or unrepresented on 18 boards, Albanian students in 10, Turkish students in 5, and other ethnic groups on 6. Macedonian students were not under-represented on any of the 60 school boards monitored. What the data does not reveal is whether satellite schools, an important issue which will be discussed in a subsequent section, were adequately represented on the school boards. The under-representation of Roma communities, as well as other non-majority communities, on school boards has been verified by other, more comprehensive reviews (OSI 2007: 238; REF 2007: 52). Their representation is particularly important given the fact that the Roma represent the fastest-growing student profile in Macedonia (OSI 2007: 193). Roma students also experience specific challenges in relation to their educational achievement, such as low enrolment and attendance rates, high drop-out rates, in-school segregation and discrimination, as well as over-representation in educational facilities for students with learning difficulties (REF 2007; Demarchi 2010; ECRI 2010). While the enhanced powers devolved to school boards may facilitate increases in the participation of Roma representatives in decision-making processes, the Roma Education Fund has warned that massive local-level capacity-building is required in municipal councils, municipal education commissions, school boards, and parents to ensure positive effects on the educational outcomes of Roma children (REF 2007: 24).

Towards a more equitable and transparent distribution of public resources

Equitable allocation of funds for education

Moving to a weighted funding allocation formula based on the numbers of students in schools, rather than the number of classes, has contributed significantly to the promotion of a more equitable distribution of state education resources. Since 2005, funds have flowed directly to where they are needed and the use of lump sum payments, in addition to weights for schools located in sparsely populated areas, ensured the higher costs of providing educational services in rural areas were met. However, an analysis of education funding completed by USAID in May 2011 suggests that the simultaneous use of both the lump sum payment and population density weights in the calculation of primary education categorical and block grants was excessive and as a result, rural municipalities received relatively too much compared to their urban counterparts (Herczyński 2011: 26). The situation was exacerbated in 2008 when changes were made to both the population density thresholds and weights, resulting in the creation of even greater disparities between categorical and block grants for urban and rural municipalities (Herczyński 2011: 14–15). While it is reasonable that per-student allocation formulas should take the higher cost of providing education in rural areas into account, the USAID analysis shows that, as a direct consequence of these changes in 2008, the differences between per-student amounts in densely populated urban and sparsely populated rural municipalities grew considerably between 2006 and 2011 (Herczyński 2011: 25). As the next chapter will examine, it may be no coincidence that the sparsely populated rural municipalities that have benefited most from these changes correlate with areas where VMRO-DPMNE electoral strength was greatest. Regardless of the need to fine-tune the current allocation formula for primary education, it is important to emphasise that per-capita funding seeks to ensure greater equity over the longer term (Levitas 2009: 24–5). Significant capital investments will also be required in areas previously neglected so that persistent regional disparities can be addressed (European Commission 2010: 62).

One area where per-capita funding is unable to address funding inequalities in education is the process by which resources are distributed at the school level, between the central school and its branches or satellites. These units are subsidiary entities belonging to the central school and are managed by the director of that school. Their unequal treatment, remarked an expert that had worked with the MoES for more than five years, 'is like a family secret, which everyone knows but nobody wants to talk about' (Herczyński 2007: 2). In primary schools the satellites often provide teaching from first to fourth grades, with older students commuting to the central school (or sometimes to a larger satellite school). Approximately two-thirds of all primary school facilities in Macedonia are satellite schools, with a large proportion providing instruction in languages other than Macedonian. A comprehensive review of the treatment of satellite primary schools located in eight municipalities was prepared at the request of the ZELS Education Committee in 2007 (Herczyński 2007). While the review acknowledged that satellite schools are not an easy subject to discuss, since considerations of equity directly contradict considerations of efficiency, it concluded that the unequal treatment of satellite schools is unacceptable on both social and moral grounds.[24]

The data in Table 3.12 illustrates the disparities in the condition of central and satellite school buildings located in the eight municipalities reviewed during 2007 (Herczyński 2007: 3).[25] The ZELS review found that pedagogical support staff such as psychologists, speech therapists, etc. tended to be concentrated in the central schools and very rarely, if ever, worked with satellite school students. The equitable distribution of teaching materials was also found to be problematic (Herczyński 2007: 5, 7). Given the significant differences in the conditions of buildings and their access to school equipment, regular co-operation between central and satellite schools is extremely important. However, the review found that in many instances such co-operation was

Table 3.12 Conditions in satellite schools in eight municipalities, 2007

Condition	Satellite (%)	Central (%)
Facilities with unsafe roofs	16.7	3.5
Facilities with inadequate school furniture	51.3	12.0
Facilities with damaged floors	52.8	34.5
Facilities with old electrical networks	61.1	13.8
Facilities with inadequate toilets	63.0	21.0
Facilities heated with wood-burning stoves	91.7	44.8
Facilities without fire protection	98.3	83.3

Source: Herczyński (2007: 4)

lacking. In order to improve conditions in satellite schools, so that students experience the equal educational standards guaranteed by the Constitution, the review recommended that schools collect and maintain data on the educational processes in each entity. School boards, which operate at the level of the central schools, could also be required to include representations from the satellite schools. Other recommendations proposed by the report were for municipalities to introduce registries of resources to monitor access to equipment, teaching aids and staff time, and request schools to submit for review and approval separate financial plans for each school entity, rather than one for the whole school (Herczyński 2007: 10). Municipalities could also employ municipal education inspectors to monitor the quality of education in the satellite facilities. It is unclear whether any of these actions have been regularly undertaken by municipalities, if at all.[26]

A further source of inequality left unaffected by changes to central government funding allocation is how much the municipalities themselves contribute to local education budgets. Within a decentralised context, central governments assume municipalities will contribute to the cost of providing education services locally. However, two separate reports commissioned by USAID in 2011 suggest that the overall level of contributions to education funds from municipal budgets in 2009 and 2010 was low (Herczyński 2011; MGLA 2011). In 2009, for example, 35 of the 66 municipalities in the second fiscal phase of decentralisation contributed 88,372,560 MKD to local primary education budgets, representing 1.3 per cent of overall municipal expenditure. In 2010, the number of contributing municipalities increased to 37 and the proportion of own-source funding increased to 1.5 per cent (MLGA 2011: 10, 17). For those municipalities responsible for secondary education functions and in the second phase, 11 provided 20,081,953 MKD to complement central government transfers during 2009. This, however, represented only 0.7 per cent of the total amount transferred to second-phase municipalities in 2009, although the amount increased to 3.7 per cent in 2010 (MLGA 2011: 14, 21). While the proportion of own-source funding for education provision is insignificant compared to central government transfers, both reports confirm that those contributing most to local education budgets were the wealthier, urban municipalities, such as Karpoš, Centar (both in the City of Skopje) and Ohrid (Herczyński 2011: 42). As municipal contributions increase in the future, it is possible educational standards in less affluent municipalities may decline as a result.

The transparent allocation of funds for education

While the use of a standardised formula should promote greater funding equity across the municipalities, it also aims to improve transparency and reduce opportunities for discretionary payments. Unfortunately, however, key financial elements of the formula have not been routinely made public, even to municipalities, and so very few people in Macedonia actually understand its impact on education financing (Levitas 2009: 24; Herczyński 2011: 5). USAID's 2011 assessment of education financing suggests certain procedural abnormalities further obscure how these funds are allocated, which fuels misconceptions within the municipalities and the general public. The assessment found excessive use of both lower and upper buffers to regulate annual payment adjustments to block grants in a way that is unclear to municipalities (Herczyński 2011: 5, 26). The fact that the allocation formula for the fiscal year is adopted in April, long before initial budget guidelines from the Ministry of Finance are issued which confirm how much funding is available and before final student numbers are known, also reduces transparency (Herczyński 2011: 12). The result is that MoES officials are no longer able to set important allocation coefficients in accordance to the actual relative needs of municipalities (Herczyński 2011: 13).

Persistent challenges to decentralised education

Ethnic segregation in schools

There is a growing trend of ethnic segregation in both primary and secondary schools, epitomising Marcel Baumann's concept of 'voluntary apartheid' (Baumann 2009). In the longer term, it threatens to undermine the cohesion of Macedonian society and ultimately the state. Rather than representing a tool for promoting mutual understanding, the education system in Macedonia currently perpetuates mutual mistrust and intolerance between the different communities (HCNM 2004: 2; MoES 2010b: 8; Schenker 2011: 20). Improvements in the provision of mother-tongue education, which necessitates students being taught in separate classes according to the language of instruction, may have been made at the expense of social cohesion (UNDP 2004b: 71; UNICEF 2009: 23). Multiple shifts, operating in most primary and secondary schools, are frequently organised along linguistic (and therefore ethnic) lines rather than by grade. In more acute cases, students of different ethnicities are relocated into separate buildings and ultimately, if local politics and resources permit, schools may split into separate legal entities. According to a review prepared by the OSCE in 2008, more than half of all secondary students attending multilingual schools were separated according to ethnicity in either different buildings[27] or monolingual shifts[28] (OSCE 2008e). Instances of ethnic separation in schools that have been given the most attention by international agencies operating in Macedonia (OSCE, UNDP, etc.) are found in Kumanovo and Struga municipalities, although further examples exist in Kičevo, Šuto Orizari, Tetovo and Gostivar. The two new secondary schools that were opened for Albanian students in Kumanovo and Lipkovo during 2010 are examples of this increase in the number of monolingual schools with Albanian-medium classes (UNICEF 2009: 55–8).[29] Efforts by international donors to prevent two further schools from dividing in Kičevo and Kruševo during 2011 have so far met with mixed success (the school in Kičevo divided, while the school in Kruševo remained united in mid-2012). In most instances, the segregation affects Macedonian and Albanian students, although the physical separation of Roma students is also a growing concern (OSI 2007: 243; Demarchi 2010: 37; Sonce 2010: 6).

Increasing ethnic segregation in schools is not a direct consequence of the decentralisation process; its roots date back to the Yugoslav system of 'separate but equal' education for the different communities, while ethnic conflict in 2001 acted as a catalyst (Petroska-Beška and Najčevska 2004: 3). However, observers have suggested that the enhanced 'voice' local politicians, teachers and parents now have in deciding important educational matters, such as the opening of new classes and schools, may have exacerbated this trend. Research suggests initial demands for segregating students have often come from parents, citing security concerns, via the school board.[30] Local politicians have also been blamed for encouraging separation, because the opening of new classes, buildings and/or schools is considered an issue of political status, as well as an opportunity to create new jobs for one's own community.[31] Splitting schools into separate entities represents a lack of trust in the discretionary powers assigned to school directors, since local communities believe that unless they have a school 'of their own' they will not receive their fair share of resources.[32] In the words of one international expert: 'The political parties are not fighting for improving the educational experiences of students. If they were, they would never allow Albanian children to learn in *that* building in Kumanovo!'[33] While the municipalities may not have been responsible for starting this trend, international observers have implied that they have done very little to reverse it (ECRI 2005: 32; Council of Europe 2008: 63). Given the extensive decision-making powers bestowed on them, municipalities could do much more to promote the construction of larger multi-ethnic schools, located in areas accessible to all communities, rather than smaller mono-ethnic ones (HCNM 2004: 2; UNDP 2009b: 63). Municipalities could also persuade local school boards to maintain teaching shifts based on class grades rather than on the language of instruction, and to implement joint school or inter-municipal projects aimed at fostering co-operation between students of different cultural backgrounds (UNICEF 2009: 10).

Entrenchment of patronage politics

A second persistent challenge to the delivery of quality, equitable education in Macedonia is the highly politicised environment within which decisions are made at the school, municipal and central levels. While progress has been made in the depoliticisation of school directors' appointments (through the involvement of school boards and creation of a school director's exam), political influences remain and affect the appointment of school administrators, teachers, even cleaning staff (HCNM 2008: 4; Bakiu 2010: 28)! Indeed, when asked by the OSCE whether the influence of politics in education has decreased or increased since the decentralisation process began, 18 per cent of municipal respondents believed it had increased, 42 per cent thought it had stayed the same and 40 per cent felt it had decreased (OSCE 2009: 65).[34] In the same survey, a citizen's poll found responses to the same question to be 23.3 per cent, 41.6 per cent and 9.6 per cent respectively (OSCE 2009: 66).

Substantial anecdotal evidence suggests that relations between the municipalities and central authorities are also affected by party politics. There is a widely held perception that centrally appointed state inspectors target opposition-led municipalities, although this has become less of a problem since the 2009 municipal elections because very few opposition-led municipalities subsequently exist. Opposition-led municipalities also experience prolonged delays in receiving responses from the MoES and there is a perception that the annual budgets they submit to the Ministry of Finance have been 'trimmed down' (Bakiu 2010: 27).[35] Finally, it is commonly assumed that those municipalities that are led by the political parties in government receive preferential treatment in the allocation of capital grants for infrastructure projects (ICG 2011: 19). Indeed, of the 54 municipalities that changed their political affiliation in the 2009 municipal elections, two-thirds received a larger allocation of capital funds once they became aligned with parties in the governing coalition.[36] While the decision to allocate capital funds to these municipalities may be based on entirely rational circumstances, in the absence of transparent criteria and the involvement of key stakeholders, such as representatives of the municipal association, decisions regarding the allocation of capital education funds are likely to remain vulnerable to political influence (ZELS: 2010b). A review of capital funding transfers in the next chapter discusses this issue in more detail.

The capacity of municipalities to manage education

Based on extensive empirical research, Donald R. Winkler and Boon-Ling Yeo (2007) conclude that simply changing the organisation of education has little, if any, impact on its actual delivery. It is how these new responsibilities are ultimately executed that has the greatest impact on service provision. Effective education provision therefore depends upon the capacity of local stakeholders. It is worth considering the fact that when an opinion poll commissioned by UNDP asked citizens who they believed could best provide educational services (central or local government), for three consecutive years the majority of respondents believed central government was best placed to do so (UNDP 2008: 81; 2009b: 78; 2010a: 94).[37] It is particularly surprising that this survey also reported that a greater proportion of Albanian respondents were in favour of central rather than local government provision than any other ethnic group (UNDP 2008: 81; 2009b: 79). The survey findings indicate a low level of public confidence in the capacity of municipalities to provide quality educational services (UNDP 2010a: 103).

In an interview for a local think-tank in 2010, former Minister of Education and Science Sulejman Rushiti confirmed the 'lack of administrative capacity' within some municipalities to effectively identify local education needs: 'Most of the municipalities count only one or two employees in the sector for education, which ... is far from sufficient' (Bakiu 2010: 28). As with own-source contributions to local education budgets, significant disparities exist regarding the administrative capacities of larger urban and less affluent rural municipalities. This is not a surprise when municipalities such as Rosoman, with a total staff of six people, and Aračinovo, with seven, were tasked with delivering the same responsibilities as Strumica and Tetovo municipalities, with 134 and 158 employees respectively (MCIC 2010). More than three years after the decentralisation of education responsibilities, less than half (40) of all municipalities employed a dedicated officer for education matters in 2009. The remaining municipalities either designated officers already employed in another area of work or had no one at all.[38] A similar practice existed with the appointment of municipal education inspectors, where only approximately 15 municipalities had appointed one by 2011.[39] Even Kumanovo, which employed 118 people and has a combined primary/secondary student population of 19,154, has only two officers working on education issues and did not employ a municipal education inspector (SSO 2011).[40] Given the inability of many municipalities to assign sufficient resources to the management of educational matters, and in the absence of much-needed inter-municipal co-operation, it is little wonder citizens were failing to notice any significant improvements in service delivery.

Summary

This chapter has examined whether decentralisation has satisfied the demands of non-majority groups for greater control over how primary and secondary education is provided. Following an evaluation of the system before decentralisation, a comprehensive analysis of the administrative and fiscal reforms introduced in 2005 was conducted. The chapter argues that the decentralisation process has facilitated heterogeneous policy-making in the provision (but not design) of educational services, although further progress has been hampered by a lack of finances and central government support. The provision of Albanian- and Turkish-medium education has, for example, generally improved, although some would argue this has come at the expense of quality. However, the experiences of the smaller communities in accessing education in their mother tongue – either as the language of instruction or in elective classes – have been less positive. Greater community involvement in decision-making processes has also improved transparency and allowed what were once highly contentious issues, such as the renaming of schools or the opening of a new school, to be generally made on a rational basis. Finally, the move to a per-capita education funding allocation formula in 2006 has facilitated a more equitable distribution of state resources. Nevertheless, challenges remain and further work needs to be done, to fine-tune funding formulae and to ensure school boards are genuinely representative of student populations, if the progress made in the first seven years of decentralisation is to continue.

Decentralisation is no panacea, however. Problems which existed in the education system before decentralisation in 2005 remain and may indeed have been exacerbated by the reforms. Ethnic segregation in schools is increasing at a disturbing rate and, despite having the legal competences to do so, the municipalities have done little to reverse this trend. The entrenchment of patronage politics, a persistent feature of the education system, is also unrelenting, and may now be more visible to citizens, given their proximity to where decisions are being made. The decentralisation process is still in its infancy and it is reasonable to expect that the capacities of municipalities to carry out new functions will require further strengthening. Nevertheless, these persistent challenges, unless adequately addressed by both the municipalities and central government, threaten to undermine the benefits of decentralised education in the longer term.

Notes

1 Other devolved public services include primary healthcare, social welfare and child protection, utilities, etc. (Official Gazette 2002: Art. 22).
2 Part of this analysis is also available in Lyon (2013).
3 Municipalities do, however, have some possibility of adapting 20 per cent of the curriculum to local needs, for example in the design and delivery of vocational training (Risteska 2013b: 200).
4 Interview with the executive director of ZELS: 8 April 2011, Skopje.
5 Interview with senior representative of the State Examination Centre: 7 April 2011, Skopje.
6 Municipalities were required to possess an adequate staff capacity for financial management, show good financial results for at least 24 months, have no arrears to suppliers or any other creditors exceeding ordinary terms of payment (Official Gazette 2004: Art. 46).

7 Other relevant treaties include Article 5 of the UNESCO Convention Against Discrimination in Education and Article 4 of the UN Declaration on the Rights of Persons Belonging to National or Ethnic, Religious and Linguistic Minorities.

8 This is reflected in the Constitution (Official Gazette 2001a: Art. 48), laws on both Primary and Secondary Education (Official Gazette 2008a: Art. 9; 2009b: Art. 4), and legislation promoting and protecting the rights of members of communities which are less than 20 per cent of the population (Official Gazette 2008b: Art. 5).

9 Two possible reasons for the reduction in the numbers of Albanian students learning in their mother tongue is the effect of lower birth rates within the Albanian community and increasing rates of migration. Interview with municipal education officer, Gostivar municipality: 22 June 2011, Gostivar.

10 Classes with fewer students can be established if the municipality concerned agrees to pay related staffing costs. Such initiatives still require approval from the MoES, however.

11 Inter-ethnic tensions between (Macedonian-majority) pupils at the secondary school 'Niko Nestor' and the adjacent (Albanian-majority) secondary school 'Ibrahim Temo' have erupted before parliamentary elections in 2008 and municipal elections in 2009. The situation has led to the parents of pupils in both schools demanding that their children be segregated in school shifts according to the language of instruction. Interviews with OSCE official: 8 June 10, Skopje; and Peace Corps volunteer at 'Niko Nestor' school: 10 June, Struga.

12 However, final approval was required by the MoES.

13 Interview with OSCE official: 12 April 2011, Skopje.

14 Interviews with: education expert, Šuto Orizari municipality: 6 April 2011, Šuto Orizari; municipal education officer, Gostivar municipality: 22 June 2011, Gostivar; secondary school director, Kumanovo municipality: 5 April 2011, Kumanovo.

15 Interview with OSCE official: 12 April 2011, Skopje.

16 Interview with OSCE official: 12 April 2011, Skopje.

17 Interview with OSCE official: 4 April 2011, Skopje.

18 Interview with OSCE official: 12 April 2011, Skopje.

19 These schools are: 'Ismet Jashari', a secondary school in Lipkovo; 'Nuri Mazari', a primary school in Delogozda, Struga; 'Sabedin Bajrami', a primary school in Kamenjane, Bogovinje; 'Mile Janevski Dzingar', a secondary school in Makedonska Kamenica; and 'Sinisa Stoilkov', a primary school in Zrnovci.

20 Interview with municipal education officer, Gostivar municipality: 22 June 2011, Gostivar.

21 Interview with a senior representative of the MoES: 7 April 2011, Skopje.

22 Interview with OSCE official: 12 April 2011, Skopje.

23 Interview with Chief of Party, USAID Schools Renovations Project: 8 April 2011, Skopje.

24 'It is difficult, indeed probably impossible, to provide adequate school equipment for extremely small school facilities, when even large schools find it hard to secure adequate furniture and teaching aids' (Herczyński 2007: 2).

25 The eight municipalities were Berovo, Brvenica, Kruševo, Pehcevo, Resen, Strumica, Tearce and Vasilievo. The report stresses that the general structure of central and satellite schools in these municipalities is similar to the national structure.

26 Although this review of the conditions experienced by satellite schools was originally commissioned by the municipal association's Education Commission, the report was subsequently not approved by them and has not been published. The recommendations included in this review were therefore not shared with the municipalities generally, or with the public.

27 Four schools (all in Kumanovo municipality), which account for approximately 27 per cent of all students attending multilingual schools.
28 Six schools in Gostivar, Debar, Struga, Tetovo and Skopje municipalities, which account for a further 24 per cent of students attending multilingual schools.
29 'Sami Frashëri' school in Kumanovo and 'Ismet Jashari' in Lipkovo; both previously part of the secondary school 'Goce Delčev' in Kumanovo.
30 Interviews with: a representative of UNDP: 25 June 2011, Skopje; representative of Forum Civil Peace Service: 25 May 2011, Skopje.
31 Interviews with: a municipal councillor, Struga municipality: 2 June 2010; and an education expert, OSCE: 12 April 2011, Skopje.
32 Interview with an international expert: 4 April 2011, Skopje.
33 The expert was referring to the ZIK building in Kumanovo, where Albanian students from 'Goce Delčev' secondary school were relocated to in 2001 (interview: 4 April 2011, Skopje). The school became an independent entity in 2010 (named 'Sami Frashëri'); however, reports suggest significant spatial challenges exist, with some classes being held in the corridors.
34 Responses to the same question one year earlier were: 13 per cent (increase), 40 per cent (stayed the same), 47 per cent (decreased) (OSCE 2008c: 17).
35 This has been confirmed by the SDSM opposition-led municipalities of Karpoš, Kumanovo, Strumica and Ohrid. OSCE official, interview: 24 June 2010, Skopje.
36 Interviews with: a representative of the World Bank: 8 April 2011, Skopje.
37 In fact, the proportion of citizens preferring central government control of education increased annually, from 52.2 per cent in 2008, to 55 per cent in 2009 and 69 per cent in 2010. In contrast, support for municipal control fell from 41.1 per cent, to 30 per cent and 28 per cent in the respective years.
38 Interview with an OSCE official: 4 April 2011, Skopje.
39 Interviews with: a senior representative of the MoES: 7 April 2011, Skopje; and an OSCE official: 4 April 2011, Skopje.
40 Interview with a municipal education officer: 5 April 2011, Kumanovo.

4 Who has the money?

Fiscal reform and local autonomy

Introduction

This chapter assesses fiscal decentralisation from a political economy perspective and considers whether the reforms have enhanced the fiscal autonomy of Macedonian municipalities. It also demonstrates the ways in which central government, in the absence of legislative changes and despite constitutional guarantees to municipal devolved competences, can interfere with anticipated improvements in the balance of power between local and central levels. As the previous two chapters have discussed, decentralisation is believed to mitigate ethnic conflict by offering spatially concentrated minority ethnic groups greater political and administrative control over their own affairs. The vertical division of power realised through decentralisation is also expected to restrain the monopoly central government has on state power and resources, and to facilitate a more balanced, inclusive system of government. An appraisal of inter-governmental fiscal relations in Macedonia is therefore essential in determining whether the political and administrative decentralisation examined in Chapters 2 and 3 is possible in the absence of sufficient fiscal autonomy and resources.

Decentralisation is an inherently political process and even when reforms are purely administrative or fiscal, it is still politicians who decide how they are conceived (Manor 1999: 53). This review begins by considering how the short-term political calculations of national governing parties at the centre may influence both the design and implementation of fiscal decentralisation. It will then evaluate the fiscal autonomy of Macedonian municipalities through an assessment of the following dynamics: the extent to which municipalities are dependent on central government for their revenues; the ability of municipalities to make independent decisions over spending; and the ability of municipalities to set independent financial contracts with private actors, such as creditors and employees. By dismantling inter-governmental relations in this way, this analysis will determine whether decentralisation has enhanced, as anticipated, the fiscal autonomy of the municipalities or has indeed facilitated the maintenance of central government control over state resources.

This chapter makes the following three arguments. First, the political-economic context within which fiscal decentralisation was conceived and implemented thus far in Macedonia has not been conducive to enhancing the fiscal autonomy of the municipalities. Second, in spite of substantial reforms, decentralisation has done little to restrain the monopoly of central government on state power and resources. This is confirmed by the limited revenue, expenditure and contractual autonomy of the municipalities, which has resulted in only the partial decentralisation of fiscal responsibility. Finally, while constitutionally guaranteed decentralisation processes may be harder to reverse than others, it is not impossible. Advances in either administrative or political decentralisation can easily be undermined by tightening controls over fiscal relations.[1]

A political economy approach to fiscal decentralisation

Fiscal decentralisation refers to a set of reforms designed to increase the fiscal autonomy of local governments and is essential if local institutions are to exercise their devolved public policy functions autonomously (Falleti 2005: 329). It can assume different forms, such as the creation of new local taxes or the delegation of tax authority that was previously held at the state level, and/or an increase in fiscal transfers from central to local governments. In his seminal work, Wallace E. Oates (1972) argues that the economic rationale for fiscal decentralisation is based on the capacity of sub-central units to improve resource allocation by delivering heterogeneous public services which are more closely aligned to local needs. Fiscal decentralisation may also promote economic efficiency by increasing experimentation, innovation and, ultimately, local competition in the design and delivery of public services. Finally, Oates suggests decentralisation will lead to more efficient levels of public spending by encouraging greater local recognition of the cost of public programmes. If local communities are required to finance basic services themselves, they are more likely to weigh their benefits against actual costs, in addition to holding locally elected officials accountable for the quality of these services, than if it were funded centrally (Oates 1972: 11, 13). What matters most, Oates concludes, is 'simply that decisions regarding levels of provision of specified public services for a particular jurisdiction reflect to a substantial extent the interests of the constituency of that jurisdiction' (Oates 1972: 17).

Research on inter-governmental fiscal relations has become increasingly conscious that these normatively inspired principles of efficiency, local accountability and democratic legitimacy are not always prominent in the minds of central governments when they choose to decentralise. Instead, and as the Introduction suggests earlier, the reasons why governments decentralise are often less benign, and the short-term political calculations of governing parties frequently take precedence over fiscal concerns. In contrast to more traditional studies, which '[treat] each level of government as a benevolent social planner, maximising the welfare of the residents of its jurisdiction', experts have increasingly taken a political economy approach to fiscal decentralisation (Lockwood 2009: 79). These studies seek to identify how political dynamics affect the design of fiscal decentralisation and, significantly, how the incentives of stakeholders may weaken, strengthen, or shift in response to changes in the political and economic environment that arise after reform begins. Decentralisation, note Eaton *et al.* (2010: xii, xv), 'is a process, not a one-time act, and the trajectory of reform is heavily influenced by how the often-conflicting incentives of different actors are pursued'.

Mindful of these considerations, one may consider why the Macedonian government decentralised power to the municipalities after 2001. Clearly, a long Yugoslav tradition of strong local government, Albanian grievances, civil unrest and the subsequent internationally sponsored peace process are significant contributory factors explaining why the reforms were adopted. However, despite pressures from below and externally by international agencies operating in Macedonia such as the World Bank, USAID, UNDP and the European Union, decentralisation was principally a 'top-down' affair, with the design and pace of reforms being negotiated at the parliamentary, rather than local level.[2] Although the government's first decentralisation programme talks of 'secur[ing] local democracy' and providing 'effective public services and economic development', the governing parties at the time may also have been motivated by short-term electoral concerns (Government of the Republic of Macedonia 2004: 4).[3] Indeed, as Kathleen O'Neill's research suggests, it seems unlikely that politicians will admit to decentralising for electoral benefits (O'Neill 2005: 12). Interviews with a senior DUI party official confirm that local party structures are considered essential for building grassroots support for parties at the central level.[4] Further interviews conducted by the ICG in April 2011 found that 'all of a sudden political parties saw decentralisation as an opportunity to gain votes' (ICG 2011: 19–20).

For the purpose of this analysis, it is important to note that Macedonia's fiscal decentralisation reforms were carried out gradually in two stages, whereby progression into the second phase was permitted only when municipalities fulfilled certain legal criteria.[5] This approach was proposed by the IMF and was motivated by the fear that poor fiscal management on behalf of the municipalities could contribute to an excessive budget deficit. During the first phase, which commenced in July 2005 and continued for two years, municipalities received earmarked grants from central government to cover only the operating costs of public service institutions. In the second phase, which began in September 2007 for those municipalities that satisfied the criteria, municipalities were entrusted with the payment of staff salaries and the earmarked grants they received from the Ministry of Finance were transformed into unconditional block grants.

Tables 4.1 and 4.2 display the election results of the largest political parties during every parliamentary and municipal election between 1998 and 2011. If O'Neill's theory holds true for Macedonia, one would expect the electoral strength of governing coalition partners SDSM and DUI to be strong at the municipal level during the time decentralisation was being designed and

Table 4.1 Parliamentary election results, 1998–2011 (percentage of vote)

Political party	1998	2002	2006	2008	2011
VMRO-DPMNE	28.10	25.02	32.50	48.78	38.98
SDSM	25.15	41.59	23.31	23.64	32.78
DUI	–	12.18	12.12	12.82	10.24
DPA	19.27	5.35	7.50	8.26	5.90

Source: European Election Database. Data available at: www.nsd.uib.no/european_ election_database/country/macedonia/ (accessed: 24 January 2012)

Table 4.2 Mayoral election results, 2000–2009

Political party	2000[a]		2005		2009	
	No. of muni-cipalities	Percentage of muni-cipalities	No. of muni-cipalities	Percentage of muni-cipalities	No. of muni-cipalities	Percentage of muni-cipalities
VMRO-DPMNE		27	21	24.7	56	65.9
SDSM		38	36	42.4	6	7.1
DUI		–	15	17.6	14	16.5
DPA		13	2	2.4	1	1.0
Independent		–	7	8.2	2	2.4
Other			4	4.7	6	7.1
Total	124		85	100.0	85	100.0

Sources: ODIHR (2000, 2005, 2009)

Note

a Results data for the 2000 local elections is incomplete.

adopted (2002–4).[6] This is clearly the case for SDSM, which controlled almost 40 per cent of Macedonia's 124 municipalities during this period. However, it is more difficult to apply O'Neill's theory to DUI, which was only established in 2002 and after municipal elections in 2000. However, elated by its landslide parliamentary victory in 2002 (winning more than 60 per cent of all Albanian votes and more than double the votes cast for its closest Albanian rival, the Democratic Party of Albanians or DPA), DUI at that time was confident it could replicate its success at the central level in subsequent local elections.[7] Clearly, the influence of international agencies in Macedonia that were actively supporting implementation of the peace agreement would also have been a significant factor in the governing parties' decision to decentralise after 2001.[8]

The data in Tables 4.1 and 4.2 also demonstrates that SDSM lost its parliamentary majority to VMRO-DPMNE in 2006 and has been in opposition ever since. However, its success in the 2005 municipal elections meant it was able to maintain control of the majority of municipalities until 2009. Based on the discussions above, SDSM's strength at the local level during this period suggests there was little incentive for VMRO-DPMNE to maintain the

Table 4.3 Gross Domestic Product annual growth rate, 2000–2010

	2000[a]	2001	2002	2003	2004	2005	2006	2007	2008	2009	2010
GDP growth rate[a] (%)	4.5	−4.5	0.9	2.8	4.6	4.4	5.0	6.1	5.0	−0.9	1.8

Source: European Commission (2011b: 79)

Note

a The figures represent the real GDP growth rate percentage change on the previous year. The amount for 2010 is based on an estimate.

momentum of the decentralisation process between 2006 and 2009, a critical period in the design and consolidation of fiscal decentralisation, which saw the start of the second phase of the reforms. To do so would mean reducing the control VMRO-DPMNE had in central government and rewarding political rivals at the local level.

While the application of O'Neill's theory to the Macedonian political context after 2009 would suggest that VMRO-DPMNE's and DUI's strength at both the central and local levels should have been conducive to greater political support for further decentralisation, the reality is that limited internal party democracy and the presence of pervasive vertical clientelistic relationships within Macedonian political parties has in fact had the opposite effect. The result is that VMRO-DPMNE's and DUI's success during municipal elections in 2009 (resulting in more than 80 per cent of municipalities being aligned with political parties in the central governing coalition), combined with their continued success at the state level, has meant they have had little incentive to consolidate Macedonia's decentralisation reforms ever since. The declining leverage international external agencies operating in Macedonia have had on influencing government decisions since the threat of renewed ethnic conflict has subsided is clearly a further contributing factor.

The effect of the global economic crisis on the Macedonian economy since 2009 adds further credence to the government's reluctance to devolve additional fiscal responsibility to municipalities at the expense of macroeconomic stability (see Table 4.3). It is therefore not surprising that decentralisation was given little or no attention in recent party election manifestos.[9] One could speculate that a success for SDSM in future municipal elections may have major repercussions for the future of decentralisation in Macedonia. VMRO-DPMNE would have little incentive to decentralise further, and may even consider reversing the progress made to date.

To summarise, the political and economic environment within which fiscal decentralisation was conceived and implemented thus far may not be conducive to enhancing the fiscal autonomy of Macedonian municipalities. Instead, the electoral strength political parties have enjoyed concurrently at the central and local levels (SDSM and DUI until 2006; VMRO-DPMNE and DUI since 2009), coupled with the existence of strong internal party discipline and vertical clientelistic relationships, suggests that governing parties may prefer to rely on (party-controlled) inter-governmental transfers and capital grants to fund devolved competences, rather than enhance local fiscal autonomy. The remaining sections will examine in detail the revenue, expenditure and contractual autonomy of the municipalities and will determine whether this hypothesis is correct.

The revenue autonomy of the municipalities

Using J. Tyler Dickovick's analytic framework for operationalising 'revenue autonomy', this section will determine how independent Macedonian municipalities are for their revenues, an essential component in any decentralised system. Dickovick (2011) recognises two main types of local revenue: own-sources (local taxes, communal fees, etc.); and inter-governmental transfers. The latter includes municipal shares of state taxes (Value Added Tax – VAT – and Personal Income Tax – PIT), grants for devolved public services and capital funds. He measures the degree of local autonomy with regard to *own-revenues* by determining the extent to which local governments are empowered to raise taxes, and asks whether central governments can ensure local dependence by refusing to devolve sufficient tax authority (Dickovick 2011: 4). If the centre grants local governments the right to enact taxes that were not previously authorised, Dickovick considers this to be more decentralising (Dickovick 2011: 17). Similarly, Dickovick determines the scope of local autonomy over *inter-governmental transfers* by assessing whether these transfers are automatic and formula-based, rather than ad hoc and discretionary. Unconditional transfers guaranteed by constitutions would clearly increase local revenue autonomy, whereas central governments' ability to impose conditions on municipalities for receiving these transfers would not. The size of the formula-based fiscal transfers is also crucial in determining the extent of local revenue autonomy, because inadequate resources will only increase local dependency on other forms of discretionary central funding (Dickovick 2011: 66).

Table 4.4 displays the extent to which municipal revenues have increased since the start of the decentralisation process in 2005. As a percentage of Gross Domestic Product (GDP), municipal revenues grew impressively from 1.7 per cent to 5.8 per cent between 2004 and 2011. Similarly, as a percentage of overall public expenditure, municipal revenues increased from 5 per cent in 2004 to 16 per cent in 2011. Both values had more than tripled since the beginning of decentralisation, while the per-capita revenues of the municipalities more than quadrupled. Such increases are almost on a par with neighbouring Bulgaria (6 per cent and 17 per cent respectively), but are less than Moldova (9.3 per cent and 25 per cent respectively); two countries with comparable levels of municipal competences (NALAS 2012: 22). Rather than assume that the increases received by Macedonian municipalities were accompanied by the desired increase in fiscal autonomy, an analysis of the main municipal

Table 4.4 Evolution of municipal revenue, 2004–2011

Year	Percentage of GDP	Percentage of public expenditure
2004	1.7	5.0
2005	–	–
2006	2.0	6.0
2007	2.7	7.9
2008	4.6	13.1
2009	4.9	14.2
2010	5.4	15.3
2011	5.8	16.0

Sources: Levitas (2011a: 9); NALAS (2012: 22)

sources of revenue will now follow. This will determine whether local government dependency on the centre for revenue has declined as a result of decentralisation.

Own-source revenues

According to the Law on Financing of the Units of Local Self-Government, Macedonian municipalities are entitled to the following forms of own-source revenue: local taxes (on property, the transfer of real-estate, inheritance and gifts), fees (utilities, administrative, etc.), charges (i.e. for urbanisation of construction land, communal activities, spatial and urban plans, etc.) and revenue from municipal assets, donations, fines and self-contributions (Official Gazette 2004: Art.4). In 2010, on average, own-source revenues accounted for 29.4 per cent of municipal revenue, the largest share being generated by property-related taxes and construction land development fees (Levitas 2011a: 14). Other important sources of revenue for the municipalities are a share of state taxes (VAT and PIT) (6 per cent), general grants (5 per cent), earmarked and block grants to pay for devolved public services (55 per cent) and capital transfers (4 per cent[10]) (Levitas 2011a: 13).

The decentralisation process assigned new revenue-generating responsibilities to municipalities. Significantly, the transfer of property-related tax administration to the local level means that municipalities are now responsible for collecting the property and property transfer taxes. Both represent a substantial proportion of own-revenue income in many, particularly urban municipalities. The municipalities also acquired discretion to set the rate of these taxes, within parameters set by the centre, while a further reform in 2008 meant that the tax base was enlarged to include properties owned by legal entities, such as businesses (Levitas 2011a: 6).[11] In the past, while all property-related taxes had been administered centrally by the Public Revenue Office and were shared 100 per cent with the municipalities, collection had been inefficiently managed and the Office had little incentive to improve collection rates (Nikolov 2007: 7; Feruglio *et al.* 2008: 23). After devolving responsibility for collecting these taxes to the municipalities, collection rates for property-related taxes more than tripled between 2006 and 2010 (Levitas 2011a: 15). Other government-led initiatives which have increased own-source revenues are the doubling of the rate of the public lighting fee and the decision to begin sharing revenue earned from the sale of urban construction land 80 : 20 in favour of the municipalities from 2011 (Levitas 2011a: 16). Own-source revenues not only represent important autonomous sources of funding for the municipalities, they also promote greater fiscal accountability between the municipality and local constituents (tax/service fee payers) – a principal objective of fiscal decentralisation (Bahl 1999: 10; Smoke 2007: 132).

These changes have resulted in significant increases in municipal own-source revenue (see Table 4.5) and have therefore increased local fiscal autonomy in spending decisions regarding to the delivery of hard municipal services, such as water and waste management, street cleansing, etc. However, some observers believe the reforms did not go far enough, especially since most of the revenue instruments assigned to municipalities have limited revenue yield (Cyan *et al.* 2012: 55). The variable range set by central government for the property tax rate (0.10–0.20 per cent), for example, was much lower than the rates set in neighbouring countries (1.5 per cent in Bulgaria and 0.3–0.8 per cent in Greece) (Šapurić 2007: 32). Others have pointed out that the number of taxes assigned to Macedonian municipalities is much smaller than in comparable countries (Šapurić 2007: 31; Levitas 2011a: 8).[12] In particular, the municipal association has been lobbying central government for more than five years to allow rural municipalities to acquire the right to manage agricultural land and forests.[13] Despite regular demands by fiscal experts that the Government introduce new revenue instruments as a means of strengthening local revenue capacities, concrete steps have yet to be taken (Feruglio *et al.* 2008: vi; IMF 2009: 30; OSCE 2011: 52).

The data presented in Table 4.5 demonstrates that, while own-source revenues have grown in absolute terms annually, they have not kept pace with an overall growth in municipal revenues.[14] Own-source revenues may have

Table 4.5 Structure of municipal revenues, 2005–2009

Year	Own-revenues of all municipalities (MKD)	Transfers and donations of all municipalities (MKD)	Total revenues of all municipalities (MKD)	Own-revenues as a proportion of total municipal revenues (%)	Transfers and grants as a proportion of total municipal revenues (%)
2005	3,488,498,031	2,070,981,673	5,573,119,704	62.60	37.16
2006	4,654,143,061	3,380,717,701	8,035,194,599	57.92	42.07
2007	5,375,216,448	5,523,015,581	11,195,984,165	48.01	49.33
2008	7,431,216,279	13,575,361,332	21,036,979,696	35.32	64.53
2009	6,803,020,251	16,299,071,076	23,139,188,375	29.40	70.44

Source: Popovska (2011: 101)

doubled between 2005 and 2009, but their relative share of total municipal revenues more than halved in the same period (Cyan *et al.* 2012: 8). This is largely the result of an increase in municipal revenues based on inter-governmental transfers, and in particular the education block grants to cover the salaries of primary, secondary and pre-school teachers (Levitas 2011a: 10). To summarise, although own-source revenues have increased substantially since decentralisation began, Macedonian municipalities remain highly dependent on central government transfers to meet their expenditure needs.

Inter-governmental transfers: share of state taxes (VAT and PIT)

To further strengthen the fiscal base of Macedonia's municipalities, the decentralisation process created two new economic activity-related sources of local revenue. The first was a general purpose grant for all municipalities, based on a percentage of the VAT collected nationwide and distributed according to a formula which seeks to consider the fiscal strength of individual municipalities. The second was a share of the PIT, calculated on a derivation basis (Official Gazette 2004: Articles 5, 9). Revenue sharing in this way attempts to realise some of the advantages of centralised taxation without relinquishing local expenditure authority (Oates 1977: 14). Previously, both taxes had been at the exclusive disposal of central government, whereas by 2010, combined, they accounted for approximately 11 per cent of total municipal revenue (see Figure 4.1). While municipal shares of both the VAT and PIT can be spent autonomously by the municipalities, it is important to stress that revenue assigned through sharing state taxes does not provide municipalities with a comparable level of revenue autonomy as own-sources. Central government retains control over determining the base rate of these taxes, discretion over the proportion shared with the municipalities and, importantly, the methodology used to allocate revenue locally. This means that municipalities may see the value of 'their' share erode as central governments amend tax rates and/or distribution formulas (Levitas 2009: 31).

An important point to emphasise regarding how the VAT and PIT are shared between the central and local levels in Macedonia is that, in both cases, the proportion allocated to the municipalities is very low (Cyan *et al.* 2012). For example, in Moldova (a country with a comparable level of decentralised competences to Macedonia) municipalities received at least 50 per cent of state PIT revenues in 2010, although they did not receive any revenue from VAT (NALAS 2012: 21). Similarly, in Republika Srpska (Bosnia and Herzegovina), municipalities received 24 per cent of VAT revenue and 25 per cent of PIT revenue in 2010 despite not being responsible for paying teachers' salaries (NALAS 2012: 21). Significant vertical imbalances therefore exist over the control of public revenue. Initially, the municipalities were assigned 3 per cent of the VAT to form the basis of a general grant allocated to each. This amount was amended in 2009 so that the local share increases gradually to 4.5 per cent by 2013.[15] However, the municipalities remain unsatisfied with

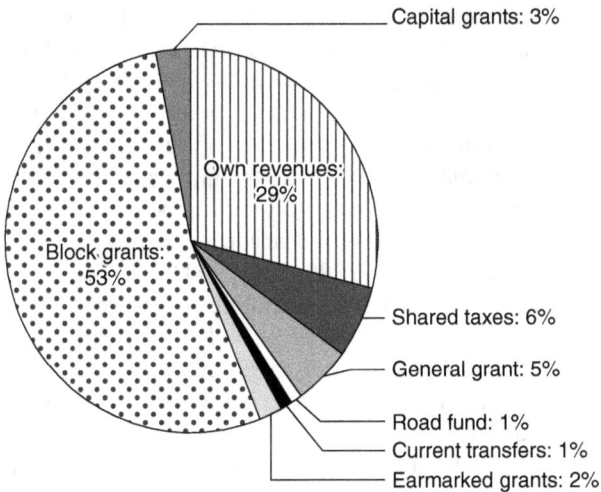

Figure 4.1 Average composition of municipal revenue, 2010

the extent of this increase, particularly since inflation jumped from 2.3 per cent in 2007 to 8.3 per cent in 2008 as a result of the effects of the global economic downturn, and the municipal association continues to lobby for at least a 6 per cent local share of the VAT.[16] In particular, ZELS points out that, while the municipal share of VAT revenue has increased moderately since 2010, the effects of the global economic crisis on income generated at the state level through VAT has meant that the amount of funds the municipalities actually receive remained almost the same.[17] Similarly, the municipalities are entitled to only 3 per cent of the PIT of local residents and 100 per cent of the PIT of independent artisans. This proportion has also been criticised for being too small or 'even trivial', because it represented only around 3 per cent of total municipal revenues in 2006 (Feruglio *et al.* 2008: 33). The local PIT yield has in fact declined by a further 10 per cent since then, largely because of the government's unilateral decision to introduce a 10 per cent flat rate on income tax in 2007 (FOSM 2010: 49; Levitas 2011a: 6). The municipalities, through ZELS, are consequently lobbying for their share of the PIT to be increased to 30 per cent on regular income and 100 per cent of PIT based on agricultural activities (OSCE 2011: 54; ZELS 2011a).

Inter-governmental transfers: grants for devolved public services

It is common for municipal own-source revenues, even when supplemented with general purpose grants, to remain insufficient to cover the full cost of providing the public services devolved to them. Inter-governmental grants, from line ministries to municipalities, are therefore an accepted way of offsetting vertical imbalances between local expenditure needs and fiscal capacity and should not be considered an 'unavoidable evil' (Prud'homme 1995: 214; Smoke 2007: 132; IMF 2009: 4). However, in practice, and particularly in countries such as Macedonia where clientelism is pervasive, these grants are vulnerable to political manipulation and may represent an instrument for maintaining local dependency on the centre (Devas and Delay 2006: 684). To overcome this risk, experts emphasise that stable, objective and transparent formula-driven transfers should be promoted, because they reduce the uncertainty and bargaining that can accompany inter-governmental fiscal relations (Burki *et al.* 1999: 29; IMF 2009: 37; Dickovick 2011: 66). Formula-based transfers also reduce the political leverage central government has over local politicians by removing its ability to exercise discretion over the distribution of funds (Willis *et al.* 1999: 22; Eaton 2001: 115). Transfer formulas should focus on the demand (clients or outputs) rather than the supply (inputs and infrastructure) of local government services in order that grants match the expenditure needs of individual municipalities (UNDP 2005a: 6). Finally, inter-governmental transfers should not be too large as to eliminate the need for local taxes, which ensure municipal accountability to citizens for spending decisions, but should provide sufficient revenue to cover expenditure needs (Litvack *et al.* 1998: 117). Inadequate transfers may force municipalities to redirect a larger proportion of autonomous own-source revenues to cover expenditure gaps than they might otherwise have done, and promote local dependency on the centre for additional sources of funding (Keefer 2005: 2).

With regard to the earmarked and block grants Macedonian municipalities receive to fund decentralised public services, the previous chapter has shown how shifting to a formula-based transfer system in June 2005 promoted greater equity in the funding of primary and secondary education.[18] This move also increased local autonomy over education revenues, since the allocation of funding on a per-student basis reduced the possibility of discretionary payments and, to a certain extent, removed municipal uncertainly over how education grants are calculated. However, the analysis in Chapter 3 also demonstrated how central government adjusted the funding formulas to suit state priorities and possibly as a means of rewarding municipalities controlled by their allies. Changes to both the population density thresholds and weights used in the education funding formulas, for example, as well as excessive use of both lower and upper buffers which regulate annual payments adjustments, have resulted in increasing funding disparities across municipalities, in addition to undermining transparency (Herczyński 2011: 14–15, 31). It may be no coincidence that those sparsely populated, Macedonian-majority municipalities that benefit most from the 2008 adjustment to the education funding formula correlate with areas where VMRO-DPMNE electoral strength is greatest.

The municipalities are also entitled to block grants to finance the provision of cultural services, social welfare and child protection. According to the law on local government financing, the methodology for calculating these grants should be 'formula-based using appropriate need indicators for each programme' and should therefore also be calculated on a per-client basis (Official Gazette 2004: Articles12.2, 22). However, this shift had not occurred by mid-2012. The allocation of grants for cultural and social welfare continued to be based on the existence of a physical facility (libraries, kindergartens, homes for the elderly, etc.) within a municipality's territory, and meant that those municipalities historically lacking such facilities received no funding for the realisation of these two competences (Levitas 2011a: 25; Risteska 2013b: 202). This approach is highly problematic because it contradicts one of the basic principles of fiscal decentralisation (that 'funds should follow functions'), and because of the inequity it creates between municipalities (IMF 2009: 25). It also prevents those municipalities lacking the required institution receiving any funding to 'buy in' services from neighbouring municipalities or the private sector.[19] Finally, when eligible municipalities do receive grants from the Ministries of Culture, Youth and Sport and of Social Welfare, observers have noted how the allocation system lacks 'an objective transparent method' for calculating the expenditure needs associated with the assigned competences (Feruglio *et al.* 2008: 3). These grants also cover only the basic running costs of institutions, and municipalities remain dependent on ad hoc funding from relevant line ministries to run specific events or programmes.[20]

Clearly, a system that allows only a proportion of municipalities to realise some of the expenditure responsibilities devolved to them is inadequate and represents a breach of both the European Charter of Local Self-Government, to which Macedonia is a signatory, and the Framework Agreement.[21] There is considerable evidence to suggest both primary and secondary education services also remained woefully underfunded, as well as municipal governments generally. While earmarked and block grants for education combined accounted for 2.8 per cent of GDP in 2010, this is considered at the low end of European norms because countries typically spend 3 to 5 per cent of their GDP on pre-tertiary education. As a consequence, many municipalities complain that the education transfers they receive do not meet expenditure needs (particularly with regard to funding student transportation) and, contrary to legal guarantees, have in fact reduced in size in recent years (FOSM 2010: 46; Herczyński 2011: 40–1; ZELS 2011a).[22] The situation became so critical that in November 2011 the municipalities threatened to collectively return responsibility for organising student transportation to central government unless sufficient funds were assured to them in the future.[23] Given the functions assigned to them, fiscal decentralisation expert Tony Levitas suggests Macedonian municipalities should receive revenues equal to at least 8 or 9 per cent of the GDP, and not 5 or 6 (Levitas 2011a: 2–3).

To summarise, since decentralisation began, grants for the delivery of primary and secondary education have been allocated according to an automatic, formula-based transfer system. While difficulties remain over the design of this formula, this move has in general increased the revenue autonomy of the municipalities and reduced the possibility of discretionary payments by the centre. However, grants for culture and social welfare remain ad hoc and discretionary, with a significant proportion of municipalities receiving no grants at all. Finally, the inter-governmental grants municipalities receive for the delivery of education, culture and social welfare are inadequate to cover local expenditure responsibilities. This has increased municipal dependence on other forms of central government funding, such as capital investments, and has forced some municipalities to supplement grants for recurrent spending with their own (autonomous) revenue. While there is nothing wrong with municipalities using local revenues to (voluntarily) enhance municipal education and social welfare budgets, forcing them to redirect autonomous revenues to cover recurrent expenditure gaps reduces the autonomy municipalities have over how their local revenue can be spent.

Inter-governmental transfers: capital grants for infrastructure projects

Capital grants are distributed to the municipalities by competent line ministries and the Public Roads Fund, and are used to finance local infrastructure investments that cannot otherwise be funded by either municipal own-revenue or block grants. Examples of possible interventions are the erection of new school buildings, waste-water treatment plants and the construction, reconstruction and maintenance of local roads. The system of grant distribution in Macedonia is uncoordinated and fragmented, with at least six ministries plus the Public Roads Fund and the Bureau for Regional Development authorised to allocate capital funding.[24] While these grants officially represented only 4 per cent of municipal revenue in 2010 (see Figure 4.1), they constituted an important source of additional funding for cash-strapped municipalities, in addition to creating considerable tension between the central and local levels, and among the municipalities themselves.[25]

Of greatest concern regarding the distribution of capital grants, and one raised by the European Commission in its 2011 Progress Report on Macedonia, is the almost complete lack of transparency upon which funding is allocated to the municipalities (EC 2011b: 9).[26] In most cases line ministries fail to respect their legal obligations and do not announce or even establish the criteria upon which municipal project proposals are assessed.[27] Application procedures and deadlines are also not commonly published (Kocevski 2009). This leaves the system highly vulnerable to discretionary decision-making, and where 'pork barrel' projects may be easily targeted to honour clientelist commitments and reward loyal constituents (Keefer 2005: 13; Remmer 2007: 375; Khemani 2010: 2). Decisions regarding the allocation of funds are also not commonly published in the Official Gazette. This means that both the public and the municipalities do not know how much individual municipalities receive from central government (Feruglio *et al.* 2008: 49; Kocevski 2009: 12).[28] The prevailing perception – real or imagined – is therefore that capital grants are largely distributed to those municipalities aligned with the governing coalition parties.[29]

There is considerable evidence to suggest that VMRO-DPMNE-governed municipalities have gained most from the current system of capital funding (Nikolov 2007: 85; FOSM 2010: 48).[30] This suggestion was verified during fieldwork interviews and personal visits to both government-aligned and opposition-led municipalities. Being aligned to the governing parties is therefore regarded as critical, especially for the smaller municipalities with limited access to independent revenues.[31] One councillor from Struga municipality even suggested that, without forming a local coalition with VMRO-DPMNE in the municipal council, the governing DUI would be unable to obtain sufficient political support centrally for its project applications to be approved.[32] When interviewed by the ICG, an official from the Ministry for Local Self-Government confirmed that the awarding of capital grants remained highly politicised. The official also suggested such discretionary practices had the potential to aggravate inter-ethnic relations (ICG 2011: 19).[33]

Significantly, the municipal association is excluded from all capital investment decision-making processes, and has lobbied central government to establish transparent, formula-driven criteria for the allocation of funds (FOSM 2010: 51; ZELS 2011a). ZELS also campaigns to participate in the setting of national investment priorities and budgets, and would like to be involved in the selection of municipal projects.[34] Ultimately, ZELS would want all capital grants to be devolved to the municipalities so that they will be able to set funding priorities independently of central government and decide which projects will be allocated funds (ZELS 2011a). ZELS is not alone in this request, with the influential Foundation Open Society Institute – Macedonia (FOSM) and others questioning the logic behind central government retaining control over decisions to build schools, construct cultural monuments and purchase educational equipment such computers, all of which fall under the jurisdiction of the municipalities:

> Such practices do not speak of the municipalities' autonomy and independence from the central government ...nor of the successful implementation of decentralisation. On the contrary, this encourages [the] politicisation of local governments, implies their servitude and obedience to the central government, which ultimately leads to [the] re-instatement of centralisation, or at least to 'centralised decentralisation'.
>
> (FOSM 2010: 44)

To summarise, despite some increase in own-source revenue, which has enhanced local autonomy in spending decisions regarding hard municipal service delivery, central government has refused to devolve sufficient tax authority to Macedonian municipalities. Instead, national politicians have designed fiscal decentralisation reforms in a way that maintains local dependency on central government-controlled revenue. The comparably low shares of state taxes assigned to Macedonian municipalities adds further support to this claim. Further, while education grants may now be allocated according to an automatic, formula-based transfer system, grants for the delivery of other public services and capital projects remain ad hoc and discretionary. The result is that the municipalities remain largely dependent on the opaque decision-making practices of line ministries, with the political leverage central government politicians have over their local counterparts being great.

The expenditure autonomy of the municipalities

Using J. Tyler Dickovick's framework for operationalising 'expenditure autonomy', this section will assess how much latitude the municipalities have in the use of local revenues. Expenditure autonomy, explains Dickovick (2011), is substantial when sub-central governments can spend revenue as they see fit, including in the form of political goods and patronage, and when they can transfer resources from sector to sector at will. In contrast, lower levels of expenditure autonomy exist when budgets are only applicable in a given sector or detailed line item, when local governments are obliged to spend on priorities established at the state level, and when unspent budgets must revert to central government. Dickovick's analytic approach is based on the assumption that sub-central governments seek greater expenditure autonomy in order to internalise the political benefits of spending. Conversely, ministers and bureaucrats seek to ensure that local governments comply with national standards, spend according to top-down directives and do not divert resources to suit other ends (Dickovick 2011: 92–4). It may be easier for states to centralise expenditure decisions than it is to centralise revenues (Dickovick 2011: 121). Examining the extent of centrally imposed restrictions on local expenditures is therefore crucial when assessing municipal autonomy in countries where increases in municipal revenue may (incorrectly) imply extensive decentralisation.

  While municipal revenues deriving from own-sources and general grants have allowed the municipalities maximum discretion over spending decisions concerning the delivery of hard municipal services (water and waste management, etc.), limited or inadequate grants to finance decentralised public services have forced the municipalities to spend a larger proportion of their autonomous revenue on what are in fact recurrent 'earmarked' expenditures (salaries, transport costs, etc.). Such circumstances have reduced local expenditure autonomy because diverting own-source revenue in this way has meant that the municipalities have fewer funds available to spend on local priorities as they see fit. Since the largest proportion of municipal revenue originates from inter-governmental transfers (earmarked, block and capital), the remainder of this section will appraise the extent of centrally imposed restrictions on how they are spent locally.

Table 4.6 Progress of municipalities to the second phase of decentralisation

Date	No. of municipalities	Cumulative total	Percentage of municipalities
1 September 2007	42	–	49.4
1 January 2008	9	51	60.0
1 April 2008	8	59	69.4
1 July 2008	5	64	75.3
1 November 2008	2	66	77.6
1 November 2009	2	68	80.0
1 April 2010	5	73	85.9
1 July 2010	1	74	87.1
1 January 2011	3	77	90.1
1 July 2011	2	79	92.3
1 January 2012[a]	5	84	98.8

Sources: European Commission (2011b: 8); Herczyński (2011: 10)

Note

a Interview with the executive director of ZELS: 20 March 2012, Skopje.

When evaluating the expenditure autonomy of Macedonian municipalities, it is important to differentiate between those municipalities in the first phase of the decentralisation process (which received earmarked grants to cover only the operating costs of public service institutions) and those that had progressed to the second phase and were entitled to receive unconditional block grants. As of March 2012 only one municipality (Plasnica) remained in the first phase, and its autonomy over spending was therefore severely restricted. However, as the data in Table 4.6 illustrates, the advance of municipalities into the second phase has been slow, with ten (almost one eighth of all municipalities) only progressing into this phase from January 2011, five of which only entered the second phase in January 2012 once the criteria for doing so had been significantly eased.[35] Such delays were caused by the inability of many municipalities to clear outstanding debts (a criteria for progression). As more than four years have lapsed since the first cluster of municipalities graduated into the second phase, many, including the European Commission and municipal association, have questioned the government's commitment to supporting the municipalities' progress with meeting the required criteria and ability to assume greater expenditure autonomy. This is particularly the case regarding the influential, opposition-led municipality of Ohrid, which was permitted to enter the second phase only in January 2012 (Feruglio *et al.* 2008: 23).[36]

Concerning the spending autonomy of those municipalities in the second phase of decentralisation and in receipt of block grants, the following observations need to be emphasised. First, comparable with restrictions placed on earmarked grants in phase one, block grants can be used only for the sector to which they are allocated (Herczyński 2011: 8; Levitas

2011a: 7). This means that the municipalities are not free to transfer resources from sector to sector. The expenditure autonomy of the municipalities is restricted further by the fact that instead of receiving a single block grant for the delivery of educational services, they receive three separate block grants for primary and secondary education, and another for kindergartens. Similarly, eligible municipalities receive three separate grants for libraries, museums and theatres, instead of one block grant for cultural programmes (Levitas 2011a: 5). In both cases, the municipalities are unable to transfer funds between these separate grants. This approach is in contrast to good practice which advises consolidating as many block grants as possible into a general grant, thereby increasing space for meaningful expenditure decisions locally (Levitas 2009: 32). The municipalities also remain unable to transfer funds between different budget lines, such as those allocated to public sector salaries and material expenditure, and are 'strongly encouraged' to return any unspent revenue to the centre at the end of each fiscal year (Herczyński 2011: 44).[37]

The second observation is that total inter-governmental transfers to the municipalities are dominated by primary and secondary education grants, and within these grants, the payment of teachers' salaries. 86 per cent of block grants for primary education, for example, was spent on teachers' pay during 2010, leaving only 14 per cent for the municipalities to use at their discretion on maintenance and student transport costs (MLGA 2011: 16). Similarly, in 2010, 77 per cent of secondary education block grants went on teachers' salaries, leaving only 23 per cent for the municipalities to spend as they wished on maintenance and transport needs (MLGA 2011: 20). The dominance of salary payments within the block grants is further compounded by the fact that both teacher employment numbers and remuneration levels remain strictly controlled by the Ministry of Finance and the state treasury system respectively (Herczyński 2011: 44). Municipalities complain, for example, that if a teacher retires or even dies, they are unable to hire a replacement, and the funds planned for their salary must be returned to the central budget (Herczyński 2011: 45). Procedures for receiving permission to employ a replacement teacher are also slow and in some instances municipalities do not receive a response from the Ministry of Finance at all.[38] Municipalities therefore have very little control over their expenditures because personnel costs, which account for the vast majority of 'unconditional' block grants, are essentially dictated by central government.

Third, several municipalities in the second phase of the decentralisation process have had their bank accounts blocked because of unpaid arrears. This may be because they have acquired debts since entering the second phase, or because some municipalities were able to graduate to the second phase by restructuring rather than clearing outstanding debts.[39] An original precondition for entering the second phase of decentralisation was that a municipality carried no debts in the 24 months prior to assessment. However, this criteria was later relaxed to allow more municipalities to advance (hence the debt restructuring) and was later removed altogether. Ohrid, for example, was permitted to move into the second phase in January 2012 with significant outstanding debts, but immediately had its account blocked upon entering.[40] Consequently, while block grants to fund devolved public services remain unaffected, the operational revenues section of a municipality's bank account is frozen and only earmarked costs for municipal overheads (salaries, etc.) can leave the account. All other revenues automatically go towards paying off the debt.[41] It is impossible to know exactly how many municipalities have had their accounts blocked at any one time because the situation changes daily and data on this issue does not exist. However, a representative of the European Union Delegation to Skopje has estimated the figure to be as high as one third of all municipalities at any one time.[42] Often the accounts are blocked for short periods (a few weeks or months) until the debt is cleared. However, for more substantial debts, the situation will take longer to resolve. While entry to the second phase of decentralisation enabled Ohrid to receive block grants for services and to borrow commercially, the long-term freezing of its account meant that the municipality had even less expenditure autonomy over its own-source revenues than it had before.

Finally, as the previous section has revealed, certain line ministries have control over capital grants to support devolved public service competences, leaving the municipalities with little or no influence over how these funds are spent. While it is reasonable that the central government remains able to promote state policies and fund expensive infrastructure projects, capital grants are being misused by line ministries to retain control over the procurement of smaller items such as computers or school furniture and cultural events. These spending decisions should be the responsibility of individual schools and municipalities. However, since the block grant payments are insufficient to meet local material needs, schools and municipalities remain dependent on supplementary capital payments in order to do so (Kocevski 2009: 26). The result is that the government's 'A computer for every child' programme, costing an estimated €50 million, distributed over 200,000 computers to schools that, in many cases, were not adequately consulted, lacked the necessary internet connects and software and had no IT administrator to maintain the machines (Hadzi-Zafirova 2011).

To summarise, the existence of stringent expenditure mandates on inter-governmental transfers (earmarked and block grants), which dwarf autonomous municipal own-source revenues, suggests that the expenditure autonomy of Macedonian municipalities remains tightly constrained by the centre. In such circumstances, for the 80 per cent of municipalities that are politically aligned with the governing coalition, locally elected officials that remain tightly controlled by party hierarchies appear to operate more like deconcentrated entities of central government. The frequent blocking of municipal bank accounts as a result of outstanding debts also undermines the municipalities' ability to take independent spending decisions.

The contractual autonomy of the municipalities

This final analysis will briefly examine the contractual autonomy of Macedonian municipalities. Dickovick defines this form of sub-central autonomy as an ability to set independent financial contracts with different sets of private actors, such as creditors and employees, in addition to the degree of legal or jurisdictional autonomy municipalities are granted (Dickovick 2011: 5). The previous section discussed how Macedonian municipalities are unable to control the wage bills of public officials under their jurisdiction. Further, since more than 80 per cent of municipalities have been aligned with political parties in the central governing coalition since 2009, the retraction of local competences by line ministries happens very infrequently and will also not be reviewed in this section.[43] In the few instances where competences have been retracted on a temporary basis, the initiative has in general been politically motivated and has disproportionately affected opposition-led municipalities.[44] It remains to be seen whether this potential threat to municipal autonomy will gain in significance if and when the political landscape changes in the future. This section will therefore focus specifically on the borrowing ability of the municipalities. Sub-central governments that control their own debt burdens are more autonomous than those who must look to central governments to set these parameters (Dickovick 2011: 5).

Shahid Javed Burki *et al.* for the World Bank note that borrowing can play an important role in sub-central financing, particularly in the financing of long-term capital development projects because costs can be spread out to match the duration of benefits to citizens (Burki *et al.* 1999: 29). It is particularly important for municipalities in pre-accession countries to the EU since they are often required to 'match' payments provided by European structural funds.[45] Significantly, access to external capital also means that municipalities are less dependent on central government for funding such initiatives. Macedonian municipalities in the second phase of decentralisation are permitted to contract debt under certain circumstances tightly controlled by the Ministry of Finance; however, their right to borrow is not guaranteed by the Constitution (Official Gazette 2001a).[46] The law on local government financing differentiates between short- and long-term borrowing. With regard to short-term indebtedness, the loan must be paid off by the end of the fiscal year and its amount must not exceed 20 per cent of total municipal revenues (flow variable) (Official Gazette 2004: Art. 19).[47] Long-term borrowing within Macedonia and from abroad is permitted only to finance capital assets or investment projects (and not to repay long-term debts), and the amount borrowed cannot exceed 15 per cent of total municipal revenues (Official Gazette 2004: Art. 20).[48] In both instances, municipalities can only borrow in domestic and/or foreign capital markets with prior consent from the Ministry of Finance.[49]

While borrowing represents an important component of municipal financing, unlimited local borrowing can destabilise macroeconomic governance and lead to central government deficits (Burki *et al.* 1999: 30). It is therefore understandable that the Ministry of Finance tightly regulates municipal borrowing and maintains a hard budget constraint (UNDP 2005a: 6; World Bank 2006: 28). However, restrictions on municipal borrowing in Macedonia have had a significant impact on both the revenue and expenditure autonomy of the municipalities, as well as obstructing progress with the decentralisation reforms. Municipalities still in the first phase of the decentralisation process, for example, were initially unable to borrow and therefore had no chance of paying off the debts that prevented them from entering the second phase. However, this issue was partly addressed by an amendment to the law on local government financing in December 2009, which permitted those municipalities still in the first phase to apply for short- and long-term loans from central government to service their debts.[50] In addition, limits on the amount a municipality can borrow, the fact that long-term borrowing is permitted only to finance capital investments (and not to clear debts) and the strict requirement that a municipality has no arrears in the two years prior to borrowing effectively blocked those municipalities in the second phase with frozen accounts from being able to clear their outstanding arrears (OSCE 2011: 71; ZELS 2011a).

Further challenges regarding implementation of municipal borrowing initiatives are also apparent. Most significantly, the effect of the global economic crisis on Macedonian state funds has meant that the government has had little if any money available to loan to the municipalities since restrictions on borrowing were relaxed at the end of 2009.[51] Additionally, there is a common perception that the assessment process for loan approval is politically biased, with the opposition-led municipality of Ohrid waiting more than four years for a response from the Ministry of Finance.[52] Even a World Bank-financed loan programme for municipal capital investments, administered by the Ministry of Finance, has been suspected of political bias in its loan approvals. A World Bank representative has noted that, despite the multi-million euro programme having sufficient funds to service all 85 municipalities with loans, only one SDSM-led municipality (Strumica) has applied to the programme since it began in September 2009. While Strumica's application was not formally rejected by the Ministry, the decision on its approval was delayed for so long that the mayor of Strumica eventually withdrew his application and funded the proposed infrastructure project locally.[53]

The record of municipalities borrowing on the commercial market and/ or issuing municipal bonds is even less impressive. According to the executive director of ZELS, Macedonian municipalities remain reluctant to take out commercial loans and, before March 2012, only three municipalities had done so.[54] The municipal association blamed the municipalities' fear of taking on too much debt in a financial crisis, along with a general cultural aversion to taking out loans. ZELS is unclear whether more municipalities applied to the Ministry of Finance for permission to arrange commercial loans and had either received negative responses or, as is the case of Ohrid, no response at all.[55] Similarly, despite being granted permission to issue local bonds in mid-2011, the municipalities had still to do so by mid-2012.[56] To summarise, while necessary, the restrictions placed on municipal borrowing, in addition to initial central government resistance to help the municipalities address outstanding debts and the reluctance of most municipalities to borrow commercially, suggests that the contractual autonomy of Macedonian municipalities remains weak.

Summary

This chapter has examined whether the decentralisation process in Macedonia has enhanced the fiscal autonomy of Macedonian municipalities, a key theoretical assumption underpinning the reform's ability to mitigate ethnic conflict in unitary states. It began by considering why the national parties governing Macedonia at the time the reforms were adopted chose to give up political and fiscal power to the local level, and suggests short-term political calculations were decisive. The chapter also suggests that fluctuations in the electoral strength of the governing parties, in particular a change of government in 2006, adversely affected central government's commitment to enhancing the fiscal autonomy of the municipalities and may continue to do so in the future. The outcome of future municipal elections will be critical for determining whether central government continues to support the decentralisation reforms or will seek to reverse progress made to date.

Detailed examination of the revenue, expenditure and contractual autonomy of the municipalities has suggested that decentralisation has done little to restrain the monopoly of central government on state power and resources. Despite some increase in own-source revenue, which has enhanced local autonomy in spending decisions regarding the delivery of hard municipal services, evidence suggests politicians at the central level may have designed fiscal decentralisation reforms in a way that has maintained local dependency on central government. Limited access to own-source revenues and an over-dependence on insufficient and often discretionary inter-governmental transfers imply the revenue autonomy of municipalities is weak. Stringent expenditure mandates for block grants and the frequent freezing of municipal bank accounts because of unpaid arrears indicate that the expenditure autonomy of the municipalities remained tightly constrained by the centre. Finally, the limited ability of municipalities to enter into financial contracts with different sets of private actors suggests that their contractual autonomy is also fragile. Since the vast majority of municipalities are politically aligned to the central governing coalition, what appear to be representative local governments are, for the most part, really only permitted to operate like deconcentrated units of central government.

Ehtisham Ahmad and Giorgio Brosio refer to such occurrences as 'partial decentralisation', because sub-central governments remain heavily dependent on the centre for their revenues and cannot therefore be held accountable for all budgetary decisions and outcomes locally (Ahmad and Brosio 2009: 9). It is not unusual for situations of 'partial' decentralisation to occur during the initial stages of fiscal decentralisation reforms, particularly if concerns exist over the fiscal management capacities of sub-central units. While in the short term, tight control of peripheral areas by central government may promote political stability, in the long term, and particularly in post-conflict environments where decentralisation is expected to provide greater autonomy to local communities, it will undermine the benefits associated with decentralisation and may even make regimes less stable. Macedonia's fiscal decentralisation reforms are therefore at a critical juncture and will require further reform to consolidate the process. At the very least, the legal requirement to calculate inter-governmental grants for all devolved public services on a per-client basis should be respected. Further, transparency in the allocation of capital grants could be enhanced if all line ministries establish and publish the criteria upon which municipal project proposals are evaluated. Ultimately, however, reforms that promote internal democracy within political parties will be crucial if local politicians are to be prevented from future subordination in party structures at the expense of local autonomy.

This chapter has demonstrated the importance of taking an integrated approach to assessing the fiscal autonomy of Macedonian municipalities. Fiscal inter-governmental relations are inherently political and political forces substantially determine the way they are designed and implemented. Similarly, without sufficient financial resources, municipalities cannot adequately carry out their newly assigned competences. The analysis has also shown that central governments, along with the political parties which constitute them, remain central players in any decentralisation process. Their motives for the reforms succeeding (or indeed failing) should therefore be prudently and continually considered. Finally, this chapter has illustrated that, while constitutionally guaranteed decentralisation processes may be harder to reverse than others, it is not impossible. Central governments can and do find ways to retain control, even as supposedly decentralising reforms proceed. Advances in either political or administrative decentralisation, examined in Chapters 2 and 3, can easily be undermined by tightening controls over fiscal relations. The potential to recentralise or, in Macedonia's case, partially decentralise, is therefore greater than the literature on decentralisation suggests.

Notes

1 Part of this analysis is also available in Lyon (2014).
2 The EU's support for the principle of subsidiarity means that decentralisation features prominently in the accession process for EU membership.
3 The largest parties in coalition at that time were SDSM and DUI.
4 Interviews with senior DUI party member: 27 June 2010 and 14 June 2011, Tetovo.
5 Municipalities were required to possess an adequate staff capacity for financial management, show good financial results for at least 24 months and have no arrears to suppliers or any other creditors exceeding those ordinary terms of payment (Official Gazette 2004: Art. 46). See also Boskovska (2010) for more information regarding the process of monitoring and assessing municipal fulfilment of these criteria.

6 O'Neill argues: 'Political parties distribute political and fiscal power to the arenas in which their political allies seem most likely to gain control of it. When political parties predict that they will be unable to control central power in a centralised governing structure and also predict that they could win a substantial proportion of subnational offices were they contested democratically, decentralisation becomes more attractive' (O'Neill 2003: 1087). See the Introduction for a more detailed explanation.

7 Interview with a member of DUI: 17 June 2012, Tetovo.

8 Decentralisation was strongly promoted by the World Bank, USAID and UNDP. The EU's support for the principle of subsidiarity also means that decentralisation features prominently in the accession process for EU membership which Macedonia is currently participating in.

9 During the 2011 parliamentary elections, only the National Democratic Rebirth Party (*Rilindja Demokratike Kombëtare* – RDK), led by the mayor of Gostivar, Rufi Osmani, campaigned on decentralisation-related issues. VMRO-DPMNE's manifesto made minimal reference to decentralisation, whereas the policy did not feature at all in SDSM's and DUI's election manifestos.

10 Including contributions from the Road Fund.

11 The Law on Property Taxes (2004) gave discretion to the municipalities to set the property tax rate between a minimum of 0.10 per cent and a maximum of 0.20 per cent of the 'market' value. Municipalities can set the rate of the property transfer tax within a range of 2 and 4 per cent of 'market' value (Feruglio 2008: 28–30). However, the executive director of ZELS confirmed that it is very rare for municipalities to increase rates above the minimum for fear of upsetting constituents. Interview: 21 June 2010, Skopje.

12 For example in Bulgaria, municipalities administer taxes on vehicle registration and on roads, while in Albania municipalities also administer taxes on vehicles and on the use of agricultural land.

13 Municipal concessions on construction land benefit urban municipalities only. Interview with the executive director of ZELS: 20 March 2012, Skopje.

14 With the exception of 2009, as a result of the effects of the global economic crisis.

15 Municipal share of the VAT increased to 3.4 per cent in 2010, 3.7 per cent in 2011, 4 per cent in 2012 and increased to 4.5 per cent in 2013.

16 Interview with the executive director of ZELS: 21 June 2010, Skopje.

17 Interview with the executive director of ZELS: 20 March 2012, Skopje.

18 Earmarked grants are assigned to municipalities still in Phase One of the decentralisation process and cover the operating costs of social service institutions. Block grants are assigned to municipalities which have graduated to Phase Two and also include employee wages. See Chapter 3 for a more detailed explanation.

19 Interview with UNDP official: 29 June 2010, Skopje.

20 Interview with executive director of ZELS: 20 March 2012, Skopje.

21 Article 9.2 of the Charter states: 'Local authorities' financial resources shall be commensurate with the responsibilities provided for by the constitution and the law' (Council of Europe 1985).

22 Article 2.3 of the Law on Local Government Financing stipulates: 'The total amount of block grants shall not be lower than the amount of the funds from the Budget of the Republic of Macedonia used for the same purpose in that area in the previous year from the year when a certain competence is transferred' (Official Gazette 2004). Examples where education grants have failed to keep up with increasing expenditures needs are: increases in student transport costs resulting from the decision to make secondary education compulsory, pay raises for teachers, and inflationary increases in the cost of heating oil and petrol. Interview with the executive director of ZELS: 8 April 2011, Skopje.

23 Such action is particularly significant given the fact that over 80 per cent of the municipalities are aligned with the national governing coalition. Interview with the executive director of ZELS: 20 March 2012, Skopje.

24 The six ministries are: Ministry of Finance; Ministry of Transport and Communications; Ministry of Education and Science; Ministry of Culture, Youth and Sport; Ministry of Agriculture, Forestry and Water Economy; and Ministry of Local Self-Government.

25 Based on official figures from the Ministry of Finance. However, there is a possibility that further discretionary payments have been made to some municipalities which are not included in this data or appear elsewhere.

26 Interview with the executive director of ZELS: 8 April 2011, Skopje.

27 Interview with the head of a USAID fiscal decentralisation project: 10 May 2010, Skopje.

28 With the exception of funds allocated for the construction of water-supply and sewerage systems (Kocevski 2009: 27).

29 Interviews with the executive director of ZELS: 21 June 2010 and 8 April 2011, Skopje.

30 Interviews with: mayor of Struga: 1 June 2010; president of the municipal council: 3 June 2010, Kruševo; municipal councillor: 25 June 2010, Kičevo; municipal councillor: 5 April 2011, Kumanovo; municipal officer: 6 April 2011, Šuto Orizari.

31 Interview with Macedonian independent researcher: 25 June 2010, Skopje.

32 Interview with municipal councillor: 1 June 2010, Struga. This is despite the fact that DUI are a junior coalition partner.

33 Ministry official: 'This makes them [central government] look like they discriminate on ethnic lines, but it is political not ethnic. Awarding your own people capital investments funds was a SDSM practice as well, so this is consistent of parties in power.'

34 Interviews with the executive director of ZELS: 21 June 2010 and 8 April 2011, Skopje.

35 These five municipalities are: Delčevo, Ohrid, Vinica, Vraneštica and Želino. Changes to the Law on Financing of the Units of Local Self-Government meant that from 2010 municipalities with unpaid arrears in the first phase were permitted to borrow money to clear debts and enter the second phase. During 2011 a decision was taken to allow municipalities to progress into the second phase without resolving significant debts first. Interview with the executive director of ZELS: 20 March 2012, Skopje.

36 Interviews with the executive director of ZELS: 20 March 2012, Skopje; and representative of the Delegation of the European Union to the Former Yugoslav Republic of Macedonia: 16 March 2012, Skopje.

37 In theory and according to the law, the municipalities are granted discretion over how surplus funds are used. However, in reality there is pressure, particularly from the IMF, to promote cost-saving measures and return unspent revenue to the Treasury. Interview with the head of a USAID fiscal decentralisation project: 10 May 2010, Skopje.

38 Interview with the executive director of ZELS: 8 April 2011, Skopje.

39 Interview with USAID project official: 14 June 2010, Skopje.

40 Interview with the executive director of ZELS: 21 June 2010, Skopje.

41 Interview with representative of the World Bank: 16 March 2012, Skopje.

42 Interview with representative of the Delegation of the European Union to the Former Yugoslav Republic of Macedonia: 16 March 2012, Skopje.

43 Since decentralisation began, local competences have been retracted only four or five times by either the Ministry of Education and Science or the Ministry of Transport and Communications. Interview with representative of the Delegation of the European Union to the Former Yugoslav Republic of Macedonia: 16 March 2012, Skopje.

44 Often there is a valid reason why the competence has been retracted, i.e. if a municipality has breached regulations. However, prohibited behaviour also happens in government-aligned municipalities and in such circumstances no action is taken. Interview with local expert working with the municipalities: 20 March 2012, Skopje.
45 Interview with USAID project official: 14 June 2010, Skopje.
46 This possibility was later extended to municipalities in the first phase of decentralisation so that they could progression into the second phase.
47 The limit was amended to 30 per cent in 2009 (CSLD 2011b: 21).
48 This limit was also amended to 30 per cent in 2009 (CSLD 2011b: 21).
49 Article 50 of the Law on Financing of the Units of Local Self-Government, for example, states: 'The Municipality may take long-term loans … after the Ministry of Finance confirms that: it has regularly submitted positively assessed financial reports for the period of at least 24 months from the day this law enters into force; and it does not have any arrears towards the creditors in the last two years from the day this law enters into force' (Official Gazette 2004).
50 Interview with USAID project official: 14 June 2010, Skopje.
51 Interview with the executive director of ZELS: 20 March 2012, Skopje.
52 Meanwhile, Ohrid is forced to pay penalty rates of interest as high as 20–25 per cent on its debts. Interview with the head of a USAID fiscal decentralisation project: 10 May 2010, Skopje.
53 Interview with representative of the World Bank: 15 March 2012, Skopje.
54 Interview with the executive director of ZELS: 20 March 2012, Skopje.
55 Interview with the executive director of ZELS: 20 March 2012, Skopje.
56 Interview with the executive director of ZELS: 20 March 2012, Skopje.

5   Subsidiarity versus state cohesion

Introduction

This chapter considers the apparent conflict between subsidiarity and solidarity, and determines whether the (limited) fiscal autonomy ensuing from decentralisation has been achieved at the expense of economic and territorial cohesion. While the previous chapter examined the differences between local revenue and expenditure, known as the *vertical* fiscal imbalance between different levels of government, the following sections review the extent of *horizontal* imbalances in municipal revenues. The chapter highlights the essential role played by equalisation transfers and other mechanisms designed to overcome such inevitable distortions, for example inter-municipal co-operation and regional development policy. It also examines whether decentralisation has indirectly addressed longstanding socio-economic inequalities which contributed to conflict in 2001 by promoting a more equitable distribution of state resources and by improving citizens' access to public services. While the Framework Agreement's primary focus was on resolving the political and cultural inequalities that existed between Macedonia's two largest ethnic communities, it fails to directly address significant socio-economic insecurities. The Agreement's emphasis on preserving territorial integrity and the unitary character of the state also neglects the importance of promoting socio-economic development and cohesion *within* the state; a key theme of the European Commission's cohesion policy (European Commission 2011a).

This analysis begins by considering the ongoing theoretical debate regarding decentralisation's ability to reduce territorial disparities within a country. It then builds upon the analysis of socio-economic disparities in Chapter 1 by examining the presence of regional disparities and rural under-development in Macedonia. Finally, the chapter discusses the impact municipal boundary changes and fiscal decentralisation has had on the municipalities' ability to deliver basic services that meet the needs of local citizens. This chapter will consider whether decentralisation in Macedonia has: led to a more equitable distribution of public resources throughout Macedonia; created the optimal conditions for expanding citizens' access to basic services (thereby reducing social exclusion); and reduced longstanding socio-economic disparities between urban and rural areas. The intention is not to evaluate the various claims that decentralisation may improve the quality of local services, promote economic development and growth through increased public sector efficiency and reduce poverty through job creation. Insufficient monitoring data currently exists in Macedonia to enable an assessment of the first claim, and it is unclear to what extent the latter claims can be ascribed to decentralisation alone. Instead this chapter argues that Macedonia's experience with decentralisation is at a critical juncture and will require further reform, particularly in the sphere of fiscal equalisation, if all municipalities (and citizens) are to benefit equally from its potential.

Decentralisation and regional disparities

Researchers have failed to reach a consensus over whether decentralisation improves or exacerbates pre-existing regional disparities within a country. The empirical evidence available, observe Andres Rodríguez-Pose and Roberto Ezcurra (2010: 626), is both scarce and inconclusive. Most single-country case studies, for example West and Wong (1995) for China and Bonet (2006) for Colombia, have found that decentralisation was accompanied by an increase in territorial disparities. In contrast, the number of single-country studies that find decentralisation is either unrelated to or, alternatively, associated with a reduction in regional inequalities is far more limited. One possible explanation for such contradictory empirical findings is that decentralisation may be less able to address regional disparities in low-income countries than in more developed states. The logic behind this assumption is that higher-income countries are less likely to have significant territorial inequalities to begin with, and are more likely to have a strong welfare state and well-established territorially progressive fiscal systems designed to address them (Rodríguez-Pose and Ezcurra 2010: 639).

Experts have argued that decentralisation may alleviate disparities between regions by promoting economic development and growth through increased public-sector efficiency. For example, Wallace E. Oates (1972) has suggested that decentralisation improves government efficiency and, as a consequence, economic growth by increasing experimentation, innovation and local competition in the design and delivery of public services. Similarly, others have suggested that devolving responsibility for local economic development to the very people that know the local business environment best means communities are more knowledgeable, motivated and able to pursue policies that will promote a more favourable investment climate (Canaleta *et al.* 2004: 74; Treisman 2007: 12). Decentralisation is also claimed to promote a more equitable distribution of state resources, either by providing the institutional channels through which remote, poor and previously under-represented areas can access resources, or by uniting poor areas with more affluent ones (Ahmad and Brosio 2009: 11). 'If urban bias is a concern', remarks James

Manor (1999: 103), 'the safest way to tackle it is to give rural areas their own decentralised authorities'. Finally, but most importantly, decentralisation is believed to be conducive to poverty reduction, because local governments are assumed to have better information and higher incentives than central government to design and deliver basic public services that effectively meet the needs of local people (UNDP 2004a: 3; Crawford and Hartmann 2008: 18).

There are, however, a variety of reasons why decentralisation may ignore and in fact even exacerbate disparities that exist within a unitary state. The most commonly cited argument is the inherent conflict between subsidiarity and solidarity, or between local revenue autonomy and state-level redistribution. Increasing the own-revenue powers of local governments almost always benefits jurisdictions with stronger tax bases, because less well-endowed regions experience greater difficulty in raising the revenues required to meet local needs (Canaleta *et al.* 2004: 75; Bakke and Wibbels 2006: 17; Spahn and Werner 2007: 104; Thede 2009: 118). This is particularly the case if local revenues are dominated by sources that favour urbanised areas, for example property-related taxes and construction fees. Further, Rémy Prud'homme has argued that in a decentralised state, existing disparities may even reinforce themselves (Prud'homme 1995: 203). Wealthier local governments may be able to lower local taxation, and in doing so further broaden their tax base by attracting additional settlement and investment at the expense of neighbouring jurisdictions. 'Decentralisation', Prud'homme concludes, 'can therefore be the mother of segregation'.

A second reason why decentralisation may reinforce pre-existing disparities is the fact that wealthier regions, with more developed local infrastructure and high quality public services, will find it easier to attract private investment, capital investment, and indeed talent (Bartlett *et al.* 2010: 150; Rodríguez-Pose and Ezcurra 2010: 625; Dragoman 2011: 666). Richer regions, observes Christian Lessman (2009: 7), are often disproportionately strong negotiators because central governments are more concerned with maintaining their political support. They are therefore more likely to wield a greater influence over central decision-making regarding the allocation of discretionary funds or even the design of formula-based grants. Wealthier jurisdictions would also have more own-source revenue at their disposal to invest in local infrastructure projects which can then be used to further improve the local investment climate. An additional reason why decentralisation may advantage wealthier and possibly more populous local jurisdictions at the expense of others is their ability to benefit from economies of scale in the provision of public services. Smaller local governments, with fewer local citizens and tax payers, will have higher average costs and will therefore be less able to deliver public services efficiently (UNDP 2004a: 9; Rodríguez-Pose and Ezcurra 2010: 622). Clearly, such disparities will impact on individual local governments' ability to provide local services in an equitable manner. Finally, but significantly, it is important to stress that decentralisation does little to address disparities that may exist *within* local jurisdictions. By facilitating local discretion in decision-making, inequalities in the distribution of resources locally may increase. This may be particularly true in jurisdictions which extend over both urban and rural areas, where urban voters outnumber their rural counterparts and where local corruption is easier to sustain (Manor 1999: 104; Crawford and Hartmann 2008: 176).

The arguments outlined above emphasise the need for decentralisation reforms to include a fiscal equalisation mechanism that would compensate for the disparities that inevitably arise from the differing fiscal capacities of local governments. While this process of revenue redistribution inevitably undermines the fiscal accountability between local governments and tax payers that decentralisation seeks to enhance, equalisation transfers are important for ensuring all jurisdictions have the necessary fiscal means to provide a comparable level of basic public services. However, the enhanced local revenue autonomy ensuing from fiscal decentralisation undermines the ability of central governments to play an equalising role, since its fiscal capacity is more limited than it would be in a centralised state (Canaleta *et al.* 2004: 75; Bird and Ebel 2007: 18; Lessmann 2009: 2). Individual local governments are also unable to equalise horizontal revenue disparities themselves, as attempts to increase tax rates in poorer regions (to compensate for narrower tax bases) would be self-defeating because local residents could move to neighbouring regions and undermine the policy (Prud'homme 1995: 202). It is not by chance, observe Richard Bird and Robert Ebel (2007: 9), that the so-called welfare state was a centralising one: 'a country cannot have both its autonomous cake and eat its redistributive one'.

Disparities within and between regions in the Republic of Macedonia

Chapter 1 has examined how an already fragile Macedonian economy was severely damaged by a prolonged process of economic transition, war in neighbouring former Yugoslav republics and a trade embargo imposed on Macedonia by Greece in 1994. Such challenges led to a significant decline in living standards, rising unemployment and increasing poverty levels, all of which contributed to a general loss of faith in the ability of the state to provide for its citizens. The analysis in Chapter 1 also demonstrated how significant socio-economic disparities between Macedonia's ethnic communities produced increasing Albanian frustration with the state and majority Macedonian community. Such disparities took on both an ethnic and territorial dimension, with persistent rural under-development representing a severe poverty trap for (predominantly Albanian) rural communities (ESI 2002b: i). This section discusses two issues that continue to polarise local development in Macedonia: the development of urban municipalities at the expense of rural ones; and the concentration of economic growth and investment in the capital city, Skopje.

Despite rural under-development being a constant feature of Macedonian life for decades, it was only with the start of decentralisation that the extent of disparities between urban and rural municipalities was comprehensively measured. An analysis of the socio-economic performance of the municipalities was completed for the first time in 2004 by UNDP (2004b, 2004c). It revealed considerable differences in social and economic development across different parts of the country, as well as between urban and rural municipalities. For example, UNDP's Human Development Index (HDI), a summary measure of human development, was found to average 0.796 in urban municipalities and only 0.765 in rural ones (UNDP 2004b: 35).[1] Skopje measured the highest, with an HDI of 0.822; while rural Zajas, Dolneni and Rosoman measured 0.737, 0.745 and 0.759 respectively (UNDP 2004b: 36). While Zajas, home to Ali Ahmeti, leader of the NLA and subsequent head of the political party DUI, was the focus of the European Stability Initiative's report 'Ahmeti's Village', an exposé of how chronic rural under-development disproportionately affects Macedonia's Albanian community, it is important to note that both Dolneni and Rosoman are both majority-Macedonian municipalities.[2] UNDP's analysis also found that average annual income levels per capita in sampled rural municipalities were around US$500 lower than in sampled urban municipalities, and at least US$300 below the national average. Unemployment, although significant throughout the country, also varied considerably between urban and rural areas, with unemployment rates exceeding employment rates by as much as two or three times in some rural municipalities (UNDP 2004b: 15).

As Chapters 1 and 3 have already discussed, rural under-development is a legacy of Yugoslav times and socialist planning's tendency to concentrate investments largely in urban areas. Throughout socialist Yugoslavia, as in many capitalist countries, infrastructure development, employment creation and public services were developed to service urban areas and socially owned enterprises at the expense of surrounding rural villages (ESI 2002b: 5; Risteska 2013b). It was assumed that concentrating public investments in the cities would encourage economic growth that would filter into outlying areas (Woodward 1995a: 66). However, there are three important consequences of this legacy which continue to impact upon local governance in Macedonia. First, in the absence of substantial capital investment in rural areas to correct the distorted infrastructure of the past, significant disparities between urban and rural areas remain. Clearly, poor local infrastructure impacts upon the ability of rural municipalities to deliver equitable public services to local citizens and to combat social exclusion. When surveyed in 2011, for example, 64 per cent of municipalities admitted that they remain unable to provide communal services to all local residents (OSCE 2011: 67). Second, the concentration of socially owned enterprises in urban areas has brought a strong spatial dimension to the privatisation process in Macedonia (Bartlett *et al.* 2010: 125). While urban municipalities may now be better placed to compete for economic investment than their rural counterparts, significant job losses in secondary towns as a result of the closure of many enterprises have exacerbated unemployment rates and made poverty an increasingly urban

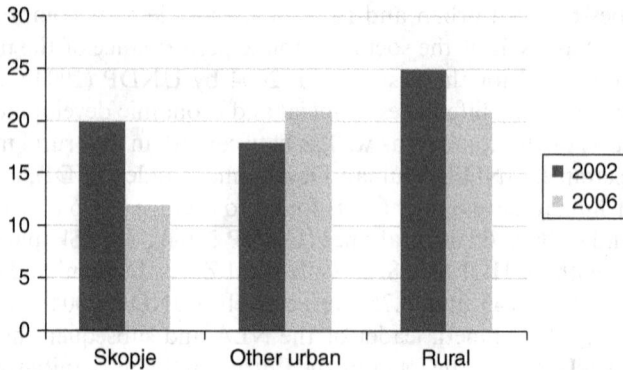

Figure 5.1 Changes in poverty rates in the Republic of Macedonia, 2002–2006 (percentages)

Source: World Bank (2009: xiii)

phenomenon (see Figure 5.1) (Ministry of Agriculture 2007: 16; World Bank 2009: 19). Finally, given the employment trends of Macedonia's ethnic communities during the Yugoslav period, where a disproportionate number of Macedonians migrated from villages to urban areas to take up jobs in newly created social enterprises, rural areas have and remain home to significant Albanian and Turkish communities. Urban–rural disparities therefore often (but not always) have unintended ethnic consequences (Poulton 2000: 132; Brunnbauer 2004: 579–86).

A second issue that continues to impact upon local development in Macedonia is the existence of persistent socio-economic disparities between regions and, in particular, between Skopje and the rest of the country.[3] The rising dominance of capital city-regions vis-à-vis the rest of the country is consistent with the broader experience of the transition countries in central and eastern Europe (Monastiriotis 2013: 227). The high level of concentration of business activities in Skopje makes it increasingly difficult for the other regions in Macedonia to compete (Bartlett *et al.* 2010: 126). When GDP is calculated on a regional, per-capita basis (see Appendix K), persistent discrepancies in levels of economic activity throughout the country are clearly apparent. The Skopje region has consistently enjoyed the highest level of GDP per capita in the country, rising to more than a third above the national average in 2010. This constitutes almost half of all economic activity in Macedonia (see Table 5.1). With the exception of Pelagonia, GDP per capita in all other planning regions was and remains below the national average. The lowest levels are found in Polog and the Northeast regions, where levels have remained consistently around half the national average since 2000. It is important to bear in mind that regional GDP values refer to production generated within the region, rather than the average income of citizens in a given

Table 5.1 Key development indicators according to planning regions, 2009

Region	Share in national GDP creation (%)	Unemployment rates (%)	Population per doctor[a]
East	7.5	17.0	703
Northeast	4.5	64.8	806
Pelagonia	12.5	33.2	528
Polog	7.2	27.3	1,106
Skopje	45.5	33.5	638
Southeast	8.0	14.4	755
Southwest	7.6	32.7	848
Vardar	7.3	39.7	622
Republic of Macedonia	100.0	32.2	713

Sources: SSO (2012c); Mojsovska (2011: 18)

Note

a These figures are for 2008.

region (UNDP 2004c: 98). Commuter flows, concentrated around major cities, may therefore have a significant influence on regional income distribution.[4] Also, official data does not capture the impact of informal economic activity or remittances from abroad, which represent important sources of income in some parts of the country. A map of Macedonia's planning eight regions is available in Appendix L.

Table 5.1 illustrates how official employment rates, in addition to basic healthcare measures, also vary significantly between regions. Although the unemployment rate in the Skopje region remained on a par with the national average in 2009, it decreased significantly in the years since 2009 at the expense of secondary cities (Figure 5.1). However, this data masks significant differences in employment rates within the Skopje region. For example, the Roma-majority municipality of Šuto Orizari in the City of Skopje experiences unemployment at least twice the national average (UNDP 2004b: 15). Interestingly, the unemployment rate in the predominantly Albanian Polog region is below the national average, despite the official data implying a low level of regional economic activity. Such discrepancies could be due to residents commuting to work in nearby Skopje, a prevalent grey economy and/ or low labour-force participation rates, particularly among Albanian and Turkish women.[5]

The data presented in Table 5.1 and in Appendices K and P suggests that a very strong mono-centric model of development was pursued in Macedonia for many decades. Unlike during the Yugoslav period, between its independence from Yugoslavia in 1991 and 2008 Macedonia had no policy for promoting balanced development among its regions (Woodward 1995a, 1995b). The only form of development support during this period was applied to highly underdeveloped, mainly rural areas, but without any coherent measures to redress disparities between regions.[6] Funds distributed by the Bureau for

Economically Underdeveloped Regions during this period were also insufficient and were generally allocated according to the political affiliation of the municipalities rather than based on need (UNDP 2005b: 146; Karajkov 2006: 10; Ministry of Agriculture 2007: 12). The lack of balanced regional development policy until 2008 therefore resulted in devastating outcomes for peripheral urban and rural areas that lag behind Skopje in terms of economic, social and cultural dimensions (Mojsovska 2011: 19).

Territorial reorganisation and the optimum size of municipalities

Experts recognise that while municipal boundary changes should be regarded as principally an administrative issue, involving considerations of scale economies and equity in the provision of services, local economic sustainability and appropriate levels of citizen participation, they are also of profound local and state-level political significance (Boex *et al.* 2004: 7; Skaburskis 2004: 43; Devas and Delay 2006: 692). As debates in the literature on power-sharing and on federalism illustrate, boundary changes may have a significant impact on community relations in multi-ethnic states – serving to either encourage integration or secure enhanced autonomy for a particular ethnic group (Meligrana and Razin 2004: 227). John Meligrana and Eran Razin distinguish between explicit and implicit goals in the design of local territorial reform. Explicit goals, they observe, are contained in official regulations or laws, while implicit goals represent the aspirations of political parties and/or population groups to gain a political advantage from the new territorial configuration (Meligrana and Razin 2004: 236).

UNDP's 2004 analysis of the economic characteristics of Macedonian municipalities provoked a debate both in the Government and with international agencies operating in Macedonia regarding what the optimal size of the municipalities after decentralisation should be. An earlier attempt at territorial division in 1996 had resulted in an over-fragmentation of local government structures, with many small municipalities being unsustainable in terms of their demographic structure, economic viability and organisational capacity (see Appendix M for an analysis of this territorial reorganisation) (UNDP 2004b: 98). For example, over a third of the 123 municipalities created had populations of less than 5,000 (see Table 5.2), the minimum threshold recommended by the Council of Europe for viable local entities (ICG 2003: 20). With the devolution of additional competences to the municipalities after 2004, in particular those related to local economic development, education and primary health, Macedonia's fragmented municipal structure required further consolidation. The *explicit* goals of the territorial reorganisation stated by the Government were therefore to make the municipalities more sustainable and effective, with boundary changes being based on ethnically neutral criteria (Kreci and Ymeri 2010: 275).[7] However, the *implicit* goals envisaged by the political parties were summarised by an Albanian politician at the time as follows:

We want to maximise the number of municipalities where Albanians make up 20 per cent of the population (and thereby make Albanian an official language) and we want to bring Albanians in connection with the urban centre; the Macedonians want the opposite – to preserve Macedonian urban control, keeping Albanians in rural areas and minimising the number of 20 per cent Albanian municipalities.

(ICG 2003: 20)

The 84 municipalities that survived the reorganisation, 16 of which still have populations less than 5,000, suggest that the process was based largely on political and ethnic compromises, rather than on establishing economically viable jurisdictions (Vankovska 2006: 22–3; Friedman 2009: 217; Kreci and Ymeri 2010: 271). According to a senior local government expert working for UNDP at the time, 'there were so many experts, so many study visits, but in the end the decisions made were political'.[8] Indeed, as the analysis in Appendix N suggests, the vast majority of these 16 municipalities were saved either because their mayor was a member of SDSM (the largest party in government at that time), or because the local population included a sizable ethnic community.

The most controversial boundary changes proposed were those affecting the municipalities of Struga and Kičevo, which were due to be enlarged to ensure Albanians became the majority in both municipalities. For Struga, expansion meant that the local Albanian population increased from 41.5 per cent to 56.8 per cent, while in Kičevo, the local Albanian population was set to rise from 30.5 per cent to almost 60 per cent (Friedman 2009). Boundaries of the City of Skopje were also extended to include rural Saraj municipality and ensure the Albanian population reached the 20 per cent threshold required to make Albanian an official language in the capital. It is no coincidence that one of the two VMRO-DPMNE-led municipalities with fewer than 5,000 residents that survived merger with a neighbouring municipality was Vevčani. It was originally selected for union with Struga, but to do so would have tipped the municipality's delicate ethnic balance in favour of local Macedonians once

Table 5.2 Number of municipalities after territorial reorganisation in 1996 and 2004

Population	No. of municipalities (1996)	No. of municipalities (2004)
Up to 1,000	5	0
1,000–5,000	42	16
5,001–10,000	24	16
10,001–20,000	26	21
20,001–50,000	15	17
50,001–100,000	9	13
Over 100,001	2	1
Total	123	84

Source: SSO (2003)

again.[9] Similarly, Kičevo's proposed enlargement, initially delayed as a result of significant local resistance, remained unrealised in mid-2012.[10] At the time the decision for amalgamation was taken in 2004, both Kičevo municipality and neighbouring Drugovo were led by VMRO-DPMNE.[11] However, the subsequent election of a VMRO-DPMNE-led government in 2006 meant Kičevo's expansion was postponed twice.

Did Macedonia's territorial reorganisation in 2004 achieve its objectives? With regard to the implicit goals held by the Albanian political parties at the time, the answer to this question is undoubtedly 'yes'. The proportion of Albanians living in municipalities where they form a majority has increased from 69.30 before the reform in 2002 to 79.33 per cent in 2004 (Kreci and Ymeri 2010: 279).[12] Further, many smaller rural municipalities have now been consolidated with neighbouring urban jurisdictions. This means that, at least in theory if not in practice, previously marginalised rural communities will benefit from the superior fiscal resources, public services and political influence experienced by the urban municipalities. However, with regard to the reform's explicit goals (scale economies, economic viability, enhancing local democracy, etc.) the verdict is less positive. The reality of Macedonia's territorial reorganisation has created two significant consequences which adversely affect the ability of municipalities to deliver basic services to citizens in an equitable and/or efficient manner.

First, while the 2004 reform significantly reduced the fragmentation of municipal government in Macedonia, a substantial number of small municipalities with questionable fiscal and organisational capacity still remain.[13] Experts had initially recommended that the number of municipalities be reduced by half to around 60 (World Bank 2003b: 16). The decision to retain as many as 84 municipalities means that approximately 40 per cent still have populations of less than 10,000 (Table 5.2). It is worth bearing in mind that no analysis of the fiscal capacity of the proposed 84 municipalities was completed at the time of the reform (UNDP 2005b: 152; Nikolov 2007: 32). In fact, neither the Government nor international experts had any idea how much revenue the proposed municipalities could generate, because fiscal records were mainly based around the original 34 municipalities.[14] The consequence is therefore the existence of significant inequalities in the size and fiscal capacities of the remaining municipalities. For example, Vraneštica municipality has a population of 1,322, a staff of 13 and had an annual budget of approximately €200,000 in 2010; while Kumanovo has 105,484 residents, 133 employees and an annual budget of €23 million (UNDP 2011b: 5, 7). As Macedonia adopted a symmetrical model of decentralisation, whereby all municipalities – regardless of their size or fiscal capacity – are required to provide the same functions and services to citizens, it is inevitable that the smaller, less well-endowed municipalities will experience serious challenges in the realisation of their competences.[15] According to an assessment published by UNDP in 2008, 'one fifth of municipalities are too small even to efficiently provide the most basic municipal services ... another one fifth ... are well above the "minimum efficient scale" for public services' (Feruglio *et al.* 2008: 6).

Second, the manner in which the political parties carried out the territorial reorganisation undermined the very values of subsidiarity and local democracy that decentralisation is intended to enhance. Contrary to Article 5 of the European Charter on Local Self-Government, there was no public consultation on the proposed boundary changes and the results of at least 40 local referenda were ignored by central government.[16] As Homi Bhabha (1990) has somewhat ironically observed, local boundaries are often constructed to serve the imaginations and interests of those at the centre. The way in which the territorial reorganisation was conducted also meant that decentralisation, while originally intended to be an ethnically blind process, became immediately ethnicised. The process raised inter-ethnic tensions to a level not experienced since the cessation of hostilities in 2001 and succeeded in tapping into deep insecurities among Macedonians, many of whom still fear their country's partition by neighbouring states. An example of this was the state referendum on the Law on Territorial Organisation, initiated by the World Macedonian Congress (a diaspora organisation), which advocated a return to the status quo of 123 municipalities. Although the referendum, held on 7 November 2004, was unsuccessful, the fact that organisers were able to collect more than the 150,000 signatures required (out of a population of only 2 million) illustrates the level of general resentment towards the process.[17] The ICG remarked at the time: 'quite literally, the process will either make or break Macedonia' (ICG 2004: 4). To a certain extent, the boundary reform has tainted the implementation of decentralisation ever since. In particular, it made it more challenging politically to discuss solutions to the disparities which exist between municipalities, for example inter-municipal co-operation or forms of asymmetrical decentralisation, in a rational manner.[18]

Fiscal decentralisation in the Republic of Macedonia: subsidiarity at the expense of solidarity?

As the previous chapter demonstrated, the revenues of all municipalities in Macedonia have increased substantially since the start of fiscal decentralisation in 2006. However, local revenue growth has been uneven across the country, and the fiscal disparities between urban and rural municipalities are intensifying. The data in Table 5.3 shows that the basic revenues of Macedonia's 21 wealthiest municipalities (represented in the fourth data quartile) increased at a much greater rate than in the other municipalities.[19] Further, revenue growth in the 21 poorest municipalities (the first quartile) has been the slowest of all. As a consequence, the ratio of total, per capita, basic revenues of the wealthiest municipalities to the poorest increased from 3.2 : 1 in 2006, to 5 : 1 in 2010 (Levitas 2011a: 20). The presence of such significant horizontal disparities impacts negatively upon the municipalities' ability to provide basic services to citizens in an equitable manner. It also limits the

Table 5.3 Per-capita basic revenues of municipalities by quartile, 2006–2010 (2010 MKD)

Municipalities	Basic revenues per capita (MKD)					Growth rate
	2006	2007	2008	2009	2010	2006/10 (%)
1st quartile	1,208	1,437	1,511	1,681	1,849	53
2nd quartile	1,841	2,236	2,668	2,731	3,184	73
3rd quartile	2,425	3,218	3,456	3,485	4,033	66
4th quartile	3,905	4,653	5,633	6,718	9,200	136
Average	2,762	3,447	4,348	4,083	5,186	88

Source: Levitas (2011a: 19)

Table 5.4 Composition of per-capita expenditure from municipal basic budgets by quartile, 2010 (2010 MKD)

Municipalities	Capital expenditures	Goods, services and reserves	Wages and benefits	Transfers, subsidies, social assistance, etc.
1st quartile	575	635	581	147
2nd quartile	1,219	1,131	736	222
3rd quartile	1,570	1,285	813	235
4th quartile	5,044	1,909	1,024	355
Average	2,238	1,506	856	375

Source: Levitas (2011a: 31)

ability of poorer municipalities to invest locally in expanding public services, fund infrastructure programmes and maintain fiscal autonomy from central government (see Table 5.4).

The principal reason for such significant disparities in the revenue-raising capacities of urban and rural municipalities is their over-reliance on three property-related sources: the real-estate transfer tax, asset income and the construction land development fee. As Chapter 4 has explained, in the absence of other potential local taxes (vehicle registration, tourism, etc.), these sources dominate municipal basic revenues. However, the extent to which they do so varies considerably between urban municipalities that have real-estate markets and their rural counterparts that do not. For example, fees on construction land accounted for approximately 25 per cent of basic revenue in urban municipalities outside Skopje in 2008 and less than 15 per cent in rural municipalities (Feruglio *et al.* 2008: 32). A second reason for such disparities is the concentration of economic activity in the urban centres, discussed earlier. Although the share of PIT municipalities receive is calculated on a derivation basis, those municipalities with more extensive commercial activity are likely to benefit more substantially than those with less economically active jurisdictions (Levitas 2009: 4). The result is that, as of 2010, the average share of tax and non-tax revenue in the principal budget of municipalities was 69 per cent in the City of Skopje, 51 per cent in urban municipalities outside Skopje (minimum = 11 per cent, maxi um = 76 per cent) and 34 per cent in rural municipalities (minimum = 5 per cent, maximum = 67 per cent) (Cyan *et al.* 2012: 55; Boskovska 2010: 91). The municipal association's efforts to increase the local share of PIT from 3 to 30 per cent of regular income will only exacerbate the revenue disparities between municipalities.

A further consequence of the municipalities' over-dependence on property-related income is the significant and increasing disparity between the capital's revenues, where property construction rates and prices are at a premium, and other urban municipalities. Property-related income accounted for an impressive 70 per cent of the City of Skopje's total basic revenues in 2010, but only 33 per cent in municipalities outside of the capital (Levitas 2011a: 17). This meant that by 2010, the ten Skopje municipalities accounted for 47 per cent of all municipal basic revenues, despite only 25 per cent of the population living in them. The result is that the average per-capita basic revenues of Skopje grew to almost three times that of all other jurisdictions in 2010 (Levitas 2011a: 16–17).

A separate but related problem is the significant inequalities in the per-capita revenues of the ten Skopje municipalities. Three of Skopje's municipalities are among the poorest in the country, while three are among the richest (Levitas 2011: 22–3).[20] As elsewhere in the country, these differences have been driven by the property market in different parts of the capital. While it is common for the per capita revenues of capital cities to exceed those of other jurisdictions, the excess is usually only 5 to 10 per cent greater.[21] The cost of providing services in the capital may be slightly higher than elsewhere and Skopje undoubtedly provides services to many commuters, in addition to local residents. However, such significant income disparities mean that, unlike in the rest of the country, the capital is able to invest substantially in improving local services and infrastructure (Table 5.5).

A second feature of Macedonia's model of fiscal decentralisation that exacerbates local fiscal inequalities is the practice of allocating cultural and social welfare grants according to the existence of a physical facility within a municipality's territory, rather than on the potential number of service users (MoLSG 2011b: 8). As the previous chapter discussed, this form of 'institutional' rather than 'functional' decentralisation means that those municipalities historically lacking libraries, kindergartens, homes for the elderly, etc. receive no grants for the realisation of these competences (Levitas 2011a: 25; Cyan *et al.* 2012: 36–7). Given socialist planning's tendency to concentrate public services and infrastructure in urban areas, this practice clearly entrenches the urban–rural inequalities inherited from Yugoslav times and limits the municipalities' ability to provide services to all citizens in an equitable manner.

Table 5.5 Disparities in per-capita expenditures from the basic budget, 2006–2010 (2010 MKD)

	2006		2007		2008		2009		2010	
	Skopje	Others	Skopje	Others	Skopje	Others	Skopje	Others	Skopje	Others
Investment	2,749	842	2,781	938	4,009	1,369	3,912	1,212	4,714	1,410
Goods and services	1,729	681	1,677	740	2,495	971	2,068	947	2,628	1,130
Wages and benefits	614	511	699	595	835	701	894	748	969	819

Source: Levitas (2011a: 30)

Table 5.6 'Institutional' decentralisation and local service delivery, 2011

Programme	No. of municipalities receiving grants	Proportion of municipalities receiving grants (%)	No. of municipalities spending without grants	Proportion of citizens 'served' (%)
Libraries	23	27	1	56
Museums	17	18	3	49
Theatres	22	26	1	48
Elderly care	3	4	2	41
Fire protection	30	35	6	81
Kindergartens	43	51	0	78
Primary education	85	100	0	100
Secondary education	32	38	0	80

Source: Levitas (2011a: 27)

Table 5.6 shows that the proportion of citizens with access to specific devolved public services varies significantly. For example, only 41 per cent of citizens have access to elderly care. The data also suggests many municipalities are either unable or unwilling to invest their own-source revenues in improving access to these services. While anti-rural bias may be offset to a certain extent by rural residents using facilities located in adjacent urban municipalities, there is no guarantee that these services will be responsive to the needs of rural residents, or that they are available on an equal basis (Feruglio *et al.* 2008: 44). Correcting such inequalities will require a considerable amount of new money to fund capital investment which, in a poor country such as Macedonia, will take many years. According to the executive director of the municipal association, ZELS, 'if rural municipalities remain unable to cover the required investment themselves, they may never have these institutions'.[22] Merely redistributing available funds in a more equitable manner may cause those municipalities already with the required institutions to receive insufficient funding to sustain them, while those municipalities without will receive inadequate funding to provide the services in a meaningful way (Levitas 2011a: 27). While central government has recognised that a problem exists, according to one local government expert, they are 'pushing it under the carpet' (MoLSG 2011b: 8).[23] A systematic solution is yet to be found and national minimum service standards have not been established.[24]

Fiscal equalisation in the Republic of Macedonia

The existence of significant and increasing disparities in the revenue-raising capacities of municipalities throughout Macedonia suggests that enhancing local revenue autonomy through fiscal decentralisation may have been achieved at the expense of economic and territorial cohesion. Fiscal inequalities among the municipalities, and between Skopje and the rest of the country, demonstrate the importance of incorporating a fiscal equalisation mechanism into Macedonia's decentralisation design. This would (ideally) neutralise the economic distortions that have arisen from the differing fiscal capacities of the municipalities, and ensure they all have the necessary means to provide a comparable level of services to residents. According to Macedonia's system of equalisation, a proportion of VAT revenue is distributed to all municipalities by means of a fixed general purpose grant of 3 million MKD and a variable amount based on pre-defined criteria. Of the VAT revenue remaining after the general purpose grants are paid out, 12 per cent is allocated to the City of Skopje, while 88 per cent is distributed to the rest of the country. Skopje's allocation is then split 40 : 60 between the City of Skopje and its ten municipalities, and the 60 per cent assigned to the City's municipalities is subsequently divided according to a formula based on population (60 per cent), surface area (27 per cent), and number of settlements (13 per cent). The same criteria are also used to distribute the rest of the country's allocation among the remaining 74 municipalities.

There are, however, a number of serious problems with the current system of equalisation which undermine its ability to neutralise fiscal disparities between the municipalities and, in some instances, actually exacerbate them. Most significantly, the formula adopted to distribute VAT funds does not take into account differences in the revenue-raising capacity of the municipalities (Cyan *et al.* 2012: 10). None of the criteria used (population size, land area, number of settlements) contains information on the relative fiscal capacity (tax base) of individual municipalities (Feruglio *et al.* 2008: 48; Boskovska 2010: 90). According to one local expert, the Government is too afraid to advocate reducing funds for those wealthier municipalities that raise revenue above a certain level.[25] A second problem with the system is that, paradoxically, poorer municipalities receive less money from the VAT Fund than their more well-off counterparts (Levitas 2011a: 21). As the data in Table 5.7 confirms, in 2010 the 21 poorest municipalities (represented in the first quartile) received less money from both the VAT Fund and the Public Roads Fund than all other municipalities, and considerably less money than the wealthiest municipalities represented in the fourth quartile. They also received significantly fewer capital transfers than the 21 wealthiest municipalities, an issue that will be examined in a subsequent section.

The reason for such a perverse outcome is the fact that, comparable to the formulas for distributing primary and secondary education block grants examined in Chapter 3, the current equalisation formula over-compensates larger and less populous municipalities at the expense of more densely populated, smaller jurisdictions (Levitas 2011a: 3; Cyan *et al.* 2009: 20). As the data in Table 5.7 confirms, the average population size of the 21 wealthiest municipalities (represented in the fourth quartile) is significantly lower than those found in the other quartiles, and particularly those in the second quartile. According to fiscal decentralisation expert Tony Levitas (2011a: 20), such results are unusual since in most countries more populous jurisdictions tend to have larger per-capita budgets. The situation is even more surprising when the 21 wealthiest municipalities are examined more closely, because 17 of these 21 municipalities have populations of less than 10,000. When the data for the other four more populous municipalities is removed from the fourth quartile, it is clear that, not only does the average population size of the wealthiest municipalities drop substantially (from 14,897 to 5,335), the per-capita VAT and Road Fund payments received by these 17 municipalities is more than three times greater than the amount allocated to the poorest municipalities (represented in the first quartile).

While it may be justifiable to include variables such as 'surface area' or 'number of settlements' in the formula to compensate for the additional costs involved with delivering services in less densely populated jurisdictions, using both simultaneously works against those municipalities with more concentrated settlement patterns (Levitas 2009: 20). The decision to incorporate a fixed general grant payment for all municipalities, regardless of population size, into the equalisation process from 2009 only exacerbated this outcome

Table 5.7 Distribution of the VAT Fund, Road Fund and capital grants among municipalities, 2010 (per capita MKD)

Municipalities	Average population of municipality in quartile	Total basic revenue	VAT Fund	Road Fund	Capital grants and other transfers
1st quartile	20,819	1,849	511	133	142
2nd quartile	34,092	3,184	534	134	245
3rd quartile	22,126	3,959	611	185	145
4th quartile	14,897	9,200	641	207	1,289
4th without the four largest municipalities	5,335	7,290	1,645	467	329

Source: Levitas (2011a: 20)

because it reduced the total funds available for distribution according to the formula (Levitas 2011a: 4).[26] As with the legacy of rural under-development during Yugoslav times and with the allocation of education block grants, over-compensating larger, less populated jurisdictions has ethnic conse-quences, because Albanian communities tend to live in smaller, more densely populated municipalities with fewer settlements.[27] (See also Appendix O for data on regional population density rates.)

A further example of where the system has failed to neutralise fiscal dispar-ities between the municipalities is that it has gradually become less equalis-ing between the City of Skopje and the rest of the country over time. While municipalities outside of the capital received approximately three times the amount of revenue per capita than those in the City of Skopje in 2006, by 2010 this had fallen to 2.4 (Levitas 2011a: 18). The reason for this is partly because the City of Skopje lobbied successfully to increase its share of the VAT Fund from 10 to 12 per cent in 2008, and partly because the decision to allocate lump sum payments to all municipalities reduced the amount avail-able to distribute to non-Skopje municipalities.

Skopje's share of the VAT funds vis-à-vis the rest of the country does not mean, however, that its ten Skopje municipalities benefit equitably from the revenue it receives, or that existing fiscal disparities between Skopje's munici-palities have been reduced. Table 5.8 demonstrates that Skopje's two poorest municipalities (Šuto Orizari and Čair) receive less money from both the VAT and Road Funds on a per-capita basis than the other jurisdictions. This is because they are both densely populated and have fewer settlements. In con-trast, another poor municipality (Saraj) fared better under the system because of its territory's size and number of settlements. It is interesting to observe, however, that while Saraj received more VAT revenue on a per-capita basis than any of the other nine Skopje municipalities, it would have received far greater funds had it not been part of the City of Skopje.[28] DUI's objective

Table 5.8 Distribution of the VAT Fund, Road Fund and capital grants revenue among municipalities in the City of Skopje, 2010 (per capita MKD)

Municipality	Majority ethnic community	Total basic revenue	Population (2002 census)	Area (km²)	No. of settlements	VAT Fund	Road Fund	Capital grants and transfers
Šuto Orizari	Roma	1,138	22,017	7	0	253	59	0
Čair	Alb.	1,441	64,773	4	1	130	56	48
Saraj	Alb.	1,513	35,804	241	0	485	92	218
Gazi Baba	Mac.	2,227	72,617	92	9	204	81	63
Butel	Mac.	3,108	36,154	58.6	0	226	95	472
Kisela Voda	Mac.	3,481	57,236	47	8	160	183	468
Gjorce Petrov	Mac.	4,079	41,634	67	5	232	106	500
Aerodrom	Mac.	7,111	72,009	21	11	136	82	0
Karposh	Mac.	7,933	59,666	35	0	158	89	51
Centar	Mac.	19,249	45,412	10	16	158	149	8,533

Source: Levitas (2011a: 23–4)

of amalgamating the Albanian-majority Saraj municipality with the City of Skopje in 2004 to ensure the capital became a bilingual city has therefore been made at the expense of its residents.[29]

In an attempt to overcome some of these challenges, UNDP began a process to improve the equalisation formula in 2008. The principal aim was to incorporate a fourth variable into the allocation formula which measures the relative fiscal imbalance of each municipality, based on the difference between estimated local expenditure needs and fiscal capacity.[30] The process proved challenging: first, because of the lack of available and reliable data upon which to base the analysis; and second, because support for amending the formula among the major stakeholders has been inconsistent.[31] In particular, the municipal association is against making any changes to the formula, since to do so would inevitably mean some of its wealthier members would lose out to the poorer ones. Such a dilemma, which is reminiscent of the break-up of Yugoslavia and the role asymmetric fiscal redistribution policies played in its dissolution, 'could tear ZELS apart' (Woodward 1995a: 61, 80).[32] Instead, ZELS (whose president is the mayor of the City of Skopje) advocates further increases in the proportion of VAT revenue available to the municipalities.[33] While such an approach may maintain the peace among ZELS' members in the short-term, increasing the overall VAT pot would do nothing to equalise disparities between municipalities and will indeed exacerbate them. Changes to the distribution of VAT revenue are further complicated by the legacy of past equalisation systems, which rewarded wealthier municipalities as a means of motivating further revenue mobilisation.[34] The result is that the wealthier municipalities, and in particular Skopje, which generated almost 50 per cent of state VAT revenue in 2009, expect money back (see VAT revenue data at Appendix P). Given the challenges experienced in improving the formula and the fact that the municipalities themselves have not pushed hard for its reform, it may be many years before Macedonia has a functioning fiscal equalisation system.

Further approaches to minimising horizontal disparities: co-operation between municipalities

The challenges imposed on Macedonian municipalities by the 2004 territorial reorganisation, along with the failure to address persistent fiscal disparities through equalisation, encouraged the pursuit of innovative approaches to facilitate the equitable delivery of public services. Inter-Municipal Co-operation (IMC), through the establishment of joint public agencies or administrative bodies and outsourcing service delivery to larger municipalities or the private sector, is considered one way of compensating for the limited fiscal and administrative capacities of the rural municipalities and of capturing scale economies (Boex *et al.* 2004: 9; Budds 2004: 6). It also represents a politically viable alternative to further municipal mergers, asymmetric decentralisation or the establishment of a regional tier of government. According to a 2011

UNDP report on local governance in Macedonia, the concept of IMC emerged as 'the only light at the end of the tunnel' (UNDP 2011b: 7). Although IMC is a relatively new concept in Macedonia, a number of successful co-operative arrangements have been established between municipalities since 2005, particularly in the spheres of fire-fighting, local economic development and tax administration (Mojsovska 2011: 11). While there have been examples of smaller municipalities co-operating among themselves to deliver basic services, it is more common for the smaller municipalities to co-operate with their wealthier, urban neighbours. For example, between 2007 and 2009, Tetovo municipality entered into an agreement with Brvenica municipality to provide tax collection and administration services on its behalf. Paying Tetovo €6,000 annually to provide this facility saved Brvenica an estimated €24,000 in administrative costs and the salaries of at least three employees.[35]

Nevertheless, IMC's potential is yet to be realised for several reasons. First, despite the efforts of UNDP and USAID in raising awareness of the concept, many municipalities remain unaware of its benefit.[36] IMC remains a voluntary process, dependent upon the goodwill of mayors, although some local experts have suggested a need to further institutionalise co-operation in some areas, for example social welfare and education inspection.[37] Second, a survey commissioned by the Ministry of Local Self-Government in 2008 found that 73 per cent of municipalities identified a lack of finances as the primary obstacle to IMC (Mojsovska 2011: 11). The stringent expenditure mandates on both block and earmarked grants, discussed in the preceding chapter, mean that the municipalities are unable to use these funds to establish co-operative arrangements.[38] Despite the law on IMC permitting the Government to 'financially stimulate and support inter-municipal co-operation between two or more municipalities', three years after this law was adopted (i.e. by mid-2012), no further action had been taken to do so.[39] Finally, it is clear that many municipalities remain reluctant to establish partnerships with their neighbours, despite being aware of the challenges they face in providing services to local citizens. This may be because rural municipalities fear losing their newly won independence, or because of the existence of ethnic or, more commonly, political animosities with their neighbours.[40] For example, while Tetovo's co-operation agreement with Brvenica made financial sense to both municipalities, it was swiftly dissolved with the election of a new mayor of Tetovo in 2009.[41] Co-operative agreements do exist between municipalities of different political and ethnic backgrounds; however, according to one local expert, 'the process runs much more smoothly if the municipalities are of the same party'.[42] It remains to be seen whether existing co-operative arrangements survive if and when the local political landscape changes after future municipal elections.

A related process, intended to correct the legacy of many years of mono-centric development policy, is the regional development agenda which began in 2008. While not directly related to improving local services, its emphasis on promoting balanced economic growth and infrastructure development among the eight planning regions should create the conditions required for equal access to public services (GTZ 2008a: 11; MoLSG 2011a: 2). In some ways the process may be regarded as undermining the spirit of localism and subsidiarity. However, as this review has demonstrated, decentralisation and municipalities acting alone are insufficient for addressing the persistent socio-economic inequalities that exist at the regional level.

The Law on Balanced Regional Development (2007) prescribed the creation of eight regions as functional territorial units for the purpose of development planning. Previously, these regions had only been used for statistical purposes. (A map of these eight regions is available at Appendix L.) The Law also instigated the creation of an institutional framework, at both the state and regional level, upon which to implement policy. At the state level, the Council for Regional Development, chaired by the Deputy Prime Minister for Economic Affairs and comprising relevant line ministries, regional representatives and the president of ZELS, is responsible for harmonising regional development policy with state strategies and for determining which project proposals receive funding. The Bureau for Regional Development, situated in the Ministry of Local Self-Government, is tasked with preparing strategic documents, such as the ten-year Strategy for Regional Development and its Action Plan (MoLSG 2009a, 2009b). At the regional level, eight Councils for the Development of the Planning Region, involving all mayors from each planning region, are responsible for creating and implementing development programmes in their respective region. They are supported in their work by eight Centres for Regional Development.

The Law states that at least 1 per cent of GDP should be reserved for the purpose of stimulating balanced regional development (Official Gazette 2007: Art. 27). Funds are allocated to finance projects that benefit the regions (70 per cent), 'areas with specific development needs' (20 per cent), and villages (10 per cent), and should be distributed on a regional basis according to the development index in Table 5.9.[43] Interesting, while the Polog region scores lowest in terms of socio-economic development,[44] its high population density means that its overall development rating (calculated by combining both indexes) is greater than that of wealthier regions, for example Pelagonia (refer to regional GDP data in Appendix K).[45] Once again, the criteria used for allocating funding seem to favour sparsely populated areas at the expense of others, a practice which has ethnic implications in Macedonia.

Macedonia achieved significant progress in developing a comprehensive legal and institutional framework for regional development in only four years. The reforms suggest the allocation of development funds is now institutionalised, with the distribution of funding based on agreed priorities and pre-determined, published criteria.[46] The progress made also implies that an important shift in central and local stakeholders' approach to development has been accomplished and is now more focused on regional, as opposed to sectorial and local priorities.[47] However, this latter assumption may be premature, since a review of the types of projects funded by the Bureau for

Table 5.9 Classification of the planning regions according to the development index, 2008–2012

Planning region	Development index	Socio-economic index	Demographic index
Macedonia	1	1	1
East	0.67	0.95	0.5
Northeast	0.56	0.33	0.70
Pelagonia	0.73	0.79	0.69
Polog	0.72	0.18	1.05
Skopje	1.48	1.86	1.25
Southeast	0.89	1.38	0.58
Southwest	0.72	0.50	0.86
Vardar	0.69	0.63	0.73

Source: MoLSG (2009a: 7)

Regional Development between 2009 and 2011 suggests most do not include a regional component and instead benefit only one or two municipalities (OSCE 2011: 46).

The regional agenda's potential for promoting balanced economic growth and infrastructure development throughout Macedonia is however severely restricted by the very limited funding apportioned to it. Despite a law requiring funding of at least 1 per cent of GDP, since 2009 approximately only 0.05 per cent of GDP has been allocated to finance regional initiatives and actual funds have in fact fallen between 2009 and 2011 as a result of the effects of the global economic crisis on the Macedonian economy (OSCE 2011: 51).[48] Moreover, in 2009 the available funds were used only to establish the eight Centres for Regional Development and not to fund projects (Mojsovska 2011: 20). The amounts allocated for regional development also represent a significant fall in funding compared to the amounts previously assigned to the Bureau for Economically Underdeveloped Regions before 2008. This is despite the fact that the Bureau also received considerably less funding than it was entitled to (see data at Appendix Q).

In response to mounting criticism, in particular DUI's pre-election demand in June 2011 that more money be allocated to regional development, Prime Minister Gruevski claimed that the Government was in fact investing 1.1 per cent of GDP in local development initiatives (ICG 2011: 7; ZELS 2011b). However, this amount was distributed through the budgets of relevant line ministries and agencies, rather than through the appropriate regional institutions. Even if this claim is true, allocating funds in this way makes it very difficult to verify whether resources are being spent according to regional priorities, especially since the Ministry of Local Self-Government has yet to establish a system for monitoring regional progress.[49] It also means that decisions over spending remain centralised within line ministries, are vulnerable to political influence and are not made in a transparent manner which respects the views of the municipalities.[50]

One further issue which undermines the balanced regional development agenda is the fact that capital investments, including those referred to by Prime Minister Gruevski, continue to be allocated unfairly throughout the country. A review completed by the Center for Local Democracy Development found that, while accounting for only 25 per cent of the population, the ten Skopje municipalities received 70 per cent of total capital investments in 2010. In contrast, the remaining 33 urban municipalities, home to approximately 50 per cent of the population, received 20 per cent of capital spending, while the 41 rural municipalities received only 10 per cent (see also the data in Tables 5.7 and 5.8) (CLDD 2011b: 22). This means that the wealthiest municipalities, most capable of funding capital projects themselves, continue to benefit disproportionately from central government funds (Table 5.5). It also means that, in the absence of substantial investment in rural areas, little progress has been made to correct the distorted infrastructure networks of the past. This reality led Rufi Osmani, then mayor of Gostivar and leader of the Albanian party 'National Democratic Rebirth', to demand in 2011 that allocation of the state budget, and particularly of capital funds, be made proportional to the ethnic make-up of the country (Zenku and Ajrullau 2011: 3). The well-respected Albanian economist Abdylmenaf Bexheti has also called for all decisions regarding the allocation of public funds to be subject to the double-majority or 'Badinter' voting procedures (Bexheti 2011: 178). As Chapter 1 explains, the use of qualified voting procedures in both the Parliament and municipal councils is currently restricted largely to cultural matters.

The main cause of such distorted funding decisions is the Government's controversial facelift of the capital city, entitled 'Skopje 2014'. Launched in February 2010, this divisive urban renewal programme includes at least 20 buildings in neo-classical style, 17 large statues, 2 bridges with 28 monuments on each, a 'triumphal' marble arch and new parliamentary and government buildings within a 1-square-kilometre precinct.[51] The project has been dubbed a Balkan-style *Pirates of the Caribbean* theme park for its inclusion of a city beach and replica wooden galleons, in addition to a London-style big wheel and double-decker red buses (Marusic 2012). It has been widely criticised for its largely mono-ethnic portrayal of Macedonian cultural heritage, for increasing tensions between ethnic communities and between socialist and nationalist political camps, the illegal manner in which urban planning was approved, claims of state-sponsored money laundering and corruption and for damaging diplomatic relations with neighbouring Greece (Marusic 2010; Mijalkovic and Urbanek 2011; Surroi 2011; Transparency International Macedonia 2011; Vangeli 2011; Graan 2013). The initiative also inspired a rival Albanian project in Čair municipality, which added to claims that Skopje is fast becoming an ethnically divided city.[52]

However, it is the vast sums spent on this project which pose the greatest threat to Macedonia's territorial cohesion, raising questions regarding the Government's priorities during a global financial crisis.[53] Questions have also been raised concerning the risk that local priorities, affecting the lives of Skopje's citizens, have been ignored as a consequence.[54] Given the opaque manner in which work was procured, cost estimates vary widely between €250 million and €500 million (Marusic 2011b; Ilijevski 2012). To put these figures in perspective, even the conservative estimate is far greater than the €131,522,523 spent on regional development projects in all eight regions during 2011. Moreover, the 22-metre-high 'Warrior on Horseback' statue of Alexander the Great, estimated to have cost €9 million, represents more than 11 times the country's entire budget for preserving cultural heritage (Marusic 2011c; Ilijevski 2012).[55] It remains an open question, remarks fiscal decentralisation expert Tony Levitas, whether the developmental needs of an entire country are best served by spending almost half of all public revenue in the capital city where only 25 per cent of the population (at least officially) reside. Indeed, Levitas believes Macedonia is at risk of falling into a vicious circle, where increasing numbers will migrate to Skopje, putting ever greater financial pressure on the capital as public services deteriorate throughout the rest of the country (Levitas 2011a: 18–19).

Summary

This chapter has considered whether the fiscal autonomy ensuing from decentralisation was achieved at the expense of economic and territorial cohesion. The analysis began by considering the ongoing theoretical debate regarding decentralisation's ability to moderate territorial disparities within a country. The literature, while inconclusive, suggests that decentralisation may be less able to do so in developing and low-income countries. Certain aspects of Macedonia's model of decentralisation, along with its impact on the ability of municipalities to deliver basic services an equitable manner, were then discussed. This analysis found that, while municipal boundary changes in 2004 may have achieved implicit political objectives, the process created a substantial number of small municipalities with questionable fiscal and organisational capacities. This has had profound consequences on the ability of Macedonian municipalities to realise their enhanced competences, particularly when they have been devolved to them on a symmetrical basis. The design of fiscal decentralisation, with its over-dependence on property-related taxes, has been responsible for significant and growing fiscal disparities between urban and rural municipalities, and between Skopje and the rest of the country. This situation is exacerbated by the adoption of 'institutional', as opposed to 'functional' decentralisation, whereby those municipalities historically lacking the required institutions are ineligible to receive the necessary funds. Finally, this review has demonstrated how Macedonia's system of fiscal equalisation has been unable to offset the disparities that exist between the municipalities and in some instances has actually exacerbated them.

Given the Yugoslav legacy of concentrating investment in urban areas, has decentralisation led to a more equitable distribution of public resources throughout Macedonia? The short answer to this question is 'so far, no'. The design of fiscal decentralisation favours urban municipalities over rural ones and, paradoxically, over-compensates larger and less populous municipalities at the expense of more densely populated, smaller jurisdictions. It also does little to compensate those areas that have been marginalised in the past. Such practices entrench the urban–rural inequalities inherited from the socialist period and have important ethnic implications in Macedonia which should not be overlooked. Meanwhile, the dysfunctional system of equalisation and grossly unbalanced patterns of capital spending mean Macedonia's model of development remains mono-centric. In view of persistent and increasing fiscal disparities between municipalities and the regions, decentralisation has also done little to create the conditions required to expand citizens' access to basic services. In the absence of substantial capital investment in rural areas, those municipalities unable to deliver services in the past remain largely incapable of doing so. Co-operative arrangements with neighbouring munici-palities have, however, alleviated this problem in some instances.

Finally, it is clear that decentralisation has so far failed to reduce long-standing socio-economic disparities between urban and rural municipalities. Notably, Macedonia's decentralisation process led to the creation of fewer rather than additional rural municipalities and therefore reduced the num-ber of institutional channels through which rural areas can access resources independently.[56] It is beyond the scope of this chapter to ascertain whether enhancing municipal discretion over local funding priorities has facilitated a reduction in disparities between urban and rural areas *within* individual municipalities. However, given the very limited own-source revenue available in most municipalities outside of Skopje, it seems likely that elected municipal representatives will choose to concentrate investment in areas where voters are concentrated (i.e. urban), and particularly where support for the govern-ing local political party exists. Decentralisation is a process, not a one-off act, and experts recognise that policies designed to indirectly address horizontal disparities between ethnic communities are often slow and partial in their impact (Stewart *et al.* 2008c: 318). Macedonia's experience with decentralisa-tion is at a critical juncture and will require further reform to consolidate the process, particularly in the sphere of fiscal equalisation, if all municipalities (and citizens) are to benefit equally from its potential.

Notes

1 UNDP's Human Development Index is based on life expectancy, literacy and school enrolment rates and GDP per capita.
2 The report 'Ahmeti's Village' examines the political economy of inter-ethnic relations in Macedonia. The population of Dolneni in 2004 was 42 per cent Macedonian, 21

per cent Albanian and 22 per cent Turkish; Rosoman's was 89 per cent Macedonian and 10 per cent Serbs; and Zajas' was 97 per cent Albanian (ESI 2002a; SSO 2003).

3 Macedonia's eight regions are referred to as either 'statistical' or 'planning' regions and do not hold any political or institutional significance.

4 While the average GDP per capita in Polog is the lowest in the country, its mean household equivalised income is above the national average and is similar to that found in the Skopje region (Bartlett *et al.* 2010: 132–3).

5 According to the 2000 Labour Force Survey, the participation rates of Albanian women were 11 per cent, compared to 51 per cent for female Macedonians (World Bank 2009: 72).

6 According to the Law on the Stimulation of the Development of the Economically Underdeveloped Regions (1994: Articles 2 and 6), eligible regions were hilly/mountainous and border regions, and those where the degree of economic development was less than 75 per cent of the national average.

7 Article 17 of the Law on Local Self-Government (2002) states: 'The territory on which a municipality is established should represent a naturally, geographically and economically linked entity, with communication among populated places and gravitation towards the common centre, and it should have infrastructure facilities as well as facilities of social standard build therein.'

8 Interview with UNDP official: 12 November 2009, Skopje.

9 Interview with representative of the Delegation of the European Union to the Former Yugoslav Republic of Macedonia: 16 March 2012, Skopje.

10 Kičevo was eventually merged with four surrounding rural municipalities (Drugovo, Zajas, Oslomej and Vraneštica) in March 2013.

11 Drugovo is the second VMRO-DPMNE-led municipality with a population less than 5,000 to survive the reform.

12 Based on population statistics from the 2002 census.

13 The reform reduced the proportion of municipalities with fewer than 5,000 inhabitants from 37 per cent to 19 per cent and increased the share of municipalities with populations between 20,000 and 50,000 from 12 per cent to 30 per cent (Karajkov 2006: 16).

14 Interview with USAID project official: 14 June 2010, Skopje.

15 The exception is within Skopje, where the City of Skopje municipality provides secondary education, health, fire-fighting and water services for the citizens of the ten Skopje municipalities (Official Gazette 2004: Art. 10).

16 Interview with OSCE official: 24 March 2009, Skopje.

17 See Marko (2004/5) and Kreci and Ymeri (2010) for detailed analysis of the national referendum.

18 Interviews with: Foundation Open Society Macedonia official: 27 May 2010, Skopje; and two UNDP officials: 12 November 2009 and 26 June 2011, both in Skopje.

19 'Basic revenues' are revenues from all sources other than capital grants and grants for social sector functions.

20 The three poorest municipalities in Skopje are Šuto Orizari (Roma-majority), Čair and Saraj (both Albanian-majority); the richest are Aerodrom, Karpoš and Centar (all Macedonian-majority).

21 Interview with the head of a USAID fiscal decentralisation project: 10 May 2010, Skopje.

22 Interview with the executive director of ZELS: 20 March 2012, Skopje.

23 Interview with USAID project official: 14 June 2010, Skopje.

24 Interview with UNDP official: 29 June 2011, Skopje.

25 Interview with USAID project official: 14 June 2010, Skopje.

26 The fixed 3-million-Denar grant greatly enhances the revenues of the smaller, less populous municipalities, but the amount is relatively insignificant in more populous jurisdictions.

27 Interview with the head of a USAID fiscal decentralisation project: 10 May 2010, Skopje.
28 Recall that in 2010, non-Skopje municipalities received approximately 2.4 times the amount of revenue per capita from the VAT Fund than those which are part of the City of Skopje.
29 Interview with USAID project official: 14 March 2012, Skopje.
30 Interview with UNDP officials: 14 March 2012, Skopje.
31 The analysis of an individual municipality's fiscal imbalance is based on local PIT revenue, the number of registered residential properties and the number of square metres of residential property. The presence of a sizable grey economy in some jurisdictions, in addition to inconsistent tax collection rates and illegal construction, has adversely affected the reliability of this analysis.
32 Interview with the head of a USAID fiscal decentralisation project: 10 May 2010, Skopje.
33 Interview with the executive director of ZELS: 20 March 2012, Skopje.
34 Before fiscal decentralisation, property-related taxes collected locally and transferred to the treasury system were subject to a public expenditure limit (PEL) or 'mini-equalisation system'. The revenues distributed to each municipality were capped according to local expenditure needs and any excess was transferred into a common fund for equalisation purposes. 65 per cent of this surplus was subsequently allocated to poorer municipalities, while 35 per cent was distributed to those municipalities that had collected revenue above the cap as an incentive for maintaining high tax-collection rates in the future. Interview with USAID project official: 14 March 2012, Skopje.
35 Information available from UNDP's online database of IMC practice: www.imc. org.mk/index.php/en/dbase-of-imc-practices (accessed: 8 May 2012).
36 Interview with USAID project official: 14 March 2012, Skopje.
37 Some forms of IMC are, however, legally required, for example fire-fighting and the use of eight regional landfills. Interview with UNDP officials: 14 March 2012, Skopje.
38 Interview with UNDP official: 29 June 2011, Skopje.
39 Interview with UNDP officials: 14 March 2012, Skopje.
40 One local expert pointed out that, particularly in an election year (municipal elections were scheduled for March 2013), some mayors are afraid their political opponents will suggest the existence of IMC agreements with neighbours proves they are unable to deliver basic services to citizens without having to rely on the support of others. Interview with UNDP official: 14 March 2012, Skopje.
41 Interview with USAID project official: 14 June 2010, Skopje.
42 For example, (Albanian-majority) RDK-led Gostivar municipality provides fire protection services to (Macedonian-majority) VMRO-DPMNE-led Mavrovo and Rostuša. Interviews with: the head of local economic development office, Gostivar municipality: 28 June 2011, Gostivar; UNDP officials: 14 March 2012, Skopje.
43 An index of 1 indicates that the development of the region is equal to the national average. An index higher (or lower) than 1 indicates the development of the region is above (or below) the national average.
44 The economic-social index is based on GDP per capita, gross value added of the non-financial sector, fiscal revenues per capita and the rate of unemployment.
45 The demographic index is based on the rate of population growth, the ageing coefficient, rate of migration and the proportion of university degrees per 1,000 inhabitants.
46 Interview with UNDP officials: 14 March 2012, Skopje.
47 Interview with a representative of the Ministry of Local Self-Government: 29 June 2011.

48 Interview with representative of the Delegation of the European Union to the Former Yugoslav Republic of Macedonia: 16 March 2012, Skopje. Funding for balanced regional development fell from 188,300,000 MKD in 2009, to 168,800,000 MKD in 2010 and 131,522,523 MKD in 2011 (OSCE 2011: 51).

49 Articles 10 and 57 of the Law on Balanced Regional Development states the Ministry will monitor the process of regional development. Interview with UNDP officials: 14 March 2012, Skopje.

50 Interview with UNDP official: 29 June 2011, Skopje.

51 The Government's promotional video of the project, entitled 'Macedonia Timeless Capital Skopje 2014', is available at: www.youtube.com/watch?v=iybmt-iLysU (accessed: 10 May 2012).

52 Interview with municipal councillor in Čair municipality: 1 July 2011, Skopje. A promotional video of the project 'Sheshi Skenderbeu' (Skenderbeu Square) is available at: www.youtube.com/watch?v=lxgGGZ4fsF4 (accessed: 10 May 2012).

53 Interview with representative of the Delegation of the European Union to the Former Yugoslav Republic of Macedonia: 16 March 2012, Skopje.

54 Centar municipality has been obliged to spend a proportion of its local budget on monuments while priorities such as the renovation of primary school buildings, canalisation and traffic management remain unfunded. Interview with a senior employee of Centar municipality: 1 July 2011, Skopje.

55 'Warrior on Horseback' ('*Voin na Konj*' in Macedonian) is the official name the Government gave to the statue of Alexander the Great in order to avoid possible retaliation from Greece.

56 Often decentralisation leads to the creation of new municipalities, for example in neighbouring Kosovo.

Conclusion

Decentralisation alone is unable to address all of the grievances raised by Albanian politicians and the NLA during Macedonia's first decade as an independent state. Given the multifaceted concerns of the Albanian community during this period, this is hardly surprising. However, the reform does have the potential to directly as well as indirectly address many of the inequalities that were responsible for raising tensions between the Macedonian and Albanian communities during the 1990s. Importantly, it may do so by remaining sensitive to the concerns of the majority Macedonian community.

Based on the empirical evidence contained in this study, this chapter assesses the extent to which decentralisation has contributed to the management of ethnic conflict in Macedonia over the years 2005–12. It evaluates whether the reform has lived up to expectations and has indeed contributed to conflict-reduction. It will also consider the extent to which decentralisation, and its combined use of power-sharing mechanisms locally, has simultaneously addressed the concerns of local minorities, including the Macedonian community residing in Albanian-dominated municipalities. The first part of this concluding chapter will finally consider whether decentralisation has had any adverse effects on Macedonia's fractious inter-ethnic relations. Decentralisation is no panacea and research findings from the few empirical studies that have examined the decentralisation–conflict nexus have so far been mixed.

Where decentralisation's potential has not been reached, the second part of this concluding chapter identifies obstacles to decentralisation's successful implementation. This analysis distinguishes between factors related to the particular design that decentralisation in Macedonia took, and the political, social and economic context within which the reform has so far been implemented. Accordingly, this book will contribute to a more nuanced understanding of the challenges facing different forms of decentralisation in the longer term. It will also offer insight into the optimum conditions required for decentralisation to promote sustainable peace in Macedonia. The chapter ends with suggestions for further research.

Decentralisation's ability to address inequalities in the Republic of Macedonia

Political inequalities

The decentralisation of 11 new competences to the municipal level has undoubtedly enhanced the ability of communities that are a minority nationally, but which constitute a majority at the local level, to have greater political (although not necessarily fiscal) control over their own affairs. The reform has addressed a significant demand of Albanian politicians and later the NLA for greater internal self-determination. Chapter 2 considered whether the decentralisation process in Macedonia has contributed to widening the effective political participation of diverse communities in local decision-making processes and has also strengthened local democracy. As Chapter 1 explained, the inability of mainstream politicians to address the political, cultural, social, and economic grievances of the Albanian community during the 1990s had led to an erosion of trust in the political class among ordinary Albanians. Broadening political participation through decentralisation at the local level creates alternative sites of power and patronage for local elites and is believed to help legitimise government institutions in the eyes of previously marginalised and disenchanted groups.

Based on the empirical findings, Chapter 2 shows that while decentralisation has certainly expanded the potential space available for citizens to participate in local governance – either directly or through elected representatives, it has guaranteed neither the participation of diverse local communities, nor that this participation is both equitable and effective. The capture of local institutions by national political parties, operating tightly controlled candidate lists, has done little to facilitate independent candidates and smaller local parties entering public life. Further, the immense resources required to satisfy horizontal clientelistic relationships between political parties and local citizens has made it very difficult for would-be challengers (either independent or opposition candidates) to establish credibility as a potential alternative source of benefits. This has significantly reduced the competitiveness of local democracy in Macedonia. A pervasive 'culture of passivity' among citizens also represents a significant challenge to the success of participatory practices at the local level. The low proportion of citizens that had either participated in municipal activities or intend to do so in the future (see Table 2.1) suggests that citizens are generally not interested in exercising their voice or in holding local political representatives to account.

Chapter 2 also appraised the effectiveness of various consociational power-sharing tools envisaged at the local level. The combined use of local power-sharing mechanisms with territorial self-government in this way represents an example of complex power-sharing and is essential for ensuring that local minorities, including Macedonians living in municipalities dominated by a different ethnic community, are not politically marginalised and become 'foreigners in their own country'.

While the implementation of local power-sharing mechanisms remains in its infancy, seven years of experience is sufficient to demonstrate how vulnerable these tools are to being highjacked by the dominant political parties and by those ethnic groups which constitute a majority locally. The result is that these minority protection mechanisms have so far not been effective in ensuring local democratic processes remain inclusive. For example, with regard to the realisation of equitable representation in municipal administrations, there is considerable evidence to suggest that mayors regularly favour their own (ethnic) party supporters in the recruitment of new employees and show little regard for candidates' skills and experience. Reports of large-scale dismissals in the wake of local elections are further evidence of the politicisation of local public administrations. As the political party governing the largest number of Albanian-dominated municipalities since 2005, DUI has equally disenfranchised Albanians who are not party members from potential positions in the local civil service and public administration.

Qualified voting procedures, designed to ensure greater consensus in municipal council decision-making, have also been made ineffective by the dominant political parties. This power-sharing mechanism is rarely used at the local level and, in most cases, political deals between the major parties on sensitive local issues are made 'behind closed doors' and long before the issue is debated in municipal councils. Such practice makes this local minority protection mechanism irrelevant. Restrictions on its use also mean that the mechanism is unable to protect the views of minority communities in many areas of importance to them, for example, education provision and adoption of the municipal work programme and budget. Further, while it is admirable that so many municipalities have established Committees for Inter-Community Relations, even though they are not all obliged to do so, their effectiveness remains questionable. The Committees' ability to facilitate institutional dialogue between different ethnic groups has been hindered by poor operational capacity, unclear competences, a lack of resources and their marginalisation by municipal councils. As with municipal administrations, their membership has also become frequently politicised and often fails to reflect the ethnic structure of the local population they are intended to represent.

It is important to emphasise that Macedonia's smaller ethnic communities, living scattered throughout the country, generally fail to benefit from these three consociational-inspired protection mechanisms. Macedonians and Albanians residing in small numbers in those municipalities where another ethnic community is in the majority are subject to a similar fate. There is also a danger that these local power-sharing mechanisms will continue to advance the interests of (some) ethnic communities at the expense of broader intra-ethnic relations, i.e. between members of different political parties.

Cultural status inequalities

Chapter 1 demonstrated how restrictions on the use of community languages and symbols at the local level represented two cultural status inequalities that increased tensions between the Macedonian and Albanian communities during the 1990s. Albanian politicians, and later the NLA, demanded that the right to use their language in municipalities where significant Albanian communities reside be reinstated, and that the Albanian flag be permitted to fly outside public buildings in Albanian-majority municipalities.

Devolving the management of controversial issues such as the use of community languages and flags to the municipal level has gone some way to diluting Albanian cultural status demands. While Albanian politicians have so far been unable to realise their request that Albanian become a second official language state-wide, reducing the threshold for the mandatory use of community languages from 50 to 20 per cent of the local population has meant that Albanian has acquired official status in 29 of the 85 municipalities, including (significantly) the capital City of Skopje. This means that the official use of the Albanian language has become mandatory in more than a third of Macedonia's municipalities. Similarly, displays of the Albanian flag alongside the state (Macedonian) flag are permitted outside public buildings in the 16 municipalities where local Albanian communities constitute more than 50 per cent of inhabitants.

However, the positive impact of having Albanian as a second 'language in official use' in so many municipalities has been restricted by the various challenges experienced in its implementation. Difficulties are particularly prevalent in the 13 municipalities where Albanians do not form a majority (but represent at least 20 per cent of the local population), i.e. where the mayor is from a different ethnic group and where the political strength of Albanian parties in the municipal council is weak. The fact that municipalities do not receive additional state resources to fund associated costs, such as the salaries of translators or interpreters, represents another significant barrier. Similarly, realisation of the enhanced use of community flags has also been beset with problems. While amendments to the 2005 law on the use of flags in 2011 eventually reconfirmed the right of local majority communities to display their flag alongside the state flag, the state flag must now be one third larger in size than the community flags.

As with the use of consociational power-sharing mechanisms locally, the dispersal of the Turkish, Roma, Serbian and Vlach communities throughout Macedonia means that in most municipalities these smaller communities fall well below the thresholds required to benefit from rights permitting the enhanced use of community languages and symbols. The use of languages other than Albanian and Macedonian is consequently obligatory in only six municipalities (approximately 7 per cent), while flags of the smaller communities may only be used in three municipalities.

Social inequalities

Dissatisfaction with the availability of Albanian-medium education during the 1990s represented a significant social inequality experienced by Macedonia's Albanian community and which exacerbated inter-ethnic tensions. The recentralisation of education provision during the 1990s also meant that decisions over spending became less transparent and exacerbated the perception that funding decisions were being made at the expense of non-majority communities. Acquiring greater local administrative and financial responsibility for the provision of primary and secondary education services, it was assumed, would reduce perceived inequalities in their quality and availability. Chapter 3 therefore examined whether decentralisation has improved access to mother-tongue education by facilitating the provision of heterogeneous local public services, enhancing participation and transparency in local decision-making and ensuring a more equitable and transparent distribution of public resources.

The empirical evidence confirms that the provision of Albanian- as well as Turkish-medium education has generally improved since responsibility for its provision was devolved to the municipalities in 2005. However, the experiences of the smaller communities in accessing education in their mother tongue – either as the language of instruction or in elective classes – have been less positive. The proportion of Albanian students attending primary education in their mother tongue was already high (97.93 per cent in 2004/5), and improved further in the following years (98.44 in 2010/11). Similarly, while the proportion of Turkish students attending primary education in their mother tongue has historically been much lower than for Albanian students, this too increased, from 58.45 per cent in 2004/5 to 67.06 per cent in 2010/11.

However, the data for secondary education shows a slightly different picture. Here, the proportion of Albanian students attending classes in their mother tongue is lower (95.02 per cent in 2010/11), but has also increased in recent years (up from 94.82 per cent in 2004/5). Interestingly, while the number of Albanian students attending Albanian-medium classes has been on the increase, so too has the total number of Albanians attending secondary school generally. The result is that the proportion of Albanian students attending Albanian-medium classes actually fell between 2004/5 and 2009/10, but improved in 2010/11 when the proportion stood at 95.02 per cent. This has not, however, been the experience of Turkish students, who have accessed Turkish-medium secondary education in increasing numbers. The official data, corroborated by municipal education officers, therefore suggests that, with the exception of a few controversial cases, since decentralisation began it has become relatively easy for municipalities to open new classes where the language of instruction is either Albanian or Turkish.

The analysis in Chapter 3 also suggests that enhanced community involvement in decision-making processes has promoted greater democratic governance within schools. It has also allowed what were once highly contentious issues, such as the renaming of schools or the opening of a new school, to be generally resolved on a rational basis. While some school boards may operate as 'mini municipal councils', with the appointment of representatives being highly politicised and discussions dominated by only a handful of members, many school boards do function well. However, ensuring their membership fully reflects the local student population they serve is an ongoing challenge, with Roma students being particularly under-represented in these structures.

A further potential benefit of decentralisation was to facilitate a more equitable and transparent distribution of education resources. The empirical evidence contained in Chapter 3 confirms that moving to a per-capita education funding formula in 2006 undoubtedly facilitated a more equitable distribution of funds through block and earmarked education grants. Basing funding calculations on the number of students attending school rather than on historical costs meant that funds flow directly to where they are needed. The use of lump sum payments, in addition to weights for schools located in sparsely populated areas, also ensures that the higher costs of delivering educational services in rural areas are met. In addition, using a pre-defined allocation formula has improved transparency in the distribution of resources and has reduced the possibility of discretionary payments from central government. Nevertheless, challenges remain and further work could be done to fine-tune the funding formulae to ensure rural municipalities do not receive too much relative to their urban counterparts. The fact that key financial elements of the formulae are not routinely made public, even to the municipalities, also suggests that greater effort could be made to ensure local stakeholders understand its impact on education financing.

Two crucial areas where per-capita funding is unable to address funding inequalities in education, and which disproportionately affect Albanian students, are the process by which resources are distributed at the school level (between the central school and its branches) and the allocation of capital expenditure to the municipalities. The analysis in Chapter 3 illustrated how approximately two-thirds of all primary school facilities are satellite or branch schools, with a large proportion providing instruction in languages other than Macedonian. Their unequal treatment is 'like a family secret', which everyone knows but does not want to talk about. Significant disparities exist in the physical condition of central and satellite school buildings, in addition to students' access to teaching materials and pedagogical support staff. This unresolved issue clearly impacts on the equity of educational standards throughout Macedonia and between the different ethnic groups.

A further issue left unaddressed by changes in the calculation of block and earmarked education grants is the distribution of capital expenditure to the municipalities. As the discussions in Chapters 1 and 5 have demonstrated, given socialist planning's tendency to concentrate public infrastructure in cities and towns, many rural areas that are home to sizable Albanian and Turkish communities remain outside the secondary school network. Significant capital investment is therefore needed to address persistent disparities in these previously neglected areas. Substantial investment is also required to counter the effects of uneven demographic growth, which has resulted in significant overcrowding in many urban secondary schools. However, capital grants for school infrastructure projects remain under the control of central government and, as the evidence in Chapters 3 and 4 suggests, their allocation lacks transparency and is highly vulnerable to discretionary decision-making. The prevailing perception – real or imagined – is therefore that capital funds are largely distributed to those municipalities aligned with the governing coalition parties. While the municipalities are legally competent to rationalise the local school network, the ability of some to access the capital investments required to build new schools or extend current facilities is severely constrained. The result is that overcrowding remains in significant problem in many schools, with some required to operate multiple class shifts in order to accommodate students.

Economic inequalities

The analysis in Chapter 1 illustrated how high levels of unemployment, a general decline in living standards, and chronic rural under-development formed the backdrop to Albanian politicians' demands during the 1990s. The economic context to inter-ethnic conflict was examined further in Chapter 5. This assessment demonstrated how significant and persistent disparities between urban and rural areas were a legacy of Yugoslav times and often had unintended ethnic consequences. The result was that citizens' access to basic public services was restricted in some rural areas, a situation which led to significant levels of social exclusion, particularly within non-majority communities. Decentralisation is believed to alleviate disparities between regions by promoting a more equitable distribution of state resources, and by facilitating economic development through increased public sector efficiency.

Chapter 5 considered whether decentralisation in Macedonia has facilitated a more equitable distribution of public resources, created the optimal conditions for expanding citizens' access to basic services and reduced long-standing socio-economic disparities between urban and rural areas. It did not, however, evaluate whether the reform has promoted economic development and reduced poverty through job creation, because it is unclear whether these claims can be ascribed to decentralisation alone, as state economic policies and rates of foreign direct investment would also clearly have an impact.

With regard to the equitable distribution of public resources, as the previous section has already discussed, significant improvements in the allocation of education funding were achieved by the adoption of a per-capita funding formula in 2006. However, and despite a legal requirement to do so, the allocation of grants to finance the provision of cultural services, social welfare and child protection remains based on historical costs. This means that funding for the realisation of these competences is dependent on the existence of a physical facility within a municipality's territory. Those municipalities historically lacking such facilities receive no funding and are unable to even 'buy in' services from neighbouring municipalities or the private sector. This form of 'institutional' as opposed to 'functional' decentralisation does nothing to facilitate a more equitable distribution of public resources, or create the optimal conditions for expanding citizens' access to basic services. Instead, it reinforces pre-existing disparities between urban and rural areas.

A second aspect of fiscal decentralisation which inhibits the reform's ability to reduce socio-economic disparities between urban and rural areas is its over-reliance on property-related taxes to provide municipal revenues. This feature, examined at length in Chapters 4 and 5, favours those (urban) municipalities with real-estate markets, rather than their rural counterparts. The same applies to the municipalities' share of PIT, which benefits those (predominantly urban) areas with more developed local economies. The result is that discrepancies in municipal own-source revenues, between urban and rural areas and between Skopje and towns outside of the capital, have actually intensified since decentralisation began. Attempts to reduce inequalities through fiscal equalisation and regional development have so far been unsuccessful and have in fact – pervasively – exacerbated current inequalities. The presence of such significant horizontal disparities impacts negatively upon the municipalities' ability to provide basic services to citizens in an equitable manner. It also limits the ability of poorer municipalities to invest locally in expanding public services and funding much-needed infrastructure programmes.

One final issue that undermines decentralisation's ability to alleviate socio-economic disparities between regions is the grossly unbalanced patterns of capital spending that favour Skopje over the rest of the country, and wealthier urban municipalities at the expense of their poorer rural counterparts. This means that the wealthiest municipalities, most capable of funding capital projects through their own-source revenues, continue to benefit disproportionately from central government funds. It also means that little progress has been made to compensate those predominantly rural areas that have been marginalised in the past. In the absence of substantial capital investment in these areas, those municipalities unable to deliver services in the past remain largely incapable of doing so. Despite (limited) efforts to establish a system of balanced regional development, Macedonia's model of development remains principally mono-centric.

Decentralisation and ethnic conflict: some counterproductive effects

To summarise, based on empirical evidence from seven years of the reform's implementation, decentralisation has positively addressed some of the inequalities that existed between the Albanian and Macedonian communities before 2001. First, devolving additional competences to the municipal level has enhanced the political control diverse communities have over the management of local affairs. Second, the creation of alternative sites of power for local elites has expanded the space available for citizens to participate in local governance. Third, devolving the management of controversial issues such as the use of community languages and flags to the municipal level has gone some way towards diluting Albanian cultural status demands. Finally, decentralising responsibility for the delivery of primary and secondary education has also contributed positively to the management of inter-ethnic tensions. Access to mother-tongue education has improved, community involvement in local decision-making processes has increased and education funds are now distributed in a more equitable and transparent manner.

However, decentralisation may also have had adverse effects on inter-community relations. For example, because the reform benefits only territorially concentrated groups, Macedonia's smaller ethnic communities, living scattered throughout the country, generally fail to benefit from its consociational-inspired power-sharing mechanisms. Macedonians and Albanians residing in small numbers in municipalities where another ethnic community may be in the majority are subject to a similar fate. The smaller communities may have been more capable of accessing primary and secondary education in their mother tongue had a more personal, rather than territorial, form of autonomy been applied. However, the Framework Agreement was never actually designed to offer equal protection to all Macedonia's ethnic communities, since its principle aim had been to address the grievances of the Albanian community and, in doing so, avert further conflict. A consequence of this may be that Macedonia has moved a step closer to becoming a bi-national state, rather than the multi-national state anticipated by its Constitution's Preamble (Engström 2002a; Vankovska 2006).

A second example where decentralisation may have had a counterproductive effect on inter-community relations is the growing trend of ethnic segregation in both primary and secondary schools, examined in Chapter 3. This threatens to undermine the cohesion of Macedonian society. While this phenomenon is not a direct consequence of the decentralisation process, the enhanced 'voice' local politicians, teachers and parents now have in deciding important educational matters may have exacerbated this trend. Similarly, improvements in the provision of mother-tongue education, which necessitates students being taught in separate classes according to the language of instruction, may have been made at the expense of social cohesion. The municipalities may not have been responsible for starting this trend; however, it appears they are doing very little to reverse it.

Third, as the previous section has mentioned, aspects of fiscal decentralisation have in fact intensified discrepancies in own-source revenues between urban and rural municipalities. Attempts to reduce inequalities through fiscal equalisation and regional development have so far failed and have actually exacerbated current inequalities. This means that some municipalities have been unable to expand citizens' access to basic services as desired and significant levels of social exclusion remain.

Table 6.1 Decentralisation's ability to address inequalities in the Republic of Macedonia

Inequalities	Addressed by decentralisation?
Political participation	
Broadened political participation by creating alternative sites of power (mayors and councillors)	**Yes/partially:** • Devolved competences have enhanced communities' political control over own local affairs • Space for citizens to participate in local governance has expanded • Party capture has reduced the competitiveness of local democracy • Weak internal party democracy and clientelism have undermined local political autonomy • 'Culture of passivity' among citizens weakens local democracy • Limited fiscal autonomy has constrained local political autonomy
Proportional representation in municipal and local public administrations	**Yes/partially:** • New jobs created in municipal and local public administrations • Politicisation of process disenfranchises non-party members (of ruling coalition) and smaller communities
Power-sharing mechanisms to protect local minorities	**Generally no:** • Qualified voting procedures are rarely used and are ineffective • CICRs are ineffective and fail to represent local ethnic communities • Mechanisms unable to protect the needs of smaller communities
Cultural status	
Use of community languages at the municipal level	**Yes/partially:** • Albanian has acquired official status in a third of municipalities • Practical and political obstacles remain regarding language use • Smaller communities rarely benefit from right to use language
Use of community flags and symbols at the municipal level	**Yes/partially:** • Albanian flag on display in 16 municipalities • Smaller communities rarely benefit from right to display symbols

Social aspects

Access to education in mother tongue at primary and secondary levels

Yes/partially:
- Provision of Albanian- and Turkish-medium education has improved
- Smaller communities less able to access mother-tongue education

Enhanced community involvement in decision-making processes

Generally yes:
- School boards have increased local community involvement
- Politicisation of membership and ethnic representation remain challenges

Equitable and transparent distribution of education resources

Yes/partially:
- Per-capita formula has improved equity and transparency
- Distribution of funds and resources remains inequitable at school level
- Inequitable allocation of capital grants for school infrastructure

Economic aspects

Improve access to public employment at all levels

Yes/partially:
- New jobs created in municipal and local public administrations
- Politicisation of process disenfranchises non-party members (of ruling coalition) and smaller communities

Rural under-development and equitable access to basic public services

No:
- Fiscal reforms exacerbate disparities in own-source revenues
- Some grants dependent on existence of a physical facility
- Inequitable allocation of capital grants reinforces inequalities
- Fiscal equalisation and regional development has been ineffective

Finally, there is evidence to suggest that the use of consociational-inspired power-sharing mechanisms at the local level has increased the saliency of ethnicity within municipalities. The empirical data suggests that some smaller communities, such as the Torbeš, are feeling the pressure to assimilate with more dominant ethnic groups. The controversial request to open Albanian-medium classes in a primary school in Podgorci, Struga municipality, where the students involved are Macedonian Muslims, is one example of such assimilationist tendencies. The fact that the 2011 population census was abandoned because it became 'marred by ethnic rows' is further evidence of the enduring contentious of nature of ethnic demographics in Macedonia. Since the recognition of community languages comes as a function of demographics, rather than as a symbolic recognition of their equal status with the Macedonian language, it is possible decentralisation may have exacerbated this longstanding tension (Marusic 2011a).

Obstacles to the successful implementation of decentralisation in the Republic of Macedonia

Design features: symmetry and an over-reliance on property-related own-source revenue

With regard to the design of decentralisation, what matters most is the degree to which the reform addresses the concerns and demands of conflicting parties, and whether it reflects the structural conditions of the conflict situation (Wolff 2012: 32). Considering the territorial distribution of the Albanian community in Macedonia, decentralisation to the local level is more suitable for addressing Albanian concerns than other forms of self-government, for example federalism or autonomy (territorial or personal).[1] The ethnic heterogeneity of Albanian-majority areas also requires that Macedonia's decentralisation model incorporates local power-sharing mechanisms. As this study has argued throughout, decentralisation, in its design and choice of devolved competences, has the potential to address most of the demands of Albanian political elites and the masses simultaneously, while remaining sensitive to the concerns of the Macedonian majority.

However, there are two particular features of decentralisation's design that have failed to address the structural conditions of the conflict situation in Macedonia. The first is the decision to devolve competences to the municipalities on a symmetrical basis, despite the existence of significant inequalities in their size and fiscal capacity. Consequently, municipalities such as Rosoman, with a total staff of six, are tasked with delivering the same functions and services to citizens as Strumica and Tetovo municipalities with 134 and 158 employees respectively. It is therefore inevitable that the smaller, less well-endowed municipalities will experience serious challenges in the realisation of their competences. A structural feature of the Macedonian environment which exacerbates this situation is the existence of longstanding socio-economic disparities between urban and rural areas.[2] So far, the success of short-term solutions, such as inter-municipal co-operation agreements, in addressing this problem has been mixed. Unless the situation is resolved in a more systematic manner, significant parts of the Macedonian population will remain marginalised, without equitable access to basic services. It is possible that these areas may once again provide fertile ground for social and political instability.

One further design feature of Macedonian decentralisation which provides an obstacle to the reform's successful implementation is its over-reliance on property-related taxes to provide municipal revenues. The consequence is that those predominantly rural areas that have been most marginalised in the past remain least capable of funding much-needed local infrastructure projects themselves. Other features of fiscal decentralisation which have been shown to exacerbate regional disparities, i.e. 'institutional' as opposed to 'functional' decentralisation and unbalanced patterns of capital spending, are the result of abuses of the reform's design, rather than of decentralisation itself, and are therefore not discussed here.

Contextual factors: a political climate that is not conducive to decentralisation

In their review of institutional designs in conflict-torn societies, Sunil Bastian and Robin Luckham point out that 'often it is not the formal institutional choices that are important, so much as the politics surrounding them' (Bastian and Luckham 2003: 305). Democratic institutions are never introduced in a political and economic vacuum. Researchers of decentralisation have become increasingly aware of how international donors tend to focus on the attainment of normatively desirable outcomes with very little consideration or understanding of the politics behind them (Manor 1999; Cheema and Rondinelli 2007). Scholars have also observed how international agencies are inclined to frame decentralisation programmes on the basis of normative Western conceptual models which embody explicit or implicit assumptions that may not always apply in developing and transition country contexts (Litvack *et al.* 1998; Connerley *et al.* 2010). It is important that this concluding chapter therefore reconsiders how the motives of political elites, changes to the national economy and the political configuration of party politics have influenced decentralisation's chances of success.

An assessment of the motives behind Macedonia's decision to decentralise power to the municipal level found that the political environment within which the reform had been conceived and implemented may not have been conducive to its success. Initially, because the reform represents part of the wider Ohrid Framework Agreement package, majority Macedonian political parties had been placed under great pressure from external actors to decentralise. As the analysis in Chapter 1 demonstrates, before conflict in 2001, there had been very little political will to devolve further political and fiscal responsibilities to the municipalities. This suggests that there may have been very little genuine enthusiasm to decentralise among Macedonian political circles at the time the reform was adopted. Given the international community's involvement, decentralisation may also have lacked legitimacy and local ownership in the eyes of citizens. Peace, note Lake and Rothchild (2005: 110), consolidates majority power, and it is possible that the dominant political parties may have used their political strength to recentralise state authority and resources once the immediate political crisis had receded.

Analysis of the electoral strength of Macedonia's largest political parties between 1998 and 2011 also suggests that fluctuations in the electoral strength of the governing parties, and in particular a change of government in 2006, may have adversely affected central government's commitment to decentralise (Roeder and Rothchild's 'transient majority problem'). SDSM's strength at the local level until 2009, for example, suggests that there has been very little political incentive for VMRO-DPMNE to consolidate the reform process since the latter came to power at the central level in 2006. To do so would mean reducing the control the party had in central government and rewarding political rivals at the local level. The electoral strength that both VMRO-DPMNE and DUI have enjoyed concurrently at the central and local levels also suggests that these governing parties may prefer to rely on (party-controlled) inter-governmental transfers and capital grants to fund devolved competences, rather than enhance local fiscal autonomy. The effect of the global economic crisis on the Macedonian economy since 2009 adds further credence to the government's preference for keeping a tight hold on public spending and maintaining macroeconomic stability rather than devolving additional fiscal responsibility to the municipalities. The outcome of future municipal elections will be critical for determining whether central government continues to support the decentralisation reforms or will seek to reverse progress made to date.

One further feature of Macedonian politics which has not made the political environment conducive to decentralisation is the overwhelming dominance of national political parties at the municipal level. As Chapter 2 demonstrated, since 2009 the four largest national parties have controlled over 90 per cent of all municipalities.[3] The number of independent mayors and candidates representing smaller, local parties has consequently declined since the start of decentralisation. Similarly, the two main parties in the central government coalition in mid-2012 (VMRO-DPMNE and DUI) controlled over 80 per cent of all municipalities. This means that there is very little room for dissent between local and state level political priorities. It also means that the municipal association 'ZELS', the only formal channel available to the municipalities for raising local concerns at the central level within the unitary state, has become dominated by mayors representing central government-aligned municipalities. According to one local government expert in Macedonia, 'ZELS' hands are completely tied'.[4]

Contextual factors: undemocratic parties undermine democratic decentralisation

Successful decentralisation requires the central government to be genuinely prepared to share power with sub-central units, and both the central and local levels must regard each other as equally authorised partners. However, high levels of central control and member discipline within Macedonian political parties implies the subordination of local politicians in party structures at the expense of local democracy. The dominance of VMRO-DPMNE and DUI at both municipal and parliamentary levels also suggests that the potential for national parties to exercise control over their local counterparts is considerable. Gordana Siljanovska-Davkova has observed how most parties in Macedonia continue to operate under organisational principles inherited from the League of Communists. Parallels can therefore be made with McGarry and O'Leary's description of the Soviet Union as a 'sham pluralist federation', in which real power lay in the tightly centralised Communist Party (McGarry and O'Leary 2011: 259). In August 2004, the ICG observed how party reform is the missing element in consolidation of Macedonia's democratic political system (ICG 2004: 10). In the absence of such reform, the question remains whether 'non-democratic parties, operating within a non-democratic structure' can bring democracy to Macedonia (ICG 2011: 9).

A second feature of Macedonian politics which undermines the autonomy of local politicians is the existence of vertical clientelistic relationships within parties. Such relations allow party leaders to maintain control over political decisions as well as state resources by nominating loyal, subservient 'clients' at the municipal level. Examples of this practice include the municipalities' fiscal dependency on discretionary, ad hoc inter-governmental transfers and on pork-barrel projects designed to reward loyal constituents. What may appear to be representative local governments, responsive to the needs of local citizens, may in reality only be a deconcentration of central government. Left unchecked, patron–client relations within political parties can undermine the benefits associated with decentralisation by limiting the effectiveness of municipal administrations and by making them less accountable to local citizens. Vertical clientelistic relationships may even weaken the legitimacy of the new democratic order itself.

Contextual factors: limited fiscal autonomy undermines political and administrative decentralisation

The detailed examination of the revenue, expenditure and contractual autonomy of Macedonian municipalities in Chapter 4 suggests that decentralisation has done little to restrain central government's monopoly of state power and resources. As a result, Macedonia's decentralisation has been only partial. Limited access to own-source revenues and an over-dependence on insufficient, and often discretionary, inter-governmental transfers imply that the revenue autonomy of municipalities is weak.[5] Stringent expenditure mandates for block grants and the frequent freezing of municipal bank accounts on account of unpaid arrears indicate that the expenditure autonomy of the municipalities remains tightly constrained by the centre. Finally, the limited ability of municipalities to enter into financial contracts with different sets of private actors suggests that their contractual autonomy is also fragile. These aspects of fiscal decentralisation are the result of a conscious political decision by central government to maintain power, rather than a general design feature of decentralisation per se. The result is that Macedonia appears to be more decentralised than it really is because the political and administrative aspects of decentralisation are more visible than the discrete and complex fiscal regulations that undermine the reform's potential.

This study confirms that while constitutionally guaranteed decentralisation processes may be harder to reverse than others, such reversal is not impossible. Administrative and political aspects of decentralisation may be constitutionally guaranteed, but a municipality's right to meaningful fiscal autonomy is not. Rules pertaining to the management of fiscal decentralisation are defined in legislation which can be easily amended, and there is evidence to suggest that central government has in fact acted contrary to its own legal procedures on some occasions.[6]

Tulia Falleti (2005) has observed how political, administrative and fiscal decentralisation may be rolled out in different sequences on the basis of politically motivated strategies. For example, where democratisation is the reform's principal objective, establishing mechanisms for the election of local representatives is likely to be a priority. When national politicians devolve powers in order to more effectively harness resources for developmental ends, fiscal aspects of decentralisation may become further advanced. Connerley *et al.* argue that when decentralisation is introduced as a security-enhancing reform, local governments are often given greater administrative control over the provision of public services, such as education, rather than enhanced fiscal or political powers (Connerley *et al.* 2010: 169). If this observation is applied to the Macedonian context, it suggests that the partial implementation of decentralisation may not be accidental, but rather represents a conscious decision on behalf of central government to maintain overall control. Non-simultaneous transfers of political, administrative and fiscal powers pose fewer threats to politicians at the centre; as does the simultaneous transfer of only *limited* amounts of administrative, fiscal and political authority (Eaton *et al.* 2010: 19).

As this integrated assessment of decentralisation's implementation in Macedonia has shown, progress in one of the reform's dimensions, i.e. administrative aspects, does not necessarily mean that improvements have simultaneously occurred in its other dimensions, i.e. fiscal decentralisation and, to a certain extent, political decentralisation. Figure 6.1 illustrates how the political, administrative and fiscal dimensions of decentralisation in Macedonia

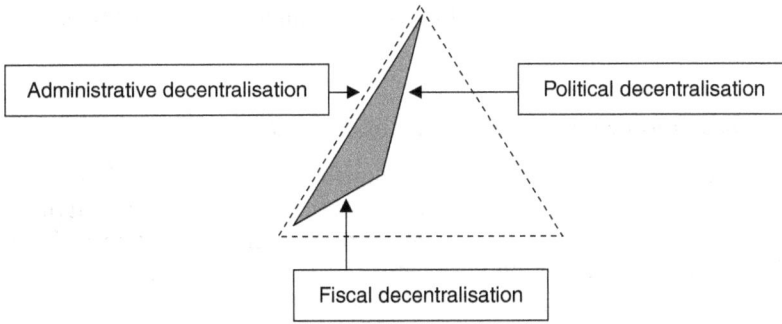

Figure 6.1 The sequencing of different decentralisation dimensions in the Republic of Macedonia

(represented by the small grey triangle) have not occurred at a balanced pace (symbolised by the larger triangle). This review has also shown that changes in decentralisation's political, administrative and fiscal dimensions may not always occur in the same direction. The increasing dominance of national parties in local politics, for example, has meant that political decentralisation has actually become more centralising over time. While the sequencing of decentralisation in a post-conflict environment may be justified in the short term, attempts to solve internal self-determination conflicts through decentralisation in the longer term will fail if self-government continues to exist only in form but not in substance.

Contextual factors: a 'culture of passivity' among citizens

The presence of a vibrant, inclusive civil society is another important precondition for successful decentralisation. Decentralisation alone is insufficient for fostering democratic processes conducive to conflict management. However, the low proportion of Macedonian citizens that had either participated in municipal activities or intend to do so in the future suggests that citizens are generally not interested in exercising their voice. This 'culture of passivity' remains a significant challenge to the success of participatory local governance and is a particularly common problem in post Communist societies.

The pervasive nature of patronage politics in Macedonia also undermines decentralisation's ability to deepen local democracy because patronage fuels voter apathy and deters local residents from becoming active in municipal affairs. Societies dependent on clientelistic exchange between parties and voters are not conducive to encouraging the development of responsive and accountable local government. This is because the voting preferences of citizens tend to be influenced by the promise of a job or financial reward, rather than a politician's success in providing collective local benefits. The absence of a vibrant civil society, serving as public watchdogs, may also encourage clientelism, which left unchecked could undermine the legitimacy of decentralised governance structures.

Albanian political elites and the politics of betrayal

As the analysis in Chapter 1 suggests, the existence of inequalities is insufficient to explain whether group grievances actually become a political issue at the state level. This will only happen if inequalities are experienced by group leaders and their followers simultaneously. Even with the presence of severe socio-economic inequalities at the mass level, the absence of political inequalities among elites may reduce the risk of violent group mobilisation because group leaders lack the incentives to mobilise their constituents for violent conflict.

There is some evidence to suggest that the blame for decentralisation's only partial success in meeting the needs of ordinary Albanian citizens may lie with the Albanian political elites that were in government between 2005 and 2015. According to leading development experts, the extent to which governments adopt mechanisms to regularly monitor the progress of reforms represents a litmus test for assessing its true commitment to its outcomes (Eaton *et al.* 2010: 64). The fact that more than ten years after the Framework Agreement was signed in August 2001, the DUI-led Secretariat for Implementation of the Ohrid Framework Agreement had failed to establish any system to monitor the implementation of equitable representation and community language use locally raises questions regarding the party's commitment to the Framework Agreement's principles. Additionally, DUI had an opportunity to improve the realisation of citizens' language rights locally when it was invited to propose amendments to the law on use of languages during parliamentary coalition negotiations in 2011. Instead, DUI proposed an amendment to the law that benefited only appointed or elected party functionaries at the expense of their constituents.

There are various reasons why DUI party elites have become engaged in a 'politics of betrayal' and have turned their back on their constituents. First, decentralisation, along with the use of power-sharing mechanisms at the state level, may have successfully integrated (DUI) Albanian political elites into state structures and they no longer feel politically aggrieved. They may also be sufficiently satisfied with the 'perks' of office, such as opportunities for personal enrichment and the dispensing of patronage, and no longer interested in pushing for further reform that will benefit their constituents. Second, DUI political elites may have entered into an agreement with their (VMRO-DPMNE) coalition partners not to pursue further reforms that will benefit Albanians at the expense of majority Macedonian voters. Instances where minority ethnic parties have been 'bought off' by the dominant community are common in ethnically divided societies. An example of this phenomenon is how Palestinian elites have postponed or effectively abandoned the struggle for Palestinian national rights in return for being given the opportunity to 'bask in the warmth of Israeli economic growth' (Khalidi and

Samour 2011: 17). Of course, another pertinent example is the behaviour of Albanian political elites in coalition with SDSM and later VMRO-DPMNE during the 1990s. Third, given the extent to which DUI has tied its polit-ical reputation to the fate of the Framework Agreement (it regards itself as the true guardian of its implementation), the party may feel it tantamount to political suicide to admit that, more than a decade later the Agreement may not have lived up to expectations and requires improving. Finally, and as greed theorists would argue, the conflict in 2001 may have in fact been driven by the private material gains of militant opportunists, with the genu-ine grievances of the Albanian community only being manipulated by them as a pretext for revolt.

Whatever the motivation, the inability of mainstream Albanian politicians to adequately address the grievances of their community during the 1990s led to an erosion of trust in the political class among ordinary Albanians. This created an opportunity for new actors, who were prepared to pursue Albanian interests outside the discredited political process, to seek to address these demands through other means. There is a danger of history repeating itself if Albanian political elites in Macedonia continue to put their own needs above those of the people they are supposed to represent.

Suggestions for further research

This study has focused specifically on decentralisation's implementation, including the effectiveness of local power-sharing mechanisms, rather than on how the reform fits within the wider Framework Agreement. An important area of further research would therefore be to take a broader look at decentralisation within the wider peace agreement, and to consider whether complex power-sharing has contributed to the management of ethnic difference in Macedonia. This study has not examined in detail the work of (limited) formal mechanisms of dispute resolution between the central and local levels.[7] The decision not to do so was based on their relative insignificance within a unitary state such as Macedonia, and because initial research findings suggested that existing mechanisms had not been utilised by the municipalities. In light of the significant financial difficulties experienced by the municipalities, it would therefore be of interest to research why no municipality brought an inter-governmental dispute to the Constitutional Court for review between 2005 and 2012.

Decentralisation is believed to promote a more equitable distribution of state resources by uniting poor areas with more affluent ones. Significantly, and unlike in other countries such as Kosovo, Macedonia's decentralisation process led to the creation of fewer rather than additional rural municipalities. It would therefore be of interest to ascertain whether the reform has facili-tated a reduction in disparities *within* individual Macedonian municipalities.

Finally, it would be beneficial to test the research findings in future studies within similar contexts, for example the implementation of decentralisation in neighbouring Kosovo as a mechanism for managing relations between Albanian and Serbian communities. There is plenty of scope for building on the implementation aspects of decentralisation. This study has provided a starting point for deeper consideration of how to fill the gap in decentralisation research in the context of ethnically divided states and societies.

Notes

1 Macedonia's Albanian community resides in compact areas in the north and west of the country, but also with sizable communities in Skopje and the eastern regions.
2 Significant socio-economic disparities between urban and rural areas do not necessarily represent an obstacle to decentralisation's successful implementation (and are therefore not discussed in the next section). However, failure to accommodate these structural features into the reform's design does.
3 VMRO-DPMNE, SDSM, DUI and DPA.
4 Interview with Foundation Open Society Macedonia official: 27 June 2011, Skopje.
5 Additionally, on the two occasions where formula-based systems have been used to allocate state resources (education funding and equalisation grants), there is evidence to suggest that central government may even have manipulated coefficients in a way that rewards those municipalities controlled by its political allies.
6 Examples include the failure to distribute cultural, social welfare and child protection grants on a per-client basis and a failure to allocate 1 per cent of GDP to fund regional development initiatives.
7 Disputes between the different tiers of government should be resolved by the Constitutional Court (Official Gazette 2002: Articles 51, 71, 87).

Afterword

Three years on from the completion of this analysis, the political climate in Macedonia has become even less conducive to decentralisation's success. Relations between governing and opposition parties have become increasingly polarised, a trend exacerbated by the forced removal of opposition SDSM MPs from the parliamentary chamber in December 2012 during a disagreement over the size of the forthcoming year's state budget. SDSM has boycotted Parliament ever since national elections were held in April 2014, the outcome of which they and other opposition parties consider to be fraudulent (Fouéré 2015). The results of municipal elections in March and April 2013 also illustrate the increasing dominance of the two main governing parties (VMRO-DPMNE and DUI) at the expense of the opposition. VMRO-DPMNE and DUI now control almost 90 per cent of all municipalities (up from 82.4 per cent in 2009), while the number of SDSM opposition-controlled municipalities has fallen from six to four.[1] The increasing marginalisation of opposition parties in local as well as national politics means that the municipal association ZELS continues to be dominated by mayors representing central government-aligned municipalities. No doubt as a consequence of this, ZELS has not prepared its annual 'Systematised Positions' (a formal list of municipal demands to central government) since December 2011.

One of the major challenges to documenting the capture of state institutions by political parties is the gaining of sufficient evidence to prove abuse of office and the existence of pervasive patronage networks. However, since February 2015 Macedonia has been embroiled in a massive wiretapping scandal, with SDSM's leader Zoran Zaev accusing Prime Minister Nikola Gruevski of orchestrating the illegal surveillance of at least 20,000 people. The release of thousands of telephone recordings (or 'bombs') by SDSM, involving ministers, judges, opposition politicians, journalists, even foreign ambassadors, suggest systematic and widespread government interference in almost every sphere of national activity. The revelations point to instances of corruption, government control of the media, electoral malpractice and manipulation of the criminal justice system by the ruling party VMRO-DPMNE and its leadership.[2]

Much of what is heard in the telephone recordings has long been rumoured and indeed claimed by many of my interviewees. For example, one recording suggests a discussion between the Minister of Transport Mile Janakieski and a cousin of Prime Minister Gruevski on how to put pressure on public employees to vote for VMRO-DPMNE and procure lists of 20 more voters for the party (Marusic 2015a). Another contains what appears to be Gruevski and VMRO-DPMNE MP group coordinator Silvana Boneva discussing a scheme to exercise control over MPs by requiring them to sign blank resignation declarations which could be activated if they disobey party instructions (Marusic 2015b).[3] Further recordings imply the extent to which the governing party interferes in the affairs of local government. In one recorded conversation, VMRO-DPMNE is purported to attempt to influence the outcome of the 2013 mayoral elections in the SDSM-led municipalities of Kumanovo and Strumica. They do this by allegedly using phantom voters, obstructing opposition activities, bribing local politicians and officials, and intimidating local businesses (Rizaov 2015b; Marusic 2015c). In another recording Gruevski apparently orders a physical assault on the newly elected opposition mayor of Centar municipality in Skopje during June 2013 and the destruction of the municipal building (Marusic 2015d). While none of these allegations are new, hearing the voices of senior government officials discussing such extensive abuse of office has left many in Macedonia deeply shocked.[4]

At the time of writing, the Government's response has been to deny all allegations and insist that the recordings have been concocted by a foreign intelligence service in order to destabilise the country. SDSM leader Zoran Zaev has been charged with espionage and attempting to stage a coup. Macedonians appear to be divided over how the national crisis should be resolved. Supporters of the ruling VMRO-DPMNE believe nothing needs to be done, whereas supporters of the opposition SDSM and the Albanian governing party DUI are split between international mediation, the creation of a technical government and early elections (Bieber 2015). At the time of writing the EU had been reluctant to get involved, although in April 2015 Members of the European Parliament facilitated two rounds of fruitless talks between senior representatives of VMRO-DPMNE and SDSM. The lack of a vibrant civil society in Macedonia that is capable of holding politicians to account, an important precondition for successful decentralisation, has meant that no significant anti-government protest took place as a result of the wiretapping scandal during its first three months and no senior government officials had resigned.[5] The public administration has also remained virtually inactive. Given that the revelations suggest many 'bought' their positions with party membership, this is not surprising as many will no doubt fear that any political change could cost them their job. Significant protests had however, been organised against proposed higher education reforms and against the Ministry of Health, so there is cause for optimism that Macedonians may be beginning to find their voice (Fouéré 2015; Rizaov 2015a).[6]

Regarding the various consociational power-sharing tools envisaged at the municipal level, little progress has been made since the completion of fieldwork in mid-2012. Unsurprisingly, these minority protection mechanisms continue to be highjacked by dominant political parties and by those ethnic groups that constitute a majority locally. Attitudes towards the use of qualified voting procedures have not changed significantly, and continued restrictions on their use mean that some decisions which may have an impact on minorities, for example local education policy or adoption of the municipal work programme and budget, remain beyond the reach of the minorities' veto. Municipal Committees for Inter-Community Relations continue to be hindered by poor operational capacity, a lack of resources and their marginalisation by municipal councils, although some do operate effectively. The use of non-majority languages remains a politically salient issue, but in spite of this the Government's DUI-led Secretariat for Implementation of the Ohrid Framework Agreement (SIOFA) has to date been unable to finalise its action plan on improving the use of community languages at the national and local levels.[7] While SIOFA did publish its first report on the implementation of the Framework Agreement in late 2012 (largely in response to criticism of its failure to publish any analysis during the Agreement's first ten years), no further analyses have been published by SIOFA since (Government of the Republic of Macedonia 2012). According to one former prime minister speaking in 2013, most politicians now regard the Framework Agreement as 'a bastard child' that has only one parent. The Albanian community glorifies the Agreement, while the Macedonian community runs away from it, leaving it to the Albanians to care for it on their own.[8]

This case study examined whether decentralisation has improved access to mother-tongue education in Macedonia by facilitating the provision of heterogeneous local public services. Three years on, the proportion of Albanian students attending primary and secondary education in their mother tongue has remained largely consistent, although the proportion of Turkish students accessing Turkish-medium language education has fallen slightly.[9] The experience of smaller ethnic communities in accessing education in their mother tongue remains less positive. In the absence of substantial capital investment, the Macedonian school network continues to be inadequate and overcrowding in urban schools remains an issue. More than half of all primary schools continue to operate multiple shifts in order to accommodate students, although the number of schools operating three shifts fell from eight in 2010/11 to six in 2012/13 (SSO 2014a: 11).[10] Funding and resource inequalities between central and satellite schools also remain. Importantly however, the trend of ethnic segregation in primary and secondary schools seems to have abated in the past three years and no new school name disputes have arisen since 2012. Student protests against proposed education reforms in late 2014 and early 2015 saw Albanian and Macedonian students protesting together for the first time.[11]

This study also considered whether decentralisation has enhanced municipal fiscal autonomy and concluded that, up until 2012, the reforms had done little to restrain central government's monopoly of state power and resources. While the amount of own-source revenue as a proportion of total municipal revenues has increased from an average of 29.4 per cent in 2009 to 41.7 per cent in 2013, Macedonian municipalities remain dependent on central government grants with stringent expenditure mandates that are in general insufficient to meet local needs (Levitas 2011a: 14; Government of the Republic of Macedonia 2014a). As agreed in 2009, the municipal share of VAT revenue increased to 4.5 per cent in 2013 and, according to the Government's programme for 2014–18, will rise further for those municipalities that succeed in increasing local tax collection rates.[12] Despite these increases, municipal revenue as a proportion of GDP and of public expenditure remains largely consistent with 2011 figures.[13] Macedonian municipalities also continue to be largely dependent on property-related taxes which exacerbate discrepancies in own-source revenues between urban and rural areas. The Government has, however, introduced some additional sources of municipal revenue since 2012 that will benefit rural municipalities. These include increases to the municipal share of income derived from the sale of state-owned land, and from mineral and water concessions. From 2015 rural municipalities will also receive 10 per cent of concessions on the sale of agricultural land, a share that is set to increase to 50 per cent by 2018 (Government of the Republic of Macedonia 2014b: 74). However, a large proportion of municipalities continue to have their bank accounts frozen because of unpaid arrears, and municipal borrowing, an important tool for enhancing municipal contractual autonomy, remains in the early stages of development (NALAS 2015: 32).

Despite the best efforts of UNDP to improve the equalisation formula in 2008, Macedonia remains without a functioning fiscal equalisation system. Little progress has therefore been made in the past three years to facilitate a more equitable distribution of state resources between urban and rural municipalities. The population census, postponed in 2011, has not yet been completed, which means there continues to be a lack of available and reliable data upon which to reform the current VAT allocation formula. While the Government's decentralisation programme for 2015–20 lists the creation of 'optimal statistical and information bases' for equalisation purposes as one of its priorities, it may be many years before Macedonia has a functioning fiscal equalisation system (Government of the Republic of Macedonia 2015: 9). Increases in the municipal share of VAT since 2012 have done nothing to equalise pre-existing disparities between urban and rural municipalities and have no doubt exacerbated them. The allocation of grants to finance the provision of cultural services, social welfare and child protection continue to be contingent on the existence of a physical facility within a municipality's territory. It is therefore inevitable that the smaller, less well-endowed municipalities continue to experience serious challenges in the realisation of their competences. Finally, Government funding to promote balanced regional development remains inadequate and remains well below the 1 per cent of GDP required by law (NALAS 2015: 58).

The Macedonian case has clear implications for our understanding of the dynamics of conflict management through decentralisation. The reform's implementation to date shows how decentralisation can indeed contribute to the reduction of ethnic inequalities that may exacerbate social divisions and lead to conflict. However, the Macedonian case also demonstrates how decentralisation's potential can be significantly undermined by the existence of undemocratic political parties, limited fiscal autonomy and a civil society weakened by pervasive clientelism. Practitioners and policy-makers in multi-ethnic states that have recently embarked upon decentralisation reforms as a means of integrating and appeasing demands for internal self-determination by territorially concentrated ethnic groups must therefore be sensitive to the political context within which they operate. Whatever the outcome of the current wiretapping scandal, Macedonia finds itself at a critical juncture. It remains to be seen whether Macedonia's decentralisation reforms can be brought back on track for the benefit of all citizens equally.

2 May 2015

Notes

1 See ODIHR (2013) for a detailed analysis of the 2013 municipal election results. This calculation is affected by a decrease in the number of municipalities from 84 to 80 plus the City of Skopje in March 2013, when the western municipality of Kičevo was enlarged to include the four surrounding rural municipalities of Drugovo, Zajas, Oslomej and Vraneštica. The decision to amalgamate Kičevo with surrounding municipalities was taken in 2004 but had been postponed for political reasons.

2 Reporters Without Borders ranked Macedonia 117th globally in its World Press Freedom Index, down from 45th in 2006 (Fouéré 2015).

3 According to longstanding VMRO-DPMNE dissident Jove Kekenovski, the party's control mechanisms are even more severe. MPs and other party officials are also forced to sign documents agreeing to forfeit their assets and possessions if they defect (Marusic 2015b).

4 Interview with Community Forums project manager: 26 February 2015, Skopje.

5 News of the wiretapping scandal is getting out, mostly via social networking sites and independent media, but the country's main media outlets have refused to air the recordings, leaving many Macedonians unable to judge the extent of corruption.

6 During December 2014 thousands of university students took to the streets in Skopje to demand the withdrawal of government plans to introduce a state-imposed exam before graduation. In February 2015 further protests were organised over the case of a nine-year-old girl who died while awaiting government approval for an operation abroad.

7 Email correspondence with an OSCE official: 23 April 2015.

8 Email correspondence with a representative of an international organisation operating in Macedonia: 27 April 2015.

9 The proportion of Albanian students attending primary education in their mother tongue was 98.23 per cent in 2012/13, down slightly from 98.44 per cent in 2010/11. The figures for secondary education have also remained largely consistent (94.28 per cent in 2012/13 compared to 95.02 per cent in 2010/11). The proportion of

Turkish students accessing Turkish-medium primary education was 62.94 per cent in 2012/13, down from 67.06 per cent in 2010/11. The proportion of Turkish students accessing secondary education in their mother tongue also fell from 50.21 per cent in 2010/11 to 46.15 per cent in 2012/13) (SSO 2014a).

10 During the academic year 2012/13, out of a total of 990 primary schools, 617 schools operated one shift, 367 schools operated two shifts and eight schools operated three shifts (SSO 2014a: 11).

11 Email correspondence with an OSCE official: 27 April 2015.

12 According to the Government's programme for 2014–18, those municipalities that improve local tax collection rates will receive increased VAT revenue by a further 0.25% in 2016, 0.75% in 2017 and 1.50% in 2018 (Government of the Republic of Macedonia 2014b: 74–5).

13 Municipal revenue as a proportion of GDP was 5.9 per cent in 2013 compared to 5.8 per cent in 2011. Municipal revenue as a proportion of public expenditure remained at 16 per cent during the same period (NALAS 2015: 59).

Appendices
Appendix A: Methodology

The majority of empirical data for this study was collected through in-depth interviews with people from a range of different backgrounds. Given this study's focus on local governance, key research participants were members of municipal administrations, locally elected figures and local civil society representatives. These were in addition to members of relevant line ministries, the municipal association, international and bilateral donors, and other NGO representatives. Over the course of a three-year period (March 2009–March 2012), 137 semi-structured interviews were conducted with at least 100 different individuals (key informants were interviewed more than once). These interviews were completed during six separate fieldwork visits, which took place in March and November 2009, May–June 2010, April 2011, May–June 2011 and March 2012.[1]

Despite the country's size, Macedonia is divided into 84 municipalities plus the City of Skopje.[2] Of these, 39 have sizable non-majority communities (above 10 per cent) and were therefore considered 'multi-ethnic' for the purpose of this study (SSO 2003). To maintain the research focus, as well as for practical reasons, data collection at the municipal level was restricted to five carefully selected municipalities: Gostivar, Kumanovo, Kruševo, Šuto Orizari and Struga (Figure A1 and Table A1). They were chosen based on the following criteria: the multi-ethnic profile of the local population, inclusion of the five largest non-majority communities (Albanian, Turkish, Roma, Serbian and Vlach), the political affiliation of the mayor (to ensure the political balance of data), proximity to the site of inter-ethnic conflict in 2001 and the municipality's level of development (urban/rural). Despite being located outside the 2001 conflict zone of north and western Macedonia, Kruševo was specifically selected for inclusion because of its local Albanian and Vlach communities, its predominantly rural characteristics and its historical and cultural significance as the birthplace of the modern Macedonian nation.[3] While not intended to be a representative sample of the entire country, concentrating the fieldwork in these five municipalities helped to clarify how formal and informal political linkages affected relations between the central and local levels. Including a mixture of urban and rural, wealthy and less affluent

Table A1 Selected characteristics of the five fieldwork municipalities

Municipality	No. of inhabitants	Area (km²)	Urban/rural	Local population by ethnicity (%)	Political affiliation of mayor	Realised budget for 2008 (MKD)	No. of municipal employees
Gostivar	81,042	519	Urban	Mac: 19.59 Alb: 66.68 Turkish: 9.86	Independent (RDK from 2011)	652,902,602	73
Kruševo	9,684	205	Mainly rural	Mac: 62.79 Alb: 21.31 Vlach: 10.53	VMRO-DPMNE (government)	100,712,209	22
Kumanovo	105,484	509	Urban	Mac: 60.43 Alb: 25.87 Serbian: 8.59	SDSM (opposition)	964,009,961	118
Šuto Orizari	22,017	7	Urban	Mac: 6.53 Alb: 30.32 Roma: 60.60	Roma Union	107,943,380	24
Struga	65,375	507	Urban	Mac: 32.09 Alb: 56.85 Turkish: 5.72	DUI (government)	715,770,999	95

Source: MCIC (2010)

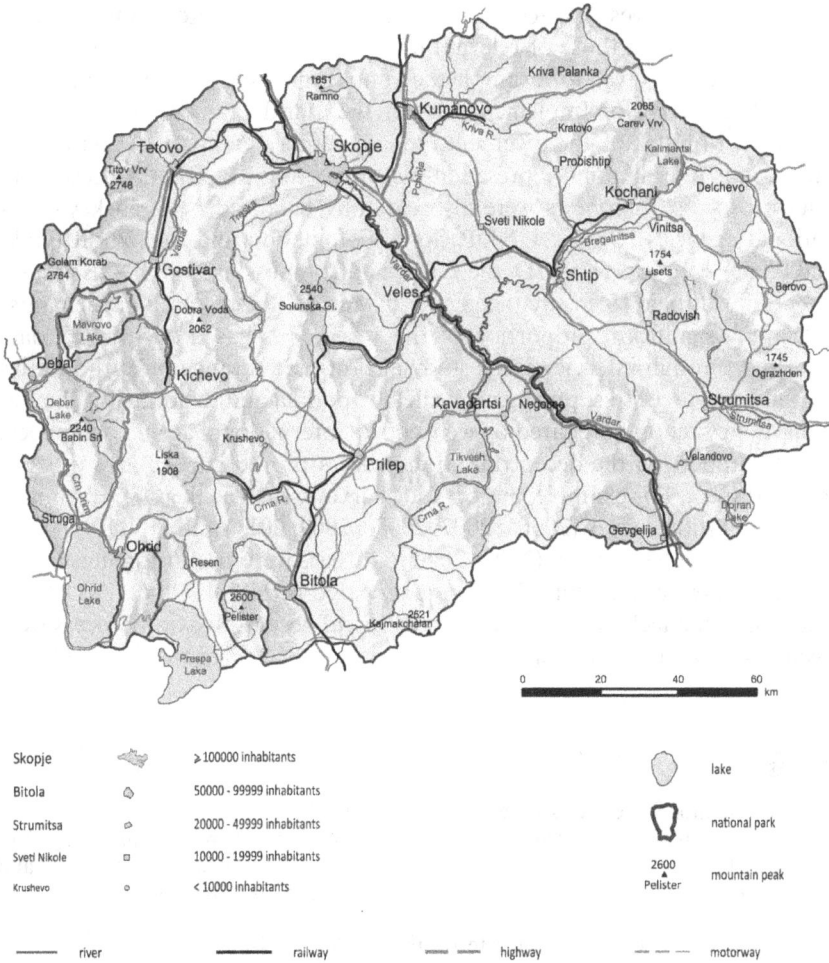

Figure A1 Location of the five selected fieldwork municipalities
Source: SSO (2014b: 8)

municipalities also enabled an assessment of how decentralisation may affect different parts of the country unequally.

Care was taken to ensure that the views of individuals from a variety of ethnic, political, professional and geographical backgrounds were docu-mented, and concentrating data collection at the local level in the five selected municipalities facilitated this process. Since the opinions of the country's two largest ethnic communities (Macedonians and Albanians) have tended to dominate accounts of Macedonia's post-conflict environment (see, for example, Neofotistos 2012), the inclusion of the perspectives of Turks, Roma, Vlachs and Serbs was an important objective of this research. The views of local representatives (elected officials, public administrators and citizens) were balanced with those of relevant line ministries and organisations working at the central level, for example the Ombudsman's Office and the government's Secretariat for Implementation of the Ohrid Framework Agreement (SIOFA). Mindful of the divergent (and sometimes competing) interests of the various international representatives supporting Macedonia's decentralisation process, interviews were also carefully balanced between key international agencies (OSCE, UNDP, Soros Foundation and the World Bank) and bilateral donors (USAID, the European Commission and SDC). Finally, attention was paid to ensure the gender balance of the research participants.

While a significant proportion of this research is based on primary data collected through interviews, the study also utilised a range of authoritative secondary sources to supplement the fieldwork data and to address its limitations. Policy reports prepared by well-known international agencies and local NGOs supporting the decentralisation process proved particularly valuable in this respect. For example, nation-wide surveys, such as the OSCE's annual decentralisation survey (2006a; 2007; 2008c; 2009; 2011) and UNDP's People Centred Analyses reports (2008; 2009b; 2010a), were useful for illustrating country-wide trends. Similarly, reports prepared by USAID and UNDP projects providing technical assistance to the fiscal decentralisation process were invaluable for supplementing budgetary data collected in the five fieldwork municipalities.

Notes

1 Some telephone interviews were also conducted between field trips.
2 In March 2013, the western municipality of Kičevo municipality was enlarged to include the four surrounding rural municipalities of Drugovo, Zajas, Oslomej and Vraneštica. The total number of municipalities decreased from 84 to 80 plus the City of Skopje as a result.
3 This mountain town was the site of the Ilinden uprising against the Ottoman Empire in 1903. For more details of Kruševo's significance in modern Macedonian history, see Brown (2003).

Appendix B: The territorial pattern of ethnic demography in the Republic of Macedonia (Turkish and Roma communities)

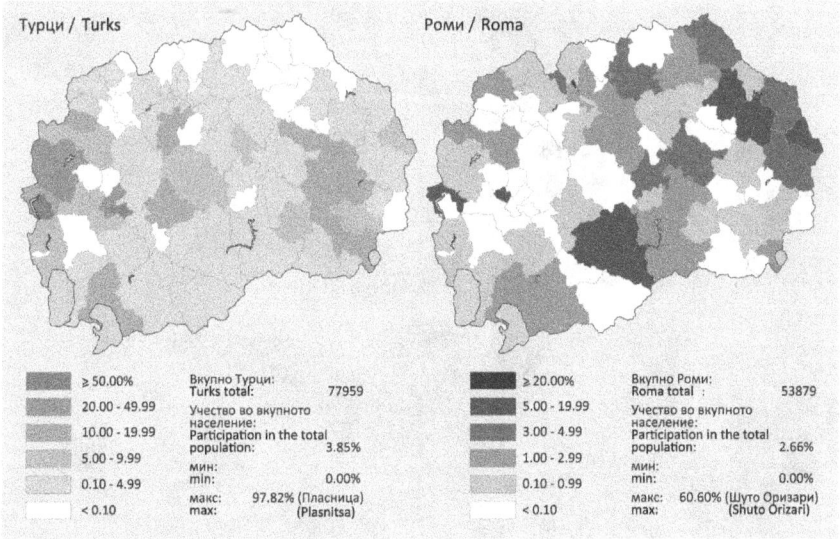

Source: SSO (2014c: 75)

Appendix C: Map of the proposed 'Republic of Ilirida' within a Federal Republic of Macedonia

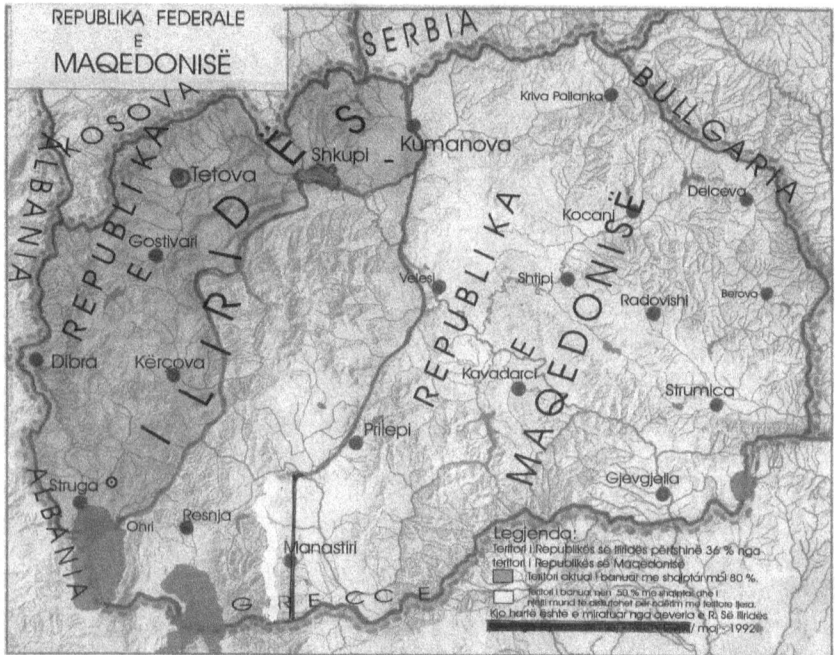

REPUBLIKA FEDERALE E MAQEDONISË

SERBIA

BULLGARIA

ALBANIA

KOSOVA

REPUBLIKA E ILIRIDËS

REPUBLIKA E MAQEDONISË

Kriva Pallanka

Shkupi

Kumanova

Tetova

Deloeva

Kocani

Gostivari

Veles

Shtipi

Radovishi

Berovo

Dibra

Kërçova

Kavadarci

Strumica

Prilepi

Struga

Gjevgjelia

Ohri

Resnja

Manastiri

GREECE

Legjenda:
Territori i Republikës së Ilirdës përbehinë 36 % nga territori i Republikës së Maqedonisë
Territori aktual i banuar me shqiptarë mbi 80 %.
Territori i banuar nën 50 % me shqiptarë dhe i cili mund të diskutohet për bashkim me kështore tjera. Kjo harte është e miratuar nga qeveria e R. Së Ilirdës
/ maj 1992

Source: Halili (1991)

Note: The map's legend explains that the dark-shaded area in the west of the country represents the proposed 'Republic of Ilirida', within a broader 'Federal Republic of Macedonia', and is where Albanians constitute more than 80 per cent of the local population. This area represents 36 per cent of the total territory of the Republic of Macedonia. The central segment, lightly shaded on the map, represents territory where Albanians constitute approximately 50 per cent of the local population and is 'open for discussion' and may represent a possible third federal unit.

Appendix D: Macedonian Academy of Sciences and Arts' proposal for the partition of the Republic of Macedonia, May 2001

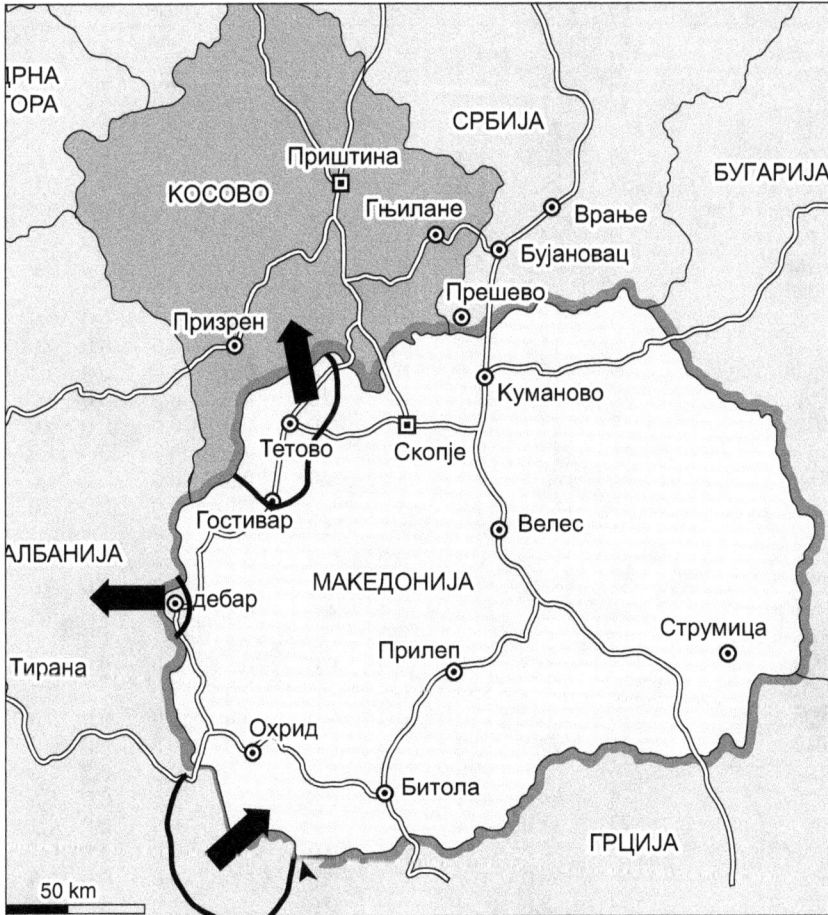

Source: Gorgevski (2001)

Appendix E: Equitable representation of ethnic communities in 15 selected municipal administrations

Municipality	No. of pop./staff	Mac. (%)	Alb. (%)	Turkish (%)	Roma (%)	Vlach (%)	Serb. (%)	Boš. (%)	Other (%)
Brvenica	15,855	37.5	61.6	0.0	0.0	0.0	0.5	0.0	0.3
2006	12	66.7	33.3	0.0	0.0	0.0	0.0	0.0	0.0
2010	16	37.5	62.5	0.0	0.0	0.0	0.0	0.0	0.0
Čair	64,823	24.1	57.0	6.9	4.8	0.1	1.0	4.6	1.5
2006	36	55.6	38.9	2.8	0.0	0.0	0.0	0.0	0.0
2010	58	29.3	67.2	5.2	0.0	0.0	0.0	0.0	0.0
Dolneni	13,568	35.9	26.7	19.1	0.1	0.0	0.1	17.5	0.6
2006	8	62.5	25.0	0.0	0.0	0.0	0.0	0.0	0.0
2010	16	56.3	6.3	12.5	0.0	0.0	0.0	25.0	0.0
Gostivar	81,042	19.6	66.7	9.9	2.8	0.0	0.0	0.0	0.0
2006	57	22.8	71.9	1.8	3.5	0.0	0.0	0.0	0.0
2010	73	17.8	76.7	2.7	2.7	0.0	0.0	0.0	0.0
Jegunovce	10,790	55.3	43.0	0.0	0.4	0.0	1.0	0.0	0.3
2006	11	90.9	9.1	0.0	0.0	0.0	0.0	0.0	0.0
2010	17	88.2	11.8	0.0	0.0	0.0	0.0	0.0	0.0
Kičevo	30,138	53.6	30.5	8.1	5.4	0.3	0.3	0.0	1.9
2006	61	88.5	8.2	3.3	0.0	0.0	0.0	0.0	0.0
2010	89	83.1	11.2	5.6	0.0	0.0	0.0	0.0	0.0
Kruševo	9,684	62.8	21.3	3.3	0.0	10.5	0.4	1.4	0.3
2006	20	75.0	0.0	0.0	0.0	20.0	20.0	0.0	0.0
2010	22	81.8	0.0	0.0	0.0	18.2	0.0	0.0	0.0
Kumanovo	105,484	60.4	25.9	0.3	4.0	0.1	8.6	0.0	0.6
2006	76	–	–	–	–	–	–	–	–
2010	118	80.5	11.9	0.0	0.0	6.8	0.0	0.0	0.8
Petrovec	8,255	51.4	22.9	0.9	1.6	0.0	5.0	17.5	0.7
2006	10	100.0	0.0	0.0	0.0	0.0	20.0	0.0	0.0
2010	21	90.5	0.0	0.0	0.0	0.0	9.5	0.0	0.0
Struga	63,376	32.1	56.9	5.7	0.2	1.0	0.2	0.2	3.8
2006	76	61.8	26.3	1.3	0.0	3.9	0.0	0.0	6.6
2010	95	41.0	47.4	3.2	4.2	0.0	0.0	0.0	4.2
Vrapčište	25,399	4.1	83.1	12.3	0.0	0.0	0.0	0.0	0.4
2006	6	100.0	0.0	0.0	0.0	0.0	0.0	0.0	0.0
2010	34	8.8	82.4	2.9	0.0	0.0	0.0	0.0	0.0
Zelenikovo	4,077	61.9	29.6	0.0	2.3	0.0	1.1	4.7	0.5
2006	8	100.0	0.0	0.0	0.0	0.0	0.0	0.0	0.0
2010	8	100.0	0.0	0.0	0.0	0.0	0.0	0.0	0.0

Sources: MCIC (2006, 2010)

Appendix F: Membership data for municipal Committees for Inter-Community Relations

Municipality[a]	Required by law?	No. of members	No. of municipal councillors	All communities represented?[b]	Equal representation of communities?
Brvenica	Yes	6	–	No: S = 0.49%	Yes
Butel	Yes	–	–	–	–
Čair	Yes	4	–	No: R = 4.76%	Yes
Čaška	Yes	5	–	No: A =35.23%, T = 5.1%	–
Čucer Sandevo	Yes	5	–	–	–
Debar	Yes	5	–	Yes	Yes
Dolneni	Yes	–	–	–	–
Jegunovce	Yes	5	5 – all	Yes	No – 3M, 2A
Kičevo	Yes	–	–	–	–
Kruševo	Yes	5	–	No: V = 10.53%	Yes
Kumanovo	Yes	12	0 – none	Yes	Yes
Mavrovo and Roštusa	Yes	–	–	–	–
Petrovec	Yes	–	–	–	–
Sopište	Yes	–	–	–	–
Struga	Yes	8	–	Yes	Yes
Šuto Orizari	Yes	5	–	–	–
Tetovo	Yes	5	–	Yes	Yes
Vraneštica	Yes	–	–	–	–
Vrapčište	Yes	–	–	–	–
Zelenikovo	Yes	–	–	–	–
Bogovinje	No	3	3 – all	No: T = 4.09%	No – all Albanian
Dojran	No	5	5 – all	No: R = 1.05% (A = only 0.47%)	No – 2A, 1M, 1S, 1T

Table Appendix F (cont.)

Municipality[a]	Required by law?	No. of members	No. of municipal councillors	All communities represented?[b]	Equal representation of communities?
Drugovo	No	3	1	No: A = 4.77%	No – 2T
Gevgelija	No	5	0 – none	Yes	Yes
Gostivar	No	4	–	Yes	Yes
Kratovo	No	5	5 – all	No: S = 0.23% (T = only 0.08%)	No – 3M, 1T, 1R
Lipkovo	No	5	2	No: S = 1.7%	No – 3A, 2M
Lozovo	No	7	2	Yes	No – 2T
Oslomej	No	5	4	Yes	No – 4A, 1M
Saraj	No	3	3 – all	No: M = 3.9%, B = 3.2%	No – all Albanian
Staro Nagoricane	No	5	2	Yes	No – 4M, 1S
Valandovo	No	6	6 – all	No: R = 6.27%	Yes

Sources: ZELS (2010a); Metamorphosis and Common Values (2011: 25–6)

Notes

a This data was collected directly from municipalities by ZELS in September 2010.

b The following abbreviations apply to the different nationalities: Albanian – A; Bošniak – B; Macedonian – M; Roma – R; Serbian – S; Turkish – T; Vlach – V.

Appendix G: Number of schools (including branches) and class sections, according to language of instruction (regular primary and lower secondary schools)

Year	2003/4		2004/5		2005/6		2006/7	
	No. of schools	Class sections	No. of schools	Class sections	No. of schools	Class sections	No. of schools	Class sections
Macedonian	764	6,578	759	6,506	748	6,986	740	6,968
Albanian	280	3,087	284	3,105	286	3,449	288	3,453
Turkish	57	272	57	274	60	353	61	318
Serbian	11	37	10	35	8	35	8	36
Total	1,012	9,974	1,010	9,920	1,005	10,823	1,000	10,775

Year	2007/8		2008/9		2009/10		2010/11	
	No. of schools	Class sections	No. of schools	Class sections	No. of schools	Class sections	No. of schools	Class sections
Macedonian	737	6,927	734	6,924	729	6,812	731	6,773
Albanian	289	3,431	287	3,440	289	3,426	288	3,403
Turkish	60	321	60	318	62	348	62	352
Serbian	8	34	7	31	7	36	7	39
Total	997	10,713	991	10,713	990	10,622	990	10,567

Sources: SSO (2006, 2008, 2009, 2010a, 2011, 2012a)

Appendix H: Number of schools (including branches) and class sections, according to language of instruction (regular upper secondary schools)

Year	2003/4		2004/5		2005/6		2006/7	
	No. of schools	Class sections	No. of schools	Class sections	No. of schools	Class sections	No. of schools	Class sections
Macedonian	89	2,441	90	2,445	—	—	93	2,418
Albanian	23	521	27	609	—	—	29	696
Turkish	5	25	8	26	—	—	8	41
English	6	45	6	54	—	—	7	64
Total[a]	96	3,032	100	3,134	—	—	104	3,219

Year	2007/8		2008/9		2009/10		2010/11	
	No. of schools	Class sections	No. of schools	Class sections	No. of schools	Class sections	No. of schools	Class sections
Macedonian	96	2,401	99	2,394	99	2,422	101	2,395
Albanian	32	722	33	781	35	853	34	912
Turkish	9	48	10	55	10	59	10	61
English	7	66	7	65	5	64	7	73
Total	107	3,237	110	3,295	110	3,398	114	3,441

Sources: SSO (2006, 2008, 2009, 2010a, 2011, 2012a)

Note

a The cumulative totals of both primary and secondary schools do not match the values included in the 'total' column because some schools are bi- or trilingual.

Appendix I: Proportion of Serbian students learning in their mother tongue (regular primary and lower secondary schools)

Year	No. of students	No. of students learning in mother tongue	Students learning in mother tongue (%)
2004/5	2,335	174	7.45
2005/6	–	–	–
2006/7	2,242	193	8.61
2007/8	2,076	177	8.53
2008/9	1,943	177	9.11
2009/10	1,871	153	8.18
2010/11	1,733	145	8.37

Sources: SSO (2006, 2008, 2009, 2010a, 2011, 2012a)

Appendix J: Number of regular and lower secondary schools according to the number of students

	No. of Schools							
No. of students	*2003/4*	*2004/5*	*2005/6*	*2006/7*	*2007/8*	*2008/9*	*2009/10*	*2010/11*
Up to 20	300	310	–	278	292	302	301	311
21–50	171	167	–	177	173	166	178	173
Total no. of schools	1,012	1,010	–	1,000	997	991	990	990

Sources: SSO (2006, 2008, 2009, 2010a, 2011, 2012a)

Appendix K: Gross Domestic Product per capita according to planning region (in MKD)

Region	2000	2001	2002	2003	2004
National average	116,657	114,916	120,768	127,478	134,050
East	89,423	80,494	83,871	90,883	96,389
Northeast	75,580	61,948	65,105	72,078	69,694
Pelagonia	131,898	135,129	150,913	160,807	153,624
Polog	57,701	51,563	55,029	66,174	64,377
Skopje	180,300	183,497	188,570	192,782	213,453
Southeast	99,128	95,993	100,269	112,626	119,194
Southwest	93,072	86,462	93,420	86,479	95,209
Vardar	104,226	114,900	118,014	132,670	131,528

Region	2005	2006	2007	2008	2009
National average	144,857	156,874	178,605	201,147	200,293
East	105,128	115,672	134,114	173,815	170,486
Northeast	73,260	82,837	92,566	122,014	104,775
Pelagonia	151,544	154,671	174,589	208,990	219,635
Polog	71,119	76,968	84,913	95,277	93,966
Skopje	235,479	254,010	294,884	314,531	312,040
Southeast	136,708	141,360	162,758	168,211	189,566
Southwest	97,861	106,970	115,083	150,771	140,262
Vardar	141,505	170,187	184,937	196,028	194,092

Source: SSO (2012c)

Appendix L: Map of the Republic of Macedonia's planning regions

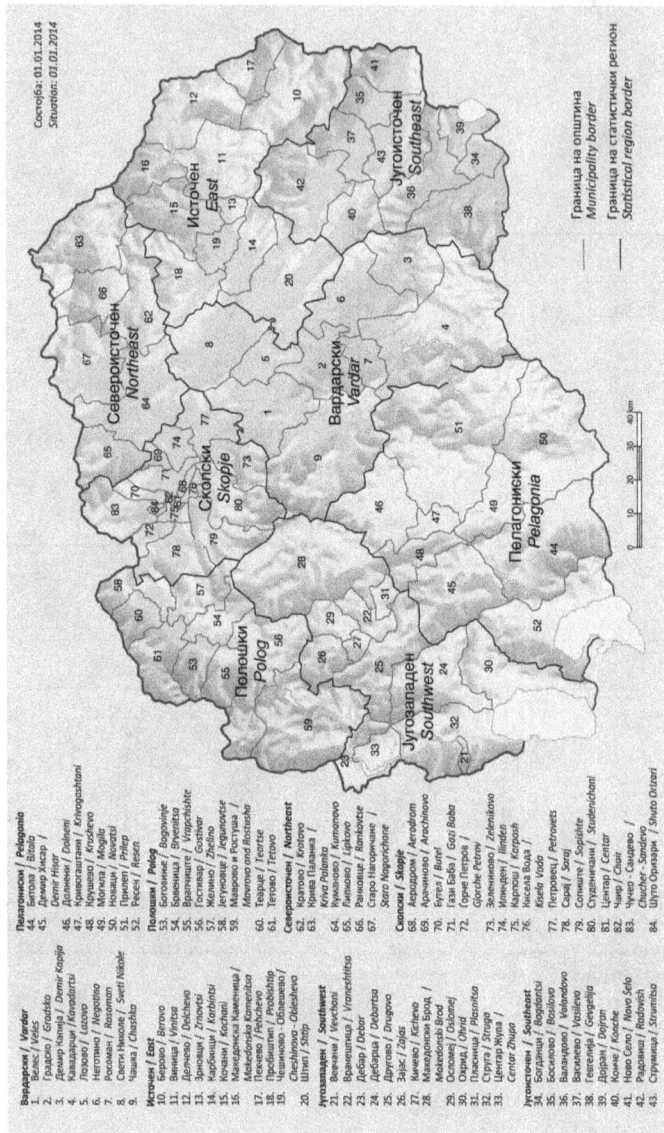

Source: SSO (2014b: 10)

Appendix M: The results of territorial reorganisation in 1996 and 2004

Planning region	32 municipalities in 1991	123 municipalities from 1996	84 municipalities from 2004
East	Berovo	Berovo	Berovo
		Pehcevo	Pehcevo
	Vinica	Vinica	Vinica
		Blatec (2,024)	
	Delcevo	Delcevo	Delcevo
		Makedonska Kamenica	Makedonska Kamenica
	Kocani	Kocani	Kocani
		Orizari (4,410)	
		Zrnovci	Zrnovci[a] (3,264)
		Cesinovo	Cesinovo-Obleševo
		Obleševo (5,076)	
	Probistip	Probistip	Probistip
		Zletovo (3,428)	
	Sveti Nikole	Sveti Nikole	Sveti Nikole
		Lozovo	Lozovo[b] (2,858)
	Štip	Štip	Štip
		Karbinci	Karbinci[c] (4,012)
Northeast	Kratovo	Kratovo	Kratovo
	Kriva Palanka	Kriva Palanka	Kriva Palanka
		Rankovce	Rankovce[d] (4,144)
	Kumanovo	Kumanovo	Kumanovo
		Klecevce (1,609)	
		Orasac (1,252)	
		Lipkovo	Lipkovo
		Staro Nagoricane	Staro Nagoricane[e] (4,840)
	Makedonski Brod	Makedonski Brod	Makedonski Brod
		Samokov (1,553)	
		Plasnica	Plasnica[f] (4,545)
	Ohrid	Ohrid	Ohrid
		Kosel (1,370)	
		Belcista	Debarca
		Meseista (2,587)	
	Struga	Struga	Struga
		Delogozdi (7,884)	
		Labunista (8,935)	
		Lukovo Velesta (1,509)	
		Vevčani	Vevčani[g] (2,433)

Planning region	32 municipalities in 1991	123 municipalities from 1996	84 municipalities from 2004
Pelagonia	Bitola	Bitola	Bitola
		Bistrica (5,050)	
		Capari (1,426)	
		Kukurecani (2,511)	
		Mogila	Mogila
		Dobrusevo (2,175)	
		Novaci	Novaci[h] (3,549)
		Bac (755)	
		Staravina (320)	
	Demir Hisar	Demir Hisar	Demir Hisar
		Sopotnica (2,332)	
	Kruševo	Kruševo	Kruševo
		Zitose (2,128)	
	Prilep	Prilep	Prilep
		Topolcani (2,923)	
		Vitoliste (494)	
		Dolneni	Dolneni
		Krivogastani (6,019)	
	Resen	Resen	Resen
Polog	Gostivar	Gostivar	Gostivar
		Cegrane (12,346)	
		Vrutok (5,999)	
		Dolna Banjica (9,467)	
		Srbinovo (3,709)	
		Mavrovi Anovi	Mavrovo-Rostuša
		Rostuša (9,451)	
		Vrapčište	Vrapčište
		Negotino-Polosko (16,865)	
	Tetovo	Tetovo	Tetovo
		Dzepciste (7,963)	
		Sipkovica (7,854)	
		Tearce	Tearce
		Bogovinje	Bogovinje
		Kamenjane (14,468)	
		Brvenica	Brvenica
		Jegunovce	Jegunovce
		Vratnica (3,563)	
		Želino	Želino

Planning region	*32 municipalities in 1991*	*123 municipalities from 1996*	*84 municipalities from 2004*
Skopje	Gazi Baba	Gazi Baba	Gazi Baba
		Aračinovo	Aračinovo
		Ilinden	Ilinden
		Petrovec	Petrovec
	Karpoš	Karpoš	Karpoš
		Gjorce Petrov	Gjorce Petrov
		Saraj	Saraj
		Kondovo (11,155)	
	Kisela Voda	Kisela Voda	Kisela Voda
		Zelenikovo	Zelenikovo[i] (4,077)
		Sopiste	Sopiste
		Studeničani	Studeničani
	Centar	Centar	Centar
	Čair	Čair	Čair
		Čučer-Sandevo	Čučer-Sandevo
		Šuto Orizari	Šuto Orizari
Southeast	Valandovo	Valandovo	Valandovo
	Gevgelija	Gevgelija	Gevgelija
		Miravci (2,631)	
		Bogdanci	Bogdanci
		Star Dojran	Dojran[j] (3,426)
	Radoviš	Radoviš	Radoviš
		Podares (3,747)	
		Konce	Konce[k] (3,536)
	Strumica	Strumica	Strumica
		Kuklis (4,449)	
		Murtino (6,544)	
		Vasilevo	Vasilevo
		Bosilovo	Bosilovo
		Novo Selo	Novo Selo
Southwest	Debar	Debar	Debar
		Centar Župa	Centar Župa
	Kičevo	Kičevo	Kičevo[l]
		Drugovo (3,249)	Drugovo[m] (3,249)
		Oslomej (10,438)	Oslomej (10,438)
		Vraneštica (1,322)	Vraneštica[n] (1,322)
		Zajas (11,605)	Zajas (11,605)

Planning region	32 municipalities in 1991	123 municipalities from 1996	84 municipalities from 2004
Vardar	Veles	Veles	Veles
		Gradsko	Gradsko[o] (3,760)
		Čaška	Čaška
		Bogomila (1,252)	
		Izvor (1,049)	
	Kavadarci	Kavadarci	Kavadarci
		Konopiste (350)	
		Rosoman	Rosoman[p] (4,141)
	Negotino	Negotino	Negotino
		Demir Kapija	Demir Kapija[q] (4,545)

Sources: SEC (1996); MoLSG (2006)

Notes

a SDSM mayor; Macedonian majority

b SDSM mayor; Macedonian majority

c SDSM mayor; Macedonian majority

d SDSM mayor; Macedonian majority

e Macedonian majority with 20 per cent local Serbian population

f Turkish majority

g VMRO-DPMNE mayor; Macedonian majority surrounded by Albanian-majority municipalities

h SDSM mayor; Macedonian majority

i VMRO-DPMNE mayor with 30 per cent local Albanian population

j SDSM mayor; Macedonian majority

k SDSM mayor; Macedonian majority

l VMRO-DPMNE mayor with 30 per cent local Albanian population

m VMRO-DPMNE mayor; Macedonian majority

n Macedonian majority with 20 per cent Turks

o SDSM mayor; Macedonian majority

p SDSM mayor; Macedonian majority

q SDSM mayor; Macedonian majority

Appendix N: Characteristics of the 16 municipalities with populations below 5,000

	Name of municipality	Population (2002 census)	Characteristics
1	Demir Kapija	4,545	SDSM mayor; Macedonian majority
2	Dojran	3,426	SDSM mayor; Macedonian majority
3	Drugovo *a	3,249	VMRO-DPMNE mayor; Macedonian majority
4	Gradsko	3,760	SDSM mayor; Macedonian majority
5	Karbinci	4,012	SDSM mayor; Macedonian majority
6	Konce	3,536	SDSM mayor; Macedonian majority
7	Losovo	2,858	SDSM mayor; Macedonian majority
8	Novaci	3,549	SDSM mayor; Macedonian majority
9	Plasnica	4,545	Turkish majority
10	Rankovce	4,144	SDSM mayor; Macedonian majority
11	Staro Nagoricane	4,840	Macedonian majority with 20% Serbs
12	Vevčani *	2,433	VMRO-DPMNE mayor; Macedonian majority
13	Vraneštica *	1,322	Macedonian majority with 20% Turks
14	Zelenikovo	4,077	VMRO-DPMNE mayor; 30% Albanians
15	Zrnovci	3,264	SDSM mayor; Macedonian majority

Source: MoLSG (2006)

Note

a Earlier proposals for the territorial reorganisation did not include the three VMRO-DPMNE-led municipalities marked with an asterisk symbol (Drugovo, Vevčani and Vraneštica).

Appendix O: Basic features of the planning regions

Region	Area (km²)	Regional population (2006)	Regional ethnic balance (2002) (%)	Pop. density (km²)	No. of municipalities	No. of rural municipalities	No. of settlements	Proportion of urban population (2002) (%)
Rep. of Macedonia	25,713	2,040,228	Mac.: 64 Alb.: 25 Others: 11	82	84	41	1767	56.7
East	3,537	180,938	Mac.: 93 Others:7	51	11	3	217	66.3
Northeast	2,310	173,982	Mac.: 59 Alb.:31 Others:10	75	6	3	192	56.6
Pelagonia	4,717	236,088	Mac.: 89 Alb.: 4 Others: 7	50	9	4	343	67.6
Polog	2,416	310,178	Mac.: 19 Alb.: 73 Others: 8	126	9	7	184	29.2
Skopje	1,812	590,455	Mac.: 64 Alb.: 23 Others: 13	319	17	7	142	71.8
Southeast	2,739	171,972	Mac.: 90 Others: 10	63	10	5	188	45.3
Southwest	3,340	222,385	Mac.: 49 Alb.: 38 Others: 13	66	13	8	286	36.1
Vardar	4,042	154,230	Mac.: 88 Alb.: 4 Others: 8	38	9	4	215	68.7

Sources: MoLSG (2009: 6); SSO (2003)

Appendix P: VAT revenue according to planning region (in million MKD)

Region	2000	2001	2002	2003	2004
East	13,681	12,328	12,436	14,217	15,150
Northeast	10,778	8,873	9,133	10,702	10,443
Pelagonia	26,880	27,532	29,244	32,815	31,472
Polog	14,602	13,148	13,620	17,367	17,087
Skopje	86,120	88,252	88,546	96,093	107,662
Southeast	14,378	13,966	13,966	16,595	17,707
Southwest	17,388	16,211	16,832	16,479	18,292
Vardar	13,515	14,916	14,816	17,583	17,548
Total	197,342	195,226	198,592	221,852	235,361

Region	2005	2006	2007	2008	2009
East	16,254	18,069	20,803	27,201	26,814
Northeast	10,851	12,443	13,842	18,461	15,991
Pelagonia	30,556	31,526	35,313	42,620	45,008
Polog	18,715	20,612	22,716	25,858	25,757
Skopje	117,853	129,487	150,310	162,869	163,477
Southeast	20,039	20,988	24,065	25,171	28,592
Southwest	18,567	20,538	21,961	29,077	27,210
Vardar	18,617	22,661	24,468	26,192	26,097
Total	251,452	276,324	313,478	357,450	358,945

Source: SSO (2012c)

Appendix Q: Approved and planned central budget funds for underdeveloped economic regions, 1994–2007

Year	Approved in the budget (MKD)	1% of GDP prescribed in the law (MKD)	Proportion of approved funds (%)
1994	418,000,000	1,464,090,000	28.55
1995	700,000,000	1,695,210,000	41.29
1996	750,000,000	1,764,440,000	42.51
1997	500,000,000	1,860,180,000	26.88
1998	520,000,000	1,949,790,000	26.68
1999	470,000,000	2,090,100,000	22.49
2000	758,000,000	2,363,890,000	32.08
2001	560,000,000	2,338,410,000	23.95
2002	850,000,000	2,388,900,000	35.58
2003	238,000,000	2,388,900,000	9.96
2004	221,132,000	2,652,570,000	8.33
2005	205,132,000	2,866,260,000	7.15
2006	166,000,000	3,076,290,000	5.40
2007	184,000,000	3,326,090,000	5.53
Total	6,541,364,000	20,303,910,000	22.60

Source: OSCE (2011: 51)

Bibliography

Ackermann, A. 2000. *Making Peace Prevail: Preventing Violent Conflict in Macedonia.* New York: Syracuse University Press.

Adamson, K. and D. Jović 2004. The Macedonian–Albanian Political Frontier: the Re-articulation of Post-Yugoslav Political Identities. *Nations and Nationalism*, 10(3), 293–311.

Ahmad, E. and G. Brosio (eds) 2009. *Does Decentralization Enhance Service Delivery and Poverty Reduction?* Cheltenham: Edward Elgar Publishing.

Ahmad, J., S. Devarajan, S. Khemani and S. Shah 2005. *Decentralization and Service Delivery.* Washington, DC: World Bank.

Akcija Zdruzenska 2008. *Monitoring of the Implementation of the Law on Equal Opportunities of Women and Men within the Local Self-Government of the Republic of Macedonia.* Skopje: Akcija Zdruzenska.

Akkaya, A. H. and J. Jongerden 2013. Confederalism and Autonomy in Turkey: The Kurdistan Workers' Party and the Reinvention of Democracy, in *The Kurdish Question in Turkey: New Perspectives on Violence, Representation, and Reconciliation*, ed. C. Gunes and W. Zeydanlıoğlu. Abingdon: Routledge, 186–204.

Amoretti, U. and N. Bermeo (eds) 2004. *Federalism and Territorial Cleavages.* Baltimore, MD: Johns Hopkins University Press.

Association for Democratic Initiatives (ADI) 2006. *Power Sharing: New Concept of Decision Making Process in Multicultural Municipalities.* Gostivar: ADI.

Bahl, R. 1999. *Implementation Rules for Fiscal Decentralization.* Altanta, GA: International Studies Program, Georgia State University.

Baiocchi, G. and P. Heller 2009. Representation by Design? Variations on Participatory Reforms in Brazilian Municípios, in *Rethinking Popular Representation*, ed. O. Törnquist, N. Webster and K. Stokke. Basingstoke: Palgrave Macmillan, 119–41.

Bakiu, B. 2010. *Education and Labour Market: Managing Education Quality in Decentralized Macedonia: Case Study Municipality of Saraj.* Skopje: Center for Research and Policy Making.

Bakke, K. and E. Wibbels 2006. Diversity, Disparity, and Civil Conflict in Federal States. *World Politics*, 59, 1–50.

Balalovska, K. 2001. A Historical Background to the Macedonian–Albanian Inter-Ethnic Conflict. *New Balkan Politics* (Online), 3/4. Available at: www.newbalkanpolitics.org.mk/cat/Issue-3–4 (accessed: 24 October 2009).

Banac, I. 1984. *The National Question in Yugoslavia: Origins, History, Politics.* Ithaca, NY: Cornell University Press.

Barker, E. 2001. The Origins of the Macedonian Dispute, in *The New Macedonian Question*, ed. J. Pettifer. Basingstoke: Palgrave Macmillan, 3–14.

Barrera-Osorio, F., T. Fasih, H. Patrinos and L. Santibáñez 2009. *Decentralized Decision-Making in Schools: The Theory and Evidence on School-Based Management*. Washington, DC: World Bank.

Barter, S. 2008. The Dangers of Decentralization: Clientelism, the State and Nature in a Democratic Indonesia. *Federal Governance* (Online), 5(1), 1–15. Available at: http://library.queensu.ca/ojs/index.php/fedgov/article/view/4398 (accessed: 15 May 2010).

Bartlett, W., H. Cipusheva, M. Nikolov and M. Shukarov 2010. The Quality of Life and Regional Development in FYR Macedonia. *Croatian Economic Survey*, 12(1), 121–62.

Bastian, S. and R. Luckham (eds) 2003. *Can Democracy be Designed? The Politics of Institutional Choice in Conflict-torn Societies*. New York: Palgrave.

Baumann, M. 2009. Understanding the Other's 'Understanding' of Violence: Legitimacy, Recognition, and the Challenge of Dealing with the Past in Divided Societies. *International Journal of Conflict and Violence*, 3(1), 107–23.

Beall, J. 2006. Decentralization, Women's Rights and Development. Presented at the FLACSO-IDRC International Workshop on Decentralisation and Women's Rights, Buenos Aires, Argentina, August 2006.

Beer, S. 1977. A Political Scientist's View of Fiscal Federalism, in *The Political Economy of Fiscal Federalism*, ed. W. Oates. Lexington, MA: Lexington Books, 21–48.

Berdal, M. and D. Malone (eds) 2000. *Greed and Grievance: Economic Agendas in Civil Wars*. Boulder, CO: Lynne Rienner.

Bexheti, A. 2011. The Equal Distribution of Public Funds in the Republic of Macedonia: Insufficient Even According to the Ohrid Framework Agreement, in *Ten Years from the Ohrid Framework Agreement: Is Macedonia Functioning as a Multi-Ethnic State?*, ed. B. Reka. Tetovo: SEEU, 159–78.

Bhabha, H. 1990. *Nation and Narration*. London: Routledge.

Bieber, F. 2004. *Institutionalizing Ethnicity in the Western Balkans: Managing Change in Deeply Divided Societies*. Flensburg: European Centre for Minority Issues.

Bieber, F. 2005a. Partial Implementation, Partial Success: The Case of Macedonia, in *New Challenges for Power-Sharing: Institutional and Social Reform in Divided Societies*, ed. D. Russell and I. O'Flynn. London: Pluto Press, 107–22.

Bieber, F. 2005b. Power Sharing after Yugoslavia: Functionality and Dysfunctionality of Power-sharing Institutions in Post-war Bosnia, Macedonia, and Kosovo, in *From Power Sharing to Democracy*, ed. S. Noel. Montreal: McGill-Queen's University Press, 85–103.

Bieber, F. 2006. *Post-War Bosnia: Ethnicity, Inequality and Public Sector Governance*. Basingstoke: Palgrave Macmillan.

Bieber, F. 2007. *Guide to Minorities and Education: Foundation of Stable Relations in the Region*. Belgrade: Civic Initiatives and the King Baudouin Foundation.

Bieber, F. 2008. Power-Sharing and the Implementation of the Ohrid Framework Agreement, in *Power Sharing and the Implementation of the Ohrid Framework Agreement*, ed. Friedrich Ebert Stiftung. Skopje: Friedrich Ebert Stiftung, 7–40.

Bieber, F. 2015. How to Make EU Mediation Work in Macedonia. *Balkan Insight* (Online, 2 April 2015). Available at: www.balkaninsight.com/en/blog/how-to-make-eu-mediation-work-in-macedonia (accessed: 1 May 2015).

Bird, R. and R. Ebel (eds) 2007. *Fiscal Fragmentation in Decentralized Countries: Subsidiarity, Solidarity and Asymmetry.* Cheltenham: Edward Elgar Publishing.

Bland, G. 2010. Elections and the Development of Local Democracy, in *Making Decentralization Work: Democracy, Development, and Security*, ed. E. Connerley, K. Eaton and P. Smoke. Boulder, CO: Lynne Rienner, 47–80.

Blunt, P. and M. Turner 2005. Decentralization, Democracy and Development in a Post-Conflict Society: Commune Councils in Cambodia. *Public Administration and Development*, 25, 75–87.

Boex, J., J. Martinez-Vázquez and A. Timofeev 2004. *Sub-national Government Structure and Inter-governmental Fiscal Relations: An Overlooked Dimension of Decentralization.* Atlanta, GA: International Studies Program, Georgia State University.

Bonet, J. 2006. Fiscal Decentralization and Regional Income Disparities: Evidence from the Colombian Experience. *Annals of Regional Science*, 40, 661–76.

Bookchin, M. 1991. Libertarian Municipalism: An Overview. *Green Perspectives* (Online), 24. Available at: http://dwardmac.pitzer.edu/Anarchist_Archives/bookchin/gp/perspectives24.html (accessed: 19 May 2014).

Boone, C. 2003. Decentralization as a Political Strategy in West Africa. *Comparative Political Studies*, 36(4), 355–80.

Boskovska, I. 2010. The Decentralization Process in Macedonia, *Analytical*, 3(1), 87–98.

Braathen, E. and S. Bjerkreim Hellevik 2008. Decentralization, Peace Making and Conflict Management: from Regionalism to Municipalism. *Journal of Peace, Conflict and Development* (Online), 12. Available at: www.peacestudiesjournal.org.uk (accessed: 26 November 2010).

Brancati, D. 2006. Decentralization: Fueling the Fire or Dampening the Flames of Ethnic Conflict and Secessionism? *International Organization*, 60(3), 651–85.

Brancati, D. 2010. *Peace by Design: Managing Intrastate Conflict through Decentralization.* Oxford: Oxford University Press.

Brown, K. 2003. *The Past in Question: Modern Macedonia and the Uncertainties of Nation.* Princeton, NJ: Princeton University Press.

Brown, K., P. Farisides, S. Ordanoski and A. Fetahu (eds) 2002. *Ohrid and Beyond: A Cross-ethnic Investigation into the Macedonian Crisis.* London: Institute for War and Peace Reporting.

Brubaker, R. 1996. *Nationalism Reframed: Nationhood and the National Question in the New Europe.* Cambridge: Cambridge University Press.

Brunnbauer, U. 2002. The Implementation of the Ohrid Agreement: Ethnic Macedonian Resentments. *Journal of Ethnopolitics and Minority Issues in Europe* (Online), 1. Available at: www.ecmi.de/publications/detail/issue-12002-65/ (accessed: 2 March 2010).

Brunnbauer, U. 2004. Fertility, Families and Ethnic Conflict: Macedonians and Albanians in the Republic of Macedonia, 1944–2002. *Nationalities Papers*, 32, 566–97.

Budds, J. 2004. *A Report on the Status of Inter-municipal Cooperation.* Skopje: OSCE.

Bunce, V. 2004. Federalism, Nationalism, and Secession: The Communist and Postcommunist Experience, in *Federalism and Territorial Cleavages*, ed. U. Amoretti and N. Bermeo. Baltimore, MD: Johns Hopkins University Press, 417–40.

Bunce, V. and S. Watts 2005. Managing Diversity and Sustaining Democracy: Ethnofederal versus Unitary States in the Postcommunist World, in *Sustainable*

Peace: Power and Democracy after Civil Wars, ed. P. Roeder and D. Rothchild. Ithaca, NY: Cornell University Press, 133–58.

Burema, L. 2013. Decentralisation in Kosovo: Defusing Ethnic Tensions or Furthering Ethnic Isolation, in *Decentralization and Local Development in South East Europe*, ed. W. Bartlett, S. Maleković and V. Monastiriotis. Basingstoke: Palgrave Macmillan, 100–17.

Burgess, M. and J. Pinder (eds) 2011. *Multinational Federations*. Abingdon: Routledge.

Burki, S., G. Perry and W. Dillinger 1999. *Beyond the Center: Decentralizing the State*. Washington, DC: World Bank.

Caca, G. 1980. *The Constitutional Development of the Socialist Republic of Macedonia*. Skopje: Grafichki zavod Gotse Delchev.

Caca, G. 2001. Status and Rights of Nationalities in the Republic of Macedonia, in *The New Macedonian Question*, ed. J. Pettifer. Basingstoke: Palgrave Macmillan, 148–66.

Canaleta, C., P. Arzoz and M. Garate 2004. Regional Economic Disparities and Decentralization. *Urban Studies*, 41(1), 71–94.

Center for Local Democracy Development (CLDD) 2011. *Report on Monitoring the Decentralization Process: Performance of the Municipalities in the Republic of Macedonia, 2008–2009*. Skopje: CLDD.

Center for Research and Policy Making (CRPM) 2010. *Achieving Gender Equality in Macedonia*. Skopje: CRPM.

Center for Research and Policy Making (CRPM) 2013. *Analysis of Internal Party Democracy in Macedonia*. Skopje: CRPM.

Center for the Study of Local Democracy (CSLD) 2011a. *Progress or Standstill? Report on Monitoring the Decentralization Process in the Fields of Local Finances, Education and Urbanism for 2010*. Skopje: Foundation Open Society Macedonia.

Center for the Study of Local Democracy (CSLD) 2011b. *Reality or Only Municipal Competence? Monitoring the Decentralization of Local Economic Development in the Republic of Macedonia*. Skopje: Foundation Open Society Macedonia.

Chanie, P. 2007. Clientelism and Ethiopia's Post-1991 Decentralization. *Journal of Modern African Studies*, 45(3), 355–84.

Cheema, G. S. 2007. Devolution with Accountability: Learning from Good Practices, in *Decentralizing Governance: Emerging Concepts and Practices*, ed. G. S. Cheema and D. A. Rondinelli. Washington, DC: Brookings Institution Press, 170–88.

Cheema, G. S. and Rondinelli, D. A. (eds) 2007. *Decentralizing Governance: Emerging Concepts and Practices*. Washington, DC, Brookings Institution Press.

Choudhry, S. (ed.) 2008a. *Constitutional Design for Divided Societies: Integration or Accommodation?* Oxford: Oxford University Press.

Choudhry, S. 2008b. Does the World Need More Canada? The Politics of the Canadian Model in Constitutional Politics and Political Theory, in *Constitutional Design for Divided Societies: Integration or Accommodation?*, ed. S. Choudhry. Oxford: Oxford University Press, 141–72.

Coakley, J. 2001. *The Territorial Management of Ethnic Conflict*. London: Frank Cass.

Cocozzelli, F. 2008. Small Minorities in a Divided Polity: Turks, Bosniaks, Muslim Slavs and Roms, Ashkalis and Egyptians in Post-conflict Kosovo. *Ethnopolitics: Formerly Global Review of Ethnopolitics*, 7(2–3), 287–306.

Cohen, J. 2004. *Linking Decentralization and School Quality Improvement*. Washington, DC: Academy for Educational Development.

Collier, P. 2006. *Economic Causes of Civil Conflict and their Implications for Policy.* Oxford: University of Oxford.

Collier, P. and A. Hoeffler 2004. Greed and Grievance in Civil War. *Oxford Economic Papers*, 56, 563–95.

Common Values 2009. *Guide on the National Legislation in the Field of Using the Languages of Ethnic Communities in the Republic of Macedonia.* Skopje: Foundation Open Society Macedonia.

Community Development Institute (CDI) 2007. *Committees for Interethnic Relations: Establishment, Mandate and Existing Experiences.* Tetovo: CDI.

Connerley, E., K. Eaton and P. Smoke (eds) 2010. *Making Decentralization Work: Democracy, Development, and Security.* London: Lynne Rienner.

Coppedge, M. 1994. *Strong Parties and Lame Ducks: Presidential Partyarchy and Factionalism in Venezuela.* Stanford, CA: Stanford University Press.

Council of Europe (CoE) 1985. *European Charter of Local Self-Government.* Strasbourg: Council of Europe.

Council of Europe (CoE) 1992. *European Charter for Regional and Minority Languages.* Strasbourg: Council of Europe.

Council of Europe (CoE) 1995. *Framework Convention for the Protection of National Minorities.* Strasbourg: Council of Europe.

Council of Europe (CoE) 2005. *Toolkit of Local Government Capacity-Building Programmes.* Strasbourg: Council of Europe.

Council of Europe (CoE) 2008. *Advisory Committee on the Framework Commission for the Protection of National Minorities Second Opinion on 'the Former Yugoslav Republic of Macedonia' adopted on 23 February 2007.* Strasbourg: Council of Europe.

Cramer, C. 2006. *Civil War Is Not a Stupid Thing: Accounting for Violence in Developing Countries.* London: C. Hurst & Co.

Crawford, G. and C. Hartmann 2008. *Decentralization in Africa: A Pathway Out of Poverty and Conflict?* Amsterdam: Amsterdam University Press.

Crook, R. C. 2002. Decentralization and Good Governance, in *Federalism in a Changing World: Learning from Each Other*, ed. R. Blindenbacher. St. Gallen: Mass Market, 299–333.

Crook, R. and J. Manor (eds) 1998. *Democracy and Decentralization in South Asia and West Africa: Participation, Accountability and Performance.* Cambridge: Cambridge University Press.

Cyan, M., J. Martinez-Vazquez and A. Timofeev 2009. *Feasibility Study: Financing Equitable Service Delivery for All Citizens.* Skopje: UNDP.

Cyan, M., J. Martinez-Vazquez and A. Timofeev 2012. *Fiscal Decentralization for Local Development: An Integral Study.* Skopje: Ministry of Finance.

Daftary, F. and E. Friedman 2008. Power-Sharing in Macedonia?, in *Settling Self-Determination Disputes: Complex Power-Sharing in Theory and Practice*, ed. M. Weller, B. Metzger and N. Johnson. Leiden: Brill, 265–305.

Danforth, L. 1997. *The Macedonian Conflict: Ethnic Nationalism in a Transnational World.* Princeton, NJ: Princeton University Press.

Daskalovski, Z. 2006. *Walking on the Edge: Consolidating Multiethnic Macedonia 1989–2004.* Chapel Hill, NC: Globic Press.

De Grauwe, A. 2004. Decentralization: Can It Improve Schools? *International Institute for Educational Planning Newsletter*, 22, 1–3.

Dehnert, S. 2010. *Elections and Conflict in Macedonia.* Berlin: Friedrich Ebert Stiftung.

Demarchi, G. 2010. *Status Report: Implementation of the Action Plan on Improving the Situation of Roma and Sinti within the OSCE Area.* Skopje: Organization for Security and Co-operation in Europe.

Devarajan, S., S. Khemani, and S. Shah 2009. The Politics of Partial Decentralization, in *Does Decentralization Enhance Service Delivery and Poverty Reduction*, ed. E. Ahmad and G. Brosio. Cheltenham: Edward Elgar Publishing, 102–21.

Devas, N. and S. Delay 2006. Local Democracy and the Challenges of Decentralising the State: An International Perspective. *Local Government Studies*, 32(5), 677–95.

Deveaux, M. 2005. A Deliberative Approach to Conflicts of Culture, in *Minorities within Minorities: Equality, Rights and Diversity*, ed. J. Eisenberg and J. Spinner-Halev. Cambridge: Cambridge University Press, 340–62.

Di Gropello, E. 2004. *Education Decentralization and Accountability Relationships in Latin America.* Washington, DC: World Bank.

Diamond, L. 1999. *Developing Democracy: Toward Consolidation.* Baltimore, MD: Johns Hopkins University Press.

Dickovick, J. T. 2011. *Decentralization and Recentralization in the Developing World.* University Park, PA: Pennsylvania State University Press.

Dimitrova, K. 2004. Municipal Decisions on the Border of Collapse: Macedonian Decentralization and the Challenges of Post-Ohrid Democracy. *Southeast European Politics*, 5(2–3), 172–86.

Dimova, N. 2008. Identity of the Nation(s), Identity of the State: Politics and Ethnicity in the Republic of Macedonia, 1990–2000. *Ethnologia Balkanica*, 12, 183–213.

Dimova, R. 2010. Consuming Ethnicity: Loss, Commodities, and Space in Macedonia. *Slavic Review*, 69(4), 859–81.

Diprose, R. 2008. Passing on the Challenges or Prescribing Better Management of Diversity? Decentralization, Power Sharing and Conflict Dynamics in Central Sulawesi, Indonesia. *Conflict, Security and Development*, 8(4), 393–425.

Diprose, R. 2009. Decentralization, Horizontal Inequalities and Conflict Management in Indonesia. *Ethnopolitics: Formerly Global Review of Ethnopolitics*, 8(1), 107–34.

Dobrković, N. 2001. Yugoslavia and Macedonia, in *The New Macedonian Question*, ed. J. Pettifer. Basingstoke: Palgrave, 79–95.

Dragoman, D. 2011. Regional Inequalities, Decentralization and the Performance of Local Governments in Post-Communist Romania. *Local Government Studies*, 37(6), 647–69.

Eaton, K. 2001. Political Obstacles to Decentralization: Evidence from Argentina and the Philippines. *Development and Change*, 32, 101–27.

Eaton, K. 2004. Risky Business: Decentralization from Above in Chile and Uruguay. *Comparative Politics*, 37(1), 1–22.

Eaton, K. and E. Connerley 2010. Democracy, Development, and Security as Objectives of Decentralization, in *Making Decentralization Work: Democracy, Development, and Security*, ed. E. Connerley, K. Eaton and P. Smoke. Boulder, CO: Lynne Rienner, 1–24.

Eaton, K. and J. T. Dickovick 2004. The Politics of Re-centralization in Argentina and Brazil. *Latin American Research Review*, 39(1), 90–122.

Eaton, K., P. Kaiser and P. Smoke 2010. *The Political Economy of Decentralization Reforms: Implications for Aid Effectiveness.* Washington, DC: World Bank.

Ejobowah, J. B. 2008. Integrationist and Accommodationist Measures in Nigeria's Constitutional Engineering: Successes and Failures, in *Constitutional Design for*

Divided Societies: Integration or Accommodation?, ed. S. Choudhry. Oxford: Oxford University Press, 233–57.

Elazar, D. J. 1994. *Federalism and the Way to Peace.* Kingston, Ontario: Queen's University.

Emerson, M. 2015. *Is There Reason to Hope for Minsk II?* Brussels: Centre for European Policy Studies.

Emurli, A. 2010. *The Public Administration Reforms in the Host Country.* Skopje: Organization for Security and Co-operation in Europe.

Engström, J. 2002a. Multi-ethnicity or Bi-nationalism? The Framework Agreement and the Future of the Macedonian State. *Journal on Ethnopolitics and Minority Issues in Europe* (Online), 1. Available at: www.ecmi.de/publications/detail/issue-12002–65/ (accessed: 16 January 2009).

Engström, J. 2002b. The Power of Perception: The Impact of the Macedonian Question on Inter-ethnic Relations in the Republic of Macedonia. *Global Review of Ethnopolitics*, 1(3), 3–17.

Engström, J. 2009. *Democratisation and the Prevention of Violent Conflict: Lessons Learned from Bulgaria and Macedonia.* Farnham: Ashgate.

European Commission 2008. *The Former Yugoslav Republic of Macedonia Progress Report.* Brussels: European Commission.

European Commission 2009. *The Former Yugoslav Republic of Macedonia Progress Report.* Brussels: European Commission.

European Commission 2010. *The Former Yugoslav Republic of Macedonia Progress Report.* Brussels: European Commission.

European Commission 2011a. *Cohesion Policy 2014–2020: Investing in Growth and Jobs.* Brussels: European Commission.

European Commission 2011b. *The Former Yugoslav Republic of Macedonia Progress Report.* Brussels: European Commission.

European Commission against Racism and Intolerance (ECRI) 2005. *Report on the 'Former Yugoslav Republic of Macedonia' (3rd Cycle).* Strasbourg: ECRI.

European Commission against Racism and Intolerance (ECRI) 2010. *Report on the 'Former Yugoslav Republic of Macedonia' (4th Cycle).* Strasbourg: ECRI.

European Stability Initiative (ESI) 2002a. *Ahmeti's Village: The Political Economy of Interethnic Relations in Macedonia.* Skopje and Berlin: ESI. Available at: www.esiweb.org/pdf/esi_document_id_36.pdf (accessed: 17 March 2009).

European Stability Initiative (ESI) 2002b. *The Other Macedonian Conflict.* Skopje and Berlin: ESI. Available at: www.esiweb.org/pdf/esi_document_id_32.pdf (accessed: 15 May 2009).

European Union 2007. *Treaty of Lisbon Amending the Treaty on European Union and the Treaty Establishing the European Community*, 13 December 2007, 2007/C 306/01.

Evertzen, A. 2001. *Gender and Local Governance.* The Hague: SNV – Netherlands Development Organisation.

Falleti, T. 2005. A Sequential Theory of Decentralization: Latin American Cases in Comparative Perspective. *American Political Science Review*, 99(3), 327–46.

Fearon, J. and D. Laitin 2003. Ethnicity, Insurgency, and Civil War. *American Political Science Review*, 97(3), 75–90.

Feruglio, N., J. Martinez-Vazquez and A. Timofeev 2008. *An Assessment of Fiscal Decentralization in Macedonia.* Atlanta, GA: International Center for Public Policy, Georgia State University.

Forum – Center for Strategic Research and Documentation (CSRD) 2008. *Commissions for Inter-ethnic Relations in Municipalities of Macedonia*. Skopje: Forum CSRD.

Forum – Center for Strategic Research and Documentation (CSRD) 2011. *Research on Transparency and Accountability of the Units of Local Self-Government*. Skopje: Forum CSRD.

Foundation Metamorphosis and Common Values 2011. *An Interethnic Relations Committees Guide*. Skopje: Metamorphosis and Common Values.

Foundation Open Society Macedonia (FOSM) 2010. *Republic of Macedonia: Centralized (Fiscal) Decentralization*. Skopje: FOSM.

Fouéré, E. 2015. Gruevski Has Made a Nightmare Out of Macedonia. *Balkan Insight* (Online, 27 February 2015). Available at: www.balkaninsight.com/en/article/gruevski-has-made-a-nightmare-out-of-macedonia (accessed: 16 April 2015).

Fox, W. and C. Wallich 2007. Fiscal Federalism in Bosnia and Herzegovina: Subsidiarity and Solidarity in a Three-Nation State, in *Fiscal Fragmentation in Decentralized Countries: Subsidiarity, Solidarity and Asymmetry*, ed. R. Bird and R. Ebel. Cheltenham: Edward Elgar Publishing, 399–434.

Friedman, E. 2009. The Ethnopolitics of Territorial Division in the Republic of Macedonia. *Ethnopolitics: Formerly Global Review of Ethnopolitics*, 8(2), 209–21.

Galiani, S., P. Gertler and E. Schargrodsky 2004. Helping the Good Get Better, but Leaving the Rest Behind: How Decentralization Affects School Performance. Washington, DC: Research Triangle Institute.

García-Guadilla, M. and C. Pérez 2002. Democracy, Decentralization, and Clientelism: New Relationships and Old Practices. *Latin American Perspectives*, 29(5), 90–109.

Georgiev, P. 2008. *Corruptive Patterns of Patronage in South East Europe*. Wiesbaden: VS Europe.

Gesellschaft für Technische Zusammenarbeit (GTZ) 2006. *Decentralization and Conflicts: A Guide*. Eschborn: GTZ.

Gesellschaft für Technische Zusammenarbeit (GTZ) 2008a. *Cooperation for a Better Future: Regions Planning their Development*. Skopje: GTZ.

Gesellschaft für Technische Zusammenarbeit (GTZ) 2008b. *From a Pilot Project to a Nationwide Approach*. Skopje: GTZ.

Ghai, Y. 2000. *Autonomy and Ethnicity: Negotiating Competing Claims in Multi-ethnic States*. Cambridge: Cambridge University Press.

Ghai, Y. 2001. *Public Participation and Minorities*. London: Minority Rights Group International.

Gjoni, R., A. Wetterberg and D. Dunbar 2010. Decentralization as a Conflict Transformation Tool: The Challenge in Kosovo. *Public Administration and Development*, 30(5), 291–312.

Gligorov, K. 2001. The Unrealistic Dreams of Large States, in *The New Macedonian Question*, ed. J. Pettifer. Basingstoke: Palgrave Macmillan, 96–104.

Gorgevski, В. 2001. Академикот Ефремов ќе ја 'спасува' државата со размена на територии! *Dnevnik* newspaper, 31 May 2001, 1.

Government of the Republic of Macedonia 2004. *Programme for the Implementation of the Decentralization Process 2004–2007*. Skopje: Government of the Republic of Macedonia.

Government of the Republic of Macedonia 2010. *Third Report Submitted by 'The Former Yugoslav Republic of Macedonia' Pursuant to Article 25, Paragraph 1 of the*

Framework Convention for the Protection of National Minorities. Strasbourg: Council of Europe.

Government of the Republic of Macedonia 2012. *Report on the Implementation Status of all Policies Deriving from the Ohrid Framework Agreement.* Skopje: Government of the Republic of Macedonia.

Government of the Republic of Macedonia 2014a. *Annual Report on Municipal Revenues and Expenditures.* Skopje: Government of the Republic of Macedonia.

Government of the Republic of Macedonia 2014b. Програма на Владата на Република Македонија 2014–2018. Skopje: Government of the Republic of Macedonia.

Government of the Republic of Macedonia 2015. *2015–2020 Programme for Sustainable Development and Decentralization in the Republic of Macedonia.* Skopje: Government of the Republic of Macedonia.

Graan, A. 2013. Counterfeiting the Nation? Skopje 2014 and the Politics of Nation Branding in Macedonia. *Cultural Anthropology*, 28(1), 161–79.

Grasa, R. and A. Camps 2009. *Conflict Prevention and Decentralized Governance.* Barcelona: International Catalan Institute for Peace.

Green, E. 2008. Decentralization and Conflict in Uganda. *Conflict, Security and Development*, 8(4), 427–50.

Gurr, T. R. 1970. *Why Men Rebel.* Princeton, NJ: Princeton University Press.

Gurr, T. R. 1993. *Minorities at Risk: A Global View of Ethnopolitical Conflicts.* Washington, DC: United States Institute of Peace Press.

Gurr, T. R. 2000. *Peoples versus States: Minorities at Risk in the New Century.* Washington, DC: United States Institute of Peace Press.

Hadzi-Zafirova, Z. 2011. A Few Keys Short of a Keyboard. *Chalkboard.* Available at: http://chalkboard.tol.org/a-few-keys-short-of-a-keyboard/ (accessed: 20 February 2011).

Hale, H. 2004. Divided We Stand: Institutional Sources of Ethnofederal State Survival and Collapse. *World Politics*, 56, 165–93.

Hale, H. 2007. Correlates of Clientelism: Political Economy, Politicised Ethnicity, and Post-Communist Transition, in *Patrons, Clients and Policies: Patterns of Democratic Accountability and Political Competition*, ed. H. Kitshelt and S. Wilkinson. Cambridge: Cambridge University Press, 227–50.

Halili, N. 1991. *Republika Federale e Maqedonisë.* Unpublished declaration.

Hartmann, C. 2010. Decentralization and the Legacy of Protracted Conflict: Mauritius, Namibia and South Africa, in *Decentralization in Africa: A Pathway Out of Poverty and Conflict?*, ed. G. Crawford and C. Hartmann. Amsterdam: Amsterdam University Press, 169–90.

Hasani, Q. 2010. E vështirë të jesh shqiptar në Manastir. *Koha* newspaper (Online, 25 October 2010). Available at: www.koha.mk/ (accessed: 27 October 2010).

Heiberg, M., B. O'Leary and J. Tirman (eds) 2007. *Terror, Insurgency and the State: Ending Protracted Conflicts.* Philadelphia: University of Pennsylvania Press.

Helsinki Committee for Human Rights of the Republic of Macedonia 1999. *Annual Report for Year 1999.* Skopje: Helsinki Committee.

Herczyński, J. 2007. *Policy Paper: Treatment of Satellite Schools.* Unpublished report.

Herczyński, J. 2011. *Financing Decentralized Education in Macedonia: Review of the National Allocation System.* Skopje: USAID.

Herczyński, J., J. Vidanovska and N. Lacka 2009. The First Careful Step: Education Decentralization and Finance in the Republic of Macedonia, in *Public Money for Public Schools: Financing Education in South Eastern Europe*, ed. C. Bischoff. Budapest: Local Government and Public Service Reform Initiative, 103–48.

High Commissioner on National Minorities (HCNM) 1996. *The Hague Recommendations Regarding the Education Rights of National Minorities and Explanatory Note*. The Hague: HCNM.

High Commissioner on National Minorities (HCNM) 2004. *Recommendations on Promoting Integration through Education*. Unpublished report.

High Commissioner on National Minorities (HCNM) 2008. *Recommendations on Promoting Integration through Education* (updated). Unpublished report.

Hiskey, J. 2010. The Promise of Decentralized Democratic Governance, in *Making Decentralization Work*, ed. E. Connerley, K. Eaton and P. Smoke. London: Lynne Rienner, 25–46.

Hislope, R. 2001. The Calm Before the Storm? The Influence of Cross-border Networks, Corruption, and Contraband on Macedonian Stability and Regional Security. Presented at the Annual Meeting of the American Political Science Association, San Francisco, USA, September 2001.

Hislope, R. 2003. Between a Bad Peace and a Good War: Insights and Lessons from the Almost-War in Macedonia. *Ethnic and Racial Studies*, 26(1), 129–51.

Hodžic, E. 2011. *Political Participation of National Minorities in Local Governance in Bosnia and Herzegovina*. Sarajevo: Analitika – Center for Social Research.

Holohan, A. 2005. *Networks of Democracy: Lessons from Kosovo for Afghanistan, Iraq, and Beyond*. Stanford, CA: Stanford University Press.

Hoodie, M. and C. Hartzell 2005. Power Sharing in Peace Settlements: Initiating the Transition from Civil War, in *Sustainable Peace: Power and Democracy after Civil Wars*, ed. P. Roeder and D. Rothchild. Ithaca, NY: Cornell University Press, 83–106.

Hopkin, J. 2003. Political Decentralization, Electoral Change and Party Organization Adaption: A Framework for Analysis. *European Urban and Regional Studies*, 10(3), 227–37.

Horowitz, D. L. 1991. *A Democratic South Africa? Constitutional Engineering in a Divided Society*. Berkeley: University of California Press.

Horowitz, D. L. 1993. Democracy in Divided Societies. *Journal of Democracy*, 4(4), 18–38.

Horowitz, D. L. 2000. *Ethnic Groups in Conflict*. London: University of California Press.

Horowitz, D. L. 2007. The Many Uses of Federalism. *Drake Law Review*, 55, 953–66.

Horvat, B. 1976. *The Yugoslav Economic System*. White Plains, NY: International Arts and Sciences Press.

Human Rights Watch 1996. *A Threat to 'Stability': Human Rights Violations in Macedonia*. Skopje: HRW. Available at: www.hrw.org/reports/1996/Macedoni.htm (accessed: 2 December 2009).

IDIVIDI 2011. Parliament Passes Amendments to Law on Use of Flags of Ethnic Communities. IDIVIDI (Online, 5 October 2011). Available at: www.idividi.com. mk/ (accessed: 5 October 2011).

Ilievski, Z. 2007. *Country Specific Report: Conflict Settlement Agreement Macedonia*. Bozen/Bolzano: European Academy of Bozen/Bolzano. Available at: www.eurac. edu/en/research/autonomies/minrig/Documents/Mirico/16%20Macedonia.pdf (accessed: 2 July 2009).

Ilievski, Z. 2008. *Between Consociational and Integrative Power-Sharing: The Case of Macedonia*. Skopje: SS Cyril and Methodius University.

Ilijevski, K. 2012. Skopje Revamp Devours Macedonian Heritage Funds. *Balkan Insight* (Online, 6 April 2011). Available at: www.balkaninsight.com/en/article/skopje-revamp-devours-macedonian-heritage-funds (accessed: 3 March 2012).

Illner, M. 1998. Territorial Decentralization: An Obstacle to Democratic Reform in Central and Eastern Europe?, in *The Transfer of Power: Decentralization in Central and Eastern Europe*, ed. J. D. Kimball. Budapest: Local Government and Public Service Reform Initiative, 7–42.

Institute for Regional and International Studies (IRIS). 2006. *The Process of Decentralization in Macedonia: Prospects for Ethnic Conflict Mitigation, Enhanced Representation, Institutional Efficiency and Accountability*. Sofia: IRIS.

International Crisis Group (ICG) 1998. *The Albanian Question in Macedonia: Implications of the Kosovo Conflict for Inter-Ethnic Relations in Macedonia*. Skopje and Sarajevo: ICG. Available at: www.crisisgroup.org (accessed: 12 December 2009).

International Crisis Group (ICG) 1999. *Macedonia: Towards Destabilisation?* Skopje and Brussels: ICG. Available at: www.crisisgroup.org (accessed: 12 May 2012).

International Crisis Group (ICG) 2001. *Macedonia: Still Sliding*. Skopje and Brussels: ICG. Available at: www.crisisgroup.org (accessed: 19 May 2012).

International Crisis Group (ICG) 2003. *Macedonia: No Room for Complacency*. Skopje and Brussels: ICG. Available at: www.crisisgroup.org (accessed: 10 December 2009).

International Crisis Group (ICG) 2004. *Macedonia: Make or Break*. Skopje and Brussels: ICG. Available at: www.crisisgroup.org (accessed: 11 December 2009).

International Crisis Group (ICG) 2011. *Macedonia: Ten Years after the Conflict*. Skopje/Istanbul/Brussels: ICG. Available at: www.crisisgroup.org (accessed: 20 August 2011).

International Development Research Center (IDRC) 2008. *Decentralization, Local Power and Women's Rights: Global Trends in Participation, Representation and Access to Public Services*. Ottawa: IDRC.

International Monetary Fund (IMF) 2003. *Former Yugoslav Republic of Macedonia: Preparing for Fiscal Decentralization*. Washington, DC: IMF.

International Monetary Fund (IMF) 2009. *Macro Policy Lessons for a Sound Design of Fiscal Decentralization*. Washington, DC: IMF.

Jeram, S. 2008. Making Decentralization Work in Ethnically Divided Societies: State and Societal Synergism. Presented at the Ethnic and Pluralism Studies Student Conference, University of Toronto, Canada, April 2008.

Judah. T. 2001. A Greater Albania? *New York Review of Books*, 48(8), 35–7.

Kälin, W. 1999. Decentralization: Why and How?, in *Decentralization and Development*, ed. Swiss Agency for Development and Co-operation (SDC). Berne: SDC Publications, 46–69.

Kälin, W. 2004. Decentralized Governance in Fragmented Societies: Solution or Cause of New Evils?, in *Facing Ethnic Conflicts: Toward a New Realism*, ed. A. Wimmer, R. Goldstone, D. L. Horowitz, U. Joras and C. Schetter. Lanham, MD: Rowman and Littlefield, 301–11.

Karajkov, R. 2006. *The Challenge of Regional Development in the Republic of Macedonia: The State of the Matter, Issues and Considerations*. Budapest: Open Society Initiative.

Kauzya, J. M. 2005. *Decentralization: Prospects for Peace, Democracy and Development*. New York: United Nations.

Keefer, P. 2005. *Democratization and Clientelism: Why are Young Democracies Badly Governed?* Washington, DC: World Bank.

Keen, D. 1996. War: What Is It Good For? *Contemporary Politics*, 2(1), 23–36.

Keen, D. 1998. *The Economic Functions of Violence in Civil Wars*. Adelphi Papers 320. London: International Institute for Strategic Studies.

Keen, D. 2001. A Response to Paul Collier's 'Doing Well Out of War' and Other Thoughts. Presented at the CODEP Conference, School of Oriental and African Studies, London, UK, June 2001.

Ker-Lindsay, J. 2011. *Kosovo: The Path to Contested Statehood in the Balkans*. London: I.B.Tauris.

Khalidi, R. and S. Samour 2011. Neoliberalism as Liberation: The Statehood Program and the Remaking of the Palestinian National Movement. *Journal of Palestine Studies*, 40(2), 6–25.

Khemani, S. 2010. *Political Capture of Decentralization: Vote-Buying through Grants-Financed Local Jurisdictions*. Washington, DC: World Bank.

King, I. and W. Mason 2006. *Peace at Any Price: How the World Failed Kosovo*. London: C. Hurst & Co.

Kitshelt, H. and S. Wilkinson (eds) 2007. *Patrons, Clients and Policies: Patterns of Democratic Accountability and Political Competition*. Cambridge: Cambridge University Press.

Klekovski, S. 2011. Охридски Рамковен Договор – Интервјуа. Skopje: Macedonian Center for International Cooperation.

Klekovski, S., E. Huredinoska and D. Stojanova 2010. Дпвербата вп Македпнија. Skopje: Macedonian Center for International Cooperation.

Kocevski, A. 2009. *Current Status of Capital Grants Allocation to the Units of Local Self-Government in Republic of Macedonia*. Skopje: USAID/MLGA.

Koinova, M. 2013. *Ethnonationalist Conflict in Postcommunist States: Varieties of Governance in Bulgaria, Macedonia, and Kosovo*. Philadelphia: University of Pennsylvania Press.

Koktsidis, P. 2012. *Strategic Rebellion: Ethnic Conflict in FYR Macedonia and the Balkans*. Berne: Peter Lang.

Kola, P. 2003. *The Search for Greater Albania*. London: C. Hurst & Co.

Kreci, V. and B. Ymeri 2010. The Impact of Territorial Re-organisational Policy Interventions in the Republic of Macedonia. *Local Government Studies*, 36(2), 271–90.

Kumanovo Municipality 2010. *Strategy for Education Development in the Municipality of Kumanovo for the Period of 2011–2016*. Kumanovo: Municipality of Kumanovo.

Kumanovo Municipality Committee for Interethnic Relations 2011. *Report of the Spatial Problems and the Needs of the Secondary Schools Where the Education is Developed in Albanian Language*. Kumanovo: Municipality of Kumanovo.

Lake, D. and D. Rothchild 2005. Territorial Decentralization and Civil War Settlements, in *Sustainable Peace: Power and Democracy after Civil War*, ed. P. Roeder and D. Rothchild. Ithaca, NY: Cornell University Press, 109–32.

Lambright, G. 2011. *Decentralization in Uganda: Explaining Successes and Failures in Local Governance*. London: First Forum Press.

Langer, A. 2008. When do Horizontal Inequalities Lead to Conflict? Lessons from a Comparative Study of Ghana and Côte d'Ivoire, in *Horizontal Inequalities and Conflict: Understanding Group Violence in Multiethnic Societies*, ed. F. Stewart. Basingstoke: Palgrave Macmillan, 163–89.

Langer, A. and G. Brown 2008. Cultural Status Inequalities: An Important Dimension of Group Mobilisation, in *Horizontal Inequalities and Conflict: Understanding Group Violence in Multiethnic Societies*, ed. F. Stewart. Basingstoke, Palgrave Macmillan, 41–53.

Langer, A., F. Stewart and R. Venugopal 2012. Horizontal Inequalities and Post-Conflict Development: Laying the Foundations for Durable Peace, in *Horizontal Inequalities and Post-Conflict Development*, ed. A. Langer, F. Stewart and R. Venugopal. Basingstoke: Palgrave Macmillan, 1–27.

Lapidoth, R. 1997. *Autonomy: Flexible Solutions to Ethnic Conflicts.* Washington, DC: United States Institute of Peace.

Latifi, V. 2001. *Macedonian Unfinished Crisis: Challenges in the Process of Democratization and Stabilization.* Skopje: Konrad Adenauer Stiftung.

Lessmann, C. 2009. Fiscal Decentralization and Regional Disparity: Evidence from Cross-section and Panel Data. *Environment and Planning*, 41(10), 2455–73.

Levitas, T. 2002. *Preparing for Education Decentralization in Macedonia: Issues, Directions, Actions.* Skopje: USAID/DAI.

Levitas, T. 2009. *Local Government Finances in Macedonia Today: Possible Reforms for Tomorrow.* Skopje: USAID/MLGA.

Levitas, T. 2011a. *Local Government Finances and the Status of Fiscal Decentralization in Macedonia: A Statistical Review 2008–2011.* Skopje: USAID/MLGA.

Levitas, T. 2011b. *Too Much of a Good Thing? Own Revenues and the Political Economy of Inter-governmental Finance Reform: The Albanian Case.* Washington, DC: Urban Institute Center on International Development and Governance.

Levitas, T. and J. Herczyński 2002. Decentralization, Local Governments and Education Reform and Finance in Poland: 1990–1999, in *Decentralizing Education in Post-communist Europe*, ed. K. Davey. Budapest: Local Government Initiative-Open Society Institute, 113–91.

Lijphart, A. 1977. *Democracy in Plural Societies: A Comparative Exploration.* London: Yale University Press.

Lijphart, A. 1999. *Patterns of Democracy: Government Forms and Performance in Thirty-Six Countries.* London: Yale University Press.

Lijphart, A. 2002. The Wave of Power-Sharing Democracy, in *The Architecture of Democracy: Constitutional Design, Conflict Management, and Democracy*, ed. A. Reynolds. Oxford: Oxford University Press, 37–54.

Lijphart, A. 2008. *Thinking about Democracy: Power Sharing and Majority Rule in Theory and Practice.* Abingdon: Routledge.

Liotta, P. and C. Jebb 2004. *Mapping Macedonia: Idea and Identity.* Westpoint, NY: Praeger.

Litvack, J., J. Ahmad and R. Bird 1998. *Rethinking Decentralization.* Washington, DC: World Bank.

Lockwood, B. 2009. Political Economy Approaches to Fiscal Decentralization, in *Does Decentralization Enhance Service Delivery and Poverty Reduction?*, ed. E. Ahmad and G. Brosio. Cheltenham: Edward Elgar Publishing, 79–101.

Lund, M. 2000. Preventive Diplomacy for Macedonia, 1992–1999: From Containment to Nation Building, in *Opportunities Missed, Opportunities Seized: Preventive Diplomacy in the Post-Cold War World*, ed. B. Jentleson. Oxford: Rowman and Littlefield, 173–208.

Lyon, A. 2013. Decentralisation and the Provision of Primary and Secondary Education in the Former Yugoslav Republic of Macedonia. *International Journal on Minority and Group Rights*, 20(4), 491–516.

Lyon, A. 2014. Challenges to Municipal Fiscal Autonomy in Macedonia. *Publius: The Journal of Federalism*, 44(4), 633–58.

Lyon, A. 2015. Political Decentralization and the Strengthening of Consensual, Participatory Local Democracy in the Republic of Macedonia. *Democratization*, 22(1), 157–78.

Macedonian Center for International Cooperation (MCIC) 2006. *Directory of the Municipalities in the Republic of Macedonia*. Skopje: MCIC.

Macedonian Center for International Cooperation (MCIC) 2010. *Directory of the Municipalities in the Republic of Macedonia*. Skopje: MCIC.

Macedonian Center for International Cooperation (MCIC) 2011. Охридски рамкОвен договор интервјуа. Skopje: MCIC.

Macedonia Local Government Activity (MLGA) 2011. *Education Funding Report*. Skopje: USAID.

McGarry, J. 2008. Power-Sharing Theory: Lessons from the Complex Power-Sharing Project, in *Settling Self-Determination Disputes: Complex Power-Sharing in Theory and Practice*, ed. M. Weller, B. Metzger and N. Johnson. Leiden: Brill, 691–719.

McGarry, J. and B. O'Leary 2004. *The Northern Ireland Conflict: Consociational Engagements*. Oxford: Oxford University Press.

McGarry, J. and B. O'Leary 2005. Federation as a Method of Ethnic Conflict Regulation, in *From Power Sharing to Democracy*, ed. S. Noel. Montreal: McGill-Queen's University Press, 263–96.

McGarry, J. and B. O'Leary 2007. Iraq's Constitution of 2005: Liberal Consociation as Political Prescription. *International Journal of Constitutional Law*, 5(4), 670–98.

McGarry, J. and B. O'Leary 2008. Consociation and its Critics: Northern Ireland after the Belfast Agreement, in *Constitutional Design for Divided Societies: Integration or Accommodation?*, ed. S. Choudhry. Oxford: Oxford University Press, 368–408.

McGarry, J. and B. O'Leary 2009. Must Pluri-national Federations Fail? *Ethnopolitics: Formerly Global Review of Ethnopolitics*, 8(1), 5–26.

McGarry, J. and B. O'Leary 2011. Territorial Approaches to Ethnic Conflict Settlement, in *The Routledge Handbook of Ethnic Conflict*, ed. K. Cordell and S. Wolff. Abingdon: Routledge, 249–65.

McGarry, J., B. O'Leary and R. Simeon 2008. Integration or Accommodation? The Enduring Debate in Conflict Regulation, in *Constitutional Design for Divided Societies: Integration or Accommodation?*, ed. S. Choudhry. Oxford: Oxford University Press, 41–88.

McGinn, N. and T. Welsh 1999. *Decentralization of Education: Why, When, What and How?* Paris: UNESCO.

Mahajan, G. 2005. Can Intra-group Equality Coexist with Cultural Diversity? Re-examining Multicultural Frameworks of Accommodation, in *Minorities within Minorities: Equality, Rights and Diversity*, ed. A. Eisenberg and J. Spinner-Halev. Cambridge: Cambridge University Press, 90–112.

Malcolm, N. 1998. *Kosovo: A Short History*. London: Macmillan.

Mandaci, N. 2007. Turks of Macedonia: The Travails of the 'Smaller' Minority. *Journal of Muslim Minority Affairs*, 27(1), 5–23.

Manor, J. 1999. *The Political Economy of Democratic Decentralization*. Washington, DC: World Bank.

Marko, J. 2004/5. The Referendum on Decentralization in Macedonia in 2004: A Litmus Test for Macedonia's Interethnic Relations. *European Yearbook for Minority Issues*, 4(1), 695–721.

Marusic, S. J. 2010. Part of 'Skopje 2014' Struck Down in Constitutional Court. *Balkan Insight* (Online, 1 July 2010). Available at: www.balkaninsight.com/en/article/part-of-skopje-2-aa4-struck-down-in-constitutional-court (accessed: 22 March 2012).

Marusic, S. 2011a. Macedonia Scraps Failed 'Census'. *Balkan Insight* (Online, 13 October 2011). Available at: www.balkaninsight.com/en/article/macedonian-population-census-fails (accessed: 13 October 2011).

Marusic, S. 2011b. Macedonia's Capital Project Costs 250m Euro. *Balkan Insight* (Online, 9 December 2011). Available at: www.balkaninsight.com/en/article/macedonia-s-skopje-2åaa4-eats-quarter-billion-euros (accessed: 2 May 2012).

Marusic, S. 2011c. Macedonia Braces for Giant Statue of Philip. *Balkan Insight* (Online, 14 December 2011). Available at: www.balkaninsight.com/en/article/macedonian-capital-embraces-for-statue-of-philip (accessed: 22 March 2012).

Marusic, S. 2012. Riverside Galleon Plan Puts Wind Up Macedonians. *Balkan Insight* (Online, 7 March 2012). Available at: www.balkaninsight.com/en/article/skopje-s-pirate-ships-cause-stir (accessed: 22 March 2012).

Marusic, S. 2014. Macedonia Contract Workers Protest Tax Increase. *Balkan Insight* (Online, 22 December 2014). Available at: www.balkaninsight.com/en/article/macedonia-contract-workers-protest-tax-increase (accessed: 1 May 2015).

Marusic, S. 2015a. Macedonia Opposition Reveals More Evidence of Election Fraud. *Balkan Insight* (Online, 10 March 2015). Available at: www.balkaninsight.com/en/article/macedonia-awaits-more-evidence-of-election-trickery (accessed: 1 May 2015).

Marusic, S. 2015b. Macedonia MPs Kept on Tight Leash, Tapes Reveal. *Balkan Insight* (Online, 20 March 2015). Available at: www.balkaninsight.com/en/article/macedonian-mps-kept-on-a-tight-leash-tapes-reveal (accessed: 1 May 2015).

Marusic, S. 2015c. Macedonia Opposition Makes Fresh Election Fraud Claims. *Balkan Insight* (Online, 2 April 2015). Available at: www.balkaninsight.com/en/article/macedonia-opposition-reveals-more-tapes-of-election-trickery (accessed: 16 April 2015).

Marusic, S. 2015d. Macedonia Opposition: PM 'Ordered Attack on Mayor'. *Balkan Insight* (Online, 20 April 2015). Available at: www.balkaninsight.com/en/article/tapes-macedonia-pm-orders-attack-against-opposition-mayor (accessed: 2 May 2015).

Marusic, S. 2015e. Macedonian Students and Pupils Unite in Protest. *Balkan Insight* (Online, 23 April 2015). Available at: www.balkaninsight.com/en/article/big-protest-unites-macedonian-pupils-and students (accessed: 4 May 2015).

Mavrikos-Adamou, T. 2010. Challenges to Democracy Building and the Role of Civil Society. *Democratization*, 7(3), 514–33.

Mehmeti, E. 2008. Implementation of the Ohrid Framework Agreement, in *Power Sharing and the Implementation of the Ohrid Framework Agreement*, ed. Friedrich Ebert Stiftung. Skopje: Friedrich Ebert Stiftung, 67–88.

Meligrana, J. and F. Razin 2004. Changing Local Government Boundaries in Different Political-Ideological Environments, in *Redrawing Local Government Boundaries*, ed. J. Meligrana. Vancouver: UBC Press, 227–39.

Metamorphosis and Common Values 2011. *An Interethnic Relations Committees Guide*. Skopje: Metamorphosis and Common Values.

Mitchell Group 2008. *Impact Evaluation of the Community Revitalization through Democratic Action Program (CRDA), Serbia Local Government Reform Program (SLGRP), and Serbia Enterprise Development Project (SEDP)*. Washington, DC: Mitchell Group.

Mijalkovic, M. and K. Urbanek 2011. *Skopje: The World's Bastard*. Skopje: Wieser Verlag.

Milosavlevski, S. 2003. Minorities in Macedonia in the Political and Constitutional Acts: From the 1903 Krushevo Manifest to the 2001 Constitutional Amendments. *New Balkan Politics* (Online), 7/8. Available at: www.newbalkanpolitics.org.mk/cat/Issue-7 (accessed: 1 February 2010).

Minchev, O. 2005. *Macedonia: Analytical Overview 2005*. Sofia: Institute for Regional and International Studies. Available at:www.iris-bg.org/files/Macedonia_Analytical%20 Overview.pdf (accessed: 20 December 2009).

Ministry of Agriculture, Forestry and Water Economy 2007. *National Agricultural and Rural Development Strategy (NARDS) for the Period 2007–2013*. Skopje: Government of the Republic of Macedonia.

Ministry of Education and Science (MoES) 2005. *National Strategy for the Development of Education in the Republic of Macedonia, 2005–2015*. Skopje: Government of the Republic of Macedonia.

Ministry of Education and Science (MoES) 2010a. *Current State of Primary Education of Students Belonging to Ethnic Communities in the Republic of Macedonia*. Skopje: Government of the Republic of Macedonia.

Ministry of Education and Science (MoES) 2010b. *Steps towards Integrated Education in the Education System of the Republic of Macedonia*. Skopje: Government of the Republic of Macedonia.

Ministry of Labor and Social Policy (MoLSP) 2007. *National Action Plan for Gender Equality, 2007–2012*. Skopje: Government of the Republic of Macedonia

Ministry of Labor and Social Policy (MoLSP) 2009. *Capacity Training Needs Assessment: Support to Women and Men Equal Opportunities Commissions at Local Government Units*. Skopje: Government of the Republic of Macedonia.

Ministry of Local Self-Government (MoLSG) 2006. *Граѓаните и Опшtината*. Skopje: Government of the Republic of Macedonia.

Ministry of Local Self-Government (MoLSG) 2009a. Акционен план за спроведување на Стратегијата за регионален развој на Република Македонија (2010–2012). Skopje: Government of the Republic of Macedonia.

Ministry of Local Self-Government (MoLSG) 2009b. Стратегија за регионален развој на Република Македонија 2009–19. Skopje: Government of the Republic of Macedonia.

Ministry of Local Self-Government (MoLSG) 2011a. *Planning Regions in the Republic of Macedonia*. Skopje: Government of the Republic of Macedonia.

Ministry of Local Self-Government (MoLSG) 2011b. *Programme for Implementation of the Decentralization Process and Local Self-Government Development in the Republic of Macedonia 2011–2014*. Skopje: Government of the Republic of Macedonia.

Mojsovska, S. 2011. *Decentralization and Regional Policy in the Republic of Macedonia: Developments and Perspectives*. London: London School of Economics.

Monastiriotis, V. 2013. The Nature of Spatial Inequalities in South East Europe and the Scope for Decentralized Regional Policy: An Analysis of Bulgaria and Serbia, in *Decentralization and Local Development in South East Europe*, ed. W. Bartlett, S. Maleković and V. Monastiriotis. Basingstoke: Palgrave Macmillan, 213–30.

Montero, A. P. 2005. The Politics of Decentralization in a Centralized Party System: The Case of Democratic Spain. *Comparative Politics*, 38(1), 63–82.

Myhrvold, R. 2005. *Former Yugoslav Republic of Macedonia: Education as a Political Phenomenon*. Oslo: Norwegian Centre for Human Rights.

Nansen Dialogue Centre Skopje (NDC) 2005. *Inter-ethnic Relations, Education and Economic Perspectives of the Municipality of Jegunovce*. Skopje: NDC.

Network of Associations of Local Authorities of South-East Europe (NALAS) 2010. *Distribution of VAT and PIT between Municipalities and Central Budget*. Skopje: NALAS.

Network of Associations of Local Authorities of South-East Europe (NALAS) 2012. *Fiscal Decentralization Indicators for South-East Europe: 2006–2011*. Skopje: NALAS.

Network of Associations of Local Authorities of South-East Europe (NALAS) 2015. *Fiscal Decentralization Indicators for South-East Europe: 2006–2013*. Skopje: NALAS.

Neofotistos, V. 2011. Going Home to Pakistan: Identity and Its Discontents in Southeastern Europe. *Identities: Global Studies in Culture and Power*, 18(4), 291–316.

Neofotistos, V. 2012. *The Risk of War. Everyday Sociality in the Republic of Macedonia*. Philadelphia: University of Pennsylvania Press.

Newman, E., R. Paris and O. Richmond (eds) 2009. *New Perspectives on Liberal Peacebuilding*. New York: United Nations University Press.

Nikolov, M. 2007. *Report on the Process of Decentralization in Macedonia* Skopje: Center for Economic Analysis.

Nimni, E. 2007. National-Cultural Autonomy as an Alternative to Minority Territorial Nationalism. *Ethnopolitics: Formerly Global Review of Ethnopolitics*, 6(3), 345–64.

Nordlinger, E. 1972. *Conflict Regulation in Divided Societies*. Cambridge, MA: Harvard University.

Norris, P. 2008. *Driving Democracy: Do Power-Sharing Institutions Work?* Cambridge: Cambridge University Press.

Novkovska, B. 2001. *Statistical Data for Background Purposes of OECD Review. Country: Republic of Macedonia*. Ljubljana: University of Ljubljana.

O'Dwyer, C. 2006. *Runaway State-Building*. Baltimore, MD: Johns Hopkins University Press.

O'Leary, B. 2008a. The Logics of Power-sharing, Consociation and Pluralist Federations, in *Settling Self-Determination Disputes: Complex Power-Sharing in Theory and Practice*, ed. M. Weller, B. Metzger and N. Johnson. Leiden: Brill, 47–58.

O'Leary, B. 2008b. Complex Power-Sharing in and over Northern Ireland: A Self-Determination Agreement, a Treaty, a Consociation, a Federacy, Matching Confederal Institutions, Intergovernmentalism, and a Peace Process, in *Settling Self-Determination Disputes: Complex Power-Sharing in Theory and Practice*, ed. M. Weller, B. Metzger and N. Johnson. Leiden: Brill, 61–124.

O'Neill, K. 2003. Decentralization as an Electoral Strategy. *Comparative Political Studies*, 36, 1068–91.

O'Neill, K. 2005. *Decentralizing the State: Elections, Parties and Local Power in the Andes*. New York: Cambridge University Press.

Oates, W. 1972. *Fiscal Federalism*. New York: Harcourt Brace Jovanovich.

Oates, W. (ed.) 1977. *The Political Economy of Fiscal Federalism*. Lexington, MA: Lexington Books.

Office of Democratic Institutions and Human Rights (ODIHR) 2000. *The Former Yugoslav Republic of Macedonia Municipal Elections 10 September 2000, OSCE/ODIHR Election Observation Mission Final Report*. Warsaw: ODIHR.

Office of Democratic Institutions and Human Rights (ODIHR) 2005. *The Former Yugoslav Republic of Macedonia Municipal Elections 13 and 27 March, and 10 April 2005, OSCE/ODIHR Election Observation Mission Final Report*. Warsaw: ODIHR.

Office of Democratic Institutions and Human Rights (ODIHR) 2009. *The Former Yugoslav Republic of Macedonia Municipal Elections 22 March and 5 April 2009, OSCE/ODIHR Election Observation Mission Final Report*. Warsaw: ODIHR.

Office of Democratic Institutions and Human Rights (ODIHR) 2013. *The Former Yugoslav Republic of Macedonia Municipal Elections 24 March and 7 April 2013. Final Report*. Warsaw: ODIHR.

Office of the Higher Representative and EU Special Representative (OHR) 1995. *The General Framework Agreement for Peace in Bosnia and Herzegovina*. Available at: www.ohr.int/dpa/default.asp?content_id=380 (accessed: 21 January 2011).

Official Gazette of the Republic of Macedonia 1991. *Constitution of the Republic of Macedonia*. Skopje: Government of the Republic of Macedonia.

Official Gazette of the Republic of Macedonia 1994. *Law on Stimulation of the Development of the Economically Underdeveloped Regions*. Skopje: Government of the Republic of Macedonia.

Official Gazette of the Republic of Macedonia 1995. *Law on Local Self-Government*. Skopje: Government of the Republic of Macedonia.

Official Gazette of the Republic of Macedonia 1996. *Law for the Territorial Division of the Republic of Macedonia and the Units of Local Self-Government*. Skopje: Government of the Republic of Macedonia.

Official Gazette of the Republic of Macedonia 2001a. *Constitution of the Republic of Macedonia*. Skopje: Government of the Republic of Macedonia.

Official Gazette of the Republic of Macedonia 2001b. *Framework Agreement*. Skopje: Government of the Republic of Macedonia.

Official Gazette of the Republic of Macedonia 2002. *Law on Local Self-Government*. Skopje: Government of the Republic of Macedonia.

Official Gazette of the Republic of Macedonia 2004. *Law on Financing of the Units of Local Self-Government*. Skopje: Government of the Republic of Macedonia.

Official Gazette of the Republic of Macedonia 2005. *Law on Use of Flags of the Communities of the Republic of Macedonia*. Skopje: Government of the Republic of Macedonia.

Official Gazette of the Republic of Macedonia 2006. *Law on Equal Opportunities of Women and Men*. Skopje: Government of the Republic of Macedonia.

Official Gazette of the Republic of Macedonia 2007. *Law on Balanced Regional Development*. Skopje: Government of the Republic of Macedonia.

Official Gazette of the Republic of Macedonia 2008a. *Law on Secondary Education*. Skopje: Government of the Republic of Macedonia.

Official Gazette of the Republic of Macedonia 2008b. *Law on the Use of a Language Spoken by At Least 20% of the Citizens in Republic of Macedonia and in the Units of Local Self-Government*. Skopje: Government of the Republic of Macedonia.

Official Gazette of the Republic of Macedonia 2009a. *Law on Inter-municipal Cooperation*. Skopje: Government of the Republic of Macedonia.

Official Gazette of the Republic of Macedonia 2009b. *Law on Primary Education*. Skopje: Government of the Republic of Macedonia.

Ombudsman of the Republic of Macedonia 2011. *Annual Report 2010*. Skopje: Government of the Republic of Macedonia.

Open Society Institute (OSI) 2007. *Equal Access to Quality Education for Roma*, vol. 2: *Monitoring Reports for Croatia, Macedonia, Montenegro, Slovakia*. Budapest: OSI.

Open Society Institute (OSI) 2009. *10 Goals for Improving Access to Education for Roma*. Budapest: OSI.

Ordanoski, S. and A. Matovski 2007. *Between Ohrid and Dayton: The Future of Macedonia's Framework Agreement*. Skopje: Forum.

Organization for Security and Co-operation in Europe (OSCE) 2006a. *Decentralization Survey 2006*. Skopje: OSCE.

Organization for Security and Co-operation in Europe (OSCE) 2006b. *Education and Decentralization: User-Friendly Guide*. Skopje: OSCE.

Organization for Security and Co-operation in Europe (OSCE) 2007. *Survey on Decentralization*. Skopje: OSCE.

Organization for Security and Co-operation in Europe (OSCE) 2008a. *An Updated Overview of the Pre-school and Primary Education Sectors*. Skopje: OSCE.

Organization for Security and Co-operation in Europe (OSCE) 2008b. An Updated Overview of the Secondary Education Sector in the Host Country. Unpublished report.

Organization for Security and Co-operation in Europe (OSCE) 2008c. *Decentralization Survey 2008*. Skopje: OSCE.

Organization for Security and Co-operation in Europe (OSCE) 2008d. *Education and Decentralization: What Stakeholders Really Know and Think about Their Roles, Responsibilities and Rights*. Skopje: OSCE.

Organization for Security and Co-operation in Europe (OSCE) 2008e. *Separation in Schools: Facts and Figures*. Unpublished report.

Organization for Security and Co-operation in Europe (OSCE) 2009. *Decentralization Survey 2009*. Skopje: OSCE.

Organization for Security and Co-operation in Europe (OSCE) 2010. *Age, Contact, Perceptions: How Schools Shape Relations between Ethnicities*. OSCE: Skopje

Organization for Security and Co-operation in Europe (OSCE) 2011. *Decentralization Assessment Report 2006–2011*. Skopje: OSCE.

Palermo, F. 2012. Central, Eastern and South-Eastern Europe and Territorial Autonomy: Are They Really Incompatible?, in *Political Autonomy and Divided Societies: Imagining Democratic Alternatives in Complex Settings*, ed. A. Gagnon and M. Keating. Basingstoke: Palgrave Macmillan, 81–97.

Palmer, S., Jr. and R. King 1971. *Yugoslav Communism and the Macedonian Question*. Hamden: Shoe String Press.

Papraniku, L. 2011. Politikat e dyfishta të MASH-it. *Koha* newspaper (Online, 19 March 2011). Available at: www.koha.mk/ (accessed: 20 March 2011).

Parekh, B. 2000. *Rethinking Multiculturalism: Cultural Diversity and Political Theory*. Basingstoke: Palgrave Macmillan.

Perry, D. 1997. The Republic of Macedonia: Finding its Way, in *Politics, Power, and the Struggle for Democracy in South East-Europe*, ed. K. Dawisha and B. Parrott. Cambridge: Cambridge University Press, 226–84.

Perry, D. 2000. Conflicting Ambitions and Shared Fates: The Past, Present and Future of Albanians and Macedonians, in *The Macedonian Question: Culture,*

Historiography, Politics, ed. V. Roudometof. New York: Columbia University Press, 259–300.

Petroska-Beška, V. and M. Najčevska 2004. *Macedonia: Understanding History, Preventing Future Conflict*. Washington, DC: United States Institute of Peace.

Pettifer, J. 2001a. The New Macedonian Question, in *The New Macedonian Question*, ed. J. Pettifer. Basingstoke: Palgrave Macmillan, 15–27.

Pettifer, J. 2001b. The Albanians in Western Macedonia after FYROM Independence, in *The New Macedonian Question*, ed. J. Pettifer. Basingstoke: Palgrave Macmillan, 137–47.

Pettifer, J. 2004a. *FYROM after the Concordia Mission*. Camberley: Defence Academy of the United Kingdom.

Pettifer, J. 2004b. *The 2001 Conflict in FYROM: Reflections*. Camberley: Defence Academy of the United Kingdom.

Phillips, J. 2004. *Macedonia: Warlords and Rebels in the Balkans*. London: I.B.Tauris.

Pickering, P. 2012. Explaining the Varying Impact of International Aid for Local Democratic Governance in Bosnia-Herzegovina. *Problems of Post-Communism*, 59(1), 31–43.

Poiana, S. 2011. Participatory Administrative Reform in South Eastern European Schools: Dream or Reality? *International Journal of Interdisciplinary Social Sciences*, 5(9), 433–52.

Popovska, J. 2011. Фискална Децентрализација во Република Македонија, in Охридски Рамковен Договор – Студии на Случај, ed. S. Klekovski. Skopje: MCIC, 97–104.

Poulton, H. 2000. *Who Are the Macedonians?* London: C. Hurst & Co.

Poulton, H. 2001. Non-Albanian Muslim Minorities in Macedonia, in *The New Macedonian Question*, ed. J. Pettifer. Basingstoke: Palgrave Macmillan, 107–25.

Project on Ethnic Relations (PER) 2003. *Macedonia's Interethnic Coalition: The First Six Months*. Mavrovo: PER.

Project on Ethnic Relations (PER) 2004. *Macedonia's Interethnic Coalition: Solidifying Gains*. Mavrovo: PER.

Prud'homme, R. 1995. The Dangers of Decentralization. *World Bank Research Observer*, 10(2), 201–20.

Putnam, R. 1993. *Making Democracy Work: Civic Traditions in Modern Italy*. Princeton, NJ: Princeton University Press.

Qian, Y. and B. Weingast 1997. Federalism as a Commitment to Preserving Market Incentives. *Journal of Economic Perspective*, 11, 83–92.

Radó, P. 2010. *Governing Decentralized Education Systems Systemic Change in South Eastern Europe*. Budapest: Local Government and Public Service Reform Initiative.

Ragaru, N. 2005. Maillage communal, frontières et nation: les imaginaires, enjeux et pratiques de la décentralisation en Macédoine. *Revue d'Études Comparatives Est-Ouest*, 36(3), 163–204.

Ragaru, N. 2008. *Macedonia: Between Ohrid and Brussels*. Paris: Centre d'Études et de Recherches Internationals.

Rahić, D. and L. Haziri 2010. *Integration of Non-majority Communities Representing under 20% of Total Population on Central and Local Level in the Institutions in Macedonia*. Gostivar: Association for Democratic Initiatives.

Rebouche, R. and K. Fearton 2005. Overlapping Identities: Power Sharing and Women's Rights, in *Power Sharing: New Challenges for Divided Societies*, ed. I. O'Flynn and D. Russell. London: Pluto Press, 155–71.

Reka, A. 2008. The Ohrid Agreement: The Travails of Inter-ethnic Relations in Macedonia. *Human Rights Review*, 9, 55–69.

Remmer, K. L. 2007. The Political Economy of Patronage: Expenditure Patterns in the Argentine Provinces, 1983–2003. *Journal of Politics*, 69(2), 363–77.

Reuter, J. 2001. Policy and Economy in Macedonia, in *The New Macedonian Question*, ed. J. Pettifer. Basingstoke: Palgrave Macmillan, 28–46.

Riker, W. H. 1964. *Federalism: Origin, Operation, Significance*. Boston: Little, Brown.

Risteska, M. 2013a. Insiders and Outsiders in the Implementation of the Principle of Just and Equitable Representation of Minority Groups in Public Administration in Macedonia. *International Journal of Public Administration*, 36(1), 26–34.

Risteska, M. 2013b. Towards Policy Entrepreneurship at Community Level: The Impact of Decentralization on Local Public Services in Macedonia, in *Decentralization and Local Development in South East Europe*, ed. W. Bartlett, S. Maleković and V. Monastiriotis. Basingstoke: Palgrave Macmillan, 196–214.

Rizaov, G. 2015a. Macedonia Health Fund Bosses Quit Amid Protests. *Balkan Insight* (Online, 24 February 2015). Available at: www.balkaninsight.com/en/article/macedonian-minister-urged-to-quit-over-girl-s-death (accessed: 16 April 2015).

Rizaov, G. 2015b. New Tapes Highlight Chicanery in Macedonian Local Poll. *Balkan Insight* (Online, 12 March 2015). Available at: www.balkaninsight.com/en/article/gruevski-used-every-trick-in-the-book-to-win-the-municipality-of-centar (accessed: 30 April 2015).

Rodríguez, V. 1997. *Decentralization in Mexico: From Reforma Municipal to Solidaridad to Nuevo Federalismo*. Boulder, CO: Westview.

Rodríguez-Pose, A. and R. Ezcurra 2010. Does Decentralization Matter for Regional Disparities? A Cross-country Analysis. *Journal of Economic Geography*, 10, 619–44.

Roeder, P. and D. Rothchild 2005. *Sustainable Peace: Power and Democracy after Civil Wars*. Ithaca, NY: Cornell University Press.

Roma Education Fund (REF) 2007. *Advancing Education of Roma in Macedonia. Country Assessment and the Roma Education Fund's Strategic Directions*. Budapest: REF.

Rossi, M. 2014. Ending the Impasse in Kosovo: Partition, Decentralization, or Consociationalism? *Nationalities Papers: The Journal of Nationalism and Ethnicity*, 42(5), 867–89.

Rossos, A. 2008. *Macedonia and the Macedonians: A History*. Stanford, CA: Hoover Institution Press.

Rothchild, D. and C. Hartzell 2000. Security in Deeply Divided Societies: The Role of Territorial Autonomy, in *Identity and Territorial Autonomy in Plural Societies*, ed. W. Safran and R. Máiz. London: Frank Cass, 254–71.

Safran, W. 2000. Spatial and Functional Dimensions of Autonomy: Cross-national and Theoretical Perspectives, in *Identity and Territorial Autonomy in Plural Societies*, ed. W. Safran and R. Máiz. London: Frank Cass, 11–34.

Safran, W. and R. Máiz (eds) 2000. *Identity and Territorial Autonomy in Plural Societies*. London: Frank Cass.

Šapuric, Z. 2001. *Report on the Fiscal Decentralization Process in the Republic of Macedonia*. Skopje: Urban Rural Consulting.

Schelnberger, A. 2010. Decentralization and Conflict in Kibaale, Uganda, in *Decentralization in Africa: A Pathway Out of Poverty and Conflict?*, ed. G. Crawford and C. Hartmann. Amsterdam: Amsterdam University Press, 191–212.

Schenker, H. 2011. Integrated Education: Emerging concepts in Macedonia. *Political Thought: The Challenges of Education Policy*, 9(33), 19–24.

Schou, A. and M. Haug 2005. *Decentralization in Conflict and Post-Conflict Situations.* Oslo: Norwegian Institute for Urban and Regional Research.

Scott, J. C. 1969. Corruption, Machine Politics, and Political Change. *American Political Science Review*, 63(4), 1142–58.

Scott, Z. 2009. *Decentralization, Local Development and Social Cohesion: An Analytical Review.* Birmingham: Governance and Social Development Resource Centre.

Shah, A. and T. Thompson 2004. *Implementing Decentralized Local Governance: A Treacherous Road with Potholes, Detours and Road Closures.* Washington, DC: World Bank.

Shefter, M. 1994. *Political Parties and the State: American Historical Experience.* Princeton, NJ: Princeton University Press.

Shoup, P. 1968. *Communism and the Yugoslav National Question.* New York: Columbia University Press.

Siegle, J. and P. O'Mahoney 2007. *Assessing the Merits of Decentralization as a Conflict Mitigation Strategy.* Bethesda, MD: Development Alternatives.

Siegle, J. and P. O'Mahoney 2010. Decentralization and Internal Conflict, in *Making Decentralization Work*, ed. E. Connerley, K. Eaton and P. Smoke. London: Lynne Rienner, 135–66.

Siljanovska-Davkova, G. 2005. Organizational Structures and Internal Party Democracy in the Republic of Macedonia, in *Organizational Structures and Internal Party Democracy in South Eastern Europe*, ed. G. Karasimeonov. Sofia: Friedrich-Ebert-Stiftung, 26–61.

Siljanovska-Davkova, G. 2009. Legal and Institutional Framework of Local Self-Government in the Republic of Macedonia. *Lex Localis: Journal of Local Self-Government*, 7(2), 107–27.

Siljanovska-Davkova, G. 2013. Political Parties, Values and Democratic Consolidation, in *Civic and Uncivic Values in Macedonia: Value Transformation, Education and Media*, ed. S. Ramet, O. Listhaug and A. Simkus. London: Palgrave Macmillan, 109–33.

Sisk, T. 2001. *Democracy at the Local Level. The International IDEA Handbook on Participation, Representation, Conflict Management, and Governance.* Stockholm: IDEA.

Skaburskis, A. 2004. Goals for Municipal Restructuring Plans, in *Redrawing Local Government Boundaries*, ed. J. Meligrana. Vancouver: UBC Press, 38–55.

Smoke, P. 2007. Fiscal Decentralization and Inter-governmental Fiscal Relations, in *Decentralizing Governance: Emerging Concepts and Practices*, ed. G. S. Cheema and D. A. Rondinelli. Washington, DC: Brookings Institution Press, 131–55.

Smoke, P. 2010. Implementing Decentralization: Meeting Neglected Challenges, in *Making Decentralization Work: Democracy, Development, and Security*, ed. E. Connerley, K. Eaton and P. Smoke. Boulder, CO: Lynne Rienner, 191–218.

Sokalski, H. 2003. *An Ounce of Prevention: Macedonia and the UN Experience in Preventive Diplomacy.* Washington, DC: United States Institute of Peace Press.

Sonce (Roma Democratic Development Association) 2010. *Shadow Report on the Implementation of the Framework Convention for the Protection of National Minorities of the Council of Europe in the Republic of Macedonia within the Third Monitoring Cycle.* Skopje: Sonce.

Spahn, P. B. and J. Werner 2007. Germany at the Junction between Solidarity and Subsidiarity, in *Fiscal Fragmentation in Decentralized Countries: Subsidiarity,*

Solidarity and Asymmetry, ed. R. Bird and R. Ebel. Cheltenham: Edward Elgar Publishing, 89–113.

State Election Commission (SEC) 1996. *Локалните Избори 1996*. Skopje: Government of the Republic of Macedonia.

State Statistical Office (SSO) 2003. *Census of Population, Households and Dwellings in the Republic of Macedonia, 2002*. Skopje: SSO.

State Statistical Office (SSO) 2006. *Primary, Lower Secondary and Upper Secondary Schools at the End of the School Year 2004/2005*. Skopje: SSO.

State Statistical Office (SSO) 2008. *Primary, Lower Secondary and Upper Secondary Schools at the End of the School Year 2006/2007*. Skopje: SSO.

State Statistical Office (SSO) 2009. *Primary, Lower Secondary and Upper Secondary Schools at the End of the School Year 2007/2008*. Skopje: SSO.

State Statistical Office (SSO) 2010a. *Primary, Lower Secondary and Upper Secondary Schools at the End of the School Year 2008/2009*. Skopje: SSO.

State Statistical Office (SSO) 2010b. *Regions of the Republic of Macedonia, 2009*. Skopje: SSO.

State Statistical Office (SSO) 2011. *Primary, Lower Secondary and Upper Secondary Schools at the End of the School Year 2009/2010*. Skopje: SSO.

State Statistical Office (SSO) 2012a. *Primary, Lower Secondary and Upper Secondary Schools at the End of the School Year 2010/2011*. Skopje: SSO.

State Statistical Office (SSO) 2012b. *Regions of the Republic of Macedonia*. Skopje: SSO.

State Statistical Office (SSO) 2012c. *State Statistical Office Online Database*. Available at: http://makstat.stat.gov.mk/pxweb2007bazi/Database/Statistics%20by%20subject/databasetree.asp (accessed: 9 June 2012).

State Statistical Office (SSO) 2014a. *Primary, Lower Secondary and Upper Secondary Schools at the End of the School Year 2012/2013*. Skopje: SSO.

State Statistical Office (SSO) 2014b. *Macedonia in Figures, 2014*. Skopje: SSO.

State Statistical Office (SSO) 2014c. *Statistical Yearbook of the Republic of Macedonia*. Skopje: SSO.

Stewart, F. 2004. *Horizontal Inequalities: A Neglected Dimension of Development*. Oxford: University of Oxford.

Stewart, F. 2008. *Horizontal Inequalities and Conflict: Understanding Group Violence in Multiethnic Societies*. Basingstoke: Palgrave Macmillan.

Stewart, F., G. Brown and A. Langer 2008a. Horizontal Inequalities: Explaining Persistence and Change, in *Horizontal Inequalities and Conflict: Understanding Group Violence in Multiethnic Societies*, ed. F. Stewart. Basingstoke: Palgrave Macmillan, 54–82.

Stewart, F., G. Brown and A. Langer 2008b. Major Findings and Conclusions on the Relationship between Horizontal Inequalities and Conflict, in *Horizontal Inequalities and Conflict: Understanding Group Violence in Multiethnic Societies*, ed. F. Stewart. Basingstoke: Palgrave Macmillan, 285–300.

Stewart, F., G. Brown and A. Langer, A. 2008c. Policies towards Horizontal Inequalities, in *Horizontal Inequalities and Conflict: Understanding Group Violence in Multiethnic Societies*, ed. F. Stewart. Basingstoke: Palgrave Macmillan, 301–25.

Sulejmani, R. 2008. Consensus Democracy and Power-Sharing in Macedonia, in *Power Sharing and the Implementation of the Ohrid Framework Agreement*, ed. Friedrich Ebert Stiftung. Skopje: Friedrich Ebert Stiftung, 131–64.

Surroi, V. 2011. Regression of Three Albanian Societies. *Südosteuropa Mitteilungen*, 51(4), 6–17.

Taleski, D. 2011. From Bullets to Ballots: Guerrilla-to-Party Transformation in Macedonia. Presented at the Political Science Departmental Seminar, Central European University, Budapest, Hungary, January 2011.

Tambulasi, R. 2009. Decentralization as a Breeding Ground for Conflicts: An Analysis of Institutional Conflicts in Malawi's Decentralized System. *Journal of Administration and Governance*, 4(2), 28–39.

Thede, N. 2009. Decentralization, Democracy and Human Rights: A Human Rights-Based Analysis of the Impact of Local Democratic Reforms on Development. *Journal of Human Development and Capabilities*, 10(1), 103–23.

Tiebout, C. 1956. A Pure Theory of Local Expenditures. *Journal of Political Economy*, 64(5), 416–424.

Tranchant, J. 2007. *Decentralization and Ethnic Conflict: The Role of Empowerment.* A Clermont-Ferrand: Université d'Auvergne. Available at: http://mpra.ub.uni-muenchen.de/3713/ (accessed: 24 October 2010).

Transparency International Macedonia 2011. *Failure to Comply with the Legislation and the Procedures for Building Memorial Landmarks.* Skopje: Transparency International Macedonia. Available at: www.transparency.mk/en/index.php?option=com_content&task=view&id=416&Itemid=35 (accessed: 12 May 2011).

Treisman, D. 2007. *The Architecture of Government: Rethinking Political Decentralization.* New York: Cambridge University Press.

Troebst, S. 2001. IMRO + 100 = FYROM? The Politics of Macedonian Historiography, in *The New Macedonian Question*, ed. J. Pettifer. Basingstoke: Palgrave Macmillan, 60–78.

United Nations (UN) 2010. *Programme to Enhance Inter-ethnic Dialogue and Collaboration. Results of a Participatory Assessment National and Local Capacities for Strengthening Inter-ethnic Dialogue and Collaboration.* Skopje: UN.

United Nations Children's Fund (UNICEF) 2009. *Child-Focused Public Expenditure Review.* Skopje: UNICEF.

United Nations Development Programme (UNDP) 1999. *National Human Development Report Macedonia.* Skopje: UNDP.

United Nations Development Programme (UNDP) 2001. *National Human Development Report 2001.* Skopje: UNDP.

United Nations Development Programme (UNDP) 2004a. *Decentralized Governance for Development: A Combined Practice Note on Decentralization, Local Governance and Urban/Rural Development.* New York: UNDP.

United Nations Development Programme (UNDP) 2004b. *National Human Development Report 2004, FYR Macedonia: Decentralization for Human Development.* Skopje: UNDP.

United Nations Development Programme (UNDP) 2004c. *Socio-economic Disparities among Municipalities in Macedonia.* Skopje: UNDP.

United Nations Development Programme (UNDP) 2005a. *Fiscal Decentralization and Poverty Reduction.* New York: UNDP.

United Nations Development Programme (UNDP) 2005b. *Fiscal Decentralization in Transition Economies: Case Studies from the Balkans and Caucasus.* Bratislava: UNDP.

United Nations Development Programme (UNDP) 2006. *Blue Ribbon Report.* Skopje: UNDP.

United Nations Development Programme (UNDP) 2008. *People Centred Analyses.* Skopje: UNDP.

United Nations Development Programme (UNDP) 2009a. *Governance in Conflict Prevention and Recovery: A Guidance Note.* Geneva: UNDP.

United Nations Development Programme (UNDP) 2009b. *People Centred Analyses.* Skopje: UNDP.

United Nations Development Programme (UNDP) 2010a. *People Centred Analyses.* Skopje: UNDP.

United Nations Development Programme (UNDP) 2010b. *The Baseline Study: Gender Dimension of Enhancing Inter-ethnic Community Relations and Dialogue.* Skopje: UNDP.

United Nations Development Programme (UNDP) 2011a. *FYR Macedonia: Local Governance and Decentralization Project Assessment.* Bratislava: UNDP

United Nations Development Programme (UNDP) 2011b. *Making Local Government Work for the People.* Skopje: UNDP.

United Nations Economic and Social Commission for Asia and the Pacific (UNESCAP) 2011. *What is Good Governance?* Bangkok: UNESCAP.

United Nations Security Council (UNSC) 1992. *Resolution 795.* S/RES/795 (14 December 1992). Available at: www.un.org/en/ga/search/view_doc.asp?symbol=S/RES/795 (1992) (accessed: 9 August 2014).

United Nations Security Council (UNSC) 2007. *Comprehensive Proposal for the Kosovo Status Settlement.* New York: United Nations.

United States Agency for International Development (USAID) 2005. Decentralization in Education. *EQ Review*, 3(4), 1–4.

United States Agency for International Development (USAID) 2009. *Democratic Decentralization Programming Handbook.* Washington, DC: USAID.

United States Agency for International Development (USAID) 2010. *School Boards Membership Data.* Unpublished report.

Van de Walle, N. 2007. Meet the New Boss, Same as the Old Boss? The Evolution of Political Clientelism in Africa, in *Patrons, Clients and Policies: Patterns of Democratic Accountability and Political Competition*, ed. H. Kitshelt and S. Wilkinson. Cambridge: Cambridge University Press, 50–67.

van Houten, P. 2004. The Political Stability of Decentralization: The Role of Parties. Presented at the Annual Meeting of the American Political Science Association, Chicago, USA, September 2004.

van Tilburg, P. 2010. Decentralization as a Stabilising Factor in Rwanda, in *Decentralization in Africa: A Pathway Out of Poverty and Conflict?*, ed. G. Crawford and C. Hartmann. Amsterdam: Amsterdam University Press, 213–31.

Vangeli, A. 2011. Nation-Building Ancient Macedonian Style: The Origins and the Effects of the So-Called Antiquization in Macedonia. *Nationalities Papers*, 39(1), 13–32.

Vankovska, B. 2006. *The Role of the Ohrid Framework Agreement and the Peace Process in Macedonia.* Unpublished paper.

Vankovska, B. 2013. Constitutional Engineering and Institution-Building in the Republic of Macedonia (1991–2011), in *Civic and Uncivic Values in Macedonia: Value Transformation, Education and Media*, ed. S. Ramet, O. Listhaug and A. Simkus. London: Palgrave Macmillan, 87–108.

Varady, T. 1997. Minorities, Majorities, Law, and Ethnicity: Reflections of the Yugoslav Case. *Human Rights Quarterly*, 19(1), 9–54.

Vasilev, G. 2013. Multiculturalism in Post-Ohrid Macedonia: Some Philosophical Reflections. *East European Politics and Societies*, 27(4), 685–708.

Vetterlein, M. 2006. The Influence of the Ohrid Framework Agreement on the Educational Policy of the Republic of Macedonia. Presented at the 8th Annual Kokkalis Graduate Student Workshop, Cambridge, MA, USA, February 2006.

Vickers, M. and J. Pettifer 1997. *Albania: From Anarchy to a Balkan Identity.* London: C. Hurst & Co.

Weiner, M. 1971. The Macedonian Syndrome: An Historical Model of International Relations and Political Development. *World Politics*, 13(4), 665–83.

Weingrod, A. 1968. Patrons, Patronage, and Political Parties. *Comparative Studies in Society and History*, 10(4), 377–400.

Weller, M. 2005. Enforced Autonomy and Self-Government: The Post-Yugoslav Experience, in *Autonomy, Self-Governance and Conflict Resolution: Innovative Approaches to Institutional Design in Divided Societies*, ed. M. Weller and S. Wolff. Abingdon: Routledge, 49–74.

Weller, M., B. Metzger and N. Johnson (eds) 2008. *Settling Self-Determination Disputes: Complex Power-Sharing in Theory and Practice.* Leiden: Brill.

Weller, M. and K. Nobbs (eds) 2010. *Asymmetric Autonomy and the Settlement of Ethnic Conflicts.* Philadelphia: University of Pennsylvania Press.

Weller, M. and S. Wolff 2005. *Autonomy, Self-Governance and Conflict Resolution: Innovative Approaches to Institutional Design in Divided Societies.* Abingdon: Routledge.

West, L. and C. Wong 1995. Fiscal Decentralization and Growing Regional Disparities in Rural China: Some Evidence in the Provision of Social Services. *Oxford Review of Economic Policy*, 11(4), 70–85.

Wilkinson, H. R. 1951. *A Review of the Ethnographic Cartography of Macedonia.* Liverpool: Liverpool University Press.

Willis, E., C. Garman and S. Haggard 1999. The Politics of Decentralization in Latin America. *Latin American Research Review*, 34(1), 7–56.

Wilson, D. 2002. *Minority Rights in Education. Lessons for the European Union from Estonia, Latvia, Romania and the Former Yugoslav Republic of Macedonia.* Stockholm: SIDA.

Winkler, D. and B. Yeo 2007. *Identifying the Impact of Education Decentralization on the Quality of Education.* Washington, DC: USAID.

Wolff, S. 2007. Conflict Resolution between Power Sharing and Power Dividing, or Beyond? *Political Studies Review*, 5(3), 363–79.

Wolff, S. 2008. Power-Sharing and the Vertical Layering of Authority: A Review of Current Practices, in *Settling Self-Determination Disputes: Complex Power-Sharing in Theory and Practice*, ed. M. Weller, B. Metzger and N. Johnson. Leiden: Brill, 407–50.

Wolff, S. 2009. Complex Power-Sharing and the Centrality of Territorial Self-Governance in Contemporary Conflict Settlements. *Ethnopolitics: Formerly Global Review of Ethnopolitics*, 8(1), 27–45.

Wolff, S. 2010. Approaches to Conflict Resolution in Divided Societies: The Many Uses of Territorial Self-Governance. *Ethnopolitics Papers* (Online), 5. Available at: https://centres.exeter.ac.uk/exceps/downloads/Ethnopolitics_Papers_No5_Wolff.pdf (accessed: 19 September 2011).

Wolff, S. 2012. Consociationalism: Power Sharing and Self-Governance, in *Conflict Management in Divided Societies: Theories and Practice*, ed. S. Wolff and C. Yakinthou. Abingdon: Routledge, 23–56.

Wolff, S. and M. Weller 2005. Self-Determination and Autonomy: A Conceptual Introduction, in *Autonomy, Self-Governance and Conflict Resolution: Innovative Approaches to Institutional Design in Divided Societies*, ed. M. Weller and S. Wolff. Abingdon: Routledge, 1–25.

Woodward, S. 1995a. *Balkan Tragedy: Chaos and Dissolution after the Cold War*. Washington, DC: Brookings Institution.

Woodward, S. 1995b. *Socialist Unemployment*. Princeton, NJ: Princeton University Press.

World Bank 2002. *The Former Yugoslav Republic of Macedonia: Toward an Education Strategy for the Twenty-First Century*. Washington, DC: World Bank.

World Bank 2003a. *FYR Macedonia Country Economic Memorandum: Tackling Unemployment*. Washington, DC: World Bank.

World Bank 2003b. *FYR Macedonia Decentralization Status Report*. Washington, DC: World Bank.

World Bank 2006. *Former Yugoslav Republic of Macedonia: Issues in Urban and Municipal Development. A Policy Note*. Washington, DC: World Bank.

World Bank 2008. *FYR Macedonia Public Expenditure Review*. Washington, DC: World Bank.

World Bank 2009. *FYR Macedonia Poverty, Jobs and Firms: An Assessment for 2002–2006*. Washington, DC: World Bank.

Xhaferi, A. 1998. Challenges to Democracy in Multiethnic States. *Albanian American Civic League*. Available at: http://blog.aacl.com/the-albanian-nation/albanians-in-macedonia/challenges-to-democracy-in-multiethnic-states/ (accessed: 1 January 2010).

Young, C. 1998. *Ethnic Diversity and Public Policy*. New York: St. Martin's Press.

Заедница на Единиците на Локалната Самоуправа на Република Македонија (ZELS) 2009. *Doracak praktik për punën e komisioneve për marrëdhënie midis bashkësive*. Skopje: ZELS.

Заедница на Единиците на Локалната Самоуправа на Република Македонија (ZELS) 2010a. *Membership Data for Municipal Committees for Inter-Community Relations*. Skopje: ZELS.

Заедница на Единиците на Локалната Самоуправа на Република Македонија (ZELS) 2010b. Систематизираните Ставови. Skopje: ZELS.

Заедница на Единиците на Локалната Самоуправа на Република Македонија (ZELS) 2011a. Систематизираните Ставови. Skopje: ZELS.

Заедница на Единиците на Локалната Самоуправа на Република Македонија (ZELS) 2011b. *ZELS Newsletter December 2011*. Skopje: ZELS.

Zenku, D. and I. Ajrullau 2011. Promovohet RDK e Rufi Osmanit. Prioritet, federalizmit Joterritorial. *Koha* newspaper (Online, 29 March 2011). Available at: www.koha.mk/ (accessed: 30 March 2011).

Index

For Product Safety Concerns and Information please contact our EU
representative GPSR@taylorandfrancis.com
Taylor & Francis Verlag GmbH, Kaufingerstraße 24, 80331 München, Germany